MW01233469

STAND WHERE THEY FOUGHT

150 Battlefields of the 77-Day Normandy Campaign

Volume 1
The American Sector

Carlton S. Joyce

AuthorHouse™
1663 Liberty Drive, Suite 200
Bloomington, IN 47403
www.authorhouse.com
Phone: 1-800-839-8640

AuthorHouse™ UK Ltd.
500 Avebury Boulevard
Central Milton Keynes, MK9 2BE
www.authorhouse.co.uk
Phone: 08001974150

Expanded Edition published by AuthorHouse 2006.

First published by AuthorHouse 3/15/2006

ISBN: 1-4259-1758-5 (sc)
ISBN: 1-4259-1759-3 (dj)

Library of Congress Control Number: 2006900882

Printed in the United States of America
Bloomington, Indiana

This book is printed on acid-free paper.

Bloomington, IN  Milton Keynes, UK

Dedication

**"On great fields, something stays.
Forms change, pass; bodies disappear,
But spirits linger to consecrate the
Ground for the vision place of souls."**

Colonel Joshua L. Chamberlain,
20th Maine Regiment
Congressional Medal of Honor

To the allied soldiers, living and dead, who fought in the Normandy Campaign, June 6 to August 22, 1944. They have consecrated these grounds with their blood and souls.

Contents

List of Illustrations

Chapter 1 Introduction

General Dwight D. Eisenhower asked me to write this book October 10, 1967. It is about heroes, thousands of heroes. In Tom Brokaw's words they are "The Greatest Generation." It is about battlefields, large and small where men died mangled or grotesquely wounded, scared and many incapacitated for life. There are the survivors who bore horrific memories into domestic normalcy. The missing thousands now lie buried on the seabed, went to oblivion in the explosion's flash or are concealed in indiscernible graves.

The invasion of Normandy was a supreme allied effort. Our generals were convinced that the way to kill the most Germans with minimum losses was to launch one great invasion with everything at their disposal.

"Saving Private Ryan" and "The Longest Day" have given us a slice of the D-Day events in a few short hours of cinematography. Steven Spielberg's realism gave the audiences an appreciation for honoring our Normandy veterans. He also showed us there were gruesome battles in the days following.

The Normandy campaign was seventy-seven days of brutal fighting over an area the size of Connecticut by an allied army consisting principally of American, British, Canadian, French and Polish troops. Ninety-six percent of their casualties occurred after D-Day, between June 7 and August 21.

Although strong, mobile, well-equipped German divisions stood prepared inland to counter the expected invasion, numerous static coastal defenses were manned by "volunteers" from Russia, Mongolia, China and Korea commanded by German non-coms who would readily shoot a "volunteer" who lacked fighting zeal.

World War II, 1939 to 1945, were my public school years. My father's large church in Canada brought me in frequent contact with veterans on leave from overseas. "Buzz" Beurling, 31 "kills" and one of the top ten allied fighter pilots of WWII came to the parsonage several evenings after church service. I sat cross-legged in awe as I listened to the "Knight of Malta" describe his dogfights. Others were from Bomber Command, a survivor of the abortive Dieppe raid, and later the Normandy Campaign veterans. University classes swelled with returning heroes. Yesterday's headlines were amongst us.

Stories of their exploits abounded. In a euthanasia debate I opposed a severely scared tank veteran, from Operation GOODWOOD, who in his rebuttal described how his Sherman tank had been hit by an 88 and as the burning fuel liquefied his flesh he attempted to shoot himself. The stories I heard needed recording and placement.

Visiting Normandy a few years later evidenced the war's trauma. Lonely, isolated gravesites with helmet topped crosses awaited re-internment. Reconstruction only partially camouflaged the destruction. Demolished tanks, trucks, vehicles, aircraft and gliders filled scrap yards as the battle sites were cleared of the carnage and returned to farming. Available literature of what had transpired was non-existent. Professional historians were writing of the events for official publication. Impatiently, I visited the national military history archives in Bonn, London, Ottawa and Washington anxious to create personal notes of the many battles throughout Normandy. As a result of my endeavors in the Pentagon, former President, General Eisenhower invited me to Gettysburg to expand my notes on his headquarter sites. He urged me to complete the research on my selected three hundred and fifty battle sites and publish the directory in dedication to the veterans and information for the public wishing to visit the battlefields.

His encouragement came from the fact that as a young lieutenant after World War I he had done similar research in France siting the battlefields for the American Battle Monuments Commission. His support facilitated my continued research. However, upgrading personal information notes to a publishing level was a major time commitment that my academic-industrial spectroscopic career would not permit. I was unable to fulfill his request at that time.

The interim years have brought forth innumerable excellent histories by outstanding and distinguished multi-national authors. **Stand Where They Fought** is a compilation and integration of informational sources to describe the actions at these battle sites. In a few instances cross-referencing indicated contradictions. I have attempted to resolve the issue through additional research or accept the most credible source.

Whether read at home or in France, with map in hand, the intent is to broaden the reader's knowledge that men died or survived numerous battles throughout Normandy after penetrating the beach defenses.

The veterans' numbers are shrinking rapidly. Through this book that goes beyond the beaches, across the countryside's expanse, readers will learn and appreciate the appalling experiences these young soldiers, WACs and nurses endured sixty plus years ago.

1.1 Acknowledgements

Researching three hundred and fifty battlefields throughout the western half of Normandy develops numerous contacts. Whether it was General Dwight D. Eisenhower, in Gettysburg or Monsieur Jules Couffey, an eye witness farmer in les Ais, their contributions to this book were immeasurable. The historical reference library archivists and the surviving veterans whose oral histories filled the gaps have made this work possible. In addition there were the professional writers, Charles Macdonald and Martin Blumenson, who encouraged and supplied information. Friends and family were the much-appreciated supportive influence on a day to day basis. Having a son, Carlton, who missed the wars has been an inducement to acknowledge and recognize the hundreds of thousands of sons who did not return. Every grave marker symbolizes mourning parents, widowed wives and/or fatherless children.

American assistance came from General Dwight D. Eisenhower, General Omar N. Bradley, General R.J. Allen, General Robert L. Schulz, Colonel W. Walker, Martin Blumenson, Charles MacDonald, Phil Brower, (GSA), Sherwood East (GSA), Hem Goldbeck (GSA), W.J. Nigh (GSA), J.R. Friedman (Historical Branch), Hannah Zeidlich (Historical Branch), Sylvia Traxler (Photo Branch), Frank Myers (AAF History), D. Schoen (USAF History) and Kurt Heilbronn (AAF).

British assistance came from Rose Combes (Imperial War Museum), B. Melland (IWM), C.E. Dornbush (IWM), D.W. King (War Office) and Colonel J.R. Harper.

Canadian assistance came from General H.D.C. Crearar, Colonel C.P. Stacey, Captain A.G. Steiger, Colonel Pierre Sevigny, Wing Commander R.V. Manning, Pilot Officer W.A. Switzer, Clarence Campbell, Colonel D.V. Currie, Dr. A. Baillergeron and Erich Henne.

French assistance came from Colonel Leonard and Mrs. Gilles, Michel and Jacques Vico, Dr. Gilles Buisson, Jules Couffey, and J. LeMoules.

Polish assistance came from Glen Jurczhki, Zygmunt Celichowski, Stan Halichi and L. Chihofsky.

I am grateful to my brother Dr. Douglas Joyce for his literary edification suggestions and resolution of opinion differences between the author and the computer's literary style.

In the final analysis, the actual creation of the book is totally due to the persistent efforts of my wife, Patricia, word processing endless hours to convert drafts into book format, to question the comprehensiveness of phraseologies and be a good friend with encouragement during the arduous writing phase.

1.2 The battlefield directory as a guide book

Each battle site story is prefaced with a route description to the site from a significant Norman town/city or invasion beach readily located on a Normandy road map with a scale of 1/200,000, such as Michelin 54, 102 or 231. The reference points are:

Caen, Normandy's largest city, west of the Seine River.
Bayeux, Route N13, west of Caen.
Carentan, Route N13, west of Bayeux.
Ste. Mere-Eglise, Route N13, north of Carentan.
Montebourg, Route N13, north of Ste. Mere-Eglise.
Valognes, Route N13, northwest of Montebourg.
Cherbourg, Route N13, north of Valognes on the coast.
St. Lo, Route D572, southwest of Bayeux.
Avranches, Route N175, southwest of St. Lo on the coast.
Falaise, Route N158, south of Caen.
Omaha Beach, northwest of Bayeux.
Utah Beach, east of Ste. Mere-Eglise.

French roads are very well marked. They combine the town name, route number and distance on their signage.

The battle site stories in each chapter relate to each other. Each chapter has an introduction page establishing the background and objectives of those battles. The reader can either travel from site to site in the book order or randomly visit any battle site. Each site story can be studied independently as they are written with an opening orientation paragraph.

The index references 2,800 towns, hills, people, military units, subjects, etc. for the reader's ease of pursuing a specific interest.

1.3 Troop Strengths

"Normandy was a soldier's battle. It belonged to the riflemen, machine gunners, mortar men, tankers and artillery men who were on the front lines. There was simplicity to the fighting: for the Germans, to hold; for the Americans, to attack." Stephen Ambrose, Citizen Soldiers.

Throughout the battle site stories the combat units are referenced frequently, i.e., squad, platoon, company, battalion, regiment, division, corps and army. One can define the size of the units by manpower and equipment but battlefield factors weakened and strengthened a unit's capability. Examples of the variables were the unit's battlefield experience; was it at full manpower strength or were there only the survivors to carry on the unit's identity; were the replacements green or experienced; was the unit in a defensive or offensive position, was artillery and air support involved; what was the available weaponry and how long had the unit been in combat conditions. Motivation was significant. Russian conscripts fighting for Germany against Americans in France had minimum motivation compared to Polish armored troops who had fled from their homeland five years before and would now return reaping revenge as they battled across the Germans' homeland.

The American and Canadian casualties could be replaced as both armies had large reserves. The British had been at war since 1939 in Europe, the Mediterranean and the Pacific. Their reserves were very low. The Polish division comprised of soldiers who had escaped the Germans in 1939 but had no replacement resources. The German army was stretched thin with occupation duties while being bled dry on the Russian and Italian fronts. Their replacement pool consisted of the young and the old. Replacement convoys and trains of men and material were interceded and delayed by the allied air forces. German units were never at their full strength after D-Day. Only 10% of their losses were replaced. They were, however, in prepared defense positions, well trained under experienced officers and better equipped.

For troop comparisons per the Table of Organization see the following:

AMERICAN

Command Rank	Unit	Soldiers
Sergeant	Infantry Squad	12
Lieutenant	Platoon	36-40
Captain	Company	190
Lt. Colonel, Major	Battalion	1,170
Colonel, Brigadier	Regiment	3,500
Major General	Division	14,300
Major General	Armored Division	11,000 (270 tanks)
Major General	Airborne Division	9,000
Lieutenant General	Corps	50,000
Lieutenant General	Army	180,000
General (4 star)	Army Group	500,000

Figure 1: Table of Organization-American

GERMAN

Command Rank	Unit	Soldiers
Unteroffizier (Sergeant)	Infantry Squad	12-15
Oberleutnant (Lieutenant)	Platoon	30-35
Hauptmann (Captain)	Company	140
Oberstleutnant (Lt. Colonel)	Battalion	1,420
Oberst (Colonel)	Regiment	4,260
Generalmajor (Major General)	Division	12,770
Generalmajor	Armored Division	12,800 – 16,500 (160 tanks)
SS Brigadefuhrer und Generalmajor der Waffen-SS	SS Division	17,000
(Major General)	1st SS Division	21,400
Generalmajor	Airborne Division	17,000
Oberst (Colonel)	6th Para Regiment	3,460
Hauptmann (Captain)	6th Para Company	230
Generalleutnant	Corps	45,700
(Lieutenant General)	Army	160,000
General der Gruppen (General 4 star)	Army Group	400,000

Figure 2: Table of Organization - German

Chapter 2 UTAH Beach

The tactical plan from the beginning emphasized the need for an adequate port for the buildup of forces and supplies in the lodgment area. General Eisenhower considered the assault on the Contentin Peninsula essential to the post invasion plans. Once a beachhead had been established the first mission was to capture Cherbourg at the north end of the peninsula. The large, protected deep-water port that accommodated ocean liners before the war would receive freighters directly from North American ports.

The objective was assigned to the 7th Corps, commanded by Major General J. Lawton Collins. The 7th Corps and 5th Corps (OMAHA Beach) became the US 1st Army under Lieutenant General Omar N. Bradley. The US 1st Army and the British 2nd Army formed the 21st Army Group commanded by General Sir Bernard L. Montgomery.

The Douve and Merderet Rivers drain the land area at the base of the peninsula. German control of la Barquette Lock and the canal north of Carentan had flooded the low-lying pastures turning them into shallow lakes. The inundation's carried north on the east side of the Contentin resulting in the UTAH Beach coastal area being isolated from the hard ground by several kilometers of marsh and lakes traversed by five elevated road ways running west from the beachfront. These were identified as beach Exit Nos. 1 to 5. Two airborne divisions (82nd and 101st) landed by parachute and gliders west of these lagoons in the predawn hours to seize enemy positions and block reinforcements from aiding the beach defenders.

2.1 UTAH Beach Assault

The beach at low tide is smooth and shallow with hard packed sand. A 10 kilometer long masonry seawall 2-3 meters high separates the beach from the sand dunes that vary from 3-7 meters in height that extend inland a kilometer to the paralleling shore road.

Field Marshal Erwin Rommel visited the area in December, January and on May 11, 1944. He was very disappointed in the defenses and progress on their improvements. He met with 23 year old 2nd Lieutenant Arthur Jahnke, the commanding officer of Resistance Nest 5 (W5) in his headquarters bunker, today's' UTAH Beach Museum. "Permitting the local citizens to pass through the defenses to get to their fishing boats must stop!" was an example of the laxity Rommel noted. Twenty days later, a week before the invasion, the 84th Corps Commander, General Erich Marcks, in front of the present day museum, awarded Jahnke the Iron Cross for his actions on the Russian front. The UTAH defenses were weaker as the Germans put more reliance on the flooded lowlands behind the beach as a landing deterrent.

On the tide flats were wood and concrete stakes tipped with explosives, steel hedgehogs tetrahedra (4-meter length tidily-winks) and "Belgian Gates", broad gates of iron rods and plates. Facing across the beach in the dunes were open concrete mortar and machine gun pits, captured tank turrets on concrete bases, pillboxes, firing trenches and underground shelters. Antitank ditches, mines and barbed wire protected the defenders. Two batteries at Azeville and Crisbecq, in concrete bunkers, five kilometers northwest could add support fire onto the beach and out to sea. Two regiments (729th and 716th) of the 709th (Static) Division manned the coastal region. An unusual remote controlled demolition device (called a Goliath) was used on this beach. It was a miniature (2 meters long, 1-meter high and 1-meter wide) robot tank filled with explosives that could be directed into the attackers' lines. The device broke down easily. (One killed 20 Americans who put a handgrenade inside not realizing they were setting off 200 pounds of TNT).

At 6 a.m., H-Hour minus 30 minutes, 276 medium Marauder bombers of the US 9th Air Force flew in, paralleling the beach, from north to south "between 500 to 1,000 feet" (150 to 300 meters) dropping 4,404 250 pound bombs. On the ground casualties were light as the small bombs had not penetrated the concrete shelters. The results on the defense firepower were devastating. Destroyed were the 50mm guns, 75mm antitank guns, the 88mm flak gun, two ammo bunkers exploded, the open mortar and machine gun nests were buried, mines were set off and the barbed wire cut. The communication wires to the Azeville and Crisbecq batteries were also cut. The garrison was either dead, wounded, dazed or in shock.

Off shore the naval force consisting of the battleship Nevada, a monitor (two 15 inch guns), five cruisers, a gun boat (three 6 inch guns) and eight destroyers bombarded the beach.

Signal flares were fired from the assault craft. The shellfire lifted. The 20 LCVPs (Landing Craft Vehicle Personnel) containing 600 men (2nd and 3rd Battalions of 8th Infantry Regiment) and eight LCTs (Landing Craft tank) with 32 tanks (A and B Companies, 70th Tank Battalion) headed in on plan and on time. The amphibious tanks were launched from the LCTs three kilometers out. One LCT hit a mine, sank losing its four tanks.

The LCVP ramps dropped. The men exited into waist deep water 200 meters from shore. Captain Leonard "Max" Schroeder, 25, Commander, F Company, 2nd Battalion, (now retired in Clearwater, Florida) is officially the first American soldier to set foot in France from the sea on D-Day. He was severely wounded by a machine gun later in the day. He did not fight again until the Korean War. Tanks tracking on the hard sand provided fire support. Only one detail was wrong. The force had landed two kilometers (one mile) south of their targeted objective.

Brigadier General Teddy Roosevelt, Jr., Assistant Commander of the 4th Division, had accompanied the first wave. Recognizing they had landed at a weaker strongpoint at Exit 2, a shorter causeway off the beach than Exit 3, he made a personal reconnaissance of the area behind the beach. "We'll start the invasion here," he told his two battalion commanders Lieutenant Colonels Conrad C. Simmons and Carlton O. MacNeely. His decision saved numerous lives and got the troops moving with a minimum of confusion. For his decisive life saving action he was awarded the Medal of Honor. The 3rd Battalion moved west on Exit 2. The 2nd Battalion moved south on the coast road and then west on Exit 1 to Pouppeville. The Germans retreating ahead of the battalion on Exit 1 hid under the road bridge until flushed out. The 22nd Regiment turned north on the coast road taking W5 (present museum area) from the rear and releasing 17 captured paratroopers. It's wounded commander, Lieutenant Jahnke was shipped to England. After the war he gave numerous interviews and wrote articles about his experiences in that early dawn hour of D-Day.

On the beach the engineers moved quickly removing or destroying the deadly beach obstacles, lifting mines in the dunes, and blowing gaps in the seawall.

La Madelaine, the coast road hamlet 500 meters north of the museum, consisted of seven homes, one with a store belonging to Paul Gazengel. In the pre-assault bombardment, the building was severely damaged entrapping his wife and twelve year old daughter, Jeannine. As M. Gazengel was working in the rubble to free his family he was seized and shipped to England (without explanation for two weeks). L Company passing in the afternoon heard the cries from inside the debris and freed the mother and daughter.

By 9 a.m. three kilometers (2 miles) of UTAH Beach was clear, the obstacles had been removed. Tanks and the follow-up waves were landing on plan. Only the batteries at Azeville and Crisbecq were actively shelling the beach but the battleship and cruisers were ranged in with merciless firepower. The 22nd Regiment was on the move north along the beach road towards the batteries. Five kilometers (3 miles) north at Hamel de Cruites they discovered Exit No. 5 west across the lagoon was undefended. At 1 p.m. the seaborne infantry crossed Exit 5 and met the paratroopers occupying the causeway's west end.

Casualties on UTAH were the lightest of all five beaches. 197 men killed or wounded of which 60 were lost at sea. One of the control vessels and the destroyer USS Corry had hit mines and sank.

The narrow beach exit causeways delayed the advance inland, not enemy action. The 4th Division Commander, Major General Raymond O. Barton and Brigadier Roosevelt had to handle the congested traffic situation as traffic directors on the shore road at Exit 2. Their tactical knowledge and authority was needed to prioritize the units' movements.

Roosevelt, 57, was the son of former President Teddy Roosevelt and a cousin of President Franklin Delano Roosevelt. He was the most senior ranking officer and the oldest man in the five beach assault waves. He had fought in WWI, was an explorer and politician.

He had seen action in North Africa and Italy. His son, Captain Quentin Roosevelt, 25, was with the 1st Division assaulting the eastern half of OMAHA Beach. Brigadier Roosevelt died of a heart attack July 12, without knowing that General Eisenhower had that day approved his appointment as commander of the 90th Infantry Division. Initially buried in a temporary cemetery near Ste. Mere-Eglise, he now lies in the US Cemetery overlooking OMAHA Beach next to his re-interned brother Quentin killed in WWI.

William Westmoreland, 9th Division Executive Officer landed on UTAH, D-Day. Twenty years later, as a Major General, he played a prominent part in the Vietnam War.

The day ended. Spasmodically the German batteries fired on the beach. Lieutenant General Lawton Collins', 7th Corps Commander, headquarters had landed as well as 23,350 men, 1,742 vehicles, and 1,695 tons of stores.

On June 8 five old freighters were purposefully sunk a kilometer (1,200 yards) off the beach in a north-south direction between Exits 3 and 4. Two were sunk, in place, by the Azeville Battery . The ships formed a breakwater (codename Gooseberry) to shelter the off loading operations. The eastern gale June 19-21 hit the breakwater broadside breaking several ships apart opening large gaps. By the 21st the breakwater had lost its value. No longer visible the hulls are still noted on marine charts.

On July 20, the day a time bomb exploded in Hitler's east Prussia headquarters Winston Churchill flew into Cherbourg's Maupertus airport, drove to UTAH Beach from where he was ferried to Port Churchill at Arromanches-les-Bains.

August 1 witnessed the landing of the Free French 2nd Armored Division across the Exit 4 beach area.

At war's end the beach had statistics rivaling a large port. 836,000 men, 220,000 vehicles, and 725,000 tons of supplies had been landed and moved across the narrow exits into the Contentin's secondary road system. A major behind-the-lines success.

Monuments and Memorials

German bunkers are easily accessible from the beach road and the beach near Exits 4 and 5. At Exit 4 is the General Leclerc, 2nd Armored Division monument.

In the vicinity of the UTAH Museum are eight memorials.

An obelisk commemorating the 4th Division landing.

A stone commemorating the 90th Division landing.

The 0.0 cylindrical milestone of "Voie de la Liberte". (The Liberty Route, with 1,182 of these markers ends in Bastogne, commemorates the US 3rd Army actions.)

A monument to the 1st Engineer Special Brigade raised in 1945 on top of one of the W5 blockhouses. There is also a barred memorial crypt to the brigade members who died on the beach clearing the obstacles. A plaque commemorates the brigade's commander Major General Eugene M. Caffey.

General Laughton Collins unveiled a stone plinth June 5, 1984, to the 7th Corps.

A plague acknowledging the heads of state here at the 40th Anniversary.

A plaque commemorating General Eisenhower.

Throughout the area are 59 road signs to the fallen of the 1st Engineer Special Brigade.

The museum is open April to September.

The Roosevelt Restaurant and Bar, across from the museum incorporated a German blockhouse in its construction. Now a food storage room, the owner, Monsieur Methivier, has preserved the numerous wall signatures of the American troops that passed through the beach.

Along the Exit 2 road to St. Marie du Mont is the Danish Seamen Memorial.

Related battle sites are: Iles St. Marcouf, Pouppeville, Audouville-la-Hubert, St. Martin-de-Vaneville, Ste Marie-du-Mont, Crisbecq, Azeville

Picture 1: Utah Beach Looking West D-Day Morning
June 6, 1944

The aircraft engine nacelle and propeller are top right. Dark patches are cloud shadows. German flooding of the low pasturelands immediately west of the beach was planned to limit American accessibility to the higher ground. Further west along the top of the photo can be seen the flooded Merderet River valley, also a defensive tactic that caused grievous losses to the 82nd and 101st Airborne Divisions. On the beach, landing craft are bringing in General Barton's 4th Infantry division. Two causeways carry vehicles and men westbound to relieve the paratroopers holding the causeways western exits. Over the following months, ships off-loaded supplies and men across the beach in volumes comparable to the port of Philadelphia.

2.2 Iles St. Marcouf

(Two piles of barren rock constitute the twin St. Marcouf Islands, situated 6 kilometers due east of the Contentin Peninsula and 9 kilometers north of UTAH Beach. There is a lighthouse on the northern island.)

The islands were overlooked by the invasion planners until three weeks before D-Day. The possibility that they could be prime sites for a German heavy battery, an artillery observation post and a minefield control point made it essential that they be occupied prior to the UTAH Beach assault. At 4:30 a.m. (H hour - 2) 132 men of the 4th and 24th Cavalry Squadrons, lead by Lieutenant Colonel E. C. Dunn, landed on the islands. Although unoccupied, as the force moved off the beach they entered deadly minefields. The islands had been strewn with mines triggered by foot pressure. The “S” mines popped into the air and exploded at waist level, sending hundreds of steel balls into the invaders bodies. By 5:30 a.m. both islands were occupied resulting in two deaths and seventeen men severely wounded. Colonel Dunn’s men had the distinction of being the first soldiers to invade Hitler’s Europe from the sea and the dubious distinction of having had the first casualties for terrain that was too little and of no value. During D-Day and for several days thereafter the islands were shelled by the German Azeville and Crisbecq (Marcouf) batteries directly west of the islands. During June and July the islands were used as a storage depot.

Related stories are Azeville and Crisbecq (Marcouf) batteries.

2.3 Pouppeville

(The village of Pouppeville is 4 kilometers southwest of UTAH Beach via the most southerly road from the beach or take D913 from UTAH Beach and turn left at the first crossroads after crossing the causeway.)

Immediately west of the UTAH Beach sand dunes is a 2 kilometers stretch of low, swampy marshland. In 1944, the Germans flooded this land to create a water obstacle to the allied invaders landing on the beach. The marsh separated the beach from the dry firm mainland of the Contentin Peninsula. Crossing the marshland from east to west are five elevated roads, which to the allied planners were classified as beach road Exit Numbers 1, 2, 3, 4 and 5 from south to north. In the predawn hours of D-Day the American 101st Airborne Division parachuted into the area immediately west of these exists, with the sole purpose of seizing and holding the western end of the beach exit roads. Unless the causeways were under American control the UTAH force would be stalemated on the beach.

The village of Pouppeville is on the western edge of designated Exit No. 1, the most southerly exit.

The town was held by 70 men of the 1058th Regiment of the German 91st Anti-Air Landing Division. The Germans had foreseen the possibility of an allied airborne division landing in the vicinity as a tactic to isolate the Contentin Peninsula. The division holding the area and the land to the north was specially trained to counter parachute landings. A kilometer southeast of Pouppeville is the hamlet of Houesville the site of German Strongpoint 101 consisting of an observation tower and artillery. It was a support position unprepared for self defense.

The responsibility of capturing and holding Pouppeville was given to the 3rd Battalion of the 501st Regiment of the 101st Airborne Division under the command of 28 year old Lieutenant Colonel Julian J. Ewell.

In the predawn hours of June 6, Colonel Ewell, his battalion and the division's headquarters staff landed in Drop Zone C, northwest of Ste. Marie-du-Mont. Many of his paratroopers were widely scattered landing far from their intended mission area. Ewell's group identifying the church tower at Ste. Marie-du-Mont to the east reassured them that they had landed accurately. Ewell, collecting only forty men of his battalion and the headquarters staff, moved off to their objective. Seven drowsy German sentries offered little resistance to their advance.

The forces' officers had increased to such a proportion due to the presence of the divisional headquarters staff that Major General Maxwell Taylor, Commander of the 14,000 man 101st Division, observed "never in the history of military operations had so few been commanded by so many."

At 9 a.m. the American force moved into the western outskirts of Pouppeville from the Ste. Marie-du-Mont road. It had been observed that the Germans had abandoned Strongpoint 101 and retreated to Pouppeville. House to house fighting ensued with rifles and grenades at close quarters. Ewell could only use his forty riflemen, as it was essential not to inflict casualties on the 20 headquarters staff. The battle converged on the village school. Ewell advanced cautiously down the street until he reached the wall surrounding the school. The German commander, a Lieutenant, ran out shooting at Ewell - he missed. The Lieutenant surrendered his force of 23 in the school. Mopping up continued until 11 a.m.. The casualties of the battle had been 18 Americans killed or wounded, 25 Germans killed and 38 captured.

Some of the Germans retreated eastward along the causeway (D913) into the face of the advancing American 4th Division's armor from UTAH Beach.

Although the bridge 0.5 kilometers to the east was prepared for demolition, the German defenders were unable to destroy the essential span. At 11:50 a.m., men of Colonel Ewell's force could see the small yellow identifying flags of the American UTAH force, lead by Captain George Maybury and Lieutenant Colonel Carlton O. MacNelly of the 2nd Battalion 8th Infantry Regiment, 4th Division. The seaborne officers were greeted by Major General Maxwell Taylor and Lieutenant Colonel Julian J. Ewell. This was the first link-up of the airborne and seaborne forces. Since landing the 4th US Division had advanced 5 kilometers.

Pouppeville became the first of many divisional headquarters sites.

On July 2, at Brucheville, 1 kilometer southwest of Pouppeville, construction commenced on an airfield (Advanced Landing Ground

A-16) by the 11th Engineering Command. Considerable difficulties were encountered. Soft areas retarded the grading progress. Eventually, the grading advanced to the point where the surface could be laid but a heavy rain on July 21 set back the timetable. It wasn't until early August that the landing strip became operational for the 36th Fighter Group, 9th Air Force. One kilometer south of Ste. Marie du-Mont, on D913, a sign marks the left hand turn to a memorial stone established in 1990 marking the location of ALG A-16.

Related stories dealing with the seizing the clearing of the beach exits are Foucarville, St. Martin-de-Varreville and Audonville-la-Hubert.

2.4 Audonville-la-Hubert

(The hamlet of Audonville-la-Hubert is 4 kilometers west of UTAH Beach on road D67.)

The defending Germans foresaw that the allies might invade across the long beaches later to be known by code name "UTAH". They therefore flooded the low-lying land west of the beach. Only a few elevated, narrow causeways crossed the natural barrier.

The allies, confident the landings would be successful, feared that well positioned German forces at the western ends of the five causeways could easily halt the westward movement off the beach and thereby "bottle-up" the UTAH force.

To prevent the situation the 82nd Airborne and 101st Airborne Divisions were dropped prior to the seaborne invasion. The divisions' responsibilities were to occupy the beach exit routes and several other causeways inland over which the mobile army would cross in the following days. In addition, the paratroopers were to occupy key positions to block German counterattacks against the beachhead itself.

In the intervening years since 1944, the marshes have been drained and the land returned to its pastoral usefulness. Only the imagination can recreate the scene, visualizing all the low land east of Audonville-la-Hubert, stretching to the dunes, as a shallow lake crossed by five slightly elevated asphalt topped roads.

The task of clearing and holding Exit No. 3 at Audonville-la-Hubert was assigned to elements of the 3rd Battalion of the 502nd Regiment under the command of Lieutenant Colonel Robert G. Cole. Cole's force had planned to parachute into Drop Zone "A" 2 kilometers to the northwest. Misdropping scattered the paratroopers. The Colonel himself landed 5 kilometers to the west, in the outskirts of Ste. Mere-Eglise. In the darkness of the predawn hours of D-Day, he secured his directions by inquiring of the local farmers.

Although his force was smaller than planned (75 men) he divided it sending the smaller unit into St. Martin-de-Varreville to secure Exit No. 4. Commanding the larger force he established a road-block position, on D67, 1.3 kilometers northeast of Audonville-la-Hubert, where the causeway meets the ascending terrain and turns sharply south from its westerly direction.

At 9:30 a.m. Germans, retreating from the beach, crossed No. 3 causeway and attacked Cole's position. Fifty to seventy-five Germans died on the road and its bordering shoulders.

A few hours later, 1 p.m., elements of the 8th Regiment, 4th Division, who had assaulted the UTAH Beach, crossed the causeway linking up with Cole's force at the roadblock.

There is no evidence of these actions to be seen today. The events can only be imagined. Dozens of German dead lying on the road and its sloping sides. American infantry and tanks filing across the length of the road back to the beach and Cole's small force of 45 paratroopers rising from behind the hedgerows to greet their compatriots. The reality of war was brought to mind in the summer of 1967 when 10,000 artillery shells were unearthed at the eastern end of this beach Exit, No. 3, at the juncture of the shore line road.

Colonel Cole, a native Texan and West Pointer, lead his battalion in an outstanding action at Carentan for which he was awarded the Congressional Medal of Honor. Three months later on September 18 along the Wilhelmina Canal in Holland, a sniper's bullet fired from a hundred meters, pierced his temple, killing him instantly.

The 7th Corps Commander, Major General J. Lawton Collins, landed on June 7 and established his headquarters 300 meters south of the Andonville-la-Hubert intersection on D14 in the Buisson farm. Contrary to the plaque on the gate this was not the first command post established in France, but it was one of the earliest.

Related stories regarding the securing of the beach exits are Foucarville, St. Martin-de-Varreville and Pouppeville. For information pertaining to Colonel Cole's actions for which he was honored refer to the Carentan story.

2.5 St. Martin-de-Varreville

(From the UTAH Beach coastal road take D423 west across the pasture land 2.5 kilometers to the village of St. Martin-de-Varreville. The story deals with the actions in the village and around the Mesieres crossroads 1 kilometer to the west at the intersection of D423 and D115. The latter location should be visited and studied first.)

The American strategy was to land two airborne divisions inland behind the UTAH invasion Beach area to secure essential bridges and causeways across the Meredet and Douve Rivers to the west. Also, they were to seize the western approaches to five of the causeways crossing the flooded marsh that separated the beach from the higher farm land and orchard country. It was planned that the paratroopers landing in the pre-dawn hours of D-Day would secure the villages to the west by capturing or destroying the German garrisons. The seaborne invasion forces would then move off the beach and inland as quickly as possible to establish a western protective defense against German counterattacks into the UTAH Beachhead.

Although the plan to drop two airborne divisions was General Omar Bradley's, its approval depended upon General Eisenhower. Against the serious considerations that the paratroopers would have 80% casualties, it was nevertheless essential that the ground west of these flooded marshes be seized prior to the seaborne assault. The Germans holding the western ends of the long narrow causeways could readily stop the western movement of the seaborne forces and "bottle up" the assault force on the beach.

St. Martin-de-Varreville's German garrison guarded the western end of Exit No. 4 causeway from the beach. Half a kilometer west of the village, on the south side of the road, German Strongpoint 108 was an artillery battery in four concrete bunkers with captured Russian 122mm guns facing seaward. The battery was a serious threat to the landings on UTAH Beach and directly could fire directly on Exits 3 and 4 thereby delaying the 4th Division's advance inland.

The invasion planners had secured detailed information about the strongpoint through the French Resistance. The chief underground organizer for the Cherbourg area was Jacques Bertin, Comte de la Houtiere. Allied intelligence requests were directed to Bertin who in turn chose the appropriate agent for the assignment. To fulfill the request about Strongpoint 108 he selected Antonin Maury, an underground agent and electrician in Ste. Mere-Eglise. Maury not only pinpointed the gun battery position but also carefully measured its dimensions by counting his bicycle wheel rotations as he cycled past. By goading a German sentry into bragging about how effective the battery would be against the "Tommies" and "Amerikans", he established the guns' caliber.

Another resistance agent, living in St. Martin-de-Varreville, established that the battery was manned by 150 men of the 1st Battalion, 1261 Army Coastal Artillery Regiment under the command of Lieutenant Erben. They were billeted in a group of farm buildings a few hundred meters west of the battery just beyond the Mesieres crossroads. So thorough was the agent's investigations that he identified the specific mess hall building.

As a consequence of this intelligence information the battery received a carpet bombing of three hundred and fifty-six tons of bombs by the RAF Bomber Command during the night of May 28 to 29. The bombing only collapsed one bunker. The three remaining guns were moved. German battery commanders were shown the site as an example of what to expect if they lowered their security precautions or did not conceal their guns thoroughly with adequate camouflage. The site was bombed again June 5.

Today several new houses bordering the south side of the road at that point most readily identify the site. The remains of the battery position is in the fields to the south of these new homes. The bunkers are hidden behind rose and raspberry rushes. Very few historians and even fewer tourists are aware of the battery's position. The farmer who owns the field is less than enthusiastic about having tourists walking amongst his crops. Nevertheless the bunkers and interconnecting tunnels are present.

Securing the battery, barracks and western ends of Exits Nos. 3 and 4 were the objectives of two battalions of the 101st Airborne Division. The 1st Battalion of the 502nd Regiment, under the command of 28 year old Lieutenant Colonel Patrick Cassidy, was to land in Drop Zone A, move out and overrun the battery and barracks then move northward to establish a perimeter defense and linkup with the 82nd Airborne Division on his western flank.

The 3rd Battalion under Lieutenant Colonel Robert G. Cole of the same regiment was also to land in Drop Zone A and move east to seize the western ends of beach Exists Nos. 3 and 4 at Audonville-la-Hubert and St. Martin-de-Varreville respectively.

The hedged fields and the absence of woods made the area ideally suitable for parachutists. The 1st and 3rd Battalion's (502nd Regiment) Drop Zone A was a meadow 3 kilometers west of St. Martin-de-Varreville, between Mesieres and Reuville.

The air armada of C-47's carrying the 82nd and 101st Airborne Divisions crossed the Contentin Peninsula from the west. German antiaircraft fire caused the pilots to take evasive action, throwing many off course. As a consequence the paratroopers of the Regiment, which had been designated for Drop Zone A, were misdropped and scattered. Not one pilot dropped his cargo in Drop Zone A. Several paratrooper "sticks" landed 40 kilometers to the north. Erroneously 20 planes dropped their paratroopers in Drop Zone C 5 kilometers to the south. The majority of the regiment landed to the north in the fields between the Cherbourg highway (N13) and the beach. A few were found in the dawn's early light drowned, entangled in their chutes and returned to the beach by the rising tide.

Cole's 3rd Battalion landed 300 meters east of Ste. Mere-Eglise. In a short time he collected approximately 75 men who, in the course of moving to their objectives, destroyed a small enemy convoy and took ten prisoners. He then marched his force towards St. Martin-de-Varreville, where he sent a small reconnaissance party to confirm the German battery was destroyed and the site deserted.

Cole split his force. The smaller group was sent into St. Martin-de-Varreville to seize Exit No 4. He with his main force moved south on Audonville-la-Hubert and its Exit No. 3.

Lieutenant Colonel Patrick Cassidy landed in the eastern outskirts of St. Germain-de-Varreville, 1 kilometer to the north. After collecting a small force and locating his whereabouts from the road signs, he moved towards the Mesieres crossroads (D14 and D423). The building on the northwest corner (objective W) was found unoccupied. After establishing his command post in the farmhouse, he checked the battery position. The battery had received many visitors in D-Day's early hours. The first American to scout the site had been Captain Frank Lillyman, leader of the division's pathfinder team and the first American soldier to land in Normandy. Colonel Cole's reconnaissance party had also checked the battery. Next Lieutenant Colonel Steve A. Chappuis with a dozen men moved in and was holding the position when Colonel Cassidy arrived. At the battery today several new homes stand on the site of the previous dwellings damaged by the RAF bombing in May and destroyed by German shellfire later in June. Just to the south of the homes past the garden are four blockhouses, two ammunition bunkers and two barracks. The battery position encompassed the area of a football field. Some buildings are hidden by bushes, others are in farm usage.

Following his meeting with Chappuis, Cassidy then proceeded with his mission of establishing the defenses at the Mesieres intersection and destroying the enemy in their barrack buildings X, Y and Z 300 meters immediately west of the intersection. For this mission he chose Staff Sergeant Harrison Summers with a platoon of 15 men.

Summers left Colonel Cassidy at his farm house command post and moved with his platoon to attack the German barracks. The barracks for the 150 German battery personnel was a collection of eleven farm buildings straddling the Mesieres road (D423) west of D14. The Germans had commandeered these buildings as they were conveniently close and large with thick stone walls for defense. Summers and his column came abreast of the first building. Unobserved Summers sprinted towards the door, kicked it open and burst in firing his sub-machine gun. Four Germans firing through slit boards in the wall fell from his fire. The other occupants, including several enemy civilians, escaped through the back door and fled to building 3. Summers, upon charging and forcefully entering another barracks (building 2) diagonally across the road found only a sick child. Private William A. Burt positioned his machine gun in front of building 2 pointing directly at the third building 50 meters away. His sweeping fire aimed at the ports kept the Germans under cover and their shooting wild. Lieutenant Brandenberger and Summers charged the third building. Unfortunately Brandenberger's shoulder triggered a booby trap causing it to explode. He was thrust to the ground with his arm badly shattered. Summers raced on to building 4. Again he kicked in the door, fired as he entered and shot six German snipers huddled inside. He rested on the doorstep for about half an hour soon to be joined by a lone 82nd Division captain. As they sprinted towards the 5th building a sniper put a bullet through the captain's heart. The Sergeant continued, kicked in another door and shot six more Germans. Private John Camin now joined Summers and as a team they attacked the next five buildings. From house to house they charged, one covering with the carbine while the other broke open the door and blasted with his sub-machine gun. Private Burt moved his machine gun along in phase with Summers and Camin, shooting at the Germans through their embrasures. Thirty Germans were killed in the five houses. Next they came to a chateau appearing building, charged it and in true Summers bravado fashion, kicked open the door and fleetingly gazed in amazement. To their surprise they found fifteen German artillery men sitting at the tables eating and seemingly oblivious to the fighting. Summers mowed them down. Eventually Summers and Camin reached the last building (number 11). This was the main barracks, a stonewalled two story structure. A high hedge on a thick bank separated the building from the road. They charged across the perfectly flat 75-meter open farmyard. By this time other Americans had joined the charge. German counterfire from the flanks killed seven and wounded four of the attacking Americans. The paratroopers fell back to the road. A hay stack near the barracks caught the attention of Private Burt who fired tracer bullets into the hay until it caught fire. The fire spread to a nearby ammunition shed and although it triggered many explosions it didn't flush the Germans occupying the large barracks. Germans did however come pouring out of the ammunition shed. Thirty were killed as they fled. Staff Sergeant Roy Nickrent with a bazooka arrived on the scene. From behind the hedgerow on the far side of the road he fired six rounds into the barracks's roof. As the bazooka would have been ineffective against the thick walls the alternative of burning the building had merit. The number of casualties among the Americans scattered along the hedgerow and ditch bordering the road increased. Five hours had lapsed since Summers had started his attack on the first building. As a result of the ranging inferno within the building the Germans were now forced to flee. Although many of them escaped, approximately fifty were shot down in the attempt. It was now 3:30 p.m. The Germans trying to escape from the firery building ran smack into a party of 502nd Regiment under Lieutenant Colonel John Michaelis. The converging of the two American bodies and the surrender of 31 Germans hiding in the bushes removed the last German resistance in the area. Summer's attack had yielded 150 Germans killed and captured. He was awarded the Distinguished

Service Cross and given a battlefield commission. (The "Sergeant York" of WWII died in the late 1980's.)

The scene of Summers action has not changed. The main house or chateau, as it is called by local inhabitants, has been repaired. The residents claim it was the battery commander's billet as well as the mess hall. Bullet holes in the doors and window frames though puttied are evident. The evenly spaced rows of holes are the result of small caliber automatic weapons. It has never been clearly established why the battery personnel were still billeted in the area two weeks after the battery site was vacated. The accuracy and precision of the RAF night bombing is evidenced by the battery damage without effect on the buildings 800 meters away.

When Colonel Cassidy ordered Summers' force to capture the barracks he also sent a force east into St. Martin-de-Varreville. Previously Colonel Cole's smaller force had moved northeast from the battery site bypassed the village and established their position at the western end of Exit No. 4. However, the Germans were in possession of the village with its church steeple containing a staffed artillery observation post. Colonel Cassidy's patrol entered the village and cleared the steeple observation post killing 12 Germans in the action. Their radio range finders and telephones were quickly disabled with a few well placed handgrenades. The village and beach exit road were cleared of Germans just as the last shots were being fired by Sergeant Summers at the barracks. Shortly afterwards the 22nd Regiment of the seaborne 4th Infantry Division crossed the causeway and passed through the paratroopers lines to move north to St. Germain-de-Varreville.

Related stories dealing with the seizure of the beach exits are Foucarville to the north, and Audonville-la-Hubert and Pouppeville to the south. The later activities of Colonel Cole and his battalion are described in the Carentan story.

2.6 Ste. Marie-du-Mont

(The town of Ste. Marie-du-Mont is 4 kilometers southwest of UTAH Beach on the D913 road to Carentan.)

In the pre-dawn hours of D-Day paratroopers of the 101st and 82nd US Airborne Divisions landed to the west of UTAH Beach to capture and hold the beach exit roads as well as the major roads crossing the Merderet and Douve Rivers to the west and southwest. Due west of Ste. Marie-du-Mont is the town of Hiesville. Drop Zone C for three battalions of the 506th Regiment and two battalions of the 501st Regiment of the 101st Airborne Division was located between these towns. One kilometer to the west and also one kilometer to the north of Ste. Marie-du-Mont were two German artillery batteries in open pit field positions. Parachutists drifting down in the dark pre-invasion hours of D-Day, landed amongst the German batteries and in the town. All were killed or captured. The Germans were now alert to the Americans presence.

The area was held by the 2nd Battalion of the 191st Artillery Regiment headquartered in Ste. Marie-du-Mont.

The church steeple was a natural observation platform affording the Germans a clear view of the beach and invasion fleet. As daylight dawned American fighter-bombers flew in low strafing the steeple and bombing the two artillery sites.

On D-Day late morning, the commander of the German 6th Parachute Regiment in Ste. Come-du-Mont, Lieutenant Colonel von der Heydte, sent the 1st Battalion to Ste. Marie-du-Mont to reinforce the artillery battalion. The gains made by the American paratroopers combined with the rapid inland advance of the 8th Regiment (4th Infantry Division) from UTAH Beach, stopped and isolated the German battalion before they could reinforce Ste. Marie-du-Mont.

The German battalion realized the batteries and town were in American hands. Their return route west had been cut off by the advancing Americans. The battalion veered south to cross the Douve marshes and regain their lines at Carentan. The battalion spent the night of June 6-7 finding and enjoying the American food rations from scattered airborne supply canisters. The next morning, June 7, the battalion divided, and in two groups attempted to cross the Douve River at la Barquette Lock and the Brevands footbridge. Both crossing points were in the hands of troops of the 101st US Airborne Division who after a fierce struggle captured the remnants of the battalion.

One kilometer west of Ste. Marie-du-Mont is a hamlet, Holdy, reached by taking the road (D80) northwest from Ste. Marie-du-Mont towards Les Forges. Seven hundred meters out of Ste. Marie-du-Mont a farm road branches to the southwest and to Holdy 800 meters along this road. Holdy was the site of one of the two German batteries with four 105mm guns. On the morning of June 6, 70 men of the US 506th Parachute Regiment were unable to make headway against the German defenses. With reinforcements and under the command of Captain Lloyd E. Patch of the 1st Battalion Headquarters Company and Captain Knuthraudstein of C Company, they re-attacked. The Germans were well entrenched within their earth embankments and gun emplacements. Assisted by American fighter-bombers the American attack was relentless. Infantry moved in from two sides and quickly rooted out the diehards.

Leaving a holding force at the battery Captain Patch moved southeast with his force against Ste. Marie-du-Mont. Simultaneously the 8th Infantry Regiment newly landed on UTAH were pressing the town from the east. (Route D913 from UTAH Beach to Ste. Marie-du-Mont was beach Exit No. 2). The two pronged attack squeezed out the defenders who abandoned the town to the Americans.

To the north of Ste. Marie-du-Mont, is the hamlet of Germain, reached by driving due north on the secondary road to Boutteville. A kilometer to the north a track leads eastwards to Germain. On D-Day the 3rd Battalion of the 8th Regiment, moving west from UTAH through La Houssaye had met little opposition. At Germain it encountered enemy dugouts, underground shelters, four 88mm guns and automatic weapons. After a short fire fight the battalion closed in. Fifty Germans were cut down as they tried to escape. One hundred were taken prisoner. The battalion then moved west to les Forges.

One and a half kilometer southeast of Ste. Marie-du-Mont is the hamlet of Brucheville. Here on July 2 a battalion of the 9th Engineering Command commenced construction of an Advanced Landing Ground A-16. Soft ground and a storm on July 21 hindered progress. Much needed but behind schedule the strip became operational in early August for the 36th Fighter Group, 9th Air Force. A commemorative plaque was placed at the site in 1990.

Numerous area plaques (14) in French tell of the D-Day actions. Three kilometers northeast of the Ste. Marie-du-Mont on D913 to UTAH Beach is the Danish Seamen Statue commemorating the eight hundred seamen who crewed in the invasion armada.

Picture 2: Vierville Road – Looking East

The road connects a major north-south highway to Utah Beach four miles east. Germans held the hedgerows and farm buildings adjacent to this tactically valuable roadway. This winding, narrow two miles is one of the most bloodied roads in the annals of the 101st Airborne Division's Normandy history. Paratroopers of Colonel Robert Sink's 506th Regiment landed outside the top of the photo. The subsequent battles to seize the road and open it up to traffic from Utah fill many pages. The converging roads at the bottom meet the Liberte' Expressway. A 2001 TV mini series, "Band of Brothers" depicted the Verville Road battle in an early episode.

Chapter 3 Utah Beachhead - Western Thrust

The invasion plan required the early capture of the transatlantic port of Cherbourg on the northern end of the Contentin Peninsula. The forces landing on UTAH Beach were to drive west, sever the peninsula at its neck, and secure the southern flank. Three divisions abreast would push northward and capture Cherbourg, providing the allies a major port capable of handling the unloading of troops and supplies arriving directly from the United States.

The German defense measure of flooding the rivers and marshes at the neck of the peninsula left only two major north-south highways as access into the peninsula. Over these roads German reinforcements and supplies would also have to pass to support the German defenders on the peninsula. Denying the Germans use of the two roads would hasten the fall of Cherbourg.

On the east, N13 passed northward from Carentan, over the Douve River marshes. The 101st Airborne Division, landing a few hours before the seaborne assault commenced, was to seize and hold the Carentan causeway.

On the west side, D900 ran north from Lessay to la Haye-du-Puits where it split into D900 and D904, both to Cherbourg.

The original plan was to have the 82nd Airborne Division land north of la Haye-du-Puits, cut the two highways and hold until it could be relieved by forces driving from the UTAH Beachhead. Division casualties were expected to be very high. Reinforcements from UTAH Beach were a long distance away. The 82nd's mission had a low probability of success. Intelligence in late May noted three new German divisions had moved into Normandy. On May 26, twelve days before D-Day, the mission was canceled. Instead, the division's objectives were shifted to the east in support of the beachhead. Landing northwest of the 101st Airborne Division, the 82nd had three functions. 1) To seize Ste. Mere-Eglise and stop German forces from moving against UTAH Beach. 2) To capture and hold the Merderet River crossings at Cauquigny (D15) and Chef -du-Pont (D70) for westward expansion. 3) To destroy the Douve River bridges southwest at Pont-l'Abbe (D24) and Beuzeville-la-Bastille (D69) thereby delaying German traffic moving north.

To achieve these three objectives the division was to parachute into three mission-specific drop zones. The 505th Regiment was to land in Drop Zone "0", the fields northwest of Ste. Mere-Eglise, then seize and hold the town and the village of Neuville-au-Plain (2 kilometers north on N13) against German counter-attacks from the north and northwest. The 507th Regiment was to land west of the Merderet River, 3 kilometers northwest of Cauquigny, move southeast to the hamlet, establish a 6 kilometers bridgehead on the west end of the causeway and move eastward to link up with the 505th at Ste. Mere-Eglise. The 508th Regiment was also to land west of the Merderet River, northwest of the Chef du Pont causeway, then establish a 6 kilometers bridgehead at the western end of the causeway. Units were to cross and hold Chef du Pont on the east bank until relieved by seaborne and gliderborne troops on D-Day afternoon. Other units, after landing, were to move south and destroy the bridges at Pont-l'Abbe and Beuzeville-la-Bastille. This plan was more feasible and less costly in terms of human sacrifice.

Its major shortcoming was the brief time available to familiarize the paratroopers with the terrain and their objectives. Unrecognized by allied intelligence the Germans had flooded the Merderet River pasturelands, as well as the Douve River valley. These two marshes at right angles to each other were to become significant factors as the paratroopers jumped in the dark hours of D-Day.

3.1 Grade Crossing 104

(2.5 kilometers west of Ste. Mere-Eglise on D15 to the railroad overpass. Walk north 1.5 kilometers along the railroad path).

In 1944 this was the 104th road crossing on the Paris to Cherbourg railroad line. Mr. Maurice Duboscq, wife, son (age 6), daughter (age 12) lived in the two story, four room house immediately adjacent to the railroad. Their responsibilities were to lower and raise the safety gate as trains came by and check the railline for debris and maintenance southward to Chef-du-Pont.

The Germans in the late summer of 1943 evaluated the low flat pasture land neighboring the house for a probable airfield. When Mr. Duboscq was sent to take soil samples he would add a little water thereby discouraging the airfield plan due to the marshy conditions. Instead the Germans, by control of la Barquette Lock, back flooded the river valley making it a marsh hidden beneath the wild tall grass and weeds

The US 507th Parachute Regiment (82nd Airborne Division) parachuted into this area and in the predawn hours of June 6. The Meredret marsh had been missed by our intelligence and reconnaissance personnel. Mr. Duboscq polled his flat bottomed boat throughout the marsh rescuing numerous paratroopers from drowning and recovering ammunition and food supplies. Mrs. Duboscq and the two children provided hot food and first aid to the wounded. Their home became an aid station to numerous Americans and several German soldiers. The marsh lapped the house's foundation. The retrieved supplies were stacked in their small garden up to the roof level. A parachute hung from the nearby telephone pole.

General Jim Gavin (82nd Division Assistant Commander) with his collected staff came by in the afternoon, having forded the marsh from the west, collected the rescued paratroopers and moved south along the railroad.

The following day an American officer, three soldiers and a German officer prisoner all in a jeep, took no heed of the Duboscq warning that there were many Germans on the other side of the marsh, attempted to cross the marsh. German machine guns opened up, the jeep nosed into the sunken river, the Americans died a hundred meters from the house. Three hours later the German officer with a chest wound crawled back to the edge of the marsh. He died an hour later in the arms of Genevieve, the 12 year old daughter. He was buried on the site at the marsh edge.

On June 10, from the attic window overlooking the marsh, Genevieve witnessed the Germans capture of the sixteen Americans holding the Cauquigny church (1.5 kilometers southwest at the western end of la Fiere causeway crossing the valley. They were marched along the marsh edge towards the Chateau Amfreville (1.5 kilometers due west of the house). 300-400 meters from the church the Germans massacred their prisoners with slashing bayonets in a indescribable horrible demonstration of inhumanity.

In January 1945, two escaped German POWs broke into the Duboscq home and stole clothing. They left two booby traps in the cooking fireplace triggered to detonate when Mrs. Duboscq prepared the evening meal. She was fortunate to spot the antipersonnel explosives hidden in the ashes and wired to her cooking crane.

As Genevieve and brother Claude were walking near the railroad bridge (1 kilometer south) after the war, August 14, 1945, at 9:30 a.m., (Claude tripped on a land mine trigger wire. He was killed instantly and Genevieve was very seriously injured. She lay unconscious for 9 days in a Cherbourg hospital only to awake to discover her face mutilated, eyes blinded, hand bones broken, throat punctured, abdomen torn open, a kneecap gone, both legs broken and multiple shrapnel wounds. Shielded from her brother's death until December 23 she went into cardiac arrest when hearing the news. She was revived but incurred some memory loss. Genevieve has spent 5 years in hospitals and had 33 operations that have restored her sight, voice, good looks and complete mobility. She's been married and has born six children.

The United States has recognized the Duboscq contribution of that June night and following days by awarding "Papa" Duboscq the Medal of Honor and the Duboscq family America's Guard of Honor.

3.2 Ste. Mere-Eglise

(13 kilometers north of Carentan on N13)

A famed horse breeding market town, Ste. Mere-Eglise, dates back many centuries. Roman roads leading to Cherbourg pass through the neighboring fields. In May 1940, a German armored division in a lightening thrust rushed up the Contentin Peninsula and seized Cherbourg thereby denying its use by the defeated British and French forces evacuating to England. The division's commander, Erwin Rommel, returned to the peninsula three and a half years later as a Field Marshal, Commander of Army Group B, responsible for the defense of Holland, Belgium and northern France against the allied invasion. For four years, the German swastika flew from the flag staff outside the town hall, bordering the old N13 road on the north edge of town.

Throughout that period, as the allies regained their strength and prepared to liberate France, the French Resistance was actively collecting information about the German defenses and troop dispositions. In the town, Antonin Maury, an electrician, was one such agent whose data about the battery at St. Martin-de-Varreville, resulted in its destruction before it could be used against the invasion fleet. Madame Maury, then a school teacher in St. Marcouf, 7 kilometers away, saw much as she traveled back and forth to her school by bicycle. Also, their young son, Georges, who did minor jobs around the German headquarters was able to pick up scraps of important information as well as having the opportunity to spit on the German's boots each night as he polished them. Using a concealed radio Antonin would transmit George's and other agents information to London.

On the night of June 5-6 an antiaircraft battery unit was holding the town with its service troops and trucks.

The pathfinders came an hour and a half ahead of the 805 aircraft carrying the 82nd and 101st Airborne Divisions. Laden with lights and beacons they were to locate the six regiments' respective drop zones. As the air armada approached the pathfinders would light and identify each of the landing zones for the pilots to maneuver their aircraft over the specified drop zone and drop their "sticks" of paratroopers accurately.

Before midnight June 5, and before the airborne operations commenced over Ste. Mere-Eglise, Mr. Hairon's villa on the south side of town square caught fire. The origin has never been determined but probably resulted from a flare or a spent antiaircraft shell. Allied air activity against radar sites had been heavy that evening in preparation for the invasion fleet crossing the channel and coming into radar range. The fire was not only consuming the villa but also threatening the nearby barn. The gutted shell of one of the buildings still stands today. The town's mayor, Alexander Renaud, sought out the German commander and was granted permission to raise the curfew enabling the residents to assist the firemen.

The parish priest, Father Louis Roulland, had the church bell rung summoning a hundred people to form a bucket brigade from the pump in the square across to the villa. (The pump, on the east side of the square is still there.) Thirty German guards flanked the line with rifles and automatic weapons. On the roof and in th belfry of thel ancient church a manned machine gun looked down on the scene, brilliantly illuminated by the flames climbing high above the buildings.

Over the crackle of the fire could be heard the drone of approaching aircraft. Cautious that the approaching aircraft might be on a bombing mission, Monsieur Renaud rushed into his pharmacy shop, on the north side of the square aroused his wife and three children in their living quarters in the rear and herded them into a passageway leading from the living room hopeful this corridor would afford more shelter. He then crossed the street and returned to the fire. (Months later Monsieur Renaud, a WWI officer, a veteran of the Verdun battles and a prolific author was presented with the Medal of Freedom by General Dwight D. Eisenhower. Monsieur Renault died on February 4, 1968 at the age of 73.)

The C-47 transport planes carrying the pathfinders came over from west to east at a height of between 150-175 meters. Looking up, both civilians and soldiers could see the blinking green jump lights through the planes' open doors. The majority of the planes had discharged their pathfinders to the west, near the intended drop zones. Two planes carrying the 2nd platoon of F Company, 2nd Battalion, 505th Regiment intended for zone "0" were still dropping their sticks as they passed over the town. Twenty came down in the square, another ten in the village. The low drop minimized the descent time during which the paratroopers, hanging in their harness, would be vulnerable to ground fire. It was 15 minutes into D-Day. The time was recorded by the first French woman to actually see a pathfinder. The town's school mistress, sixty year-old Madame Angele Levrault almost bumped into Private R.(Bob) M. Murphy when he landed in her garden.

In the square, confusion reigned. A ground to air crossfire was created as the Germans and descending paratroopers fired at each other with their sub machine guns. German bullets ignited a pathfinder's Gammon grenades. A burst of light, a tremendous explosion and an empty parachute weightlessly floated slowly ghostlike into the market place. Air currents feeding the fire sucked Private Charles Blakenship and another pathfinder into the burning building on the south side of the market square. Their ammunition and flares exploded leaving no traces and two "Missing, Presumed Dead". With parachutes and shroud lines tangled in the trees of the square, their comrades also died quickly.

Private John Steele dropped over the church. As he descended his chute caught on the west side pinnacle of the belfry. He drifted and the shrouds twisted around the spire on the southwest corner. Hanging helpless he played possum. The German machine gunner on the church roof assumed Steele had been killed and traversed his fire along to the corpses hanging in the trees. A German soldier in the square looked up, aimed his gun and fired. The bullets ripped into Steele's jump boots and feet. Fearing any movement on his part would attract more bullets he suppressed his pain and anguish and hung limply, feigning death. Meanwhile, the bells in the belfry of St. Vincent de Paul tolled, deafening him for several days thereafter. A German observer in the belfry pulled Steele in and made him a prisoner. Steele was abandoned in the morning when the Germans withdrew.

Private Ken Russell's parachute was also caught on the steeple. A German on the square was about to shoot Steele and Russell but was killed by his dying victim Sergeant John Ray whom he had shot moments before. Russell cut his shrouds, fell into the marketplace then raced across the square, the street and into the trees with machine gun bullets whistling by.

The slaughter in the square quickly ended. A dozen troopers were either killed (Charles Blankenship, H. T. Bryant, Harold Cadish,

Van Holsbeck, John Ray, Penrose Shearer and Landislaw Tlapa) or captured. The remainder managed to land beyond the light of the fire and had a moment to get out of their harness and defend themselves to advantage.

Between 1 and 1:30 a.m. the air transports carrying the 82nd Airborne Division crossed the west coast of the peninsula. Visibility was good over the channel, enabling the planes to stay in their tight formation. However, cloud banks over the peninsula caused the formations to spread out to avoid air collisions. German antiaircraft fire further dispersed the formation as the planes increased speed, twisted and turned to avoid the flack.

Of the division's three drop zones the 505th Regiment targeted for "0" was the most successful in having its men land close together although 3 plane loads were dropped 28 kilometers to the north. The majority landed as planned west and northwest between Ste. Mere-Eglise and the Merderet River.

Lieutenant Colonel Edward C. Krause's 3rd Battalion could only collect 108 men (25%). Dividing his small force into two companies, Krause headed southeast towards the town. En route, a local Frenchman told him of the German roadblocks guarding each of the town's entrances. Not wishing to become engaged and held up outside the town Colonel Krase had the Frenchman lead the force into the town's center through a sunken path unknown to the Germans. Six small detachments were directed out to the roads entering the town to fend off German reinforcements entering the town center. In the town, not wishing to reveal their own positions, the Americans used only knives, bayonets and handgrenades. The battle was quiet and quick. Eleven Germans died and thirty were captured. The young German Lieutenant Zitt commanding the flack unit misjudged the size of the American force and withdrew his battery southwards along old N13.

Climbing a telephone pole on the southwest corner of the square, one of the paratroopers hacking at the cable with his bayonet severed the German's main communications cable to Cherbourg.

Krause took over the town hall, pulled down the swastika and raised the old torn regimental flag that they had flown over Naples at the time of its capture October, 1943. The stars and stripes now flew over the first town liberated by the Americans in France. (The flag is on exhibit in the town hall). It was 5 a.m., June 6. The German main reinforcement and supply road (N13) had been cut. The American force now 360 strong strengthened their defense positions anticipating counterattacks to reopen this vital link.

An American roadblock 200 meters south of the last house on old N13 was positioned at the point where the hedgerow arching in from the northwest joins the highway hedgebank. At 9:30 a.m. a German force of two companies, three light tanks and two self-propelled guns preceded by mortar and machine gun fire, approached along the road behind a herd of cattle. An American outguard ahead of the roadblock, Private Dominick de Tullio, waving his field jacket dispersed the herd and then fired into the surprised and unprotected infantry. (Tullio was killed the following morning on a mercy mission to obtain water for the wounded). The German force split and attempted to outflank the roadblock through the bordering fields.

The timely arrival of the regiment's 2nd Battalion gave Krause the opportunity of moving more of his men into the southern perimeter to counter the strong German attack. The 2nd Battalion under the command of Lieutenant Colonel Benjamin Vandervoort had a relatively successful landing in their "0" Drop Zone. Although Vandervoort himself had broken an ankle he had collected 575 of his 650 men. The German attack was pressed without gains, until noon. Colonel Krause was wounded, German artillery fire caused damage and casualties in the town.

Fauville, the elevated village a kilometer south of Ste. Mere-Eglise was the origin of the German attack. After repulsing the German attack of that morning Colonel Krause, in the early afternoon, sent the eighty men of Item Company south down the secondary road D67 to outflank the German position from the west. The winding road bordered by the hedgerows caused the company to cut eastwards prematurely, bringing it in front of the German positions. Although ineffective in attacking the defenses the company destroyed a small convoy, misleading the Germans as to their size and strength. The German attack force still facing the roadblock pulled back into their Fauville pocket and Item Company withdrew to Ste. Mere-Eglise. The widening of N13 and the Ste. Mere-Eglise/Fauville exit ramp, from the Liberte Expressway have altered a portion of this battle site area.

The German 709th Division holding the UTAH sector was ordered to retake Ste. Mere-Eglise on D-Day. Two battalions (1058th

Regiment) attacking from the north along old N13 were held up 2 kilometers north at Neuville-au-Plain (separate battle site story). In the late afternoon the small American force was forced to withdraw into the Ste. Mere-Eglise perimeter.

During the evening and night German units moved into the area north of the town in preparation for the next day's attack. The German strength became formidable; four battalions and ten 75mm self-propelled guns. (456th, 457th, battalions of the 1058th Regiment, 3rd battalion of the 243rd Regiment, the Strum Battalion and a company of the 709th Battalion.)

German artillery softened the American defenses for the D+1 morning attack. In the first two days of liberation German shells and mortars killed sixty civilians, who had endured the four long years of occupation.

At dawn the tempo of the shelling showed a marked increase. At 7 a.m., June 7, two battalions attacked the American positions on the northern edge of town. Paralleling the road, the Strum Battalion on the west side and the 1058th on the east supported by self-propelled guns attempted to regain the town and reopen the highway to Carentan.

The 1058th Regiment's battalions were unsuccessful on their side of the road but on the west the Strum Battalion battled its way into the northern outskirts. American antitank gunners shot it out at close quarters with the self-propelled 75s. The German attack had become a serious threat. The 82nd's Commander, Major General Matthew B. Ridgway, requested armor. The 746th Tank Battalion (Lieutenant Colonel C. G. Hupfer) in reserve at Reuville (3 kilometers east) moved into Ste. Mere-Eglise mid afternoon. The American tank column moved north out of the town, along the road but was blocked by German armor and antitank guns. Seven hundred meters northeast of the town, on the Baudienville road (D15), Colonel Hupfer discovered an undefended trail leading north into Neuville-au-Plain, paralleling N13. Rushing a company of tanks along the trail he outflanked the German line of attack. Simultaneously, the 2nd Battalion (8th Regiment, 4th Division) and the 2nd Battalion of the 505th Regiment attacked the hamlet of Sigeville, 0.5 kilometers north of Ste. Mere-Eglise on old N13, successfully capturing 300 Germans and causing the remainder to retreat. With American tanks in Neuville-au-Plain and the loss of

Sigeville, the German attack ceased and their force withdrew northward.

The Germans left the remnants of the 1058th Battalion as a rear guard, hidden in the sunken road east of N13, connecting with the highway in the town's north outskirts. Easy Company (505th Regiment) blocked its exits while tanks diverted from the road poured artillery and machine gun fire through the hedgerows. The casualties were tragic. Recognizing his impossible position, the German commander surrendered with his remaining 160 men. By midnight German threats to recapture Ste. Mere-Eglise had been eliminated. Colonels Krause and Vandervoort received the Distinguished Service Cross for their actions and leadership.

Although the 82nd gains on D-Day were unspectacular, they gained the time necessary for the seaborne forces to land and move inland. Glider-delivered reinforcements strengthened the division until 4th Division forces moving west from UTAH Beach took over the airborne positions, enabling them to direct their attention to new objectives westward.

In the following days as casualties mounted, two cemeteries were established to the east and west of the town. Cemetery Number 1 site is 0.7 kilometers east on the Reuville road and Number 2 site is on the road to Chef-du-Pont (D67) approximately 1 kilometer southwest of the town square. Commemorative tablets mark both sites. The remains were buried here until transferred to the American, St. Laurent Cemetery overlooking OMAHA Beach or returned to the United States. In 1948 re-internments were completed and the temporary cemeteries were closed.

Several airstrips were built near Ste. Mere-Eglise for refueling and rearming close support fighter aircraft, for incoming supplies and evacuation of wounded. One such Advanced Landing Ground, A-6, was located 3.5 kilometers to the northeast (road D17) at Beuzeville-au-Plain on the LeLonde Farm. In the late evening of D-Day, Lieutenant Colonel McCrory, of the 9th Engineers Command, leading a small party, attempted to reconnoiter the area to site the first ALG. After clearing the edge of the proposed site, they were stopped by withering German fire. Early the next morning the Germans laid down a nebelwerfer (mortar) barrage forcing the Americans to move their heavy equipment several fields to the north. A little later, Master Sergeant Charles A. Lane was able to reach the proposed site and although subjected to sniper and antitank gun fire, succeeded in making a reconnaissance of the proposed site. At dawn, on June 8, a detachment of the 819th Battalion, consisting of 4 officers and 105 men proceeded to Beuzeville, where they met the previous detachment and commenced construction of the ALG at 10 a.m. Throughout the day they worked. Enemy aircraft and sniper fire prevented them from continuing through the night. The first aircraft to use the field were three Royal Air Force Spitfires, of a Polish squadron, on June 10. The following day American airplanes, including five gliders with ammunition and reinforcements, landed. On the 12th twenty tons of urgently needed ammunition was parachuted into the field. Initially the A-6 airfield was developed as a rearmament and refueling strip for fighter aircraft. Its importance and usefulness expanded rapidly. The addition of pierced steel planks (PSP) to the runway and hardstands was completed by June 14 enabling C-47 cargo planes to re-supply close to the front lines. The field was used for the evacuation of the 82nd Airborne Division in mid July after four continuous weeks of front line duty. Today the fences and gates in the area are fabricated from the abandoned runway and hardstands. Steel mesh bears mute evidence of the ALG's presence 55 plus years ago.

There is much in Ste. Mere-Eglise today reminding us of its 1944 battles. The church of St. Vincent de Paul bears the patchwork of repaired damages. The pillar as you enter has bullet holes. Two stained glass windows commemorate the actions of the paratroopers and the town's place in American history. From the church belfry Private Steele's plastic effigy hangs in its parachute harness. Railings around the square show bullet hits. Although Mr. Renaud has died, his thriving pharmacy remains. Standing at its front door, facing directly across the square one can envision the scenes of those dramatic early hours of D-Day. In 1963, General Eisenhower revisited the town and recorded a filmed interview with Madame Renaud sitting on a bench with the church as a backdrop. In June 1964, the twentieth anniversary, the interview was part of the 20th Century Hour on television.

The honor of being the first town in France liberated by the Americans is well celebrated each year at the June 6 fete. On the east side of the square the skeletal structure of the barn still casts its morning shadows across the square. An outstanding Airborne

Museum has been built on the south side of the market square. Designed by the same architect who planned the Arromanches Museum, Mr. Francois Carpentier. It's roof is shaped and molded to resemble a huge convoluted parachute from which a glider wing juts forward forming the entrance canopy. Upon entering one passes through the foyer, a WACO glider containing dummy pilots and glider troops. The building corner stone was laid by General James Gavin June 6, 1961, and opened on the 20th Anniversary, June 6, 1964. The C-47 "Argonia" stands on the site of Mr. Hairon's burned home.

The square, Place d'Eglise, was used in the filming of scenes for the movie "The Longest Day" the adaptation of Cornelius Ryan's book of the same name. A camera mounted in a helicopter simulated a paratroopers view as he descended into the face of death from the German machine guns. The town's electric power had to be cut off to permit the use of a crane to lower the parachutists into the desired positions. The 4-meter high monument commemorating the landing adjacent to N13 was camouflaged under a pathfinder's parachute. It is a masterpiece of realism. The veterans, civilians and technical advisors recreated those few minutes with precision and accuracy.

In front of the town hall a monument commemorates the names of the town's citizens who gave their lives for liberation. Also, in front is "0" kilometer marker of the Liberty Route that follows the route of the Free French 2nd Armored Division through France. There is also a plaque in recognition of Generals Ridgway and Gavin. There are 13 memorial plaques in the town area commemorating the events and forces involved.

Picture 3: Ste. Mere Eglise

American paratroopers of the 82nd Airborne Division erroneously parachuted into the town square in the early hours of D-Day. M. Hairon's burning barn, top mid-photo, illuminated the scene making it easy for the Germans in the square to shoot the descending troopers. Private John Steele's parachute caught on the steeple. He survived by feigning death until the town was occupied in the daylight hours. His parachute effigy still hangs on the steeple. The airborne museum stands on the site of Hairon's barn. The town has been a gathering point for returning veterans of all divisions.

3.3 Foucarville

(The village of Foucarville is 6 kilometers northwest of UTAH Beach)

It's significance lay in the fact that the road paralleling the beach road passes through the village and it was the westerly end of beach Exit No. 5 which continued west through Ste. Mere-Eglise and across the Merderet River valley.

To the east, the marshes separating Foucarville from UTAH Beach had been flooded. Germans holding the western approaches of the five beach exit roads could readily delay the invasion timetable by denying the American seaborne forces access to the Contentin Peninsula across these causeways. As a counter move against this German defense strategy, paratroopers of the 101st Airborne Division were dropped to the west of the marshes, with the objective of capturing and holding the westerly ends of the beach exits until the seaborne infantry on UTAH Beach was able to cross the exit causeways and move inland to consolidate their gains.

Foucarville's situation controlled all movements along the main north-south road, the road German armor would have to use to reach the beachhead. Elements of the 101st Airborne Division parachuted into the area at 1:20 on D-Day morning. A fortified position on the hill at the northwest corner at the Foucarville intersection dominated the town.

Nine paratroopers who landed on the fortified hill were immediately taken as prisoners. Lieutenant Joseph Smith fought hard but was wounded. Two others captured were Sergeant Charlie Ryan and Private Hewitt Tippins of A Company (502nd Regiment). Others landing near the causeway, discovered that this, the most northerly exit and a direct road westward, was undefended and not mined.

The plan called for B Company (502nd Regiment) with 250 men to occupy the town in the early hours. Captain Cleveland Fitzgerald was only able to muster eleven of the misdropped paratroopers and arrived at the village at 2 a.m. The resulting skirmish around the courtyard of the German headquarters has been reported as the first unit battle on D-Day by the 101st Airborne Division. The intense small arms fire forced the Americans to withdraw 700 meters to the south. Captain Fitzgerald, with 25 of his men, re-entered the town at daybreak. Fitzgerald killed a German at close range but received a bullet through his chest. (Assuming his wound was fatal he asked his men to move on. He recovered but was killed in Reims (France) a month after the war ended in an auto accident.) The German soldiers took up advantageous positions in the houses from where they easily "picked off" the Americans in the streets. The stubborn resistance of the garrison supported by automatic weapons from the fortified hill forced the attackers to withdraw. Simultaneously, the Germans withdrew from the village into the fortified position. When US patrols reentered the town to collect their wounded, they discovered the village was unoccupied. Although the American force was small they immediately established roadblocks.

Roadblock #1 was by the church where the lane from the church joins the street. Lieutenant Wallace Swanson and his three riflemen faced eastward. Their meager firepower consisted of a grenade rifle and a machine gun. Germans, retreating from UTAH Beach occupied the hedgerows facing the roadblock position. Others entered the church through the rear door and climbed to the belfry, from where they snipped at Swanson's force below. Several more paratroopers arrived on the scene that were dispatched to clear the church. Four German snipers emerging from the church were shot by a paratrooper lying in wait outside the door. In the early evening Sergeants W. Willis Sweibl, Charles Assay and Private Leroy Nicolai darted into the church, killing a fleeing German, and fired up through the belfry floor boards into the German position, killing its occupants.

Roadblock #2, also under the command of Lieutenant Swanson, was established at noon at the Foucarville intersection, and consisted of 6 riflemen, a bazooka team and a rifle grenade. It faced to the east protecting their flank against retreating Germans from UTAH and to the northwest, facing the fortified hill.

Roadblock #3 was also established at noon 300 meters west of the Foucarville intersection on the Haut Fornel road (D19) at the fork where the secondary path leads southwest through the orchards. It was under the command of Sergeant C. Theiland, with 12 riflemen and 2 machine guns. At 3 p.m. the Germans on the fortified hill attempted to outflank the position from the west, coming into the roadblock from the field to the north. At 10 meters the American riflemen fired through the hedgerow into the surprised Germans who stampeded back up the hill. The embankment along the north side of the road protected the paratroopers until German antitank gun fire, from the hill position, tore up the protective hedgerows. Private J. T. Lyell and two comrades crawled to the crest of the hill and located the antitank gun between two dugouts. With a few well aimed handgrenades Lyell knocked out the gun and crew, but in the skirmish that followed he was severely wounded, resulting in his death later in the day.

Roadblock #4 was established in the late afternoon 600 meters west of the Foucarville intersection on the Haut Fornel road. The twelve riflemen with two machine guns, two bazookas and 15 lbs. of explosive faced west. At 5:30 p.m. a German convoy of one car and five trucks from Haut Fornel was ambushed at the roadblock. All trucks were destroyed and the men they carried were either killed, captured or escaped back to Haut Fornel.

The fortified hill was 40 meters to the northwest of the village intersection. A sea of barbed wire enclosed the German positions. The slope was studded with concrete shelters and pillboxes. To the rear, screened by tall trees, was a motor park. Machine gun platforms were located in the trees. From these elevated positions, automatic weapons sprayed death down into roadblock #2 at the intersection.

At 10 p.m. the Germans raised the white flat and 87 men and a woman paraded down the slope. Lieutenant Smith being held captive in the commander's pillbox had told the Germans of a scheduled bombardment of their position at 10:30 p.m. The surrendering Germans paraded down the slope and the diehards headed north. The 17 American prisoners quickly seized guns and fired on the retreating Germans, killing fifty. Smith killed the German commander, a major.

Today, there is little evidence of the concrete pillboxes that were embedded in the slope. The slope if rough and uneven due to shellfire at the time of battle and the subsequent removal of the German fortifications. Loop holes can still be seen in the church tower, but the doors and the floorboards, through which the Americans machine gunned the Germans, have since been replaced.

Two and a half kilometers west of Foucarville, on the Haut Fornel road, is the hamlet of Beuzeville-au-Plain. Here, in the late evening of D-Day, Lieutenant Colonel McCrory, of the 9th Engineers Command with a small party attempted to reconnoiter the area to site the first Advanced Landing Strip (A-6) for the air force. After clearing the edge of the proposed site, they were stopped by withering

German fire. Early the next morning the Germans laid down a nebelwerfer (mortar) barrage forcing the Americans to move their heavy equipment several fields to the north. A little later Master Sergeant Charles A. Lane was able to reach the proposed site and although subjected to sniper and antitank gun fire, succeeded in making a reconnaissance of the proposed site. At dawn, on June 8, a detachment of the 819th Battalion consisting of 4 officers and 105 men, proceeded to Beuzeville, where they met the previous detachment and commenced construction of the Advanced Landing Ground at 10 a.m. Throughout the day they worked. Enemy aircraft and sniper fire prevented them from continuing through the night. On June 10 three Spitfires piloted by Poles of the Royal Air Force landed. The first American plane used the strip on June 11. Five gliders landed with ammunition and reinforcements on the same day. On the 12th, twenty tons of urgently needed ammunition was parachuted into the field. Initially the A-6 airfield was developed as a rearmament and refueling strip for fighter aircraft. Its importance and usefulness expanded rapidly. Tracking of the runway and a marshaling area beside the field were completed by June 14. The field was also used for supply and evacuation of the 82nd Airborne Division in mid July.

Related stories are St. Martin-de-Varreville, Audonville-la-Hubert and Pouppeville. All these villages are to the south at the western ends of the beach exit routes.

3.4 Neuville-au-Plain

(2 kilometers north of Ste. Mere-Eglise on N13)

The US 82nd Airborne Division had been assigned the tasks of establishing a 6 kilometers deep bridgehead west of the Merderet River, capturing Ste. Mere-Eglise, Neuville-au-Plain, and Baudienville and thereby secure the northern perimeter defenses until seaborne forces could come to their relief.

The three battalions of the 505th Regiment were to parachute into Drop Zone 0, 2 kilometers southwest of Neuville-au-Plain. Lieutenant Colonel B. H. Vandervoort's 2nd Battalion, after landing, would strike off to the northeast, capture Neuville-au-Plain and Baudienville and hold until relieved. In these positions the battalion would act as an outer defense ring to Ste. Mere-Eglise's important crossroads and stop German attempts to move against the UTAH Beachhead from the northwest.

Clouds over the Contentin Peninsula and German antiaircraft fire broadened the troop carriers flight path. Consequently the entire battalion did not land in the designated drop zone but became scattered and dispersed. As the darkness of June 6 gave way to dawn the paratroopers gathered and shortly thereafter about half the battalion had collected and moved off to their objectives.

The exact purpose of Vandervoort's 2nd Battalion's redirection to Ste. Mere-Eglise is uncertain. The 3rd Battalion in Ste. Mere-Eglise was holding off a concerted German attack from the south, consequently Colonel W.E. Ekman, the regiment's commander, ordered the 2nd Battalion in to support the 3rd Battalion. Possibly poor radio communications during the critical hours of 5 to 8 a.m. left doubt as to whether the 3rd Battalion had taken Ste. Mere-Eglise. The 2nd Battalion was directed to make certain the key town had actually been captured. Regardless, the 2nd Battalion was redirected from its primary objectives and served an important function in supporting the 3rd Battalion.

Colonel Vandervoort, mindful of his objectives, sent the 3rd Platoon of Dog Company to Neuville-au-Plain to clear the hamlet, mine the highway to the north, and establish a defensive position.

Lieutenant T.B. Turnbull, nicknamed "Chief" , with forty-one men in two parallel columns flanking the highway, trotted north along

N13 2 kilometers to Neuville-au-Plain. Slight opposition in the hamlet was overcome. The north edge of the village appeared to be a suitable site for his defensive positions. The village tops a rise that descends to the north channeling their would-be attackers up the ascending slope.

Lieutenant Turnbull stationed two riflemen and a bazooka man in the village to defend against a potential armored breakthrough.

A few meters north of the Baudienville road (D15E), a hedgerow runs eastward to the woods, while an open field, affording no cover, stretches north. Behind the hedgerow, and spread along its full length, he placed the main body of the platoon and the machine gun.

Further north 100 meters, down the slope and west of the highway a sunken road bordered by a wall enclosed orchard provided an excellent defensive position for a squad.

Shortly thereafter, at 10:30 a.m., units of two battalions of the German 1058th Regiment, in column formation, approached Neuville-au-Plain along N13 from the north. The 91st Division had been ordered to recapture Ste. Mere-Eglise. Unaware the Americans had occupied Neuville-du-Plain the Germans whistled and sang as they ascended the slope to Turnbull's positions.

Lieutenant I. Michaelman's squad, west of the highway moved across the sunken road into the orchard and barn. Before his squad could begin flank fire into the unsuspecting column, a volley from Turnbull's main body sent the column into the ditches. Not realizing Michaelman's squad was positioned in the orchard and barn, a German platoon moved into the orchard to outflank Turnbull's position from the west. A sharp fire fight in the orchard and around the barn ensued at which time the Lieutenant was wounded. His squad pulled back across the sunken road into their previous positions.

Moments later the balance tipped in the American's favor as Colonel Vandervoort arrived by jeep with two 57mm antitank guns in tow. One was dropped at the crossroads and the second positioned to the east of the long barn on the Baudienville road. The jeep and its Colonel sped off to Ste. Mere-Eglise.

Immediately a duel commenced between the antitank gun at the intersection, supported by the bazooka man and a German self-propelled gun (SP) and a Mark IV tank on the road north of the apple orchard. The SP was destroyed, the Mark IV damaged and the bazooka man killed.

Over the next few hours German mortar fire pounded the Americans creating casualties and weakening their defense. In the afternoon, as the mortar barrage continued along the American line, the Germans made a second advance. Moving out wide around both flanks a giant pincer was developed. Through the woods to the east and around the chateau to the west the attackers bypassed the paratroopers line. With increasing casualties Turnbull was unable to deploy his troops to defend wider area, and thus halt the envelopment.

The vice tightened on Turnbull's men. Sniper fire was now being effectively directed into his line. A machine gun, in the barn in the orchard, was cutting down the few remaining men, while the opportunity was still available he withdrew his twenty-three men. At dusk, on the southern outskirts of the village, the extricated force joined with a platoon of Easy Company, sent north to assist in his withdrawal. In the darkness the sixteen men of the original forty-two re-entered their lines at Ste. Mere-Eglise.

The following morning Turnbull was killed in the northern outskirts of the town during a German attack. The value of his platoons fight at Neuville-au-Plain was incalculable. By stopping the German advance he gave the defenders of Ste. Mere-Eglise the necessary time to halt the major morning attack of June 6 from the south. If the defenders had been compelled to defend against attacks from the north and south simultaneously it is conceivable that Ste. Mere-Eglise would have fallen back into German hands, re-opening the highway and allowing the flow of German reserves into the sector.

Throughout June 6 evening and the night June 6-7, German infantry and armor entered Neuville-au-Plain in preparation for their attack to retake Ste. Mere-Eglise on June 7. The attack was launched at 7 a.m. On the same afternoon the American 746th Tank Battalion was thrown into the battle. Its commander, Lieutenant Colonel C. G. Hupfer, discovered a sunken road paralleling N13, the axis of the German attack and connecting Ste. Mere-Eglise with Neuville-au-Plain. Pressing a column up the road the American tanks entered Neuville-au-Plain via the Baudienville road (D15E). The battle that followed in the village knocked out two American and two German tanks. Sixty prisoners were taken and nineteen captive paratroopers, including several of Turnbull's platoon were released.

This outflank, coincidental with a similar effort to the northwest, blunted the German attack on Ste. Mere-Eglise, causing them to withdraw. The American tanks held Neuville-au-Plain until 9 p.m. then withdrew from their exposed positions. The Germans reoccupied the hamlet during the night of June 7-8.

The following morning the American 8th Infantry Regiment (4th Infantry Division) attacked north from Ste. Mere-Eglise. Artillery fire fell on the attackers until they entered Neuville-au-Plain in the mid afternoon. A sharp skirmish followed and for the third and last time the town fell into American possession. Pressing on, by nightfall, the 8th Regiment was 3 kilometers, north of Neuville-au-Plain.

3.5 les Forges

(3.5 kilometers south of Ste. Mere-Eglise)

On D-Day morning the US 4th Infantry Division successfully assaulted UTAH Beach. The division's 8th Regiment commanded by Colonel James A. Van Fleet moved westward across Exits 1 (Pouppeville), 2 (la Houssaye) and 3 (Audonville-la-Hubert). The 2nd and 3rd Battalions crossing Exits 1 and 2 respectively passed to the north of Ste. Marie-du-Mont and joined D70 on the town's west side. Continuing west, paralleling the road's north and south sides, the battalions arrived at the les Forges crossroads in the mid-afternoon. G Company moved south down N13, through Blosville (1 kilometer) and established their perimeter on the southern edge of the village. The 3rd Battalion moved north a few hundred meters along N13, and spread out in the fields facing north. The 2nd Battalion moved southwest into the fields a hundred meters from the crossroads.

A little later 90 men of the 325th Glider Infantry Regiment, a platoon of the 4th Cavalry Reconnaissance Squadron and a company of tanks (746th Tank Battalion) entered the crossroads from Ste. Marie-du-Mont.

The tanks were heading to Ste. Mere-Eglise to reinforce the 505th Regiment (82nd Airborne Division). The glider troopers were the seaborne vanguard, arriving to prepare the area to receive glider landings that evening.

Pre-planned before the invasion commenced, the les Forges crossroads was the center of Glider Zone W with a diameter of 3 kilometers. That evening and the following morning two groups of gliders were scheduled to land the entire regiment.

The airborne landing of the 82nd Division north and west combined with the westward advance of the forces from UTAH Beach had compressed a reinforced German battalion into a pocket that included a section of N13 between les Forges and Ste. Mere-Eglise. The southern perimeter of the Fauville pocket was just 2 kilometers north of the crossroads, its slightly elevated position enabled the defenders to overlook the glider landing area.

At 5 p.m. Colonel Edson D. Raff, Commander of the 82nd Airborne Division's reinforcement tank battalion, had accompanied the tank company into les Forges. He sent a scout car and tank on a reconnaissance along N13. Three hundred meters north of the crossroads a high velocity 88mm shell from a German battery hit the scout car head on. It didn't explode, however, the impact pushed the car backward into the tank, disabling the latter by dislodging a tread.

A concerted effort by the tanks and infantry to dislodge the Germans was unsuccessful, resulting in the loss of two tanks west of the highway in the triangular field between the northwest farm road and the highway.

Precisely at 9 p.m. as scheduled, the sixty gliders cut loose from their tugs and silently soared into the no man's land between the German and American forces. The German gunners could hardly believe their eyes. Antiaircraft guns and heavy machine guns concentrated on the slow airborne gliders. Mortars, artillery and automatic weapons swept the fields harboring the landed gliders. The American tanks and mortars fired a counter barrage into the German lines attempting to lessen their fire. For the glider troops, the serenity of England and the flight were now mere memories. As they neared the ground, bullets, shrapnel and shells ripped their wood and canvas "birds" apart. Damaged, their structure snapped on impact and their contents were flung across the fields at 100 kilometers per hour. The survivors scurried to the hedgerows for protection. Confused and disorganized they huddled until darkness had fallen and then, dragging their wounded, they entered the American lines. One hundred and sixty of their comrades lay dead in the fields to the north amongst the shattered carriers. The wounded were concentrated at the crossroads for treatment and transferred to England from UTAH Beach.

The next morning June 7 the 8th Regiment attacked the pocket from the south and east, successfully overrunning the defenders.

Shortly afterwards the second flight of gliders brought in the remainder of the 325th Regiment without losses. The regiment's three battalions then moved west to clear a German pocket at Carquebut (two kilometers southwest) and reinforce the paratroopers at Chef-du-Pont, la Fiere and Ste. Mere-Eglise.

The casualties of this battlefield and others in the vicinity were buried at the temporary wartime cemetery No. 3 at Blosville (one kilometer south on N13). A commemorative marker erected January 21, 1958 identifies its location. After the war the bodies were either returned to the United States or reinterned in the St. Laurent Cemetery overlooking Omaha Beach.

3.6 Fauville Pocket

(1.5 kilometers south of St. Mere-Eglise on N13)

On the morning of June 6, the US 4th Infantry Division successfully assaulted UTAH Beach. The division's 8th Regiment, under the command of Colonel James A. Van Fleet, moved westwards rapidly.

The landing of the paratroopers of the 82nd Airborne Division north and west of Fauville cut off German escape from the pressure of the advancing seaborne forces.

Consequently the 795th German "Georgian" Battalion and elements of German units became pocketed on the ridge running from a point 1 kilometer west of Fauville to Turqueville, 3 kilometers to the east, with a north-south depth of about 1 kilometer.

By D-Day afternoon, to the south (2 kilometers) at the les Forges crossroads, the 3rd Battalion (8th Regiment) with a company of 749th Battalion tanks was pressing northward trying to get through to Ste. Mere-Eglise. The regiment's 2nd Battalion was maneuvering into position south of Ecoqueneauville, and to the east the 1st Battalion was pressing the "Georgians" conscripts from the Russian State of Georgia at Turqueville.

Before this tight envelopment, the German force had consumed much of its strength in the late morning hours when two companies, three tanks, and two self propelled guns had attacked north from Fauville up N13 into the American lines at Ste. Mere-Eglise. Without much gain the force was greatly weakened. In the early afternoon the American paratrooper I Company (505th Regiment), destroyed a convoy on the highway in Fauville, further weakening the German force. The afternoon developments by the US 8th Regiment pulled the string tight around the pocket.

Weakened, but still defiant, the encircled battalion denied the Americans the ridge and the highway through to Ste. Mere-Eglise.

Unknowingly, their elevated position overlooked the American Glider Landing Zone W to the south, the designated area to be used D-Day evening by the 325th Glider Infantry Regiment.

Unsuccessful US attempts to capture the feature left the Germans and Georgian's in a dominant position. At 9 p.m. sixty gliders soared into the no man's land between the opposing forces. The German fire killed 160 and wounded many more. A second glider landing was scheduled for the next morning.

Before the defenders of the pocket had a second opportunity to enfilade the landing zone, the 8th Regiment attacked synchronously with its three battalions in the early morning of June 7. At Turnqueville to the east the 1st Battalion fought tenaciously, eventually succeeding when one of its Russian-speaking members persuaded the Georgians' to surrender.

On the south side of the ridge the 3rd Battalion was stopped by heavy machine gun and artillery fire at the creek over which N13 passes at the low point in the road.

East of the 3rd Battalion, the 2nd Battalion moved against Ecoqueneauville along D387, out of Sebeville. Their attack carried and they outflanked the ridge positions that were holding up the 3rd Battalion at the foot of the slope.

The three battalions mopped up the pocket and continued north to Ste. Mere-Eglise.

3.7 La Fiere Causeway

(3 kilometers west of Ste. Mere-Eglise on D15)

The elevated causeway is the one kilometer east-west roadway (D15) crossing the lower flat grazing lands of the Merderet River valley. Both ends and the causeway saw furious fighting. The flooded river valley focused the action along the deadly causeway. The narrow, meandering Merderet River rimming serene pastures is a silent witness to the carnage that occurred in the surrounding farms, fields and marshlands that claimed 600 American casualties.

The US 82nd Airborne Division, under the command of Major General Matthew B. Ridgway was assigned the task of parachuting its three regiments into the western sector of the UTAH Beachhead in the predawn hours of D-Day. The 507th and 508th Regiments landing west of the Merderet River were to establish a bridgehead, 6 kilometers deep initially, to stop German reinforcements from entering the beachhead from the west and later to be used as a jump off point to drive west and sever the Contentin Peninsula. The division's third regiment, the 505th, landing east of the river and northwest of Ste. Mere-Eglise was to seize the town and block German attempts to enter the beachhead from the north. Its 1st Battalion moving south from its Drop Zone 0 was to capture the eastern end of the causeway. With the 507th and 508th Regiments on the west bank the causeway would be secured and available for the planned movements west.

Rivers, lowlands and flooded marshes were a major problem at the base of the peninsula. To forestall the Germans from bottling-up and containing the UTAH Beachhead behind these natural obstacles, both the 82nd and 101st Airborne Division were parachuted into the beachhead in the early hours of D-Day to capture and secure the key causeways by surprise.

The air armada, in excess of four hundred C-47 transports, carrying the 82nd Division paratroopers made landfall on the Contentin's west coast, about 1 a.m. Flying due east, the tight formations spread out as cloud banks and antiaircraft fire increased the hazards of the flight.

As an aid to landing in the regiments' respective drop zones, pathfinders had dropped earlier with beacons and lights to mark the fields for the pilots' identification. The majority of the pathfinders for the two Drop Zones T and N, west of the Merderet River, were rapidly killed or captured by units of the German 91st Division specifically trained and positioned to handle airborne landings. Consequently the airplanes were severely scattered and unguided when the paratroopers jumped. Drop Zone T, 3 kilometers northwest of the causeway, received only three plane loads of paratroopers and one of those was planned for Drop Zone N, 4 kilometers south. Twelve plane loads of the 507th Regiment landed over 25 kilometers away. The broad dispersion had one positive result. The German high command, collecting the many reports of paratrooper landings, were confused as to the strength, magnitude and focus of the airborne activities.

Allied aerial reconnaissance and intelligence had overlooked a significant fact. Back flooding of the Douve River had also flooded its major northern tributary, the Merderet River. The tall reeds and marsh grass had camouflaged the 700-meter wide lake over which the la Fiere causeway now crossed. Thirty planes overshot their jump point by 2 kilometers, 30 seconds late, the "sticks" jumped into the "Merderet Lake". Weighted down with equipment, supplies, ammunition and rations the paratroopers were dragged below the surface. Many drowned before they could free themselves from their harnesses. The drained lake, now grazing marsh land, still holds a few of the "missing" and their equipment, swallowed up by the mire.

The division knew the Douve River valley had been flooded but not realizing the Merderet River also had overflowed its banks, many were misled by these two waterways and believed they had landed 10 kilometers south in the Douve River marshes. In the darkness the troopers searched for their landmarks. In the distance the elevated railroad embankment, crossing diagonally above the Merderet valley, a kilometer north of the causeway, attracted their attention. Gravitating to this dry rise of ground contrasted by the low wet marsh, the men collected on the railline and moved south (read and visit Grade Crossing 104). These movements brought the regiment to the east side of the river. Their objective was to establish a defense of the bridgehead, to a depth of 6 kilometers, on the western side. The original west bank seizure plan was no longer feasible.

Throughout the dark hours the paratroopers pulled their comrades out of the marsh and recovered equipment when possible. The light of dawn forced the abandonment of these activities as

German snipers, on the west bank, picked off the exposed paratroopers.

One such American who ended up on the wrong side of the river was the 82nd's Assistant Commander, Brigadier James M. Gavin ("Slim Jim"). Landing on the west side of the "lake" he believed he was on the south side of one of the Douve's convoluted banks. He erroneously moved across the valley and arrived on the east bank. (Thirty-seven years old at the time, General Gavin was later to become Chief of US Army Research and later US Ambassador to France under President J. F. Kennedy.)

The eastern end of the causeway was dominated by a large farm. Half a dozen barns and a massive four-story home, the Manoir la Fiere, was owned and occupied by Mr. Louis Leroux and his family. With its thick stone walled buildings, interconnected by three-meter high stone fences, its defense value to the Germans was obvious, yet throughout the four years of occupation it had not been considered by the Germans as a strongpoint or resistance nest. Defenses for the causeway had been positioned on the west side of the Merderet River valley. On D-Day the Leroux family farm and its neighboring fields would become one of the bloodiest small battlefields in US military history. The tall turreted, manor house, backing against a ridge, provided excellent fire positions for its defenders.

The causeway commences a few meters west of the farm's gate after crossing the river bridge. The height of the river is seasonable. A hundred meters along, the road bends 30 degrees to the right and starts its gentle incline towards (one kilometer) the hamlet of Cauquigny. The road's shoulders are flanked by two rows of stunted poplars. At the far end, facing across the valley on the north side of the causeway, stood two, two-story stone houses and a church in the midst of its cemetery. Paths running north and south border the marshland. A hundred meters further the highway forks. The north side of the fork was overshadowed by a two-story farmhouse and two barns enclosed in a stone walled yard.

Lieutenant Colonel Charles J. Timmes, Commander of the 2nd Battalion, (507th Regiment) landed 800 meters northwest of the Cauquigny church and quickly collected 50 of his men. Certain of his location and his objectives he moved his force into the undefended Cauquigny hamlet. Dawn was breaking, his position was quiet, but to the west the sound of small arms fire indicated his troops could be of more use elsewhere. Vacating the hamlet at 7 a.m., he moved off northwest to the village of Amfreville (2 kilometers) where he was repulsed by its large German garrison. He reassembled his force a few hundred meters east in an orchard and established a defensive position.

The loss of radios in the night drop and the limited visibility created by the hedgerows contributed to the poor communication between groups. While Timmes's force withdrew from the critical west end of the causeway to seek out a more useful mission, American forces on the east side of the river prepared to attack Cauquigny, under the belief it was well defended by a German force. Three days of fighting would be needed to regain the Cauquigny position voluntarily vacated when it should have been consolidated.

After establishing his defenses in the apple orchard east of Amfreville, Colonel Timmes reconsidered his vacating of Cauquigny. In mid-morning he directed Lieutenant Louis Levy to take a ten man platoon with a machine gun back to the hamlet and dig in around the churchyard until reinforcements arrived. En route Levy's force joined with a force of twenty-one men also heading for Cauquigny. Arriving at 11:30 a.m. they established defensive positions around the churchyard. Forty more stragglers drifted in giving Levy a sizable force, with machine guns, and a bazooka. Looking east across the marsh and causeway Levy could see there was fighting in the manor house vicinity.

On the east side Brigadier Gavin took stock of the forces that had collected. He had set up headquarters where D15 passes over the railroad. Only the 1st Battalion of the 505th should have been there. He and the units of the 505th, 507th and 508th were in the wrong place. The division's commander, Major General Matthew B. Ridgway, and the 508th Commander, Colonel Ray Lindquist, also arrived on the scene.

Of all the units to parachute into Normandy on D-Day only the 1st Battalion's Able Company (505th Regiment) landed as designated, that was a kilometer north of the causeway and east of the river. Within moments of landing the company was organized and off to its respective objectives, missing only two men. A platoon of Able Company, led by Lieutenant J. H. Wisner, ventured off at 2 a.m. to seize the Leroux Manoir and prevent the Germans destroying the bridge.

The German 91st Division, specialized in countering an airborne assault, had ignored the Leroux Manoir's defensive potential until an hour and a quarter before the American pathfinders dropped into the area. At 11 p.m., June 5, Monsieur Leroux, his wife and their three children were aroused by a pounding on their door. Twenty-eight heavily armed German soldiers had come to occupy the farm complex. Eight hours later, a force ten times larger would try to take the position.

Lieutenant Wisner's platoon was the first to feel the effect when it moved against the farm early D-Day morning. The American's were repulsed.

Another of the company's platoons led by Lieutenant G. W. Presnell, moved against the farm from the north along the secondary road paralleling the river bank joining the highway between the farm gates and the bridge. At 7 a.m., as the platoon came down the road, German fire from the farm building directly ahead drove the platoon into the field next to the river. Attempts to move up to the road using the hedge as cover were stopped by fire from the manoir buildings and a machine gun on the causeway that raked Presnell's men.

At the same time a small company of Colonel Timmes's 2nd Battalion, (507th Regiment) who had landed on the wrong side of the river, was also attacking the farm. Captain F.(Pappy) V. Schwartzwalder, the company commander, was primarily interested in crossing the causeway but the German force in the farm was blocking his route. The open slopes between the buildings and his position near the river were being swept by machine gun fire. The company was also stopped.

A third force, under Colonel Lindquist, (Commander of 508th Regiment) was approaching the farm from the east along the Ste. Mere-Eglise road (D15). At the bend his lead scouts although in the ditch and hugging the hedgerow, came under fire from the manoir's tower and a machine gun perched on the ridge. Withdrawing eastward Lindquist circled around and re-approached the farm from the south, meeting Schwartzwalder's company just pulling back from their abortive attack.

From the north side A Company made another attack. Using 60mm mortars they preceded the assault with a softening-up bombardment. Against the massive stone walls, the effect was negligible. Lieutenant John "Red Dog" Dolan planned his three-pronged simultaneous assault from the north and south. A platoon circled around to the east and approached the farm from the south. There they met the Lindquist and Schwartzwalder forces. A second platoon followed Lieutenant Presnell's earlier route to position themselves to allow an assault across the road and into the farmyard through the entrance road. The remaining platoon, the third prong, would attack across the field directly north and across the road from the farm, launching their attack from the hedgerow at the far end of the field.

All three attacks made little headway. The German guns were well sited and difficult to locate. Crisscrossed supporting lines of fire from the farm and causeway presented walls of fire difficult to penetrate. Dolan's platoon charging across the open field was chopped down as it left the hedgerow start line. Not a man made it across the field to the road.

As the morning wore on, senior commanders were able to mold all the forces now surrounding the farm into an adhesive, coordinated powerhouse. At noon a double pincer movement was successful. A reinforced platoon commanded by Lieutenant Oakley attacked from the river bank up the slope to the stone wall. A mortar shell had created a gap providing access into the farm yard. Synchronously Captain Schwartzwalder's company fought into the farm yard from the southeast, past the long barn and stable. Combat was brief. By 12:30 p.m. the farm was cleared and eight of the original twenty-eight man garrison were taken prisoner.

Colonel Lindquist, now in charge of the available forces, established his command post in the farm and planned his follow-up moves.

Captain Schwartzwalder with his company of 80 men however were eager to find their battalion somewhere on the west bank. After a brief rest, lunch and tending their casualties they left the farm yard, headed for Cauquigny across the causeway. It was 1:45 p.m. From the manoir, field glasses showed manned rifle and machine gun pits dug in the causeway's shoulders at irregular intervals along its full length. Schwartzwalder expected the causeway to be a tough battle. A hundred meters west of the bridge a nearby sniper winged the company's point scout, Private J. L. Mattingly. Quick to respond, the paratrooper unleashed a few rapid fire shots from his carbine into the German's position concluding with a handgrenade for good measure.

In the German rifle pit one man died and two were wounded. Unbelievably the remaining Germans manning the pits along the causeway, impressed by the American's speed of response and ability to kill, surrendered. Collecting his prisoners Schwartzwalder sent them back to the farm while he pressed across the captured causeway. The time was then 2:15 p.m., thirty minutes after the fracas had begun, one man had captured the causeway!

Reaching the west side the force joined Levy's enlarged platoon holding the church and road fork. All was quiet. Lindquist's large follow up force, organizing to cross, was but a few hundred meters away. After a brief exchange of news and information Schwartzwalder, his company and sixty of Levy's group struck off to the northwest to find Timmes in his Amfreville orchard. Lieutenant Levy, Lieutenant J. Kormyko and eight men, remained to hold Cauquigny and greet Lindquist's column soon to cross the causeway.

All was quiet at the intersection for the next quarter of an hour. Then, to every ones surprise, a German ambulance entered the junction from the southern Pont-l'Abbe road and stopped. Unbelievingly the driver stared at the Americans then pulled hard to the left, shifted gears and sped down the Amfreville road.

Within minutes, in quick succession five shells exploded on the road fork. Withdrawing from their positions at the fork and in the adjacent farm the paratroopers crossed the field and the dirt track, and dug in deep amongst the churchyard's tombstones and hedge bordering the narrow dirt road. Today a meter-high stone wall has replaced the hedge. Shortly afterwards three light German tanks entered the scene from the Amfreville road. All three had been captured from the French and Russians and integrated into the 100th Panzer Replacement Battalion, 1057th Regiment (91st Division). The battle that followed was brief (10 minutes). Although the bazooka knocked out two of the tanks, Levy's force was annihilated. Only Levy and a couple of his patrol were able to escape north along the marsh bank. The dirt track in front of the church was strewn with German and American dead. The tank shellfire left the church a roofless skeleton with only its four walls standing. The cemetery had been plowed up, the tombstones overturned and tombs laid open.

The German force then shifted their attention back to the causeway where they intercepted the forty-man vanguard of Able Company just entering Cauquigny from the causeway. Open and exposed on the road, the company scattered and retreated. Those attempting to withdraw across the causeway were struck down by murderous tank shell and machine gun fire. Those attempting to wade back across the marsh were either shot or drowned. Not one survivor made it back, nor was a prisoner taken to tell the story of the slaughter.

By the late afternoon of D-Day the Germans were firmly established in Cauquigny. Chances and opportunities of the day had been lost by the invaders. Already fifty had died on the west end. In the next two days the casualties would increase.

After Private Mattingly captured the causeway single handedly and Schwartzwalder's company moved west to join Colonel Timmes, Colonel Lindquist deployed the decimated Able Company of the 505th's 1st Battalion, in defense positions along the causeway.

Along the causeway's straight-away, the banks and shoulders are relatively broad. Twenty-five meters west of the bridge the company occupied the vacated German rifle pits and spread out into the shoulders to the waters edge. A bazooka team dug in amongst the bushes on the road's south shoulder close to the west end of the bridge. A second bazooka team was across the road on the north side. Forward, antitank mines were dug into the road bed. East of the bridge a disabled German supply truck on its side, provided cover for riflemen.

At 5:30 late afternoon, two German tanks, with supporting infantry, approached the American causeway positions from the west. The bazooka teams knocked out the lead tank. The second tank twisted off the road onto the north side shoulder hoping for some camouflage and cover from the poplar trees. A second rocket swished over the distance, penetrated the armor and exploded. Black, oily smoke engulfed the demolished tanks. The German infantry, void of their cover, were gunned down as they retreated to Cauquigny.

The battles of the day were over, but death still stalked the marsh. Throughout the late afternoon and evening, misdropped paratroopers, attracted by the battle noises to the east, attempted to ford "Merderet Lake" unaware that German snipers held its west bank. Helplessly the Americans along the causeway witnessed the death of many comrades. Burial parties later dragging the lake to remove the bodies of those killed and drowned, were surprised by the number of fatal face and head wounds.

Shell and mortar fire fell upon the Americans on the causeway and in the Leroux farm during the night, softening the defenders for the next day's attack.

The following morning, June 7, Wednesday, at 8:00 a.m. the tempo of the German mortar fire increased. With a high degree of accuracy the American positions were pounded in a systematic pattern. Heavy machine gun fire from the west bank kept the men in the rifle pits under cover. After an hour the barrage lifted and four captured French light tanks followed by German infantry began to cross the causeway. Antitank fire knocked out the lead tank, which, when combined with the two tanks of the previous day, provided the attacking infantry with ample cover. Able Company spread out along the road shoulders took heavy casualties and slowly dwindled to fifteen men. A German breakthrough appeared imminent and plans for a withdrawal were being considered. Ammo was low, casualties were high, some soldiers retreated. The presence of Major General Matthew Ridgway and the exemplary heroism of Sergeant W. D. Owens did much to hold the line. Just as the American line was about to collapse, a red cross flag fluttered from the German side. A 30 minute truce was called for removal of their wounded. Taking the opportunity of the cease fire the attackers pulled back to Cauquigny.

On June 8 a flooded road just beneath the marsh surface was discovered 2 kilometers to the north leading to Colonel Timmes position on the west bank. The one time farm road standing elevated above the lower pasture land of Merderet River valley, was slightly submerged by the German flooding of the valley. General Ridgway, grasping the opportunity had the 1st Battalion of the 325th Glider Infantry Regiment cross and enter Timmes's position via the sunken road at 10:30 p.m. June 8.

Striking out from Timmes's bridgehead the battalion ran into strong resistance. Casualties were high, little gains were made. By dawn June 9, the operation was concluded unsuccessfully.

General Ridgway was now under pressure. The US 90th Division was approaching from disembarking on UTAH Beach. It was to spearhead the westward advance to cut the Contentin Peninsula hastening the fall of Cherbourg. The causeway and a bridgehead on the west bank were essential for the division's start line. Although costly, Cauquigny would have to be taken by a frontal assault across the causeway.

The 325th's Commander, Colonel Harry L. Lewis, moved the 3rd Battalion up from Chef-du-Pont. The attack was to start at 10:45 a.m., June 9.

George Company leading the attack moved into the Leroux farm area from the Ste. Mere-Eglise road. From the point where the road turns to pass the farm and moves to the straightaway, German heavy machine guns from across the marsh peppered their ranks. The company cut through the hedge behind the farm, passed through the orchard and collected in the farmyard between the stable and long barn. The blasted hole in the wall bordering the farm road to the main road, through which Oakley's platoon had entered on June 6, was under constant surveillance by the machine gunners on the west bank.

At 10:30 a.m. US mortars and twelve tanks, located in the fields north and south of the causeway on the eastern shoreline, opened up a barrage on the west bank. While the shellfire kept the Germans down in their gun pits, George Company troops dashed past the gap in the wall, one by one. Collecting in the farms entrance roadway its commander Captain John B. Sauls organized his assault platoons.

Sauls, with Staff Sergeant W. L. Ericsson's platoon, was on the left, Lieutenant D. B. Wason's platoon on the right. At 10:45 a.m. Sauls blew his whistle, the two platoons trotted out of the farm driveway onto the road, and as quickly as possible raced across the causeway. Overhead the flat trajectory fire of the tanks whined by. As they neared the opposite side a smoke shell signaled the halt of the bombardment. Only the platoons were crossing, the rest of the company held back. An American tank, crossing in support, blew a tread on one of its own unlifted mines placed there three days previously. The disabled German tanks, a truck and the Sherman tank cluttered and confused the lines funneling through steel-like doorways that focused German machine guns. The charging platoons took heavy casualties. The follow up troops saw what lay ahead and held back.

Once across Ericsson's remnant platoon turned left along the first trail to clear out the gun nests along the bank housing snipers firing on the causeway. Lieutenant Wason's platoon did the same on the right side. Wason was killed as he turned onto the path. His platoon stopped and took cover behind the poplars lining the causeway.

Reinforcements were not crossing. The crisscross fire on the road and its shoulders piled up the dead and wounded. Westerly movement stopped completely. General Ridgway, General Gavin and Colonel Lewis came forward and encouraged the men. With these efforts the assault line proceeded.

Ericsson's efforts had cut down the flank fire. The force in the bridgehead grew. More men aided the clearing of the left hand trail. Captain Saul's George Company headed through the fork down the Pont-l'Abbe road. Lieutenant Rufus Broadaway and another lieutenant, who had only recently joined the 507th Regiment, proceeded cautiously. A German "potato masher" handgrenade came over the hedgerow exploding noisily but harmlessly. Broadway tossed over a grenade which was followed by an explosion and a scream. Both officers peered over the hedgerow. A German bullet pierced the skull of the new arrival who died in Broadway's arms. As a retired surgeon, Broadway still ponders fate's selectability that allowed him to live through this and numerous other close calls.

The Germans in the ruins of the church and its cemetery were pinned down by a machine gun. Enlargement of the bridgehead was fast but expensive. German strength was still formidable. North of the causeway, along the marshes, the Germans had not been subdued and continued to fire on the causeway creating high casualties amongst those of Easy Company who were trying to cross. Lieutenant R. B. Johnson lead an attack on the thirty Germans dug in around the church. The mortar and artillery barrage had torn the place apart. Graves' contents and tombstones were scattered about the neighboring fields. An American "short" shell hit the church wall killing and wounding half a dozen Americans. Advancing up the church road the company cleared the large farm capturing twenty-seven Germans.

Fox Company moved along the Amfreville road against the main German strength. A unit actually entered les Heliquets (called le Motey in 1944) but American artillery fire bracketing the area to thwart a German buildup caused the unit to pull back.

George Company, without too much opposition, was well along the Pont-l'Abbe road.

The dead and wounded along the causeway held up the vehicular traffic until noon. At 12 o'clock the first tanks entered the bridgehead. Unaware of the depth of the bridgehead and aware that German resistance pockets had been bypassed, a tank fired into the first field on the left side of the roadway. Mistakenly identifying the tops of the helmets over the hedgerow, the shell exploded in an American command post, killing five.

By evening a firm and broad bridgehead had been established. Colonel Timmes's 2nd Battalion near Amfreville and the 1st Battalion (325th Regiment) had linked up with the Cauquigny bridgehead forces. To the south, the 1st Battalion of the 508th Regiment, which had crossed the causeway and moved southward, were battling in Guettenville (one kilometer south of the Cauquigny intersection). A general depth of 2 kilometers had been achieved. The stage was set for the next phase, driving west to cut the peninsula.

The shelling of Cauquigny had resulted in many of the homes being reduced to hollow skeletons. The houses have been rebuilt, the church is new. All stand on their former sites. A few depressions along the bank and causeway shoulders are the collapsed rifle and machine gun pits. Unexploded shells and handgrenades made the causeway and marshes dangerous for decades after the war. The sparseness of the trees in the center of the causeway are the result of shellfire. The gap in the farmyard wall has been noticeably repaired as well as barn roofs. All the signs are there, silent evidence of the story.

On the east bank a dominant memorial, a larger-than-life bronze paratrooper facing across the serene Meredret River valley pastureland, commemorates the actions of the men of the 82nd Airborne Division who fought here.

In 1994, on the 50th D-Day Anniversary, thirty-eight of the original veterans made a commemorative jump from a camouflaged C-47 into the area. Following closely behind were nine-hundred, 1994, 82nd Airborne paratroopers jumping from a dozen C-130 cargo planes.

Picture 4: la Fiere Causway - Looking West
August 13, 1947

The low land over which the causeway passes was flooded in 1944. Many American paratroopers drowned here. Others were shot by snipers as they waded across the marsh. The road was important as the Utah invasion forces pushed west across the Contentin Peninsula. Captured intact without losses in D-day, it was left unguarded to be occupied later that day by the Germans recognizing its strategic value. The defenses occupying the farm buildings to the east end, foxholes along the causeway, and the western bank took a very heavy toll on the 82nd Airborne over a three day period. General "Jumping Jim" Gavin's wartime foxhole is preserved along the road in the foreground. The "Iron Mike" airborne memorial is in the field across from the Leroux Manior (foreground) overlooking the Merderd River valley.

3.8 Amfreville

(5 kilometers west of Ste. Mere-Eglise, on D15. then right on D126)

The allied invasion plan called for the dropping of airborne divisions prior to the seaborne assaults to seize bridges, causeways and bridgeheads. The 82nd Airborne Division was to land two regiments west of the Merderet River valley to stop German reinforcements from entering and attacking the UTAH Beachhead from the west. Subsequently their bridgehead would be used a few days later as the start line for driving west and cutting the Contentin Peninsula, thereby hastening the fall of Cherbourg on its northern end. The fields east and northeast of Amfreville were designated as Drop Zone T for the 507th Regimentof the division. Loss of pathfinders, cloud conditions and antiaircraft fire caused severe misdropping and scattering of the 140 aircraft carrying the paratroopers. All but two aircraft went astray.

The arrival of dawn on D-Day saw the regiment’s 2nd Battalion Commander, Lieutenant Colonel C. J. Timmes, and fifty of his men organized and off to their objective, the hamlet of Cauquigny, to the southeast 1.2 kilometers, on the west end of the la Fiere causeway. Arriving shortly thereafter, and finding no Germans, the group headed northwest towards the sounds of battle where they hoped to serve a more useful purpose.

Cutting across the fields, 2 kilometers, they arrived on the eastern outskirts of Amfreville and attempted to take the village. German resistance was strong, and from their elevated positions on the roofs and the church tower, decimated Timmes's meager force.

Withdrawing east along the winding secondary road the force took up positions in an apple orchard 700 meters from the village with their backs to the flooded Merderet River valley. To the north 500 meters the tall chateau, nicknamed the "Grey Castle", looked down upon them. It was a well defended and manned headquarters. Timmes's men were not in a position to press their attack.

Although his force was small, he was concerned about having vacated Cauquigny. In mid morning he sent Lieutenant Louis Levy, a bazooka man and eight paratroopers south to hold the hamlet.

At 3 p.m. a Captain with a company of 140 men joined Timmes's battalion in the orchard.

The Colonel and his force succeeded in holding his limited position and thereby accomplishing one of the regiment's objectives, establishing a bridgehead on the west bank. Except for sniper and machine gun fire from Amfreville and the Grey Castle the pressure was insufficient for him to contemplate a withdrawal across the marsh to his rear.

On June 8 evening, two scouts from his position, crossing the marsh to contact the division headquarters on the eastern bank, discovered a usable submerged roadway across the flooded valley. Once a farm track, flooding had covered the road just below the water level. This invisible bridge was a usable find. The division's commander, Major General Matthew B. Ridgway, saw this route as a way to outflank the German's who had retaken Cauquigny and were holding back the American westward thrust.

On June 8 at 10:30 the 1st Battalion of the 325th Glider Infantry Regiment crossed the ford and entered Timmes's foothold position by 1 a.m. (June 9).

Charles Company moved north and attacked the Grey Castle at 3:30 a.m. After successfully clearing the castle they withdrew back into the orchard. The Germans reoccupied the castle.

Able Company followed the dirt road southwest to les Helipiquets (le Motley in 1944), arriving at its junction at 3:30 a.m. The area was thick with Germans. Unable to hold the intersection, the company returned to the orchard.

Returning from the Grey Castle Charlie Company proceeded south along the dirt road to les Helipiquets, but 400 meters along the road the company cut southeast across the fields, crossed the Amfreville - Cauquigny highway and proceeded towards the Cauquigny fork, in the fields bordering the road, on its south side. German resistance stiffened at the road fork 400 meters further along the road. It was then 4:30 a.m. Meeting this impasse and seeing no further gains in sight, the force retraced its steps to Timmes's orchard.

Baker Company moved directly southeast against Cauquigny where it arrived at 3 a.m. The hamlet was strongly held with armored supported troops. The night fight in the farm adjacent to the road fork was confused. Unsuccessful, the company returned to the orchard.

What the battalion lacked in gains it reaped in casualties. Remaining in the orchard the battalion reinforced Timmes's position and prepared for further action. A frontal assault against Cauquigny, from across the causeway, the same morning was successful. That afternoon the battalion moved south out of the orchard and then west against Amfreville. Its southern flank neighbored the regiment's 3rd Battalion that had successfully crossed the causeway and taken Cauquigny.

The following day, June 10 saw front line changes. Three fresh regiments faced west and Colonel Timmes's 507th Regiment pivoted to face northwest.

By midnight the 357th Regiment (90th ID) was in Amfreville's eastern outskirts. The next morning the village fell.

3.9 Chef-du-Pont Causeway

(3 kilometers southwest of Ste. Mere-Eglise on D67)

The lush pasture land of the Merderet River valley of today falsifies that it afforded such difficulties to those who attempted its crossing in 1944. Southwest from Chef-du-Pont, the arched stone bridge passed over the 300-meter wide river bordered by 1-meter deep banks. The bridge, too weak to carry the military traffic was reinforced and topped with a Bailey bridge in 1944. The road is slightly elevated above the pastures and flanked by two rows of stunted poplars. One hundred and fifty meters past the bridge a secondary tree-lined road branches to the northwest, crossing 800 meters to the higher land to the north. The highway continues southwest another 1.5 kilometers over the pasture land before reaching the higher ground.

Defensive flooding by the Germans throughout their occupation had made the present low-lying pasture land a lake, camouflaged by the growth of marsh grass and weeds. Crossing the marsh was restricted to the Chef-du-Pont and la Fiere Causeways (3 kilometers to the north).

The plan following the establishment of the UTAH Beachhead was to drive American forces west to cut the Contentin Peninsula off at its base and, while holding a southerly defense line drive north, to capture the port of Cherbourg.

The causeways across the flooded Merderet valley were key to the rapid success of this plan. The US 82nd Airborne Division landing on the east and west banks of the valley was to assure the early capture of the causeways. The secure bridgehead on the west bank on D-Day would be the start line for the westerly thrust on D+1.

The 508th Regiment would secure the bridgehead on the west end of the Chef-du-Pont causeway at the same time as a battalion of the 505th Regiment secured the east end.

The operation commenced in the first hours of D-Day. Misdropping caused extensive scattering of paratroopers. The hedgerows created communication problems and made it difficult to collect the men into sizable forces.

On the west bank the 508th Regiment was unable to achieve its objectives, however a large force did collect on a slight rise (Hill 30) distracting the German attention and drawing some of their available forces away from the two causeways.

On the east bank the Regiment, scheduled to land in Drop Zone 0, 4 kilometers north of Chef-du-Pont, were not as badly scattered and did form into cohesive battalions quickly. The redirecting of these forces into critical areas blunted the original plan. A few planeloads landed east of Chef-du-Pont but soon became embroiled in local skirmishes. They did not move towards the causeway but instead joined the concentration of American paratroopers to the north between the la Fiere causeway and Ste. Mere-Eglise.

The division's Assistant Commander, Brigadier James Gavin (Slim Jim), from his position at the intersection of D15 and the railroad line, 2 kilometers west of Ste. Mere-Eglise, directed Lieutenant Colonel A. Maloney, with a small company of 75 men, to move south and capture Chef-du-Pont and its causeway.

Moving down the railroad line, Maloney's company swung east around Chef-du-Pont seeking another crossing point to the south. Behind him, Lieutenant Colonel E. J. Ostberg, with a similar sized force proceeded directly into the town along the railroad line. The town was lightly held. After a few minutes of firing from doorways the Germans moved to prepared positions along the causeway shoulders between the village and the bridge. The creamery parking lot (south side of the road to the causeway) was a portion of the German positions. While a German platoon settled into the pits east of the bridge, the remainder of the force crossed the bridge taking up positions along the shoulders west of the bridge.

The Americans pressed through the town and onto the causeway. The two Germans in the first pit raised their hands to surrender. The paratroopers fired, killing both. No one else attempted to surrender, as it appeared the Americans were not taking prisoners. To retreat across the exposed bridge would be suicidal. The only option for the German defenders was to fight 'til death and kill as many American paratroopers as possible. This produced what later was described by veterans as "tenacious German troops". As a result of this rash "take no prisoners" act by the trigger-happy paratroopers many lives on both sides were wasted.

Ostberg and Maloney's forces had several outstanding sharpshooters. Their sniping at the German heads as they presented themselves over the next few hours slowly cleared the pits east of the bridge. Although the Americans were now up to the bridge, its hump restricted their firing at the defenders on the west side. Ostberg, leading a platoon, charged across the bridge. A machine gun readied and awaiting such an action, cut down the first six men. The Colonel pitched into the marsh. Colonel Ostberg was rescued shortly afterwards and after recovering from his wounds rejoined the regiment. A second charge was attempted but it was halted by handgrenades hurled at the attackers.

Fighting to the north recalled Colonel Maloney and a sizable proportion of the remaining force. Captain Roy E. Creek with an undersized company of 34 men were left to hold what had been gained.

After Maloney left, Creek could see a German company to his south, on his side, at le Port preparing to attack. Shellfire from the west bank was "softening up" his positions along his southern perimeter, presently occupied by the dairy and the three fields east of it. He requested reinforcements from la Fiere and waited. Overhead the gliders of the 325th Glider Infantry Regiment had cut loose and were heading into their landing zone, 3 kilometers to the east at les Forges. One straying off course, apparently confused, landed to the north of Chef-du-Pont. It carried a 57mm antitank gun. As Creek's men rushed to position the gun, a reinforced company of 100 men arrived from la Fiere. The Germans, within firing range were quick to feel the added firepower. They pulled back a kilometer to le Port.

In the early evening Creek did a reconnaissance of his position looking for a crossing point. A hundred meters to the north, a finger of land jutted 20 meters into the marsh. Today this is a tree lined roadway leading to an industrial plant nestled in a loop of the river. He rushed a machine gun and his best marksmen onto the finger from where they could snipe at the causeway defenders west of the bridge. Before dark his marksmen had tallied forty Germans. His paratroopers were able to charge across the bridge without losses, pull out the German bodies and use the foxholes to the Americans' benefit. Five Germans making a hasty retreat down the road were shot. His company established itself along the causeway to the intersection of the road leading northwest to Caponnet. At midnight reconnaissance troops of the 4th Infantry Division from UTAH Beach entered Chef-du-Pont bringing some relief and supplies.

Two kilometers along the road an American pocket (Hill 30), isolated and surrounded, and commanded by Lieutenant Colonel T.J.B. Shanley, absorbed much of the German strength over the next few days. Captain Creek's force, though lacking sufficient strength to establish a bridgehead, could adequately hold the bridge. Available forces were concentrated on capturing the la Fiere causeway. Both causeways could not be taken simultaneously.

Throughout June 7 to 9, Creek's force held their gains while available units secured the area south to Carentan. The June 6 airborne and seaborne assaults had cut off German lines of retreat, creating resistance pockets that had to be flushed out before the drive west could be mobilized.

On June 9 the la Fiere Causeway was taken. The 325th Glider Infantry Regiment fanned out from the Cauquigny bridgehead, joining Colonel Shanley's force on Hill 30 late in the afternoon.

The following day, June 10, the 358th Regiment, fresh from disembarkation across UTAH Beach, passed through Chef-du-Pont, across the bridge, and advanced westward, encountering little resistance.

There are two memorial markers near the bridge commemorating the actions of the 508th Regiment.

Picture 5: Chef du Pont Causway - Looking North
August 13, 1937

This is one of the most southerly causeways crossing the flooded marshlands of the Merderet River. The other, la Fiere Causeway, is two miles north towards the top right in the photo. The elevated roads crossing the marsh were flanked by German manned foxholes. Attempts by the 75 paratroopers of the 505th Regiment were stopped at the bridge as the men left the town of Chef du Pont. American snipers took up positions around the smoke stacked factory picking off Germans lining the road. Other paratroopers who had landed in the fields west of the marsh (top of photo) attached the Couffey farm (center left) successfully. The causeway was cleared by D-day +3 allowing the Utah landed troops and tanks to move west to cut off the Contentin Peninsula.

3.10 Hill 30

(6 kilometers southwest of Ste. Mere-Eglise via D15 to Gueutteville, left to Caponnet then right .0.5 kilometers to the hilltop. The Americans were in the left hand orchard.)

The 507th and 508th Regiments (82nd Airborne Divisions) were to parachute into the area west of the Merderet River in the predawn hours of D-Day. By destroying the bridges across the Douve River (Pont-l'Abbe and Beuzeville la Bastille) and occupying the west ends of the two Merderet causeways (la Fiere and Chef-du-Pont) the regiments would obstruct a German attack against the UTAH Beachhead from the west, and at the same time create a bridgehead from which to push west to cut the Contentin Peninsula.

The 508th Drop Zone N was 2 kilometers west of Hill 30. Low clouds, antiaircraft fire and the loss of the pre-dropped pathfinders caused the regiment to be widely scattered. Only 7 of the 140 planeloads landed as planned. This misdropping was so expansive that five "sticks" landed 28 kilometers to the north and twelve landed 10 kilometers east near UTAH Beach.

The 2nd Battalion's Commander Lieutenant Colonel Thomas J. B. Shanley was one of the few to land on target. In the next few hours he was able to collect a "mixed" force of paratroopers. His planned objective was to capture Pont-l'Abbe (2 kilometers to the southwest) and destroy its bridge across the Douve River. When in position his force would be 18 kilometers west of UTAH Beach, the most westerly of all the invasion forces. They were to hold until relieved by seaborne troops moving west from the beach.

Realizing his force of 250 men was too small to successfully compete their mission they moved east towards the Merderet valley to establish a bridgehead between the two causeways. The hedgerows slowed their progress. Visibility was limited to the far end of the field. Radio communication was minimal. Much of the equipment had been lost and the communicating parties could not accurately establish their location. Assembling the lost paratroopers was difficult because of the dense hedgerows and the presence of German forces combing the area.

Initial response by the Germans had been slow. The 91st Division's Commander, Major General Wilhelm Falley had left his

Chateau Haut headquarters, 2 kilometers west of Hill 30, late June 5 for a "war game" the following day in Rennes. The increased allied air activity caused him to return, arriving in the chateau's driveway at 8 a.m. Lieutenant Malcolm Brannen with several paratroopers opened fire then faded into the undergrowth. The killing of Falley delayed the German offensive reactions. The division had been specifically trained to counter an airborne landing. By dawn of D-Day the Germans realized sizable forces had landed west of the river. The 1057th Regiment was ordered to eliminate the Americans.

Throughout D-Day, brief skirmishes slowed Shanley's force as it moved to the east from field to field along the Picauville-Caponnet road. By late evening his men had reached the Hill 30 area.

To cover the force's movement to the hill, Shanley had moved a three man flank guard into Gueutteville, a kilometer northwest. The men held off a German tank supported battalion for two hours. Corporal Ernest T. Roberts, Privates John A. Lockwood and Otto K. Swingman were captured. Prisoner Swingman was killed in December. All three were awarded the Distinguished Service Cross for their action that provided the time needed for Shanley to prepare a strong defense on Hill 30 against the attacks that were to follow.

Hill 30 is 30 meters above sea level. The Merderet valley is 10 to 20 meters above sea level. The elevation is difficult to distinguish. The high, dense hedgerows and tall trees further camouflage its slopes and elevation. The hill is topped by an orchard. The American position was nestled in this orchard on the road's south side. From this vantage point the east side of the marsh and Chef-du-Pont were clearly visible. The attacks of June 7- 9 came across the fields from the north and northwest. The road was no man's land.

Isolated on the hilltop, being attacked from the northwest, Shanley arrived at a plan to stop German movements toward the Chef-du-Pont causeway, as well as deter the Germans from slipping around to his south side and squeezing his force in a military vice. Around the southern slope of the hill 300 meters away a narrow farm road (greatly improved today) encircled the hill and bordered the marsh (now pasture land). From a T junction a road leads off to a causeway where it joins the Pont-l'Abbe-Chef-du-Mont causeway road (D70). Close at hand, straddling the narrow farm road lay the hamlet of les Ais 300 meters west of the T-junction to the causeway.

At the first light on June 7 Shanley directed a fifty-man platoon down to the hamlet where they established a roadblock facing east and west.

Radio communication with headquarters across the marsh acknowledged his position and its value. Although low on essential medical and ammunition supplies and with a serious mortar barrage falling into his position, he was ordered to hold and await forthcoming supplies.

On the morning of June 8 a German company approached the hamlet and roadblock from the west through adjacent fields. A mortar bombardment preceded the attack. Shanley's evaluation of the tactical significance of the roadblock led him to the conclusion that it wasn't worth the resulting casualties at that time. His large force was capable of reclaiming the position later if it became necessary. The platoon withdrew to positions up the hill. The Germans passed through the hamlet and continued to the T junction where they occupied the Jules Couppey farm on its southeast corner.

On the hill surrounded, the American position was becoming desperate. German pressure was depleting the reserve ammunition supplies. Casualties required bandages and plasma. There was no food.

Headquarters promised a supply column would cross the Chef-du-Pont causeway if the German occupied Couppey farm at the foot of the hill commanding the road to the causeway was cleared.

The clearing operation was arranged for that night (June 8). A barrage on the farm would precede the way for the assault to follow. The artillery fire didn't materialize nevertheless at 30 minutes after midnight, June 9, Lieutenant Woodrow W. Millsap and twenty-three men moved down the south slope of the hill to attack the Couppey farm.

Reaching the road west of the fork they crossed the road and advanced east arriving in the orchard west and across the causeway road from the farm. It was 2:30 a.m. The Germans were waiting. Flares illuminated the scene. A German machine gun on the road's north side amongst the buildings a hundred meters east fired into the orchard. The Americans charged out of the orchard across the road, over the ditch, through the hedge and passed through the orchard immediately adjacent to the farm buildings. Facing them across the driveway was a machine gun nest to the left and rifle pits straight ahead (a garden today). The defenders were shot, bayoneted and grenaded. Within the buildings the Americans were killing everything in sight. A mass psychoneurosis took over. Even the animals had their throats slit. The killing continued until Millsap ordered the blood bath to stop. Not a German was left alive. Six Americans died, seven were severely wounded.

Leaving a small holding force, Millsap proceeded along the road to the causeway and then over to the east bank. Although he confirmed the road was open, previous German mortar and artillery fire had threatened its destruction. The supply convoy was canceled. Instead, during the day plasma supplies were ferried over the marsh and carried up the hill into Shanley's position.

During the morning on June 10, the 3rd Battalion of the 325th Glider Infantry Regiment forced a bridgehead at Cauquigny (2 kilometers north). In the afternoon the battalion's companies followed across the causeway enlarging the bridgehead. The 1st Battalion of the 508th Regiment (82nd Airborne Division) entered the bridgehead, turned south and fought into Gueutteville. The Germans facing Shanley on the north withdrew as the threat of encirclement became apparent. The American forces joined.

Shanley's battalion's ordeal was over. During his four day siege he had attracted much of the German forces away from the two causeways and thereby directly assisted the Americans in gaining their foothold at Cauquigny on June 9. Whatever efforts were made to supply or rescue his force had been unsuccessful. His force although large had been low on supplies. Doubtless receiving the necessary equipment would have enabled him to move north or south to seize the west end of one of the causeways sparing many lives. There is a marker on Hill 30 commemorating Shanley's battalion's actions.

Chapter 4 Cutting the Contentin Peninsula

The small Norman ports were inadequate to handle the supply and reinforcement demands of the large mechanized armies. The fabricated Mulberry harbors for OMAHA Beach and Arromanches could only satisfy a portion of the port facilities required. Ocean sized freighters were required to transfer their cargoes to smaller craft to be ferried to the shore. The allies need for a major port was obvious.

The capture of the transatlantic deep-water harbor of Cherbourg was essential. Its many established docks and piers would enabled ships from America to unload their troops and cargo port side for immediate and rapid inland dispersal by rail and road.

German resistance and defense of the fortified city was expected to be strong. Their supply lines to the south had to be cut to weaken their defense capability.

As a preparedness measure the Germans had flooded and inundated the base of the Contentin Peninsula to barricade the American forces behind water barriers.

The allies utilized this condition advantageously to maintain a strong southern defense with a minimum number of troops. Offensive divisions would be available to move north and capture Cherbourg.

The general plan of operations for Major General J. Lawton Collins' 7th Corps was to gain a foothold on the peninsula, isolate, occupy it and capture Cherbourg speedily.

On June 9 the 82nd Airborne Division established a bridgehead on the west bank of the Merderet River. In conjunction the US 9th Division recently landed and the 101st Division on its southern flank, the division was to drive west and sever the German northbound supply roads. As the front lines moved west the regiments of the 82nd Airborne Division would advance south towards la Haye du Puits and Mont Castre to increase the 7th Corps southern defense depth.

4.1 La Chateau Bastille

(5 kilometers southwest of Ste. Mere-Eglise, via D67 to Chef-du-Mont, via N13 and D70, 2 kilometers. The chateau is on left hand side)

On June 9 the US 82nd Airborne Division established a bridgehead on the west side of the Merderet River at Cauquigny. The 7th Corps commander directed the 90th Infantry Division to exploit westwards the following day.

The 358th Regiment moved into Chef-du-Pont late June 9. The causeway to the west had not been completely cleared. The American positions along the causeway were only a few hundred meters west of the Merderet River bridge. German strength to the west was unknown. The regiment's objective was Pont-l'Abbe on D70, 5 kilometers west of the Merderet River.

The chateau and grounds adjacent and south of their advance line, 1 kilometer ahead, was an obvious German strongpoint for the remaining stretch of the causeway.

The 1st Battalion moved out from the forward positions on the causeway as dawn was breaking (June 10). By 5:30 p.m. the battalion had passed the chateau and was across the causeway moving towards Picauville. They had encountered only sporadic small arms fire from the chateau grounds.

The 3rd Battalion following detached Item Company to attack the chateau which now threatened the supply line. The battle for the chateau and its grounds was a costly affair for both sides.

Related story is Chef-du-Mont Causeway.

4.2. Picauville

(7 kilometers south of Ste. Mere-Eglise, via the Pont-l'Abbe road, D15)

The town played a part in two phases of the operations to occupy the Contentin Peninsula on June 6 (airborne landings) and 10 (drive to cut the peninsula).

The first phase of the invasion plan called for the airborne troops to secure a bridgehead west of the Merderet River and destroy bridges along the German counterattack routes.

The 82nd Airborne Division's 508th Regiment was to land in Drop Zone N, 1 kilometer north of Picauville. Units were to then move southwest and southeast to destroy the Douve River bridges at Pont-l'Abbe and Beuzeville la-Bastille, respectively. Simultaneously another unit would occupy the west end of the Chef-du-Pont causeway while the main body of the regiment cleared the general area and established a defense line west of Pont-l'Abbe.

The division "jumped" into Normandy in the dark, early hours of D-Day. The 508th Regiment was badly scattered and was unable to proceed with its plan and achieve the objectives.

Picauville was garrisoned by a strong German force of three infantry companies, an artillery battery and four medium tanks. The noise of the eight hundred plane armada and the antiaircraft barrage fully alerted the Germans. Into their bivouac area parachuted a plane load of paratroopers. All died still in their parachutes.

The German 91st Division, holding the central core of the peninsula , was specialized and trained to handle an airborne invasion. Field Marshal Erwin Rommel and Hitler, in the two weeks prior to the invasion, were inclined to believe it would take place in Normandy. As a consequence, another division had been inserted into the Atlantic Wall, an armored division had been moved closer, and "anticipatory preparedness conditions" were in place.

The 91st's headquarters was 800 meters north of Picauville, on D15, in the Chateau Bernaville. Emphasizing the need for constant alertness, General Rommel, on May 17, when visiting the headquarters, lectured the division's officers not to expect the invasion on a beautiful day but on a stormy night.

To sharpen their defenses and alertness, German officers held war games on map boards in which they would emulate the allies invading Normandy. By placing themselves "on the other side", they were more critical of their own preparations and adjusted their defenses accordingly.

General of Artillery, Erich Marcks, Commander of the 84th Corps, holding the invasion area, had called for a war game at Rennes for June 6, his birthday. He was to play the part of General , his division commanders would defend and counter his "invasion".

Major General Wilhelm Falley, the 91st Division's Commander, left his Chateau Haut headquarters late June 5 to drive to Rennes for the next days "game". The increased allied air activity during the night drive gave him concern. Ordering his driver to turn the Horch around, they sped back to his headquarters with the division's red and white pennant fluttering on the fender. As he drew closer to Picauville, he saw more and more activity and the sound of small arms fire. Increasing their speed, they raced along the roads, the slits of the cars blackout lights illuminating but a few meters of road ahead and nothing else. Pulling into the chateau's driveway at 8 a.m. the car was halted along the stone wall. Lieutenant Malcolm Brannen with several other paratroopers opened fire. Falley and his driver were hurled back against the side of the car under the impact of the volley. The paratroopers disappeared into the underbrush. The first general to die in Normandy hadn't issued an order. Falley's body was discovered a short time later and was temporarily buried in the paddock behind the chateau, until re-interned after the war.

The largest American force to hold a bridgehead on the west side of the Merderet River, throughout the next few days, held the summit of Hill 30, 2 kilometers to the east. While German forces tried to overrun Lieutenant Colonel Thomas J. B. Shanley's positions on the hill June 7, 8, and 9, American forces east of the river battled to cross the la Fiere causeway (4 kilometers northeast). On June 9 the causeway was seized, a bridgehead at Cauquigny was established, and preparations were made to attack westward the following day.

The Chef-du-Pont causeway, 4 kilometers due east of Picauville was crossed by the 1st Battalion, 358th Regiment (90th Division) at 5:30 a.m. On June 10, half the battalion entered Picauville from the east (D69) and proceeded west while the second half of the battalion headed towards Pont-l'Abbe along D70. Picauville offered little resistance. Five hundred meters west of the town a heavy German barrage hit the battalion. The companies spread out, dug in, and became defensive as ordered by the regiment's commander, Colonel James V. Thompson.

A German counterattack in the mid-afternoon was repulsed. American artillery blasted the German lines and four US companies attacked towards Pont-l'Abbe. Quick to recover from their abortive attack and bombardment, the Germans held and stopped the American advance with mortar and 88mm fire. What little gains had been made were held.

Only a few roads pass north to south at the neck of the Contentin Peninsula. Of the eight, five were still in German hands. Essential for supplying their forces on the peninsula , they fought tenaciously to hold each one. Pont-l'Abbe, a crossroads, commanded one such important route.

On June 11, the 358th Regiment's three battalions were moved to the start line. Four battalions of divisional artillery were in support. At 1:30 p.m., the attack was launched behind a rolling barrage advancing at the rate of 100 meters every 5 minutes. Nearing the northern and eastern outskirts of Pont-l'Abbe, German automatic weapons and artillery fire stopped the advance. Although partially encircled, the town still hadn't fallen.

On June 12, while one battalion contained the town, two battalions attempted to move past to the north. German fire stopped the battalions advance causing the Americans to reconsider their plan. German fire from Pont-l'Abbe to the causeway at Beuzeville-la-Bastille (4 kilometers east), which the 508th Regiment was preparing to cross, further increased the need to capture Pont l'Abbe.

At 5 p.m., a squadron of P47 fighter-bombers struck the town. Again at 7 p.m. artillery blasted the already rubbled town. Half an hour later, the infantry attacked and occupied the ruins. Defensive positions were established on the town's perimeter that night.

Prior to the regiment's movements west the next morning (June 13) short bombing by several support aircraft disrupted the organization and delayed the scheduled 7 a.m. jump off time. A noon attack was stopped cold by the German defense.

The regiment attacked west astride D15. By early afternoon the regiment was to the D24 junction a kilometer west of Pont-l'Abbe On

June 14, at 9 a.m., two battalions of the 358th. Units (508th and 325th Regiments) of the 82nd Airborne Division passed through the 358th and continued the attack west. The 90th Division disengaged and moved to the northerly portion of the line.

On June 19 near Picauville a company of the 826th Battalion (9th Engineer Command) commenced construction of an aircraft landing strip A-8 to accommodate 75 fighter-bombers and 36 night fighters. The 1,500-meter runway was laid and completed in 36 hours.

4.3 St. Sauveur-le-Vicomte

(14 kilometers west of Ste. Mere-Eglise via D15)

On June 16, the 82nd Airborne Division moved to within 2 kilometers of the town's eastern limits. The division's 325th Regiment was south of the D15 highway, holding Rauville-la-Place (1 kilometer east). To its north, the 507th Regiment held the division's right flank.

Northward, through the town, ran the German supply highway N900, one of the two major roads open for supplying their northern divisions.

Between 5 and 8 a.m. the following morning (June 17), the 325th Infantry Regiment, supported by Able Company of the 746th Tank Battalion, attacked across the fields to the bank of the Douve River. By noon, the 505th and 508th Regiments had also moved up. Seeing the Germans withdrawing, artillery fire bombarded the exit roads. A battalion crossed the river into the town. Little opposition was encountered, and by nightfall a bridge spanned the river, and the 505th and 508th were 3 kilometers west of the town. The airborne division's success was a pacesetter and motivator to the offensive action of the 9th Division to their north driving westward.

Situated on a major German supply route the town had received considerable attention by the allied air force and artillery. As a result it became the most damaged town on the peninsula. After its capture, German artillery pounded it, trying to slow down the flow of supplies to the American point columns.

Rubble strewn in the streets was too extensive to be bulldozed back into the ruins of the crumpled homes. Instead, bulldozers packed it and made a temporary route across the masonry and stones. Gauntly silhouetted against the sky, the building skeletons produced pictures reminiscent of the World War I shelled towns after months of siege. Heavy bombers had created craters in the fields large enough to envelop complete buildings.

Although damaged, the historic castle and its moat were spared. The grave site of the great French writer Barbey d'Auerevilly, remained undisturbed.

4.4 Orglandes

(14 kilometers west of Ste. Mere-Eglise via D15 to Cauquigny, D126 to Amfreville and Orglandes)

June 9 witnessed the establishment of an American bridgehead on the west bank of the Merderet River. From this foothold two US divisions (90th and 82nd)) launched a drive west to cut off the Contentin Peninsula and by so doing isolate the German forces and hasten the fall of Cherbourg.

Radiating from the UTAH Beachhead streamed a huge, full splayed, military fan of man and might. The 82nd Airborne Division was on the southern flank of the drive skirting the north bank of the Douve River. The 9th Division, in the middle, was to its north as the 90th Division moved northwest. The 4th Division was driving north along the peninsula 's east coast.

Ahead of the divisions' westward drive there lay several natural barriers, which, if utilized by the Germans to their fullest advantage, would delay the American advance. A kilometer west of Orglandes the village of Hautteville-Bocage, picturesquely nestled atop high ground, provided the Germans with a valuable natural observation lookout, their last east of the Douve River. Involuntarily Orglandes' 400 villagers protected the Hautteville-Bocage defense position's eastern flank.

By midnight, June 15, two US regiments were closing in on the two villages. The 47th was spread out 500 meters south and paralleling the Hautteville-Bocage to Orglandes road, (D126) facing north. The 359th was 1.4 kilometers southeast of Orglandes and approaching up the les Ancres road (D325) and its neighboring fields. There was a gap of 2 kilometers between the two regiments.

The following day, July 16, the 2nd Battalion of the 47th pushed north, crossed the road (D126) and fought into the churchyard and the village. Resistance was stubborn but by nightfall the houses were in American hands.

Simultaneously the 1st Battalion, following a costly struggle to the west of Biniville, had captured its objective.

Meanwhile at Orglandes the 39th Regiment had moved forward. While the 359th changed its direction from northwest to north, the 39th crossed in front of the 359th along the Amfreville road D126 and attacked Orglandes from the east. The leading 1st Battalion fought across the fields on the east side of the north-south Valognes road (D24). Throughout the latter part of the day the road was no man's land. With the 47th Regiment behind them on the Hautteville-Bocage road, the Germans in Orglandes were confined to the houses, fields and orchards in the village's northwest corner. That evening the 1st Battalion (39th) was forced back from the Valognes road (D24) by strong German fire.

The impasse was broken the following morning (June 17) when American artillery shelled the town. Able and Baker Companies of the 1st Battalion attacked and eliminated the remaining resistance.

The regiment's 3rd Battalion passed through the crumpled village to Hautteville-Bocage where it took over the 2nd Battalion's (47th Regiment) positions.

On June 19, the recently landed 79th Infantry Division commanded by Major General I. T. Wyche, became a part of the drive north to capture Cherbourg. Orglandes became divisional headquarters and bivouac area for its reserve regiment (314th).

On July 12 the 830th Battalion (9th Engineer Command) moved into Biniville (2 kilometers west) to construct a transport airfield (A-24C). Unsurfaced, the field became operational on the 17th and completed on the 19th. Lacking a hard surface its use was limited in the rainy latter half of July.

The last ground held by the German defenders of Orglandes became their final resting place. North of the village, on the Valognes road (D24), west side, is one of the six German Normandy cemeteries. It contains 10,152 graves. The six German cemeteries in the Normandy battlefield area (June 6 - August 21) total 77,967 gravesites. An additional 2,336 graves are in ten British cemeteries.

4.5 Ste. Colombe-Nehou Causeway

(12 kilometers southwest of Valognes via D2 to D42 then west on the Ste. Colombe-Orglandes road)

June 16 and 17 were significant days in the battles to cut the Contentin Peninsula. As the US 9th and 82nd Divisions pressed west, German resistance on the northern flank stiffened. Recognizing the possible loss of their forces on the peninsula and the significant port of Cherbourg a determined resistance was made by the German forces to stop the American tide.

On June 16 while two regiments of the 9th Division fought for Orglandes, Hautteville-Bocage and Biniville, its 3rd Regiment, the 60th, drove west along D42 from the D2 intersection towards Ste. Colombe. The 2nd Battalion and tanks of the 746th Tank Battalion, under the command of Lieutenant Colonel M. B. Kauffman, lead the advance.

A machine gun nest in the field south of the road, in front of the first buildings of the hamlet temporarily delayed the point platoon as it attempted to advance beyond the road bend towards the church. Overcoming the resistance the battalion advanced through the hamlet and across the tree lined road traversing the Douve River valley.

At this point the Douve River was not a significant obstacle. One bridge and two culverts span its three branch streams. The first bridge and first culvert were crossed without incident. Surprisingly the buildings beside the first culvert were not defended although their four-story height and tower offered excellent observation and firing positions.

As Easy Company moved forward past the buildings artillery fire fell on the three companies spread out along the causeway. The last culvert had been blown by the retreating Germans. The tanks, now sitting ducks, pulled back into Ste. Colombe. The company continued forward, waded across the river and dug in on the west bank. Heavy machine gun fire and self-propelled guns east of Nehou fired into its positions. Easy Company, precarious and low on ammunition was reinforced by platoons of F and G Companies that moved across the causeway from the village. German fire on the causeway forced the platoons to dig in and take cover.

Ammunition supplies came in from regimental headquarters. G Company crossed over into E Company's bridgehead.

During the night the 3rd Battalion moved into the exhausted 2nd Battalion's positions. The following morning, June 17, its attack into Nehou was successful.

The crossing of the Douve River here and at Ste. Sauveur-le-Vicomte (4 kilometers south) by the 82nd Airborne Division on June 16 were the decisive battles for cutting the peninsula.

Four kilometers northeast of Ste. Colombe at Biniville, the 9th Engineer Command established an airfield, A-24C, for supply and evacuation transport aircraft. Construction by the 830th Battalion was started on July 12 and completed on the 19th although operational on the 17th. As a grass strip, its use was limited throughout the rainy weeks of July.

In early July General George S. Patton, Jr., one of the US Army's most outstanding field commanders, moved his headquarters from England to Nehou. This quiet hamlet became the nucleus for the 3rd Army that became operational August 1 when it burst into Brittany. Patton established his headquarters in a neighboring orchard to benefit from the camouflage of the trees. Only a solitary tree remains today and a memorial stone with his immortal words "Do not take counsel of your fears."

4.6 St. Jacques-de-Nehou

(14 kilometers southwest of Valognes via D2 to D42 then west on the Ste. Colombe-Orglandes road)

On June 17 the US 60th Regiment (9th Division) occupied Nehou (5 kilometers east), in their drive west to cut the Contentin Peninsula. German resistance was sporadic from isolated groups as the regiment moved along D42 towards Barneville-sur-Mer. In its wake came the 1st Battalion, 39th Infantry Regiment with the responsibility of holding the northern flank.

German strategy had originally tried to hold back the American drive west and not allow its forces to the north to be cut off. With two US divisions across the Douve River the Germans attempted to hold open a corridor through which its best troops, the 77th Division, could move south and escape inevitable capture.

With the headlong westward advance of the US 60th Regiment on June 17 the roads leading south, now to the American rear, had to be closed to stop withdrawing German columns from escaping.

In the late afternoon (June 17) Lieutenant Colonel Tucker's 1st Battalion (39th Regiment) entered St. Jacques de Nehou. His men spread out in a line facing north 450 meters north of the village. His right flank included the secondary road (D87) out of the village's northeast section.

Moving south towards St. Jacques-de-Nehou was the 3rd Battalion and part of the 2nd Battalion of the German 1049th Regiment (77th Division) commanded by Colonel Rudolf Bacherer, a man destined to be the division commander after his commander was killed on June 18. The force was trying to cut through the American east-west line.

At 4:30 a.m. (June 18) the Germans attacked all along the battalion's front. Mortars and machine guns pounded both the attackers and defenders. The ardent fight was confused. A breakthrough on the American right flank, along the secondary road, caused Colonel Tucker to pull his line back into the village. Platoon by platoon, covered by heavy machine gun fire, they fell back to the stone walls and houses across from the church and bordering D42. The Germans occupied the fenced churchyard and the houses facing the American positions. An American counterattack was organized.

At 9 a.m. divisional artillery and heavy mortars bombarded the German positions. The infantry moved forward against the dazed but resolute Germans. Their former lines were regained, resistance decreased, they continued their advance 3 kilometers north to the Seye River. Two hundred and fifty dead and 60 wounded German soldiers were counted in the fields. The US had recorded 39 casualties in the German attack and 5 in the counterattack. Bacherer and his remnant battalions retreated north. They regrouped and continued to probe for a breakthrough point. In the late afternoon, June 19, they succeeded at St. Lo-d'Ourville (10 kilometers southwest near the coast) where N903 crosses the Ollande River. The German 1050th Infantry Regiment's 1st Battalion charged the US 2nd Battalion, 47th Regiment, holding the bridge. The bridge was captured. The German force, with 250 prisoners and twelve captured jeeps, moved south and entered their own lines. These 1400 men and a few scattered groups were all that escaped. The remainder retreated north into fortress Cherbourg.

4.7 St. Pierre-d'Artheglise

(18 kilometers southwest of Valognes via D902 to D242, east 2.5 kilometers to St. Pierre-d'Artheglise)

On June 17 the US 60th Infantry Regiment (9th Division) crossed the Douve River at Nehou (11 kilometers east) at 6 a.m. Advancing on St. Pierre-d'Artheglise late the same night the 2nd Battalion passed north of the town while the 1st Battalion passed to the south.

The road D242 west of St. Pierre-d'Artheglise descends sharply between two high points. The northern elevation is called Point 145 and the southern Point 135 in reference to their height in meters above sea level. The 1st and 2nd Battalion occupied the south and north points respectively during the early hours of June 18. The 3rd Battalion having descended D42 towards Barneville-sur-Mer had reached its destination at 5 a. m. (June 18) and thereby blocked the last German escape route south. To the south the 47th Regiment had cut the same road at Grande Huanville. All German escape routes from the Contentin Peninsula had been blocked, although units of the 77th Division were to the north trying to penetrate. The division commander, Major General Rudolf Stegmann, was killed that day by fighter-bombers as he attempted to direct the southerly movement and organization of his division near Bricquebec. Without approval for such a withdrawal south, the division merely organized and readied itself while awaiting their orders.

Far to the east on June 17 Hitler had come to Margival (northeast of Paris) to discuss the Normandy invasion front with Field Marshals Gerd von Runstedt and Erwin Rommel. There, in the bunker built in 1940 as a command post for the German invasion of England (now a French Army communications center) the Field Marshals argued for permission to allow the 77th Division to move south while it was still possible so that it would not be cut off in the peninsula . Although permission was not granted, sufficient ambiguous orders were issued which, when acted upon, moved the division south June 18. The presence of the American forces on the two hilltops west of Ste. Pierre-d'Artheglise, overlooking and dominating route D902 and the countryside, meant the Germans were one day late and a division would be lost.

In the morning, June 18, a German column with units of the 77th Division's artillery, moved down D902 from Bricquebec in an effort to do an end-run ahead of the American point troops.

The leading vehicle was abreast of Point 145 when the guns of the American 60th Field Artillery Battalion opened fire. Antitank guns, heavy machine guns and mortars joined the barrage. The guns adjusted and back-tracked into the trapped column. With the lead vehicles destroyed the column became immobile. The gun caissons in tow were impossible to turn and too cumbersome to reverse. The barrage crept 10 kilometers along the road almost to Bricquebec. When the bombardment stopped there remained the debris of thirty-five vehicles, ten artillery pieces, machine guns, mortars, wagons, trailers, motorcycles, caissons, bicycles, horses, a tank, half tracks, cars and trucks.

Had the column moved south the previous day it would likely have been partially successful in its end-run.

It is unlikely that the entire column would have regained their lines as American fighter-bombers patrolled the routes constantly throughout the daylight hours, taking a heavy toll of mobile equipment and forcing movement to be restricted to the night hours.

4.8 Barneville-sur-Mer

(25 kilometers southwest of Valognes via D902)

Driving west from the Douve River at Nehou (16 kilometers east) on June 17, by nightfall the US 60th Infantry Regiment was on the high ground overlooking Barneville-sur-Mer from the southeast.

Aerial reconnaissance throughout the day had spotted a few German units slipping south ahead of the American westward drive to occupy the "neck" of the Contentin Peninsula. In general, however, allied fighter-bombers and the indecision of the German high command had kept the roads relatively inactive. Capitalizing on the German's dilemma, the American field commanders seized the opportunity to close the escape route.

Although weary form their advance of the day the 3rd Battalion pushed on from the crossroads (D42 and D50) south of le Valdecie (8 kilometers northeast) at 10 p.m. (June 17). K Company riding five tanks of B Company (746th Tank Battalion), four tank destroyers of A Company (899th Tank Destroyer Battalion), and four half tracks, drove down D42 towards St. Maurice-en-Contentin. Crossing the bridge over the stream, 1.4 kilometers northeast of the village a German antitank gun opened fire knocking the tread off the lead tank destroyer. The tanks retaliated, the antitank nest was silenced. Pushing the disabled vehicles aside, the armored squadron continued.

At the fork and crossroads north of St. Maurice-en-Contentin, the force rather than turning west onto D130, the direct route to Barneville-sur-Mer, continued directly through St. Maurice-en-Contentin to the hamlet of Villot (Quilbec) arriving at 2 a.m. (June 18). The armor turned west taking the paralleling ridge road to N903 which lead them to its high point overlooking the town arriving by 5 am.

While the remainder of the battalion closed up along the ridge, K Company, the tank and tank destroyers moved into the seemingly deserted town. A few German MP traffic controllers were captured. Moving north the company established roadblocks 200 meters beyond the town limits on D904 and D902.

The first attempt to break the American line came from the southeast that morning at 10 a.m. (June 18). L Company repulsed the attack taking 85 prisoners.

Later in the day two more attacks were defeated at the roadblocks north of town. This terminated German efforts to capture the town. However, numerous skirmishes developed to the east and west as small groups attempted to slip through the American held territory.

In front of the Barneville town hall stands a tall, black monument containing a photograph of K Company's Commander, Captain Pat Williamson, as a bemedaled Major. The French honored their liberator "to symbolize the American youth who came to fight in Europe for them and who paid with their lives and wounds."

A memorial on D903 south of the town commemorates the cutting of the Contentin Peninsula here on Sunday, June 18, a significant milestone in the battle of Normandy.

Only the monuments evidences the war. Uniquely, Barneville-sur-Mer was not bombed or shelled by either the Americans or Germans. In contrast, St. Sauveur-le-Vicomte (16 kilometers east) has the distinction of being the heaviest damaged town on the peninsula .

The capture of Barneville-sur-Mer on June 18 ended exactly four years of occupation. On the same date in 1940 the German 7th Armored (Ghost) Division under General Lieutenant Erwin Rommel passed northward through the town in his drive to Cherbourg which fell the following day.

4.9 Bricquebec

(13 kilometers southeast of Valognes via D902)

Two American soldiers were hanged in the nearby hamlet of Hameau-Pigeon just inside the gate of la Ferme des Galeries, February 10, 1945. The execution was witnessed by local residents and hundreds of American servicemen guarded by armed MPs.

To reach Hameau-Pigeon drive north from Bricquebec to Quettot (3 kilometers, D900). Go west on D23, the Les Pieux road, 1.5 kilometers to the D367 turnoff. Left 1.5 kilometers to the collection of farm buildings close to the road, the Hameau-Pigeon hamlet.

On August 1, 1944, Privates Waiters Yancy and Robert Skinner of the 1511 Engineer Water Supply Company, bivouacked in Bricquebec, entered the farm house of Monsieur Xavier Hebert and demanded cider from the housemaid Marie Isouf, 19. After gulping down five glasses of the potent Calvados they left but returned for more. Armed and intoxicated they followed Marie into the cider shed. Skinner hit Marie on the head several times and dragged her screaming into the courtyard. Madame Hebert rushed to her aid but was threatened by Yancy holding his carbine against her. Madam Hebert wrestled the gun away and ran to her nearby neighbors Monsieur and Madame Augusta Mace. Yancy chased Madame Hebert and shot Augusta Mace in the arm as he exited his house to investigate the commotion. Xavier Hebert and his workman Auguste Lebraillier, 19, also hearing the screams ran into the courtyard but were cut down by Yancy's rifle fire at the gate entrance. Xavier was hit in the back and Auguste in the stomach. Auguste died the following day in the 101st Evacuation Hospital.

Skinner, at knife point then dragged Marie across the road into the field and raped her while Yancy stood guard. They then changed places and raped again.

The court martial was held in Cherbourg on November 7. Skinner for rape, Yancy for rape, bodily harm and murder. Both were found guilty and sentenced to hang.

The execution site chosen was the la Ferme des Galeries in Hameau-Pigeon. A gallows was erected immediately inside to the left of the farm field gate. The hanging was by strangulation. The second man watched his friend die over a six minute period before his trap door dropped him into oblivion. The execution was witnessed by the victims, their families and hundreds of soldiers. The MPs firing in the air forced the curiosity seekers away.

Forty-seven US servicemen were executed in France between D-Day and the end of the war for similar offenses.

Chapter 5 UTAH Beach - Northern Thrust

The D-Day objectives of the 4th Division were to establish a UTAH Beachhead, then advance north and northwest 10-12 kilometers creating a secure lodgment area for the 7th Corps buildup of troops, supplies, airfields, etc. The coastal village of Quineville, 10 kilometers north of UTAH Beach, was the northerly objective. The 101st Airborne Division to the south, and the 82nd Airborne Division to the west, were responsible for the expansion and securement of their lodgment areas.

By midnight on D-Day, the 4th Division had not reached its objectives. Their front line ran from Ste. Mere-Eglise east to the beach hamlet of Hamel de Cruttes 4 kilometers north of the UTAH Beachhead. Batteries that should have been overrun (Azeville and Crisbecq) were operational, still dueling with the invasion fleet and laying down harassment fire on the Beach.

To the north of these batteries the terrain rises gradually to the Quineville-Montebourg ridge. A German defense line ran southwest from Montebourg along the ridge and railroad line.

After securing the beachhead and cleaning out resistance pockets on D-Day and D+1, the 4th on the right and 82nd Airborne Divisions (on the left) drove northward to the Quineville-Montebourg line.

Much would depend upon the success of this drive. Harassment fire on the beaches would cease, a start line for the drive to Cherbourg would be provided, and a broader base for the 7th Corp's thrust west across to the Contentin Peninsula would be established.

5.1 Magneville

(6 kilometers northwest of Ste. Mere-Eglise via N13 4 kilometers to the Fresville road, D269, then left 2.5 kilometers)

On June 8, at 8 a.m. the 8th Infantry Regiment (4th Division) began its advance northward from positions to the west of Neuville-au-Plain (4 kilometers southeast).

The 3rd Battalion moved into the southern outskirts of Magneville in the early afternoon. Item Company proceeded to clear the village and the fields to the north.

Unknowingly the company was a few hundred meters south of a significant German defense line. The line ran from the west through Magneville continuing east to the coast including the batteries at Azeville and Crisbecq. German bicycle troops of the 243rd Division and the Sturm Battalion had hurriedly rushed down from Cherbourg to reinforce the line.

As the American company moved out of town through the orchards and fields towards the huge airship hangar on the opposite side of a stream (Merderet River tributary), it came under heavy artillery and mortar fire from the les Landes area (1 kilometer northwest). (The large airship hangar, fortified by the Germans was adjacent to the Magneville-Ecausseville road (D510) at the dogleg turn as the road runs between Magneville on the south and les Landes to the north. The hangar was bordered on its north by the Ecausseville road and on its south by the stream that flows into the Merderet River a kilometer away.) From dugouts and pits around the hangar and along the stream small arms and machine gun fire cut through the hedgerow flanking the farm road paralleling the stream. The company retreated back into the village digging in along the lateral road.

Throughout the night, the regiment spread out. The highway N13 (2 kilometers east) was shelled by German 88s, mortars and the multi-barrelled nebelwerfers.

On June 9 at 6 a.m.,US artillery from three battalions opened up against the German defense positions north of the creek. Half an hour later the infantry advanced. Counterfire fell amongst them as the men crossed from Magneville to the stream. L and I Companies abreast, L to the left, arrived at the stream together. L was held up but I skirting around to the east of the hangar, raced across the field over the Ecausseville road (D510) across the adjacent field into the orchard. From the hamlet of les Landes on the far side of the field and the houses across the field to the northeast machine guns and rifle fire stopped the company's advance. While dashing across the flat open fields the company had received fire from behind (the hangar), from overhead (les Landes' artillery) and from the flank (farm buildings northeast). In this triangle of fire their casualties had been severe. However two platoons, the company command post unit and mortars had reached their temporary orchard objective.

Meanwhile L Company had crossed the creek. After a brief fierce fight in the orchard immediately west of the hangar the company battled and subdued the positions in and around the hangar.

With the fire to its rear eliminated I Company, feeling a little out on a limb in the orchard, fell back to the ditches and hedgerow of the Ecausseville road (D510). L Company, its mission at the hangar completed; moved up to the road left of I Company.

Again both companies advanced into the orchard and dug in for the night. K Company moved up to I Company's right flank in readiness for a counterattack.

The next day, June 10, the Americans in the orchard were heavily shelled. Recovering quickly, the battalion moved to the northeast, took the farm and circumvented les Landes.

Advances to the west by the 1st Battalion, 505th Regiment (82nd Airborne Division) made the les Landes position untenable and the Germans withdrew without a struggle.

Related stories are Ecausseville, a kilometer north and le Ham 2 kilometers west.

5.2 Ecausseville

(7 kilometers northwest of Ste. Mere-Eglise via N13 7 kilometers to Ecausseville road on D510, turn west 1 kilometer)

Commencing from its positions west of Neuville-au-Plain on the morning of June 8, the 8th Regiment, commanded by Colonel James Van Fleet, attacked north towards the east-west Montebourg-Quineville (coastal village) German defense line.

That evening the 1st Battalion stopped along the Magneville-Ecausseville Road, a kilometer southeast of the village. To its west the 2nd and 3rd Battalions held the line to Magneville.

The following day, June 9, the 1st Battalion was to continue along the road passing east of Ecausseville while the village would be taken by the 2nd Battalion.

Reconnaissance patrols reported the town unoccupied. The 1st Battalion was being held up at the junction of N13 and D510, while the 3rd Battalion was meeting stiff resistance at the Magneville hangar. Colonel Van Fleet ordered the 2nd Battalion to advance due north into Ecausseville.

An east-west stream separated the Americans from their objective. The German defense positions were on the stream's north slope. At Magneville the defenders were causing high casualties and slowing the advance. The Ecausseville area was seemingly void of defenses and clear.

From N13 the creek passes west and south of Ecausseville. Immediately west of the village it turns sharply south for a few hundred meters then again turns to the west, passing north of Magneville. A farm road on the south side parallels the stream's course from Magneville to the Ecausseville road near N13.

At 2 p.m. two platoons of Easy Company emerged from their Magneville-Ecausseville road position, crossed the fields and entered the farm road at the point where it bends north towards Ecausseville. The point scouts moved ahead to the stream. On signal the Germans opened fire on the platoons along the road. Machine guns swept the flank from the northwest. Artillery and mortars, accurately registered on the road firing air burst charges, quickly littered the road with dead and dying. Efforts to silence the closer German positions were thwarted by crisscross lines of fire. Pressing along the road to the right hand turn and moving east was of no avail. Wherever the Americans moved, accurate well placed shells followed. The German ambush had been thoroughly executed.

The toll had been heavy. Discouraged and harassed Easy Company troops returned to their start line and conceded the loss of fifty to sixty of their men, all of their mortars and the destruction or abandonment of half of their machine guns.

To the east, at 7 p.m., the 1st Battalion with two platoons from A Company, 70th Tank Battalion, moved up the Magneville-Ecuasseville road and across the stream. The farm at the road bend into Ecausseville was a potential antitank gun nest. As they passed their machine guns tore through the doorways and windows. Moving into the fields they attacked Ecausseville from the northeast. Halting in the fields they weakened the German defenders with 15 minutes of shellfire while 88's in the village returned the fire. The tanks withdrew to the rear of the farm aware that its buildings sheltered many Germans. The armor attacked the buildings. Able Company moved in to complete the task. The battle ended at 9 p.m. A hundred prisoners shuffled back to the prison cage at UTAH Beach.

During the night the Germans abandoned Ecausseville. The 3rd Battalion at les Landes and the 1st Battalion at the farm, threatened encirclement or decimation if they attempted to withdraw in daylight.

Related stories are Magneville, one kilometer south and le Ham, 3 kilometers southwest.

5.3 Le Ham

(8 kilometers northwest of Ste. Mere-Eglise on N13, 3 kilometers to the Fresville road, D269, then west 6 kilometers)

The German defense line ran from Quineville (12 kilometers northeast) on the coast, through Montebourg (5 kilometers northeast) to Montebourg Station (1.5 kilometers northeast where D42 crosses the railline) ending at le Ham, its southwest anchor.

Prior to June 1944 Montebourg was connected to the Cherbourg-Paris railline by a railroad spur line that started at the D42 road, railroad intersection. That area was Montebourg Station. The railline paralleled D42, 500 meters to its north into the town of Montebourg. Heavily damaged by shelling in mid June, it has since been removed and not replaced.

The hamlet of le Ham, the defense line's west end anchor was isolated by the flooded Merderet River tributaries east, south and west. The grazing pasture land of today was a 400 meter wide marsh in June 1944 cleverly developed by the Germans in their defense strategy. During the four year occupation their war games had created excellent tactics. le Ham, elevated 10 meters above the marsh on three sides became a significant strong point.

Moving north from the UTAH Beachhead, the American forces were approaching the Quineville-le Ham line by June 9. The 3rd Battalion, 325th Glider Infantry Regiment, occupied positions between the Merderet River and Magneville (3 kilometers southeast of le Ham). Passing through the 3rd Battalion's positions on June 10 the 1st and 2nd Battalions of the 505th Regiment attacked north into Montebourg Station.

In support of their advance the air force bombed le Ham to subdue the German fire positions throwing flank fire into the advance.

The attack carried. The Americans entered Montebourg Station at 7 p.m. The Germans withdrew, some northward, the remainder to le Ham. The 2nd Battalion pivoting west attempted to follow the retreating Germans down D42 into le Ham but was stopped at the les Landes road fork 200 meters from the station.

The next morning, June 11 at 10:15 a.m., the 456th Field Artillery Battalion shelled the German positions east of the village for 15 minutes. While the 2nd Battalion (505th Regiment) on D42 maintained pressure and feint attacked from the station, the 2nd Battalion (325th Regiment) attacked across the marsh from the southeast.

American casualties were high but the swollen tributary was crossed and the battalion moved into the fields, orchards and hedgerows. Stopping to regroup, distribute ammunition, and re-supply, the Germans were seen to be withdrawing from their gun pits into le Ham. Artillery fire was called in. Machine guns fired at the retreating Germans.

A follow-up attack at 6 p.m. overran the rear guard holding the fortification and carried through to le Ham. Two hours later only dead Germans remained. Pushing west along D42 200 meters the bridge across the second tributary was secured intact.

June 12 was spent clearing the sector of bypassed resistance pockets to the south, between le Ham and the forks of the Merderet.

The two regiments (325th and 505th) of the 82nd Airborne Division were pulled out of the line the following day and replaced by the 359th Regiment (90th Division).

Related stories are Magneville, 2 kilometers east and Ecausseville, 3 kilometers northeast.

5.4 Taret de Ravenoville

(The hamlet of Taret de Ravenoville is on the east coast of the Contentin Peninsula 7 kilometers north of UTAH Beach)

On D-Day the 3rd Battalion (22nd Regiment of the 4th Division) moved north after landing at UTAH Beach to secure the German resistance nests along the beach front. By the evening of June 7th the battalion had advanced to a point 3 kilometers south of Taret de Ravenoville to Hamel de Cruttes. Between the two hamlets the Germans held Strongpoints 55, 102, 103 and 104.

A strongpoint consisted of a reinforced concrete blockhouse with one or two machine guns in steel cupolas on its roof. The outer defenses consisted of barbed wire, minefields, pillboxes, trenches and artillery pieces. Support fire from neighboring strongpoints and the Azeville and Crisbecq batteries all interconnected through deep sunk telephone cables, made the capture of each strongpoint a major and costly endeavor. The method of attack coordinated naval shellfire and close in tank support. The foot soldiers had to do the rest. The Germans after surviving the barrage held fire until the infantry was close in then the support fire from the two batteries, neighboring strongpoints and their small arms would open up. Months of preparedness and practice had optimized the destructive effects on the infantry. The open beach, sand dunes and flooded marshlands provided little cover for the attackers.

As the battalion faced Strongpoint 55 at Hamel de Cruttes it received orders to move inland in regimental reserve in anticipation of a German counterattack, against the shattered 1st and 2nd Battalions holding to the west. Lieutenant Colonel Arthur S. Teague, commander of the battalion, left K Company facing Strongpoint 55. He moved the remainder of his battalion inland 2 kilometers to the village of Ravenoville. The beach Strongpoint 104, 2.5 kilometers east, at Taret de Ravenoville had been heavily shelled by the navy. A number of Germans had slipped out to surrender reporting that many of their comrades were willing to surrender but were being prevented by their officers. On the basis of this information Colonel Teague moved his battalion east across the broad marshy expanse and closed in on the rear of the strongpoint. A prisoner, who was sent ahead, returned with the entire garrison of 82 Germans. That night the battalion billeted themselves in the strongpoint. Three strongpoints separated the battalion force in Taret de Ravenoville and its K Company at Hamel de Cruttes. On June 8 one of the strongpoints surrendered.

On June 11, K Company captured the two remaining strongpoints. For two days they had hammered at the two positions. Finally the company learned from prisoners that the heavy American shellfire had only served to force the garrison to shuttle through a tunnel from one section to another.K Company fired 50 rounds of 57mm on the first fort then switched suddenly to 80 rounds into the adjacent stronghold. Resistance ended in both forts. Ninety three prisoners were marched to UTAH Beach.

On June 12 two companies of the 2nd Battalion (39th Regiment) entered the beach area through the positions of the 3rd Battalion (22nd Regiment) at Taret de Ravenoville. The companies assaulted and captured the first strongpoint north of Taret de Ravenoville.

5.5 Crisbecq (Marcouf Battery)

(Crisbecq is 8 kilometers north of Ste. Mere-Eglise. From Ste. Mere-Eglise take D15 to Ravenoville and north on D14 to St. Marcouf. At the church take the right hand fork to Crisbecq.)

The Crisbecq Battery is 300 meters west of the village of Crisbecq. The secondary road passes through the battery site as it ascends the slope towards D140. German literature refers to this emplacement as the Marcouf Battery. American historians favor the term Crisbecq Battery because of its proximity to the village.

The extended view of the Bay of the Seine afforded the Germans an excellent observation and fire control position for bombarding the allied invasion fleet. The Crisbecq and Azeville (2.5 kilometers to the southwest) Batteries were strategically located to affect the beach landing operations. This vantage point dictated the positioning of the Azeville Battery's observation post and fire control bunker within the defense perimeter of the Crisbecq Battery.

The Crisbecq Naval Battery was planned as the showpiece of Hitler's Atlantic Wall and was specifically designed for bombarding the invasion fleet if it appeared. Its offensive and defensive armaments were to consist of; four, 210mm long barreled guns housed in four meter thick concrete emplacements with steel cupolas enclosing the gun aperture; six, 75mm antiaircraft guns and one 150mm field run in an open firing pit. Ammunition storage was underground. Communication trenches interlaced the area between bunkers and machine gun nests. Barbed wire and minefields defined the outer defense limits.

The elaborately proposed plans did not materialize as anticipated. German ordnance failed to provide the necessary guns. French Resistance handicapped the completion stages by sabotaging trains while the allied air force bombings further contributed to the operation being somewhat less than the planned "showpiece". The first 210mm gun was installed on April 19, 1944. From then on the battery was bombed nightly. The first evening without a bombing raid was June 5 but at 11 p.m. 100 bombers dropped 600 tons of bombs on the fortifications in a 35 minute period. Although not affecting the three 210mm guns in their casements the raid did destroy the six 75mm antiaircraft guns. The chateau in St. Marcouf, a

German billet, was damaged, killing the wounding many of its occupants. The gun crews lived at the battery site. The auxiliary staffs were housed in Crisbecq and St. Marcouf.

Although the three 210mm guns were operational, their defenses were incomplete. The steel face plates protecting the gun embrasures had not been installed or received. This left the casements although tremendous in size and protective thickness with an opening 6 meters by 3 meters on the seaward side. Neither the radar nor modern fire control equipment had arrived.

The first shots fired in combat were in the predawn hours of D-Day when a misdropped stick of US paratroopers landed east of the battery and engaged the battery's protective infantry. The paratroopers withdrew to their specified objectives.

Three US battleships, Nevada, Arkansas and Texas mounting a total of ten 14-inch guns, twelve 12-inch guns and twenty-five 5-inch guns had the battery on their target list. At 5 a.m. D-Day the three casement guns of the battery dueled with the battleship Nevada and one of her escort destroyers. Three hours later one of the battery's guns was damaged and ceased firing. (The guns was repaired and returned to action on the morning of June 8.) At 9 a.m. the duel with the Nevada resulted in number 2 casement receiving a direct hit through the open gun aperture. The Nevada's shell exploded amongst the ammunition, stacked behind the gun breach. The effect can only be imagined. The gun crew was obliterated and the gun destroyed.

Damage to the 150mm open pit field gun position was extensive. Its capability of ranging out to sea had been lost so it was redirected to harassment fire against UTAH Beach. On D-Day morning the battery engaged the destroyer USS Corry, anchored close into UTAH Beach providing inshore fire support for the assault forces. The Corry's Commander, Lieutenant Commander G. Hoffman, weighed anchor and in the maneuver of withdrawing to deeper water hit a submerged mine. The destroyer sank with a loss of 13 lives and 33 wounded. There were more casualties in this single action than had been sustained by the assault force on the beach to that time. This was the only major US navy loss on D-Day.

On the morning of June 7 the US 22nd Infantry Regiment in its northward advance from St. Germain de Varreville (4 kilometers south of St. Marcouf) were just 2 kilometers south of the battery at Bas Village de Dodainville. Shellfire from the Crisbecq Battery halted the advance. At 7 a.m. the 1st Battalion of the regiment attacked towards the battery incurring heavy losses due to flank fire from the open pit gun position inside the battery's perimeter.

The battalion entered St. Marcouf from the south. At the village church they took the right hand fork. A few hundred meters along they branched onto the left fork, the road to Dangueville.

The battalion fought along the poplar lined and hedge enclosed track to the battery site at the intersection of the Crisbecq road. The battery's perimeter defenses of minefields, barbed wire, machine gun nests and trenches had been shattered by the air force bombings and the naval bombardment. The Crisbecq road became the front line with both sides lobbing handgrenades across the hedges.

U .S. infantry climbed on top of Crisbecq's Battery observation and fire control bunker, and attempted to dislodge the German occupants by thrusting explosive charges into the ventilator shafts and apertures. The Crisbecq Battery commander Lieutenant Ohmsen, requested the Azeville Battery to fire antipersonnel shells into his positions. The support fire literally blew the surprised US infantry off the bunker. The Americans withdrew abandoning valuable equipment. German reinforcements (6th Company of 919th Infantry Regiment) commanded by Lieutenant Geissler arrived from the north, crossed the Crisbecq road and flank attacked the Americans along the Dangueville road. The German counterattack was pressed through St. Marcouf to the US line at Bas Village de Dodainville. Ninety Americans were captured. The Germans continued their attacks throughout the night of June 7 and 8, but against the stubborn defense their attacks faltered.

The next day, Thursday, June 8 at 1:30 p.m. following a twenty minute naval and artillery bombardment of the area between Bas Village de Dodainville and the battery, the American battalion advanced behind a rolling artillery barrage. The advance and rate of fire were well coordinated permitting the battalion to reach the fortifications with few losses. Once again the infantry entered the defense perimeter and surrounded several of the casements and pillboxes. By attaching demolition charges to long poles and thrusting them through the gun slits, they were successful in reducing much of the German resistance. However, on the large casements the demolition charges were ineffective.

Shellfire from the Azeville Battery coordinated with a German infantry counterattack on the American west flank forced the Americans to withdraw to their lines at Bas Village de Dodainville.

In this two day action the 1st Battalion had suffered 50% casualties.

Throughout the battle the besieged Germans were in direct contact with their higher command in Cherbourg. Miraculously, a loosely buried telephone cable, one meter deep, had survived the bombing and shelling. Over this wire on June 11, Lieutenant Ohmsen, the battery commander, was given permission to withdraw his beleaguered force north to their lines at Quineville. While one battalion of the American regiment fought to reduce the battery the other battalions were rushing north towards Cherbourg. By this date the front lines were 6 kilometers to the north. Ohmsen's decimated gun crews, reduced to 67 men from an original 400 on D-Day, withdrew under the cover of darkness on the night of June 11 and 12.

The battery was occupied on the following morning at 8:20, June 12, by elements of the US 39th Regiment. No opposition was offered by the 21 wounded Germans and their noncommissioned officer serving as a medical orderly. Although the battery had been operational six days longer than the allied timetable had planned, the severe damage of June 6 naval bombardment had reduced its effective firepower to that of beach harassment.

Today the bunkers and antiaircraft guns open pits are visible. There is a Battery Museum on the site.

On the north side of the road, the two casements are severely damaged. The most northerly received the shell through its embrasure. The walls have been blown out and the roof has collapsed into the confines of the casement itself. The concrete walls are cracked and pock marked showing evidence of the large navy shells that bombarded the area. South of the road, on the inside of the hedge, is the observation post used by the Azeville Battery for fire direction control into the Bay of the Seine. The west side of the control bunker bears the pock marks of the shelling it received from its own Azeville Battery. In the roof there is a large crater as a result of the US demolition team's efforts. Around the walls is evidence of the small arms fire and bazooka explosions blasted against the walls. One hundred meters to the south in the field is the barracks bunker semiconcealed in the ground. Relics of the battle, 20mm shell cases can be found in the rubble.

North of the D69 intersection, 7 kilometers on D14 (west side) is a monument to the 365th Fighter Group that operated from an Advanced Landing Ground nearby.

Related stories are the Azeville Battery and UTAH Beach.

5.6 Azeville Battery

(The village of Azeville is located 6 kilometers north of Ste. Mere-Eglise. The village is most easily reached by driving north from Ste. Mere-Eglise, on N13 3.5 kilometers to the Azeville road, which branches to the east. The battery position is 200 meters east of the village on the road of St. Marcouf, which passes through the site. There are four large concrete blockhouses, two on each side of the road.)

During the early hours of June 6 American paratroopers landed in the area overcoming an open pit field gun position and its crew lazily sleeping in tents beside their weapons.

Other paratroopers engaged German troops returning to Azeville from night training exercises whose ammunition pouches only contained blank charges. The encounter was in the village churchyard with green troops of the German 709th Infantry Division. The Germans crawled along the road and ditches into the American positions among the churchyard tombstones. The battle proceeded from tombstone to tombstone with the paratroopers withdrawing towards the church. By morning the Americans had surrounded their attackers. After effecting heavy casualties on the Germans the paratroopers withdrew.

Throughout June 6 to 8 the Azeville Battery created harassment fire on UTAH Beach.

The battery consisted of four 122mm guns in concrete casements manned by the 9th Battery of the 945th Army Coastal Artillery Regiment commanded by Lieutenant Kattnig. The position was a permanent coastal battery position prepared for land attack and defense, consisting of concrete blockhouses, underground ammunition storage with inter-communication defense and communication trenches. The area was ringed with barbed wire. Ground defenses included automatic weapon pits. Even the outpost sentry boxes were constructed of concrete.

On June 9 at noon the US 22nd Regiment, commanded by Colonel Harvey A. Tribolet, attacked the battery position after a 1500 shell bombardment. German records indicate that naval shellfire secured a direct hit on casement no. 3. The 3-meter concrete walls were smashed the gun and its crew were buried in the rubble.

German harassing support fire from the Crisbecq Battery (2.5 kilometers northeast) was minimal as it was in a self-survival duel with the battleships, cruisers and destroyers of the invasion fleet.

Two companies of the 22nd Regiment circled the Azeville Battery and attacked from the west across the barbed wire and minefields protecting the battery. The defensive automatic weapon pits faced south and therefore machine gun fire was not serious. The gun casements resisted demolition charges and flame throwers used by the US infantry, but the positions were finally subdued due in part to the actions of Private R. G. Riley. Single handed, Riley completed the mission. Dashing toward the casement he sprayed his flame thrower into the base of the door until he heard the explosion of the ammunition within. The blockhouse door opened and a captured American paratrooper officer escorted the German commander and his 169 men from the casement. Riley was awarded the Silver Star.

Today the batteries are still present surrounded by grazing cows. All the blockhouses are of similar design, with the rear access protected by a machine gun loop hole covering the entrance corridor. In the first casement north of the road the ventilation blower is still in tact. and on the south wall five holes as a result of US field artillery fire can be seen. Otherwise there was little damage. To the west a few meters on the north side of the road is a bunker. This was a barracks and control bunker with an observation post and machine nest on its northwest corner, under a cement roof. The second casement to the north of the road clearly shows evidence of a shell having passed along the entrance corridor, penetrated the machine gun embrasure and exploded amongst the small arms ammunition supply. Navy shellfire weakened the roof. Internal damage was slight resulting only from the close small arms and hand to hand fighting. The first casement on the south side of the road was damaged around the embrasure facing east. There is no further evidence of a large caliber shell entering the casement. On the west side, from which the Americans attacked, there is little or no damage. The second casement south of the road bears evidence of artillery shelling on the west wall around the door and exhaust ventilator. On the east side there is shell damage on the roof overhang, which protected the gun opening against incoming shells.

There does not appear to be any evidence of the German commander's claim that a direct hit by a naval shell entered through the gun embrasure and blew the roof off the No. 3 casement. In the fields nearby are machine gun pillboxes which were the defense for the battery position. Several ammunition bunkers between the casements and underground barracks can still be seen. The observation and fire control bunker for the Azeville Battery was located on the site of the Crisbecq Battery (2.5 kilometers northeast), because of the better visibility from Crisbecq. It is advisable, because of the interrelation of the batteries and the fighting which ensued in the two areas simultaneously, to also visit the Crisbecq Battery.

Shortly after, on June 16, a battalion of engineers commenced construction of Advanced Landing Ground A-7 in the Azeville area. Although the Germans kept shelling the proposed runway area during construction, no casualties or damage resulted. Due to terrain difficulties and the prohibitive amount of earth that would have to be moved the completed runway was somewhat shorter than the anticipated 1,600 meters. Within two weeks the strip became operational for refueling and rearmament.

5.7 Quineville

(11 kilometers northeast of Ste. Mere-Eglise via N13 to Montebourg and east on D42 to the coast)

Northerly advances by regiments of the US 82nd Airborne and 4th Infantry Division on June 8, 9 and 10 had moved the US northern flank to the le Ham-Montebourg road (D42). Along the coastal road (D421) the German strongpoints built as beach defenses against seaborne assault were difficult to subdue resulting in less spectacular gains. Backed by marshes, flanked by open beaches and accessible only across elevated causeways the 39th Regiment (4th Division) was compelled to take each one separately with close support from tanks, artillery and warships.

Ozeville (4 kilometers southwest) the last barrier to Quineville was captured on June 12. Leaving Fontenay-sur-Mer (2 kilometers southwest) the 3rd Battalion (39th Regiment) moved northeast towards its objective. As it neared the Quineville-Montebourg road (D42) German and American artillery fire falling on its lead platoon halted the advance for the day.

On June 14, 9 a.m., the attack was re-launched.

On the 3rd Battalion's left flank, the 22nd Regiment moved north clearing the east-west road (D42, the Montebourg road). D42 from Montebourg descends into Quineville. Four hundred meters before reaching the coast is the Quineville church and cemetery. South of the church, 300 meters, is the Quineville Chateau. Passing the church D42 continues its descent into Quineville-les-Bains on the coast.

By 3 p.m. the battalion was to the southwest of the hamlet and the Quineville church. German fire halted the American advance. An American artillery barrage fell on the German forward positions causing appreciable damage to the Quineville Chateau, its farm buildings and the houses around the church and the road junction.

An hour later K Company resumed their attack and took the chateau and the hamlet.

Between Quineville and Quineville-les-Bains the flat open fields were mined and covered with barbed wire entanglements running north and south. On the north side of the road, a hundred meters east of the Quineville church, a concrete casement facing northeast housed an 88mm gun.

K Company moved from the Quineville Chateau across the two fields and took the casement bordering D42 from the rear. Continuing east slight resistance at the farm bordering the sharp road bend was overcome and the company entered Quineville-les-Bains.

The village spread out along the sandy seashore was well fortified and designated on German maps as Strongpoint 105. Along the shoreline a long seawall holds back the seawater in times of high tides and eastern gales. Dotted along its length were four concrete machine gun nests and a thick walled casement housing a 75mm gun facing north to enfilade the beach. Two barracks bunkers submerged and camouflaged were dug into the grounds of the large sea coast chateau. Several Tobruk type mortar pits, machine gun nests and a steel turreted antitank gun were scattered around the chateau's outside garden walls. Around the rim of the concrete mortar pits were photos overlaid and indexed for the mortar's position to fire on prefixed non-visible targets. For night fighting the descending road was indexed to fire at the noise of trucks shifting gears.

Quineville's beach defense were exemplary of the might and strength of the Atlantic Wall. Cement tetrahedra, element "Cs", Belgian gates and mine tipped stakes presented a labrinyth of destruction for landing craft attempting to beach.

The concrete 75mm gun emplacement was ingeniously camouflaged as a barn complete with a peaked shingled roof and dummy shuttered windows. Through the perpetually open doors peered the gun's muzzle.

Entering the village at the first street the 3rd Platoon turned right and headed towards the beach, a hundred meters ahead. An antitank ditch running north-south from the Sinope River (north) to the marshes (south) cut their path. The 47mm turreted antitank gun at the end of the street, on the beach, swung in their direction and fired. The platoon scattered taking cover amongst the buildings.

The 1st Platoon passed through the intersection and along to the northeast corner of the village where it positioned its machine guns to fire at a gun nest on the far side of the river mouth on the beach.

Suffering from high casualties, K Company was virtually cut off from the remainder of the battalion at Quineville. Attempts to move up Companies I and L were handicapped by the mines and wire in the separating fields. Crossfire from the strongpoint on the south edge of

Quineville-les-Bains had closed off the exposed road from Quineville.

While US artillery bombarded the strongpoint three US tanks made it through to the village. The antitank gun on the beach firing up the street across the impassable antitank ditch forced the tanks to take up defensive positions to support the infantry. The smoke shells request by the 3rd Battalion's Commander, Lieutenant Colonel William P. Stumpf, was fulfilled. A barrage from divisional artillery shrouded the strongpoint. K Company's two platoons attacked in the late evening. Finding the Americans swarming over their position's at close quarters, the garrison surrendered.

To the south, along the coast, the regiment's 1st Battalion had spent the day clearing out and capturing the pockets of resistance bypassed by the American advances inland. During the night patrols of the 1st Battalion linked up with the 3rd Battalion at Quineville completing the rupture of the Quineville-le-Ham defense line.

By June 14, the objectives of June 6 had been achieved.

Many of the fortifications are still present. Only time or demolition can remove the thick concrete bastions. Along the sea wall are the gun pits and the casement. Within the chateau's garden are the barracks. Earthworks and the antitank ditch have been leveled and are but a memory to a few of the older citizens. There is a Liberty Museum in Quineville les Bains.

Picture 6: Quineville sur Mer - Looking West
July 6, 1948

Strong beach defenses (strongpoint on beach shoreline mid-photo and along the top of seawall). The chateau, bottom left, the 88,, casemate, mid-photo, near the ascending road and the church further up the hill witnessed strong German resistance on D-day +6 when attacked by the 3rd Battalion of the 22nd Regiment. The attackers came across the fields from the top left in the photo, descending upon the church and chateau 300 yards south. After subduing the Germans, K Company descended the road, battled the cement casemate gun crew but were stopped at the farm at the sharp corner. The capture of the seaside town was hard fought.

5.8 St. Floxel

(2 kilometers east of Montebourg via D71)

The village fell without battle on June 18. The northern sweep of the US 12th Regiment (4th Division) through the gap between St. Floxel and Montebourg and the 22nd Regiment passing east of the village left the Germans little choice but to withdraw.

The skirmish, which developed within the village, early D-Day is militarily and historically interesting.

The headquarters of the 3rd Battalion of the German 919th Regiment (709th Division) was located in St. Floxel. Its commander, Lieutenant Colonel Hoffman, was in his command post when the eight hundred plane air armada swept over the Contentin Peninsula from west to east. Most of the traffic was 9 kilometers to the south passing over the Ste. Mere-Eglise area.

Many aircraft strayed and became scattered. Those carrying the 502nd Parachute Infantry Regiment (101st Airborne Division) were to drop their sticks of paratroopers in Drop Zone A in the fields east of Ste. Mere-Eglise.

At 2 a.m., as the Colonel stood before his command post six C-47 transports flew overhead at less than 200 meters. The sticks of paratroopers hit the silk, floating down around St. Floxel. One of the earliest skirmishes in the battle of Normandy had begun. A few casualties resulted but the majority of the remaining paratroopers faded into the darkness. Not realizing these were misdrops he reported the incident to his regimental headquarters. A master map board at 84th Corps Headquarters in St. Lo denoted the landings by flagging the village of St. Floxel. This erroneous reporting and notation of the paratroop concentration, like hundreds of other similar reports, served to confuse the German command for several hours.

In the British sector, small rubber dummy parachutists were dropped setting off firecrackers when hitting the ground, imitating machine gun fire. These were dropped south and east of the 6th British Airborne Division landing zones to further confuse the size and focus of the airborne invaders on the German map boards.

Chapter 6 The Drive on Cherbourg

June 6 to 18 had witnessed the enlargement of the UTAH Beachhead. The westerly drive had cut the Contentin Peninsula, isolating the remnants of four German divisions (77th, 91st, 243rd and the 709th). Captured field orders of the 84th Corps outlined the German plan to withdraw the divisions into the defenses of Cherbourg.

The American line ran from Barneville-sur-Mer on the west coast to Quineville on the east coast. The battles and resulting casualties had disorganized many of the German frontline regiments. A rapid, decisive broad front thrust to Cherbourg could turn their withdrawal to fortress Cherbourg into a rout.

The German force was estimated at 25,000 - 40,000 men consisting of army, air force, navy, antiaircraft, rocket site and Todt construction organization personnel.

On June 18 the US 1st Army Commander, Lieutenant General Omar N. Bradley, the 7th Corps Commander, Major General J. Lawton Collins and the division commanders planned for the northern offensive.

Using the full width of the peninsula , from west to east the 9th, 79th and 4th Divisions would drive towards Cherbourg. As the 4th Division moved north to its objective, the east coast and northeast corner of the peninsula would be cleared by the 4th Cavalry Group. Between the 9th and 79th Divisions, the 4th Cavalry Squadron would advance.

The drive was to start July 19. The 4th Division would jump off at 3 a.m., the 9th and 79th 2 hours later.

6.1 Montebourg

(7 kilometers southeast of Valognes on N13)

Montebourg is a new town. Ninety percent destroyed between June 6 and 19 many of the original facades still stand. A US Army photo of the main street in June 1944, shows every building standing but internally destroyed. Today, comparison photographs depict the same buildings with reconstructed interiors.

Straddling the major north-south highway (N13) Montebourg was bombed and shelled to block the flow of German reinforcements. The east-west, Quineville to le Ham, German defense line passed through the town as well as east-west supply roads. Consequently the town was vulnerable and destined to destruction.

The advances by the US 12th Regiment (4th Division) June 6-10 brought its 2nd Battalion to the eastern edge of Montebourg on June 10. The German defenses were very strong, stopping the battalion's attempt to enter and capture the town.

The 1st Battalion passing to the east reached the Quineville road (D42) and withstood a strong counterattack.

On June 11, the regiment's three battalions established themselves between Montebourg and St. Floxel facing north and west from along D71. The same day the 4th Engineer Combat Battalion established roadblocks one kilometer south of Montebourg on N13.

The next day the German Artillery Group Montebourg moved into the woods north of the town. Commanded by Major Frederick Wilhelm Kuppers the group consisted of four 122mm, two 105's, a 105mm self propelled, mortars and flak guns. For the Germans a sizable concentration and a great support for the front line infantrymen.

An American reconnaissance patrol on June 12 reported Montebourg to be lightly held. It had not spotted the nineteen guns in the woods. The 4th Division Commander, Major General Raymond O. Barton, requested Colonel James A. Van Fleet to have his 8th Regiment take the objective with a minimum of casualties. A task force of two companies with engineer platoons, heavy machine guns, mortars, antitank guns and tank destroyers, all under the command of the regiment's executive officer, Lieutenant Colonel Fred Steiner, moved against Montebourg at 9 p.m. along N13. Automatic weapon fire from the buildings along the south edge of town stopped the night attack.

The next morning (June 13) at 7 a.m., with a company on each side of the road, the attack was resumed. Nearing the stream, 88mm fire stopped the advancing tank destroyers. Foreseeing a costly street battle developing, General Barton ordered the force to advance no further but contain the town.

The drive to Cherbourg was scheduled for June 19.

By midnight June 18 the town was hemmed in on two sides and part of a third. To the southwest the 8th Regiment held the south side of D42 to le Ham. K Company of the 22nd Regiment was 600 meters south, across N13. East, the 1st Battalion, 12th Regiment was a kilometer along the St. Floxel road (D71). To the northeast the 2nd and 3rd Battalion, 12th Regiment, were spread out along the Vaudreville road (D25).

On schedule the 8th and 12th Regiments launched their attacks simultaneously at 3 a.m. (June 19). The 12th's line of advance was west to seize the hill 2 kilometers north of Montebourg. Paralleling the Vaudreville road (D25) on its west side was a railroad line since removed. Heavy artillery and Nebelwerfer fire on the railroad delayed the 12th's advance. After it was crossed the battalion moved ahead, overcoming the resistance. At 10 a.m. Point 100, the high point on D115, 1.5 kilometers north of Montebourg, was taken and at 4 p.m. Point 119, 800 meters further to the northwest fell. Continuing, the lead battalion proceeded northwest to Point 118 3 kilometers east of Valognes, where they dug in for the night.

Meanwhile on June 19 southwest of Montebourg, the 8th Regiment encountered stubborn resistance attempting to move north and bypass the town. The railroad (since removed) 500 meters ahead and paralleling the front line was well defended by entrenched Germans. The night attack became somewhat confused and a little disorganized. Consequently, the gains anticipated were delayed. Companies E and F slipped through crossed N13 and dug in forming a defensive pocket northwest of the town. Other units of the 2nd Battalion circled around and entered Montebourg from the northwest. The Germans withdrew and ran into E and F's defense pocket. Caught between the pocket and their pursuers, the Germans suffered high casualties. Surrounded, the town fell at 6 p.m. to the 3rd Battalion, which promptly released the three hundred inhabitants from their cellars where they had taken refuge from the bombardment of the past week.

6.2 Lieusant

(3 kilometers south of Valognes on D2)

On the morning of July 19 the US lines 4 kilometers to the south were held by the 79th Infantry Division.

Launching their northward advance to Cherbourg, the division's 315th Regiment attacked from Urville (3 kilometers southeast) at 5 a.m. (June 19). The 1st Battalion was to pass to the east and the 2nd Battalion to the west. Their day's objective was to cut the Valognes-Cherbourg highway (N13) northwest of Valognes.

To the east of Lieusant, at Flottemanville Bocage (2 kilometers) the 1st Battalion ran into strong resistance and was temporarily stopped.

On the west the 1st Battalion after crossing the D2 highway, was counterattacked along the highway by a German force from its positions south of Lieusant.

These two actions held up the regiment until early evening. The 3rd Battalion entered the area in the early evening, flushing out snipers and taking the village.

By midnight the 315th Regiment was 1.7 kilometers north of Lieusant and the 313th Regiment under cover in the Bois de la Brique, 4 kilometers west of Valognes. The days delay at Lieusant had denied the regiment its objective.

6.3 Valognes

(20 kilometers southeast of Cherbourg on N13)

On D-Day the German 709th Division was headquartered here. It's commander, Major General Karl W. von Schleiben, a gourmet, had wisely chosen this 18th century town, the Versailles of the Contentin Peninsula. The Beaumont mansion, not destroyed in the war, was the center of the Norman 18th Century aristocracy.

Late evening June 5, members of the French Resistance severed the cable connecting von Schleiben's headquarters with the 84th Corps in St. Lo. This delayed the transmission of reports and commands in the critical hours of D-Day, delaying German counter moves.

Site of a divisional headquarters, straddling N13, a junction of crossroads and a supply center made it a prime target for the allied air force, navy and army artillery from June 6 to 19. Seventy-five percent destroyed, the rubble of a thousand buildings clogged the streets. Regrettably, yet miraculously, only 300 of its 5,000 population perished during the bombings and bombardments. The modern reconstruction bears witness to the city's destruction.

Not wishing to be delayed by a street battle, the American drive to Cherbourg planned to bypass the city, with the 4th Division to the east, the 79th on the west.

Jumping off at 5 a.m., June 19 from Golleville (8 kilometers southwest), the 313th Regiment's 2nd Battalion was into the Bois de la Brique (3 kilometers west) by 2 p.m. German strength between the woods and the northwestern outskirts of Valognes necessitated bringing in the 315th Regiment to contain the sector while the division continued its drive north. On the east, the 8th Regiment was in la Victoire (1 kilometer southeast). On the regiment's east flank the 12th Regiment was further north at Huberville (2 kilometers northeast).

On the peninsula 's western half, the US 9th Division's gains of the day had been spectacular. The 60th and 39th Regiment's had advanced 13 kilometers and were pressing the outer defense zone of Cherbourg, 9 kilometers to its southwest.

Von Schleiben, now commander of the four remnant divisions on the Contentin realized that the 9th advances had outflanked the

Germans positions on the eastern half of the peninsula . He had the forces holding the Valognes sector break off and withdrew to Cherbourg during the night of June 19-20.

The following morning the 315th Regiment west of the city, cleared the area of rearguard resistance pockets while the 8th Regiment entered the deserted demolished city from the east.

Under German harassment shellfire the clearing of the road of rubble to reopen the highway took two days. German batteries, 12 kilometers north, ranged on the church tower, delayed the engineers bulldozing the streets. A team set charges and demolished the tower. When the German fire became less accurate the work proceeded more rapidly.

After the fall of Cherbourg, allied communication cables were laid under the channel from England. In late July Valognes became the Communication Zone headquarters.

The Pipeline Under The Ocean (PLUTO), carrying the essential fuel and oil for the allied mobile armies from England into France through Cherbourg, passed to the west of the Valognes railroad line.

There is an intact rocket site at Montaigu-la-Brisette 8 kilometers northeast of the Quettehou road, D902. Because the early V-1 rocket sites were readily identifiable on aerial reconnaissance photographs a less visible "modified site" was designed. The Montaigu-la-Brisette is an intact modified site. The launch ramp (a concrete farm road), the targeting non-magnetic square, firing hut, assembly building and fuel depot are as they were. Inquire in the village for directions to the "Vay-Un Construction". For more rocket site background see Rocheville.

6.4 Rocheville

(9 kilometers west of Valognes via D902 6 kilometers to D519. Rocheville is 3 kilometers north)

On July 18, Troops E and F of the 4th Cavalry Group were holding Blandamour (10 kilometers south). The group was between the 9th Division to the west and the 79th Division to its east.

In the drive north planned for the following day the troops were to reconnoiter between the flanks of the divisions and maintain contact.

Launching on schedule at 5 a.m. the two troops advanced rapidly against slight resistance. During the night the Germans had withdrawn into the Cherbourg defenses leaving only rearguards to delay the American pursuit.

As Troop A passed to the east of Rocheville, it came under artillery, mortar and small arms fire. A reinforced platoon with two depressed antiaircraft guns, had been left holding the village. Troops A, C, E and F were now on the scene. Troop E provided artillery support while Troop F's tanks attacked with the dismounted personnel from Troops A and C. The town was cleared and the troops rushed on to catch up with the 39th Regiment now well ahead at Rauville-la-Bigot (6 kilometers northwest), and close their open flank.

The following day, June 20, the 313th Regiment (79th Division) moving northwest, on the west side of N13 took Sottevast (2 kilometers north) overrunning an unfinished rocket site.

The site is on the la Ferme les Fontaines (the Fontaine farm) bought in the 1950s by Monsieur Adam Albert. The V-1 site was still under construction when overrun by the Americans. Little had changed when Monsieur Albert made his purchase. He has bulldozed and filled in trenches and top dressed over the exposed concrete. A partially blocked doorway gives accessibility to the largest bunker. The magnitude of the site and its buildings are very apparent. Metal objects used in the construction abound.

As an aid to inquiring about the location of a rocket site the locals refer to it as "Vay-Un Construction" (V-1 construction).

The original V-1 rocket sites were easily recognizable from aerial reconnaissance photographs by the double tracked inclined cement launch ramp. From December 4, 1943 British and American heavy bombers started a campaign to destroy the sites. German General Heineman of the 64th Army Corps designed a "modified site" that would not be recognized from the air. Straight farm lanes were cemented and only four or five submerged bunkers were constructed. The metal ramp built remotely could be added to the prepared farm road in six days. All construction was done by German personnel and convict labor to avoid the French underground spy network.

Related rocket site episodes are Hill 171, Coulville, le Gravelle, Bois du Rondou, Cherbourg, Valognes.

Northwest and northeast of Sottevast are numerous rocket sites. A few are:

1. Bois du Rondou - 8 kilometers northeast
2. Martinvast - 9 kilometers northwest
3. Equeurdreville - Cherbourg western suburb
4. Belhamelin - near Cherbourg. The first "modified site" to be identified on aerial photographs
5. Montaign-la-Brisette - 15 kilometers southeast of Cherbourg. A "modified site". This site is in its original construction condition with a concrete targeting non-magnetic square, launch ramp foundation in the farm road, firing hut, assembly building and the fuel depot. From Valognes go northeast on D902, one kilometer to Montaigu-la-Brisette. Inquire, "le ferme avec le Vay-Un Construction, s'il vous plait?"

Hitler's V-1 rocket campaign against England started June 12, 1944. The last firing from a French site was September 1. All 10,492 rockets were aimed at London's Tower Bridge. Only 2,419 reached London killing 6,184 people.

All the sites in the Cherbourg area were overrun before becoming operational.

6.5 Couville

(10 kilometers southwest of Cherbourg via D904, 9 kilometers to D27, the Teurtheville-Couville road, southeast 3 kilometers)

The village and the highway junction (3 kilometers northwest) were taken by the 39th Regiment (9th Division) June 19 evening, following a 14 kilometer drive north that day from the Seye River. The Germans had withdrawn into Cherbourg. The village fell without a fight.

During the German occupation the Alsatian schoolmaster, Monsieur Utterreiner, unobtrusively served as a member of the French Resistance. Although German batteries and fortifications were camouflaged and under tight security, he was able to collect considerable information which aided the Americans in their battle for Cherbourg June 21 to 26.

6.6 Barfleur

(27 kilometers east of Cherbourg via D901)

In August 1942 the allied war situation had so deteriorated due to consistent military reverses, that considerable pressure was brought to bear on the allied forces in England to launch an attack across the English Channel and open a second European front against the German forces. Such action if carried out on a sufficiently large scale hopefully would relieve pressure against the Russians on the eastern front and the British in Egypt.

The available allied military strength in England although building up rapidly was still concerned with controlling the Atlantic sea lanes, keeping the German surface raider force contained in the North Sea and maintaining heavy offensive bombing raids nightly against German industrial sites.

Although a second front could not be initiated and maintained it was essential for military and political reasons to launch a large scale raid against the German forces occupying France.

On August 19, 1942, six thousand allied troops (Canadian infantry, supported by British commandos and a small number of US rangers transported by the Royal Navy) in 237 boats attacked the French port of Dieppe and neighboring coastal towns along the Normandy coast east of le Havre.

This density of boats and men in the Dieppe area was the greatest concentration ever organized in an amphibious assault. Not even the invasion of 1944, although numerically the largest armada and the greatest amphibious force organized by man, could compare with the concentration of men and ships in the limited confines of the Dieppe raid.

As a feint to mislead the defending Germans along the French coast about the allied landing intention a commando raid was made a few days before the Dieppe raid against the Normandy coastal town of Barfleur.

The six man commando force landed from a motor gunboat at the mouth of the river, a kilometer north of the town at 3 a.m., August 15, 1942. Between the river and the town was Strongpoint 122, manned by seven men. Four commandos loomed over their parapet and fired. All but the section's sergeant were killed. The commandos faded away to attack a four man flak battery a hundred meters away. They also were killed.

An hour and forty minutes after landing the gunboat with the six commandos sped away leaving behind supplies and equipment suggestive of a larger force. For a long period afterwards the German defenders on the Contentin and along the shores of the Bay of the Seine maintained a first degree of readiness. At Dieppe, where the Germans considered an invasion unsuitable, undesirable and unlikely, only normal precautions prevailed. The feint had been successful.

The lessons learned from the Dieppe raid were applied two years later to the invasion. Much of its success and the relatively low casualties were attributable to the Dieppe raid.

In 1942, '43 and '44, the German Atlantic Wall developed. Ninety-two radar stations were located in the area assaulted in 1944. These radar stations, medium and long range, scanned the sky and channel for planes and ships carrying the invasion forces. The defenders expected to have a twelve to twenty-four hour warning. French Resistance Agents pinpointed the radar bunkers. Allied bombers destroyed them. A week before the invasion, the radar site at Barfleur was accurately bombed and obliterated. It never saw the four thousand ship fleet that sailed past Barfleur into the bay.

As the American forces moved against Cherbourg, June 19, from the south, all the German forces on the peninsula withdrew into the Fortress Cherbourg. Barfleur was vacated and its defenders who had trained and waited to fight here moved to Cherbourg where they were either killed or captured when the port fell on June 27.

The next day, a squadron of the US 24th Reconnaissance Battalion entered Barfleur seeking out stragglers and holdouts. The two Strongpoints 121 and 122 had been abandoned.

Hitler's Thousand Year Reich disintegrated in May 1945 but its pillboxes and bunkers may survive a millennium. Two kilometers north of Barfleur at Gatteville-le-Phare huge battery concrete bunkers look out over the English Channel mute evidence of a battle never fought.

Chapter 7 The Capture of Fortress Cherbourg

The availability of Cherbourg's port facilities was an invaluable asset to the allies supply line. The harbor and wharves could accommodate deep draught freighters from America with dockside unloading. Through the port could pass reinforcements and supplies to augment those being discharged on the beaches and ports already in allied hands. Being the closest point in the beachhead to England communication cables and a fuel pipeline could be laid across the English Channel to Cherbourg. Cherbourg, a major facility, was required by the allies to provide massive quantities of material and tip the balance of power in their favor.

Two fabricated harbors had been towed across the channel and installed at OMAHA Beach and Arromanches-les-Bains. In addition, at UTAH, JUNO and SWORD Beaches breakwaters had been formed by sinking old ships to provide calm waters for beach unloading.

On June 19 a record breaking high tide combined with a four day storm to destroy the OMAHA Beach Mulberry harbor, severely damage Port Churchill at Arromanches-les-Bains and greatly curtail all other unloading. The decrease in the flow of supplies warranted restrictive use of ammunition.

The immediate importance of seizing, establishing and maintaining the port and city of Cherbourg as an operational gateway became increasingly imperative to the allies.

Field Marshal Erwin Rommel advised his planners that - "the American and British will not sail into le Havre or Cherbourg on the Queen Mary, but assault the beaches in specialized craft." Once a toehold had been established, he reasoned, a port facility would be required by the invaders to continually furnish and strengthen their forces with men, might and essential supplies. It was a priority that this requirement be denied the allies. To this end orders were dispatched to fight to the last cartridge, demolish the facilities and mine the ruins.

In a semi-circle, 8-10 kilometers around the landward side of Cherbourg, on commanding ground, a "landfront" was built by the Germans. The early defenses of the port faced out to sea. Benefiting from the British loss of Singapore in 1942 by the Japanese landward attack, German preparations in late 1943 and the five months of 1944 were put into its landfront defenses.

The belt of steel and concrete positions stretched from Cap Levy (10 kilometers northeast of Cherbourg) in a great arc around the south to Greville-Hague (14 kilometers west of Cherbourg). Cherbourg's outer defense line consisted of twelve strongpoints, and over one hundred resistance nests. Behind, in support, were twenty-four batteries. Once through the landfront the attackers faced a series of fortresses rimming the outskirts of the port. Within the port and harbor were another 30 resistance nests.

Although the landfront appeared formidable it contained inherent weaknesses. Many of the positions did not have telephones or radios, others were not visible to their neighbors and lacked supporting lines of fire. The cities historical forts were outmoded in defense against the air and artillery firepower of 1944. The weaknesses had been recognized and tested in early May by the Germans themselves. At that time Assault Battalion Messerschmitt successfully penetrated the landfront through the Bois du Rondou and Bois du Coudray. From this exercise the German defenders profited, however their experiences did not adequately prepare them for the American assault, which broke their line at the same point on June 21, and 22.

The defending General von Schleiben, divided his force into four regiments each under the command of an officer familiar with his sector. Miscellaneous stragglers of depleted and mauled units were dispersed into the regiments. The overall efficiency and morale were low. All the regiments had suffered heavy casualties following lengthy sustained battles since June 6. The manning of the landfront was conducted by troops who had withdrawn ahead of the advancing American steam roller. Administrative and headquarter staffs were placed in gun pits foreign to their training. The "heaven" of captivity further dissuaded "fight to the last cartridge" policy as reports infiltrated amongst the frontline soldiers regarding the excellent treatment prisoners were receiving.

Three divisions might have held out for several weeks. Four battle torn regiments were completely inadequate.

Ammunition supplies, deep in the fortress caves, were augmented by German air drops and speeding E-boats from Brittany.

In a two day drive (June 19-21), General Collin's 7th Corps moved north from the Carteret-Quineville line to the Cherbourg landfront. The General, fresh from the slow slugging battles of the dense jungles of the Pacific Theater, had taken advantage of the openness of the Contentin Peninsula and hastily driven his mobile forces to the port's outer defense ring.

By midnight, June 21, three US divisions were pressing against the landfront. The fleet stood off shore dueling with the coastal batteries and sealing off the port's last vital life line. The air force shot down the incoming German supply aircraft and provided tactical support.

On the night of June 21 General Collins sent a "surrender or else" ultimatum to General von Schleiben for reply by 9 a.m. the next morning. Von Schleiben chose to ignore the message. Collins ordered his attack plan to be set in motion at 2 p.m. At 12:40 p.m. four squadrons of rocket firing Typhoons followed by six squadrons of RAF Mustangs approached and for twenty minutes strafed the landfront positions. At 1 p.m. the Typhoons and Mustangs were replaced by 562 planes of the 9th Air Force. P-47s, P-38s and P-51 fighter-bombers again strafed and bombed frontline positions for 55 minutes. At 2 p.m. the infantry attacked. Three hundred and eighty-seven medium bombers now supported the infantry by bombing strongpoints ahead of their advancing line. This was the first time during the invasion the air force was employed in tactical close ground support. Its effectiveness was disappointing. The airborne "rolling barrage" was not sufficiently concentrated on pinpointed targets to destroy them. Lessons were learned that were applied later at Caen and in Operation COBRA more successfully. Although the physical destruction was not as extensive as hoped, German communication lines were cut and morale dropped.

The three US divisions attacked simultaneously. The 4th Division on the east was to keep east of the Trotebec River and clear to the coast. It would only enter the eastern outskirts of Cherbourg. The 9th Division was to stay west of the Divette River and send spearheads northeast into Cherbourg, through Octeville, and north to the coast. The western half of Cherbourg and all the land west to Cap de la Hague was the division's area of activity. Between the 4th and 9th Divisions, the 79th was to attack along the axis of highway N13 and seize the eastern half of the port city.

7.1 Carrefour des Pelles

(9 kilometers southwest of Cherbourg via D64 at the intersection of D22)

The hamlet of Carrefour des Pelles is a road junction on high ground providing clear lines of fire to the south and west.

Designated on military maps as Crossroads 114 (it is 114 meters above sea level). A section of the German outer defensive line, landfront Cherbourg, ran from Sideville (3.5 kilometers southeast) across the fields, through Carrefour des Pelles and northwest of Acqueville (1 kilometer northwest).

Nine resistance nests with artillery support were entrenched within that stretch. At Crossroads 114 was Resistance Nest 470. Number 471 was 500 meters north along D22. Number 469 was 500 meters east at Junction 130, the intersection of D64 and D406, the Flottemanville-Hague road.

On June 18 and 19 the US 9th Division had moved rapidly up the west coast of the Contentin Peninsula from its start line on the Saye River. The 47th Regiment, following behind the 60th had driven up D37 as far as Vasteville (3 kilometers west). Spread out along the highway, the regiment pivoted east along the two secondary roads passing along the north and south sides of the Bois de Nerest. This change of direction brought the 47th Regiment into Cherbourg from the southwest, while the 60th Regiment proceeded due north towards Cap de la Hague.

In the early afternoon, June 20, the 2nd Battalion advanced from Vasteville along D64 towards Carrefour des Pelles. Leaving Boivin and approaching the Carrefour intersection the battalion received fire from the resistance nest in the hamlet. From Crossroads 130, 88mm shells and 20mm cannon shells added their support and decimated the two American lead Companies E and F. An 88mm shell landed amongst the battalion's command group. The battalion commander, Lieutenant Colonel James D. Johnston, a platoon leader and the artillery liaison officers were killed. Fox Company's commander, its executive officer, a radio operator and two runners were wounded. The battalion pulled back and dug in. Heavy German fire continued to fall on the American positions forcing them to abandon their plan to seize the crossroads and high ground to the east, that day.

On June 22 the entire 7th Corps opened a three division attack on the landfront defending Cherbourg. The 9th Division concentrated its efforts on punching through a hole between Acqueville and Sideville i.e. seize the nine resistance nests. The 47th Regiment, three battalions abreast jumped off at 2 p.m. in the sector Carrefour des Pelles to Sideville. The air bombardment had been successful. Thirty minutes later the crossroads was being held by the 2nd Battalion. Moving north from the crossroads, G Company cleared Resistance Nest No. 471. By nightfall the American frontline was 3 kilometers northeast of the secured crossroads.

7.2 Flottemanville-Hague

(7 kilometers west of the Cherbourg suburb, Octeville via D123)

The village of Flottemanville-Hague occupies a significant elevated position on the eastern end of a 150-meter high ridge. As a portion of the German landfront defense line of Cherbourg this point was a significant defense position. German Resistance Nest 536 was located to the north of the village along the road (D152) to Tonneville. The present day radio transmitter at the high point 178, one kilometer to the northwest was originally constructed as a German transmitter bunker. In the slope of the descending hill towards Acqueville, 3 kilometers southwest, three more nests were dug in to stop American advances towards Cherbourg from the southwest.

At mid-day, June 22, as part of the 7th Corps attack against Cherbourg, the village and resistance nests were bombed and strafed by fighter-bombers in the preliminary softening-up operations.

Advancing from the southwest the 1st Battalion of the 60th Regiment advanced to within a kilometer and a half by nightfall. The nests on the slopes stopped the American advance.

Throughout the next day the battalion waited for a bombardment to reduce the enemy defenses. At 8 p.m. the awaited air and artillery bombardment pounded the slopes and village. The 1st and 2nd Battalions attacked, clearing the area in two hours.

With the landfront broken the way was now clear to advance on Cherbourg.

7.3 Ste. Croix - Hague

(11 kilometers west of Cherbourg via D901 and south on D118 1 kilometer)

During the years of German occupation, the French Resistance agents collected intelligence information and relayed it to the allied planners in England. The schoolmaster of Ste. Croix, Monsieur Richard and his wife were very effective in securing valuable information pertaining to the heavy batteries around Cap de la Hague to the northwest.

On June 21, the 9th, 79th and 4th Divisions were tightening the noose around Cherbourg. The 60th Regiment (9th Division) moved against Ste. Croix Hague from the southeast. The 2nd Battalion's lead patrols were unable to break into the village. Two German Resistance Rests (Nos. 538 and 98) half a kilometer to the southwest threw out a wall of fire supported by artillery from the rear.

Battle lines were drawn, and except for patrol activity, the 60th Regiment kept the Germans contained while the corps concentrated on capturing Cherbourg.

On the afternoon of June 26 with Cherbourg's capture imminent, the Germans holding the Hainneville - St. Croix - Hague - Vauville defense line fell back to their prepared positions linking Querqueville-Branville-Vauville. The next morning the 60th Regiment occupied St. Croix-Hague.

7.4 Crossroads 167

(13 kilometers west of Cherbourg via D901 to the intersection of D37)

On June 19, when the American 8th Corps directed its attention northward to the capture of Cherbourg, the extreme left flank of the advancing line was turned over to the 60th Regiment (9th Division). The 3rd Battalion coming from the south was to advance up D37 and seize the crossroads, thereby defending the divisions western flank against German attacks from the northwest.

The crossroads was part of the outer defense landfront around Cherbourg. Seven tenths of a kilometer south of the junction on the east side of D37 was Resistance Nest No. 481. In the field immediately north of the junction was Resistance Nest No. 482. Running in a straight line north to Gruchy, at half kilometer intervals, were Resistance Nests Nos. 483, 484, 485 and 486.

After a rapid two day advance north on D37 the 3rd Battalion arrived at a point 1 kilometer south of Crossroads 167 where D237 feeds into D37. The remainder of the regiment had encountered resistance at Goubesville (5 kilometers southeast) causing the 3rd Battalion to stall and wait for the 1st and 2nd Battalion's arrival.

During the following week the corps concentrated its efforts on Cherbourg. On June 28, with the primary objective realized, namely the capture of Cherbourg and the obliteration of its defense forts, the 9th Division directed its interests northwest and the clearing of the Cap de la Hague Peninsula.

On June 29 the 1st Battalion (60th Regiment) attacked Crossroads 167 from the east along the axis of highway D901. The Germans had made the crossroads an important defense position in a defense line across the neck of the peninsula . A line that arced south from Gruchy on the channel coast to Vauville on the Contentin's west coast. A north-south antitank ditch butted up to a stream creating a significant obstacle. Antitank guns and emplacements to the southwest on the forward slopes of the Lande de Beaumont escarpment. The open fields provided clear lines of fire for the small arms and automatic weapons of the defenders in the resistance nests and on the slopes. The Americans were stopped. To the north the 3rd

Battalion was more successful and fought its way into Greville-Hague (2 kilometers north) as an outflanking maneuver.

On June 30 the 2nd Battalion took over the attack. E Company under Captain Sprindus crossed D37, attacked the hills to the west in a dramatic charge and continued directly through to the Beaumont area. Meanwhile F Company and tanks of C Company, 746th Tank Battalion moved against the crossroads along the fields to the north of D901. Tanks also moved into the crossroads from the east along the highway. The German defenders surrendered allowing the Americans to proceed and capture Beaumont by mid-day.

7.5 Hill 171

(6 kilometers southwest of Cherbourg. From Cherbourg's southwest suburb, Octeville, take the road D64 southwest to Vasteville 6 kilometers to the crossroads hamlet of le Saussey. Turn south (left) onto D152, the road to Sideville. Hill 171 is one kilometer on the north side.)

The hill topped by the Bois du Mont du Roc was an integral part of Cherbourg's landfront defense perimeter. Its western and southern slopes covered with patchwork fields was dotted with resistance nests and machine gun pits. The le Saussey-Sideville road (D152) cut across the German defense positions.

June 6 to 21 had witnessed the rapid advance of three American divisions from the UTAH Beachhead to the Cherbourg landfront. By midnight, June 21 the 47th Regiment (9th Division) was in position 2 kilometers to the west. On June 22 air and artillery bombarded the forward slopes to "soften-up" the defenders. Two companies of the 3rd Battalion jumping off from Beaudenville hamlet, 1 kilometer southwest, crossed the Caudet River and advanced up the slope of Hill 171. By evening the road D152 delineated the American forward positions. Somewhat extended ahead of their flank battalions, the companies dug in and waited for the 2nd Battalion to move up on the left. The Germans, low on supplies spread their forces thin and attempted to conserve ammunition whenever possible.

On June 23 the division continued its advance puncturing the landfront defense line in many places.

On the hill, the Americans pressed up the slope and into the woods. Four hundred prisoners were taken. The way was clear to advance against Cherbourg's southwestern suburb, Octeville.

The northern part of the Contentin Peninsula due to its proximity to England had numerous V-1 rocket sites. (See the Rocheville story for additional information and site locations and/or see Rocket Sites in the Index.) One site was 3 kilometers southeast at Martinvast in the grounds of the 16th century chateau. The concrete blockhouses new and exposed in 1944 are now aged and grown over. From Hill 171 continue south to highway D904 then go north 2 kilometers to the Martinvast exit.

7.6 Octeville

(Southwest outskirts of Cherbourg bordering D904)

Octeville, straddling the highway from the southwest and Hill 102 to the east, defended the approaches of Cherbourg from the southwest. Only two resistance nests were in Octeville but to its southwest, one kilometer, north of N64 at the old fortress was a four gun antiaircraft battery. The battery, Strongpoint 532, could lower its guns for use against men and tanks.

On June 22 all three divisions of the US 7th Corps attacked against Cherbourg's semi-circular defense positions. The 47th Regiment (9th Division) was at that time in the Bois du Mont du Roc (4 kilometers southwest). Between it and Octeville lay the strongpoint. In December 1943, the French Resistance had carefully determined its strength and specific location. Well before June 22 the Americans knew what lay ahead. On their maps it had been labeled Strongpoint C. Before the attack started the strongpoint was bombed and shelled.

The 39th Regiment to the south, moved up into line beside the 47th and advanced against the strongpoint. On the June 24 the 2nd and 3rd Battalions easily cleared the strongpoint and moved into the outer houses of Octeville.

German resistance stiffened and the advance halted. Artillery fire was called in which broke the defenders resistance. The battalions moved down the slope into Octeville.

The next day saw few gains by the regiment. The 2nd Battalion received enfilading fire from the north slowing its advances. On the east flank German infiltration drew much of the 3rd Battalion's attention. By midnight the regiment had occupied all of Octeville and was on the edge of St. Sauveur lying between it and the houses of Cherbourg.

Meanwhile, other regiments of the corps had also squeezed the Germans back into Cherbourg. On the east, south and west house to house fighting was ensuing. The fortifications and resistance nests in the city were coming under fire.

A few hundred meters ahead of the 39th Regiment lay Strongpoint 259, the underground battle headquarters of the German Naval Commander, Admiral Walther Hennecke. Dug into the north slope of the hill in St. Sauveur, 300 meters east of D3 (Rue de Roger Salengro), the great cave contained two large galleries. The one on the right served as a hospital, the left hand one contained map rooms and command posts. From here telephone lines ran to every coastal battery on the peninsula as well as direct to the Fuherer's headquarters in East Prussia. Steel doors under a cement canopy protected the entrance. The villa directly above the entrance was Admiral Hennecke's headquarters.

Nine days before, when the Americans cut the peninsula, the Germans isolated to the north were destined to be the fodder of fortress Cherbourg. All units came under the command of Lieutenant General Karl von Schlieben of the 709th Division.

The fighting and bombardments of June 25 had forced von Schlieben to withdraw into Hennecke's command post along with the few remaining battle weary troops and their wounded.

During the night (June 25-26) and the morning, the 39th Regiment entered St. Sauveur. E and F Companies surrounded the underground headquarters. Attempting to smoke the Germans out, the Americans lowered demolition charges down the air intake and outlet vents. Soldiers, sailors, staff officers and medical personnel were crammed within the "tomb". At the exits, small arms fire was attempting to hold back the American tanks and tank destroyers, maneuvering to fire the death blow. Poisonous fumes from the demolition charges were spewing down the ventilators. The wounded were dying from asphyxia.

American machine gun fire rattled against the three exit doors. Tank destroyers fired point blank into the entrances. Demolition experts hurried to set charges to blow the face off the hill.

Von Schlieben, realizing the futility of prolonging the entombment and its consequential useless loss of lives, dispatched an officer bearing a white sheet tied to his rifle barrel. The American guns fell silent. It was Monday, June 26, 2 p.m. The surrender was limited only to the headquarters. Out filed the General, the Admiral, their staffs, medical doctors and nurses and 800 miscellaneous troops. Cherbourg with its many strongpoints and resistance nests, had yet to be subdued. The Germans were determinedly delaying the fall of the port.

Among the women was a singer Frau Wist. On June 5 evening she had given a concert at the Cherbourg officer's mess. The invasion had prevented her safe return to Germany; she awaited her inevitable capture. Frau Wist and a number of nurses were later transferred to Germany as members of an exchange group in return for the release of captured British nurses.

Von Schlieben and Hennecke were whisked off to General Eddy's (9th Division) command post on the hill at Octeville and then to General Collin's (7th Corps) headquarters, 30 kilometers south. The propaganda leaflets with his surrender picture were dropped on resisting German forces the following day. Although a senior commander, he lost the privilege of dining with General Bradley (1st Army Group) because of his prolonged resistance and associated loss of American lives. Von Schlieben, the gourmet, could only be content with his souvenir menu and reminiscences of the dinner in Cherbourg, the previous month, when he was the guest of honor (lobster hollandaise, pate'de'foie gras, baked bluefish, roast leg of lamb, peaches and cream, chateau wines, vintage champagne and Napoleon brandy). He did not consider the American K rations and his temporary showerless farmhouse prison befitting an officer of his rank.

Further inconveniences and deprivations befell him. His trunk of uniforms and personal articles fell off a truck in transit and scattered on the road amongst a column of soldiers. Before the MPs could stop the souvenir seekers, not a shred of the uniforms remained.

The General's and Admiral's aids were moved from a prison camp near Cherbourg to rejoin their commanders at the US headquarters at Yvetot. Traveling with a trigger happy guard, the jeep hit a mind. The guard's submachine gun went off. Of the six in the jeep, only two badly wounded Germans survived.

With St. Sauveur captured the 39th Regiment entered Cherbourg the same afternoon occupying a major portion by nightfall.

Today the headquarter's tunnel is blocked and the villa above has once again reverted to a private residence. The area is private property.

7.7 La Gravelle

(5 kilometers south of Cherbourg on N13, the Route de Liberte)

The hamlet of la Gravelle astride the main highway was the center of a major German strongpoint, a segment of Cherbourg's landfront outer defense perimeter. Manned by troops of the 739th Regiment, as part of Combat Group Kohn, it consisted of six Resistance Nests (Nos. 447 to 452) spread out in the fields a kilometer east and west of the highway where the road bends abruptly north. From that point a zigzag antitank ditch cut east and west to the Trotebec River and Douve River respectively.

The US 313th Regiment (79th Division) moved up to within a kilometer of the strongpoint on June 21. In the preliminary bombardment of June 22 the sector received a lot of attention yet resisted fiercely as the 313th advanced on it at 2 p.m. The 1st Battalion made a frontal assault while the 3rd Battalion moved in from the west and "rolled up" the nests one after the other. The 2nd Battalion east of the highway simultaneously advanced across the antitank ditch and ferreted out the Germans in the woods.

The regiment's advance continued and by midnight was fighting for Junction 177, the crossroads of D122 and N13. The concrete antitank gun pit (Resistance Nest No. 492) on the northeast corner of the intersection was captured and the Americans advanced another 400 meters along N13 before digging in for the night. The next day they moved against the German strongpoint at la Mare a Canards, 800 meters further along N13.

There were numerous V-1 rocket sites in the area. Three close to la Gravelle are:

1. Bois du Rondou, 5 kilometers east. South on N13, 3 kilometers, to Delasse. East on D56 40 kilometers. (For details see Rocheville)
2. le Mesnil-au-Val, 5 kilometers northeast. North on N13, 1 kilometer, to D122. East 4.5 kilometers, through Luce to D87, south 1 kilometer.
3. Martinvast, 5 kilometers west. North on N13, 1 kilometer to D122. West 5 kilometers. (For details see Hill 171)

7.8 La Mare a Canards

(3 kilometers south of Cherbourg on N13, the Route de Liberte)

Designated on American maps as Strongpoint "F" it consisted of three Resistance Nests (Nos. 521, 524 and 548) and an antiaircraft battery manned by platoons of the German 739th Regiment. Although a defense position on the Cherbourg highway it was not integrated into Cherbourg's landfront defense perimeter. The three nests bordered the road at la Mare a Canards, the la Loge intersection and Rouges Terres, i.e. spread out over a kilometer length of the highway. The battery was in the field 500 meters west of the la Mare a Canards hamlet.

The antiaircraft battery was bombed first on June 21 and then the complete strongpoint on June 22 when all the German defenses ringing Cherbourg were "softened" before the infantry attack started.

By 2 a.m. June 23 the US 313th Regiment was straddling N13, dug in 800 meters to the south. At dawn, the 313th shifted its line of advance to the east and the 314th Regiment faced Strongpoint F from the southwest. At 9 a.m. the strongpoint was bombed. The 3rd Battalion followed and advanced into the southwestern edge of the German positions. Able Company by-passing the strongpoint to the west, proceeded north and captured la Loge (1.5 kilometers northwest). La Mare a Canards continued to hold, another bombing was called for June 24. As planned at 8 a.m. twelve P-47 dive-bombers hit the strongpoint. The 2nd and 3rd Battalions (314th Regiment) attacked and cleared the resistance after a tough two and a half hour battle. From here they could easily see their next objectives Fort du Roule and Cherbourg.

There are V-1 rocket sites in the vicinity:

1 le Mesnil au-Val, 5.5 kilometers east. South on N13, 1.5 kilometers to D122. east 4.5 kilometers through Luce to D87, south 1 kilometer. (For details see Rocheville)

2 Martinvast, 5 kilometers southwest. south on N13, 1.5 kilometers to D122. west 5 kilometers. (For details see Hill 171)

7.9 Bois de Rondou

(8 kilometers southeast of Cherbourg via N13 to Delasse, D56 east 4 kilometers)

The road (D56) skirting the north edge of the woods (Bois de Rondou) and as far as the la Bourdonnerie junction (Crossroads 148, the intersection of D56 and D87) was a portion of Cherbourg's landfront outer defense perimeter. Along this stretch of road five resistance nests were positioned in the adjacent fields, also, two operative V-1 (buzz bomb) launching sites and a third under construction. The elevation provided an ideal setting for the construction of these launching sites, aimed to fire directly to England with defensive positions facing south. On the northwest corner of the Bois de Rondou, on the north side of D56 was Point 178 the highest point of the elevation.

From Crossroads 148 the German defense line swung northeast to the channel at Cap Levy. This, the eastern quadrant of the Cherbourg landfront, was manned by remnants of the 729th and 739th Regiments (709th Division) and miscellaneous troops organized into Combat Group Rohrback. Their advantageous positioning compensated for their lack of zeal.

During the evening of June 20 the 8th Regiment (4th Division) moved into the area, after a days drive from Valognes' eastern outskirts.

Approaching from the southeast, towards Crossroads 148, along D87, the 3rd Battalion attacked Ruffoses (500 meters south of Crossroads 148) from the east, occupying it at dusk. The 2nd Battalion, further east arrived at D56, 600 meters east of the crossroads.

There were two resistance nests, one at the crossroads, the second 700 meters north on D87. A few hundred meters further along the road in the field west of the road was a rocket site.

The next day, June 21, the 2nd Battalion crossed D56 and with two companies abreast pivoted west, advancing against the resistance nests on the north-south road. George Company became pinned down by fire from along the road but Easy Company crossed and continued pushing west to link up with the 1st and 3rd Battalions battling through the Bois du Rondou. Easy's hold was tenuous, as the crossroad's resistance nest was now to the rear leaving the American company out on a limb. Fox Company with tank support moved up from reserve and reopened the corridor to Easy Company. By evening contact had been made with the 3rd Battalion which had crossed to Point 178 after a difficult battle on the northwest corner of the woods.

Throughout the night June 21-22, German squads from the crossroads harried the companies rear positions. At dawn the Germans attacked the 2nd Battalion's command post.

Fox Company then organized to clear the crossroads. A platoon moved through the Bois de Rondou and attacked the crossroads form the south. Simultaneously, after an eight minute mortar barrage, another platoon attacked the woods northwest of the crossroads where the launch site was located. Both attacks were successful and yielded three hundred prisoners.

While this action was taking place 2 kilometers to the west, the 1st and 3rd Battalions were in positions north of the road (D56) and preparing to attack northwest against a resistance nest a kilometer away. Several local German counterattacks were repulsed, but by 2:30 p.m. the battalions were able to move. The 1st Battalion on the left made little headway but the 3rd moved ahead. Passing west of the rocket site, the battalion took heavy casualties from machine guns and tree burst shells originating from the resistance nest in the hamlet of la Boissais. The "path" from D56 to the hamlet was the axis of the attack although the severe casualties occurred in the woods 500 meters east of the houses. By dark the nest was captured at a cost of thirty-one Americans killed and ninety-two wounded.

On June 23 the 3rd Battalion sent a company back to clear the rocket site bypassed the previous day. Using explosives to blast the Germans out of the blockhouses, 228 surrendered.

Simultaneously the 1st Battalion on the 23rd continued pressing west from the Bois de Rondou and by 2 p.m. had gained a kilometer. A German counterattack threw the Americans back to the road (D56). Reorganizing, the battalion attacked again on the 24th, regaining its previous positions and continuing northwest several kilometers.

Two kilometers west of the Crossroads 148 on D56, on the north side, a concrete driveway leads into a pasture and farm, probably one of the very few cement farm roads in France. The original intention of the German engineers was somewhat different. From the asphalt of D56 the trucks carrying the delicate V-1 rockets would bring the missiles to the rocket bunker where they would be fueled and readied for firing. From there they would be dollied to the launch platform, angled and directed towards England. The buildings and platform are still present, although the steel rails have been removed and the concrete supply buildings are now stables and barns. The farmhouse was a barracks.

A kilometer north of Crossroads 148, another cement road connects the roadway with a rocket site (rocket site le Mesnil au-Val). A rocket "garage" stands a the entrance which, unlike the other site, is now overgrown with bushes and trees.

For more information about the rocket sites see Rocheville.

7.10 Luce

(5 kilometers southeast of Cherbourg via D121 to la Glacerie then east on D121 one kilometer)

Situated on high ground the hamlet intersection of Luce was the last strongpoint guarding the southeasterly approach into Cherbourg. Sloping off to the west the wooded slopes fall to the valley of the Trotebec River.

An attack would have to advance from the south along the ridge road or from the east. The German entrenchment's included several 88mm guns, four 105mm field guns, a 40mm cannon, 20mm antiaircraft guns, mortars and machine guns. All were well sited and expertly camouflaged.

On June 24 the 2nd Battalion (8th Regiment) attacked along the axis of the road entering the intersection from the south. Twelve P-47 fighter-bombers, each carrying two 500-lb. bombs, preceded the battalion. Twenty-three landed on target, the most accurate mission witnessed to that time. As the planes departed, a fifteen-minute artillery barrage blanketed the strongpoint. As the mortar and artillery plummeted the intersection the American infantry advanced, two companies abreast, on both sides of the road. In spite of the bombing and shelling the German counterfire was very effective. The companies were stopped.

The Americans withdrew, regrouped and two hours later resumed their attack. Support tanks to the right of the Americans broke into the eastern perimeter along the la Croix Fresville road (D122). Pressing into the crossroads the resistance crumbled. About a hundred prisoners were taken and although German casualties had been high, the artillery ordinance stood intact and operative. The regiment had suffered 37 killed including the 1st Battalion's Commander, Lieutenant Colonel Conrad Simmons.

As the American ring around Cherbourg tightened the semi-circle decreased. Regiments were squeezed out of the frontline by advances on their flanks. On June 25, after consolidating the Luce area, the 8th Regiment halted to allow the 12th Regiment and 313th Regiment on its two flanks to move in around Cherbourg. This battle terminated the regiment's actions on the Contentin Peninsula. Held in reserve it awaited the division's capture of the eastern sector of the Cherbourg defense perimeter.

There is a rocket site 2 kilometers southeast at le Mesnil-au-Val. From Luce go east on D122, one kilometer to D87, turn south for 2.5 kilometers. A cement farm track, the launch track joins the paved road. For more details see Bois de Rondou and Rocheville.

7.11 Hill 158

(8 kilometers east of Cherbourg on D901)

Hill 158 dominates the surrounding countryside. Its highest point is a kilometer east of the D320-D901 intersection. Part of Cherbourg's landfront, it was a strongpoint with three antiaircraft batteries positioned on its southern, northern and western slopes. Units of the German 729th Regiment held the hill. To its east and northeast were major German defense strongpoints and coastal batteries. The main German supply road D901 between Cherbourg and its outer defenses crossed Hill 158. Its capture was vital to the rapid seizure of Cherbourg.

On June 21, the 22nd Regiment (4th Division) was in le Theil (4 kilometers south). Moving north along D320 and its adjacent fields at 4 p.m., the 1st and 3rd Battalions advanced on their objective behind a curtain of artillery fire. By 8 p.m. they were 500 meters short of their objective and receiving heavy artillery fire from the depressed 88mm antiaircraft batteries on the hill now firing on the tanks of 70th Tank Battalion's Baker Company. Pressing up the southern slopes, the battalions occupied the hill by midnight. The 1st Battalion remained along the eastern slope with the 3rd across the highway and dug in along the northern crest.

German infiltrators moved in from Gonneville (2 kilometers southeast) to cut the American supply line along D320. Although in American hands the hold was tenuous. During the next few days, until advances were made on the 22nd Regiment's flanks and the resistance pockets to the rear were cleared, the two battalions on Hill 158 were out on a limb. Supply convoys under shellfire had to be escorted by tanks. One was attacked and had to turn back. Another turned erroneously off D320 onto D413 at the crossroads a kilometer southeast of the hill. The road led into Gonneville still under German occupation. Ambushed, the supply convoy lost two light tanks, three half-tracks, three 57mm antitank guns and several jeeps. It was planned that on June 22, the 3rd Battalion would leave its positions on the hill and drive westward along D901 to Tourlainville (5 kilometers west). Before the plan could be realized a strong German counterattack engulfed the hill that threatened its recapture. The regiment's 2nd Battalion, holding a line to the south along the le Theil road, was summoned to clear the Germans from the southern slope and reopen the communication lines. By nightfall the entire regiment was on the hill manning an all around defense.

Instead of the hill becoming a start point for a drive into Cherbourg from the east, it reverted to a blocking position. That is, while the 12th Regiment and the 2nd Battalion (22nd Regiment) moved against Cherbourg from the southeast on June 24, the 1st and 3rd Battalions contained the German forces to the east, stopping them from threatening the rear of the Cherbourg attack.

Policing the area and keeping open the supply line to le Theil was entrusted to the 1st Battalion. Meanwhile, on June 25, the 2nd and 3rd Battalions attacked north against the coastal positions.

The following day, the 1st Battalion captured Gonneville and the section of D901 between Hill 158 and the Maupertus Airfield, thereby eliminating the remaining threats to the hill position.

7.12 Maupertus Airfield

(11 kilometers east of Cherbourg on D901)

The airfield and its defenses comprised a section of the Cherbourg landfront defense ring. The airfield was encircled by five antiaircraft batteries and fourteen resistance nests. The area was Strongpoint No. 505, called "Flugplatz Theville".

The US 7th Corps' Commander, General J. Collin's tactics were to drive into Cherbourg from the southwest, south and southeast without delay or interference from the northern flank, and secure his prime objective, Cherbourg.

On June 21, the US 22nd Regiment (4th Division) moved into Hill 158 (1.5 kilometers west) from the southeast. This move closed D901 between the airfield and Cherbourg, isolated the German landfront north to Cap Levy and permitted the Americans to advance on Cherbourg without being delayed by battles of no tactical value. While the 22nd Regiment held Hill 158 and struggled to keep open its supply lines, the 24th Reconnaissance Squadron, the 4th Reconnaissance Troop and a company of the 801st Tank Destroyer Battalion contained the airfield and Gonneville (1 kilometer south), the southern limit of the strongpoint.

While containing the airfield the Americans attempted to send combat patrols north to the coastal road to cut the railroad line running east along the coast. Their efforts were repulsed by the greater strength and positions of the German defenders. (The railroad at that time paralleled D116 and D210 to St. Pierre Eglise but has since been removed.)

On June 26, while the 4th Division's 12th Regiment was battling into Cherbourg, the 22nd Regiment directed its attention against the airfield. The 1st, 2nd and 3rd Battalions attacked from the south, west and north concurrently at 11 a.m. June 26. The well-sited resistance nests supported by the depressed dual purpose 88mm antiaircraft guns made the American advance slow and costly. Not until the following day was the airport subdued. Leaving the final clearing of a few last ditch entrenched diehards to the 2nd Battalion, the 1st and 3rd moved north to clear Strongpoint Osteck, the Hamburg Battery and Strongpoint Seadler.

Today many of the bunkers can still be seen. Skirting D901 to the west of the airfield's main entrance is a defense pillbox (No. 505-H). Bordering the driveway to the administrative-terminal building is a submerged barracks tier. On the southeastern edge of the airdrome property, the junction of D612 and D901 is another submerged bunker. A kilometer north of D901 on D612 on the left-hand side dug in on a rising slope, is a single battery bunker (No. 506-H). Aimed across the open pasture it undoubtedly delayed the 1st Battalion as it attempted to capture the southern defense positions.

With the airfield in American hands on June 27, Able Company of the 850th Engineer Battalion (9th Engineer Command) moved in immediately and repaired the field. As a delaying tactic the Germans cluttered the 270 acre field with cumbersome two wheeled farm carts strewn at regular intervals. Fearful the carts were booby trapped caused each one to be carefully scrutinized by the sappers before it could be removed. The time wasting efforts were in vain. All carts proved to be "clean". An uncratered strip was marked out, the tall grass was mowed and the debris of the battle cleared off. The following day, June 28, the transport strip became operational. Beside the runway stood a pile of bombs, shells, duds and 600 mines lifted from the field.

The airfield, identified as ALG (Advanced Landing Ground), 5 was later extended to 2,000 meters for medium bombers. This was started on July 9 by the 850th Battalion and rushed to completion two days later by the arrival of the 877th Battalion, specialists in laying the PSP (pierced steel plank) runway.

On July 20, Prime Minister Winston Churchill flew into Maupertus from England, the beginning of a three-day visit to Cherbourg, then south to UTAH Beach and ferried over to Arromanches-le-Bains to see the fabricated port (Port Churchill) in operation.

During General Charles de Gaulle's second visit to France since the invasion he landed here on the afternoon of August 20. Having flown non-stop from Algiers his Lodestar "France" had became lost. He landed with only two minutes of fuel remaining. General de Gaulle drove into Cherbourg, where he spoke, while the plane was refueled. Continuing his flight, he proceeded to General Dwight D. Eisenhower's headquarters (SHELLBURST) near Tournieres. The previous day, August 19, the Free French in Paris had commenced their uprising against the Germans. De Gaulle's mission was to persuade General not to bypass Paris but to divert forces to enter and support the French uprising.

There is a memorial to the 9th Air Force near the terminal building.

Picture 7: Maupertus Airfield - Looking North
August 3, 1947

The airfield, five miles east of Cherbourg, was an integral part of Cherbourg's land-side defenses. Cherbourg's outer port breakwater can be seen in the top left. The airport, Strongpoints Ostek and Seadler and the Hamburg Battery are in the center. The three battalions of the 22nd Regiment started their attack from the south and east D-day +19. It fell the following day. The airfield, designated ALG (Advanced Landing Ground) A-15 became operational D-day +21 although beside the runway stood a pile of bombs, shells, duds and 600 mines lifted from the airfield. Prime Minister Churchill landed her on July 20 as did General Charles de Gaulle on August 20.

7.13 Hill 138

(11 kilometers northeast of Cherbourg via D901, 11 kilometers to the Fermanville road, D612 then north 3 kilometers)

Leaving D901 driving north on D612 towards Fermanville, one passes through the hamlets of la Rue and la Brasserie. The few houses of the la Brasserie hamlet are most easily identified as the junction for Carneville, 1 kilometer to the east. Continuing past la Brasserie, 1 kilometer, the road (D612) forks. The right hand road leading to Fermanville, the left road to la Village. Immediately north of the junction on the la Village road, a dirt track from the west joins the asphalt road. Following the dirt tract brings one into a field wild with overgrowth and dotted with dozens of concrete pillboxes and bunkers.

This is Hill 138 with the structures of Strongpoint 235 "Osteck". Within a 2 kilometers radius of this point was the highest concentration of batteries and fortifications of any location along the Atlantic Wall from Spain to Denmark.

South of Osteck was Maupertus Airfield with 30 resistance nests and 5 flak batteries. Between the airfield and the hill was Strongpoint Ritter with two flak batteries. Northeast of the hill was the Hamburg Battery housing four 240mm naval guns. Directly north 2 kilometers lay Strongpoint Seadler, a battery of 105s and four resistance nests. To the east, through Carneville (1 kilometer) ran the Cherbourg landfront in a north-south arc anchored at Cap Levy. In the 5 kilometers sector of the landfront between the highway D901 and Cap Levy were an additional twenty-three resistance nests.

American intelligence had accurately determined German strength in the Maupertus Airfield-Cap Levy area, and in their drive to capture Cherbourg had left containing forces south and southwest of the airfield while concentrating their main effort on the port's capture, June 25-27. While the last battles for Cherbourg on June 26 and 27 were in progress the US 22nd Infantry Regiment (4th Division) supported by the 44th Field Artillery Battalion opened its offensive to clear the Maupertus Airfield-Cap Levy area.

The airfield was overrun on June 26 with mopping up of the last ditch diehards on the 27th. While clearing was still in progress the regiment's 1st and 2nd Battalions moved north from the airfield against Osteck. On the northeast corner of the airfield, bordering D162 lay Strongpoint Ritter No. 503, consisting of two antiaircraft batteries depressed as antitank guns. With its open fields of fire the strongpoint could not be bypassed.

American tanks and infantry attacked from the south and west. Two tanks were destroyed by 88mm fire before the Americans broke into the strongpoint. As the tanks mingled in the German positions, panzerfaust rockets destroyed two more. The American attack faltered briefly but was resumed and successfully overran the position.

Holding the airfield and Strongpoint 503 placed the Americans behind Resistance Nests 409 to 416 to the east and facing east. Companies moved east across the several hundred meters to the landfront and took the resistance nests from behind.

Strongpoint 235, Osteck, was now to receive the full attention of the 1st and 3rd Battalion plus the guns of the 44th Field Artillery Battalion, the navy off shore and the fighter-bombers waiting to be called in.

Osteck and Westbeck (west of Cherbourg) were two of the most modern "forts" built to defend Cherbourg. Whereas many of Cherbourg's defense strongpoints were modifications and improvements of the existing French fortresses, these two were planned and built by the TODT organization as superb examples of a 20th century landfront. Osteck was tactically located on high ground overlooking the airfield to the south and the possible invasion beaches to the west.

The diamond shaped strongpoint was a kilometer long on each side. A road led into it from D162. Four, six embrasure turrets marked the north, south, east and west corners. On each side, between the turrets were two mortar positions with automatic fire control and a flame thrower position. On the northwest side an observation post looked across to Cherbourg harbor. In the center was a periscope bunker, a command post bunker, a radar station, a dressing station, two auxiliary command posts, antiaircraft gun position and ten living quarter bunkers. Thirty-five structures, buried in the ground were carefully camouflaged and interconnected by underground tunnels. Antitank guns guarded the entrance road. Around the strongpoint were rings of barbed wire, a saw toothed antitank ditch, a minefield and entanglements of barbed wire encircled the area. The strongpoint was the toughest obstacle the Americans had yet to penetrate since landing on UTAH Beach. As the Atlantic Wall was built up and strengthened under the critical eyes of its commander, Field Marshal Erwin Rommel, the demand for mines grew excessive and could not always be met. Many fields contained only a sign "Achtung Minen", while cattle grazed peacefully, awaiting the mines to be laid and the field to become a deathtrap. In less supply were the detonators required to activate the mine's charge. More mines than detonators were received, consequently many mines were buried minus detonators and therefore non-lethal unless fired upon. Osteck's minefield had a large proportion of mines without detonators. A fact not realized by its commander, Major Kuppers, until he saw American tanks freely crossing the minefields, unhampered.

Manning the strongpoint were units of the 729th Regiment (part of Combat Group Rohrback) as well as remnants of the 1261st and 1262nd Army Coastal Artillery Regiments.

A powerful support from the Hamburg Battery (1 kilometer northeast) had been organized. One of the batteries flanking guns had blown off its roof to allow it to traverse southwest. If necessary, it could direct support fire around Osteck.

As the American tanks and infantry advanced on Osteck from Maupertus sur Mer and along D162, the fire from the Hamburg Battery and Osteck threw up a curtain of death. Tanks blew up and the infantry dug in. The allied navy opened fire on the two positions while fighter-bombers swooped in to drop their bombs on pinpointed battery targets. Shifting to the east and northeast, the Americans attacked from Carneville (1 kilometer). German batteries hit the lead tanks and stopped this advance. The next attack came from the south across the fields adjacent and north of the airfield. It was stopped but some gains had been made and the vice tightened.

The Germans in the south corner embrasure turret ran up the white flag of surrender. Elderly reservists, they had no desire to be dead heroes on a bypassed battlefield. Major Kuppers, from his periscope bunker, ordered the flag shot down by a battery salvo. American tanks were pushing through the southwest perimeter, having crossed the minefield without loss and maneuvered in and out of the antitank ditch.

On the east, tanks scored a direct hit on the east point embrasure turret, killing its occupants. They then began to duel with the antitank gun bunker at the entrance to the strongpoint. On the south a company of American infantry were pouring across the antitank ditch and into the strongpoint. The Germans in their underground concrete bunkers called in fire upon themselves from the flank gun at the Hamburg Battery. An American observation post had unknowingly set themselves up on Kuppers camouflaged periscope bunker. A carefully aimed shell blew the Americans off the roof while inside the bunker only a slight rumble was felt.

Now Americans were everywhere but outside, not inside. Doors were being blasted open and positions were falling. A group attempted to blast open the doors on the periscope bunker. Kuppers led a charge and cleared the entrance way.

Night fell (June 27). Throughout the dark hours Americans telephoned over captured lines and demanded the besieged force surrender. Loud speakers added to the war of nerves by proclaiming the fall of Cherbourg and the destruction of Osteck at sunrise.

At 3 a.m. (June 28) an American officer arrived by jeep and demanded its unconditional surrender. Kupper refused. Again at 8 a.m. a jeep appeared followed by others. Driving up to the periscope bunker down stepped the US 4th Division Commander, Major General Raymond O. Barton with his personal staff. Barton spread out a map displaying minute intelligence details of Osteck's fortification as well as the plan of attack if it should be needed. The Germans were amazed at the accurate detailed information the Americans had received through the French underground. Even the names of officers commanding pillboxes had not been omitted. American preparedness and available power was overwhelming. Kuppers surrendered at 1:30 p.m. Wednesday, June 28. Nine hundred and ninety prisoners marched the long road south to UTAH Beach where they embarked for British and American prison camps.

Since the war many of the blockhouses have been demolished and the tunnels caved in by French demolition personnel practicing and expending much of the remaining German ammunition. The tall grass and thick bushes have closed the open vistas that once prevailed. Standing on top of the periscope bunker, with its now empty periscope collar, affords one a good panoramic view of the battlefield in all directions. The dirt path now twisting and turning around the growth follows the general line of the original German entrance road.

Returning to the road fork and taking D162 to Fermanville, at the foot of the hill, before joining coastal road D116, is the Hamburg Battery. Under command of Lieutenant Gelbhaar the battery consisted of four, 240mm guns with flak and flanking guns. It surrendered at the same time as Osteck.

A huge blockhouse lies to the east of the road. The gun and its protective roof shields have been removed. The gun room now empty is the size of a small auditorium. Wide corridors connect it to the ammunition rooms and its control room on the roof. Casements and pits nearby were for the smaller caliber flank guns and antiaircraft batteries. Buried barrack bunkers are accessible by descending the steep tunneled steps.

North of Fermanville, on the lighthouse road empty blockhouses and pillboxes of Strongpoint 201, (Seadler) can be seen. In the village itself are pillboxes, part of the Cherbourg landfront and the coastal defenses. Houses built since the war hide many of the old fortifications. There are thirteen fortifications in and north of Fermanville, including a four 105mm battery between D116 and the hamlet of le Perrey.

7.14 Digosville

(5 kilometers east of Cherbourg via D901, 6 kilometers to D120, the Digosville road)

On June 22 and 23 the 1st and 3rd Battalions of the US 12th Regiment, 4th US Infantry Division, advanced from the Bois de Coudray (3 kilometers southeast), along the axis of the Hameau Gallis-Tourlainville Road (D63). In their advance the battalions overran five resistance nests, breaking through the outer landfront defense perimeter of Cherbourg.

The 1st Battalion moved north out of the Croix Fresville crossroads (1.5 kilometers south) towards Digosville (D87). A kilometer out of the crossroads German fire stopped their advance on Digosville from the south.

On June 24, K Company of the 3rd Battalion (12th Regiment) attacked the village from the southeast, along the le Theil road (D120). Two hundred meters from the objective the lead scouts came under fire from German machine guns. The American four supporting tanks deployed, opened fire and overran the outer positions. German fire from their rearward positions zeroed in on the American attack. Twelve P-47 fighter-bombers streaked in. Simultaneously the fighters released their bombs while the tank fire further saturated the German positions. The infantry and tanks followed up the bombardment and soon managed to occupy the village. A few Germans escaped leaving behind machine guns, six 155mm field pieces and 150 prisoners.

Meanwhile to the south, three quarters of a kilometer, the 2nd Battalion, 12th Regiment occupied the concrete fortifications flanking the D120 road. Three hundred prisoners were taken.

Continuing their advance the Americans gained the D901 highway to the east of Tourlainville by nightfall.

7.15 Tourlainville

(3 kilometers east of Cherbourg on D901)

A kilometer northeast of the town on the bluffs overlooking the channel was situated the Brommy Battery. Sheltered in massive concrete bunkers three, 150mm guns faced out to sea. Ammunition sheds, barracks and fire control bunkers were contained within the strongpoint's complex. Further north along the beach between le Bequet and Cherbourg's outer harbor jetty were numerous pillboxes, gun emplacements and beach assault defenses.

Tourlainville, the battery and beach defenses, were the objectives of the 12th US Regiment (4th Division) as outlined by General J. Collins' (7th Corps Commander) orders of June 22.

Attacking from the Bois de Coudray (5.5 kilometers southeast) on June 23, the 12th Regiment's battalions advanced northwest along the axis of the Tourlainville-Gallis road (D63). By evening of the June 24 the 1st and 2nd Battalions were on the higher ground one kilometer southeast of Tourlainville. The 1st Battalion's right flank was on D901 near the Tourlainville water tower (1 kilometer east). Before darkness fell, the 3rd Battalion with tank support, passed through the 2nd Battalion's positions to occupy the town without opposition. The night was spent organizing the following morning's actions.

At daybreak (June 25) the 1st Battalion, still positioned in the water tower area, moved north from the intersection of D901 along D120 towards the coast. Ahead lay the Brommy Battery, Strongpoint 245. At 9 a.m. P-47 fighter-bombers attacked ahead of the advancing infantry. Only thirteen bombs were dropped, but enough to cause the defending garrison to raise two white flags. In spite of their intention to surrender, fighting broke out as the Americans crossed the hedge enclosed field immediately south of the strongpoint.

The strongpoint site was "L" shaped. One leg paralleled the west side of D120 and the longer leg ran west from D120 along the bluff's edge for a distance of one kilometer. The American infantry shifted to the west of D120 and descended into an orchard filled draw. This maneuver brought them to the rear of the German positions along the bluffs. Anticipating such a move German mortar fire, 88mm guns and machine gun fire was pumped into the three orchards and their neighboring tree lined fields. American tanks entered the battle providing counterfire. Throughout the day surrender flags appeared and then suddenly disappeared. The fighting continued.

Not until 4 p.m. did a lasting surrender take place. Four hundred Germans surrendered abandoning their three 150mm guns, 20mm guns, several 88s and mortars.

From the road D120, a dirt track leads past a concrete guardhouse into the strongpoint. At the time of battle the area was void of trees and bushes. The concrete buildings stood naked on the bluffs. Now thick, high bushes and shrubs hide the buildings and casements almost completely. From the beach can be seen the battery's observation post and fire control bunker, undamaged, recessed into the crest of the bluff.

On the east side of D120, a footpath leads into a field containing concrete auxiliary bunkers, open cement emplacements, the remains of Resistance Nest No. 244.

While the 1st Battalion was engaged in its battle the 2nd and 3rd Battalions cleared the Tourlainville area and its Resistance Nest No. 246. Completing this, they advanced west towards Cherbourg.

With the area cleared by 6 p.m., the regimental commander, Colonel James S. Luckett, ordered the 2nd and 3rd Battalions to advance into Cherbourg that evening.

7.16 Cherbourg

(North end of the Contentin Peninsula)

The projection of the peninsula into the English Channel formed a protective inlet and a natural deep water harbor for Cherbourg, one of the major channel ports with established docking facilities to accommodate ships plying the Atlantic. Its unique position was further enhanced by the large calm water basin created by the construction of the 8 kilometers long breakwater that arcs across from Pointe de Querqueville to Pointe des Greves. The breakwater was started in 1776. Louis XVI was a spectator to its slow development. Storms delayed progress and it wasn't until 1853 that the breakwater was finally completed.

The naval portion of the port was commenced by order to Napoleon I and completed in 1858 under the reign of Napoleon III. The following year, the first transatlantic steamship unloaded its American cargo at the Gare Maritime.

During World War II Cherbourg was twice besieged. The first battle was in 1940.

On May 10, 1940 the German 7th (Ghost) Division commanded by Generalmajor (Major General) Erwin Rommel crossed the Belgian frontier. The events of the succeeding five weeks witnessed the fall of France and the British retreat at Dunkirk. Rommel's division captured the bulk of the British 51st Highland Division after a desperate battle at St. Valery and sped west to the Contentin Peninsula. From the base of the peninsula his forces moved north along the west coast roads against Cherbourg.

On June 18 the division passed through Barneville-sur-Mer (30 kilometers southwest), les Pieux (18 kilometers southwest) and drove to Cherbourg's western outskirts along highway D904. As the German column neared their objective at 4 p.m., the artillery of the port's forts, in combination with British warships offshore, opened up a deadly barrage against the attackers on the approach roads. Rommel set up divisional headquarters at the Chateau Sotteville (14 kilometers southwest on D904) where he organized the assault on the city. The chateau's previous occupant, the Commandant of Cherbourg, had left a full collection of maps denoting Cherbourg's fortifications in "secret" drawers discovered by Rommel's staff. At 9 p.m. the 7th Rifle and 25th Panzer Regiments moved north against Querqueville (5 kilometers west of Cherbourg). Rommel's tactics were to seize the high ground overlooking the port and dominate the city. The last British troop ship had withdrawn five hours before.

Throughout the night of June 18-19 the German divisional artillery amassed in preparation for a support mission in the assault slated for dawn. The next morning, the forts and strongpoints on Cherbourg's western outskirts surrendered, one after the other. Regardless, the Port Militaire and the city held out refusing to surrender. The German bombardment of the military targets continued until 4 p.m. when a surrender agreement was reached.

The formal surrender took place at 5 p.m. in the courtyard of the Prefecture Maritime between Rommel and Admiral Abrial, Commander of the French Channel Fleet. Thirty thousand French sailors and soldiers marched into captivity down the long road D904. On the Gare Maritime, the British had abandoned hundreds of new trucks and useable vehicles.

In January 1944, Rommel, then a Field Marshal of great fame was made Commander in Chief of Army Group B responsible for the defense of the Atlantic Wall from St. Nazaire to Holland. He visited the length and breadth of his area of responsibility and was shocked and discouraged by its weak defenses. The German propaganda machine had sorely misrepresented the factual situation. Only Cherbourg's defenses met his standards but he observed that "he did not expect the allies to launch their invasion by sailing into a major port on the Queen Mary."

Hitler reasoned the allies would require major port facilities to sustain their divisions, consequently he ordered each major channel port become a fortress.

The allies possession of the beaches and coast would be insufficient. Ships had to transfer their cargoes to landing craft and then to trucks. A tedious, time consuming procedure dependent upon the weather. German intelligence had not discovered the artificial ports being built in England for use at OMAHA Beach and Arromanches- les-Bains. Conclusively, the German high command believed the capture of one or two major ports would be the early objective of the invasion. Logically the ports had to be denied and held to the last cartridge. The last act when seizure was imminent was to demolish the wharves, warehouses, railway lines, etc., rendering the facilities useless for many months afterwards.

Cherbourg, Napoleon's dream as the French Gibraltar, was well situated for defense on its seaward and landward sides. After capture in 1940, the Germans strengthened its existing defense and added hundreds of resistance nests.

As the TODT Organization built the bunkers and the army prepared its defenses, the port served as an aggressive German naval base.

High speed E boat flotillas based here could range up and down the channel sinking coastal steamers hugging the English coast. Small convoys being piloted through the mined shipping lanes would suddenly come under attack by the wooden hulled E boats skimming over the magnetic sensitive minefields. Much of the U boat warfare of the Battle of the Atlantic was waged against the submarines from Cherbourg.

As the Germans used the port and prepared its defenses the French underground carefully studied the developments sending all the information to England. Heading the French Century agents in the Cherbourg district was Yves Gresselin, a grocer in the city. After collecting the observations from his agents he would have it transmitted to England. Located as he was in the city and with the constant roving German radio detection trucks, he could not keep the transmitter in his home. Much of the American knowledge of Fort Roule's defenses was due to Gresselin's personal surveillance.

When the Americans attacked, their guide maps included the names of the German officers in charge of resistance nests. Their knowledge of the German defenses was more exacting than that of the defenders. A major portion of this information came from Gresselin's Century agents.

Aside from collecting intelligence information, Gresselin and his agents were involved in sabotage activities. The demolition of the railway line and trains between Cherbourg and Caen became so common place that the Germans conscripted twenty French hostages to travel on each train, believing the resistance would hesitate killing their fellow countrymen. The Hotel de Cherbourg was commandeered for housing the hostages. In the late evening of June 5 upon receiving a secret coded signal from England, Gresselin and his agents blew up sections of the railline between Cherbourg and Carentan.

A few weeks later when the American encirclement of the port was developing, Gresselin slipped across the lines and presented the Americans with the latest intelligence information and explained the lay of the land. For his invaluable contribution to saving many American lives, he was awarded the American Bronze Star.

The Allied High Command realized that supply lines crossing the beaches and entering through the numerous small ports or landing at the two artificial harbors would be beneficial and logistically manageable. As the front lines advanced, the supply lines from the ports and beached would be lengthened and more divisions would be landing. Each division would require approximately 2,000 tons of supplies per day. It was estimated that fourteen divisions could be adequately furnished with necessary supplies by the network of highways and railroads serving the port of Cherbourg.

The campaign was a war of material. Supply attrition by mobile armies is high. The allied buildup had to exceed the German buildup, therefore, as anticipated by the German strategists, Cherbourg was a primary objective once the UTAH Beachhead had been secured. Lieutenant General Omar Bradley (US 1st Army) estimated it would take 10 to 30 days to capture the port.

Major General "Lightning" Joe Collins, (7th Corps) tactics were, after landing, to cut the Contentin Peninsula at its base (accomplished June 18) and while holding his southern flank, drive north and capture Cherbourg. Transferred from the close jungle battles of Guadacanal, he was quick to seize upon the opportunities of the open fields and roads of the peninsula .

On June 19, a record breaking 3 day gale, slowed down the unloading operations, smashed the OMAHA Beach artificial harbor and created a critical supply problem. With the decrease in the inflow of fresh supplies, the stockpiles began to dwindle. Artillery fire became restricted as shells were rationed. With only the beaches, small ports and Port Churchill (Arromanches-les Bains) as supply entrances, the balance of power threatened to tip to the Germans. Also, during the gale, the allied air force had been grounded and less effective in stopping German vehicular traffic delivering their supplies. The weather had given the Germans a respite that they used to build up their front lines and reserves. As the allied rate of buildup decreased, the German rate increased. The capture of Cherbourg became more important than originally anticipated.

By June 25, three US divisions (9th, 79th and 4th) had ringed Cherbourg's landward side, the allied navy lay off the coast and the air force was at hand.

In the afternoon the navy task force consisting of three US battleships, two US cruisers, two British cruisers and eleven US destroyers, all under command of Admiral M. L. Deyo, USN, opened fire on the Cherbourg defenses from off shore 18 kilometers. Only three 280mm German batteries could reply. Located to the west at Cap de la Hague, their accuracy forced the navy to change from its bombardment mission to that of a duel with the batteries that could not be ignored. After three hours, the navy withdrew. The battleship Texas, cruiser Glasgow and three destroyers had been hit. Although diverted from their original intent this action had kept the German batteries from rendering support fire to their beleaguered comrades in Cherbourg.

The air force had given the port with its E-boats and U-boats much attention before the invasion. During June the raids became more frequent and were climaxed on June 25 by carpet bombing with medium bombers and fighter-bombers. In local close support missions the fighter-bombers were effective and useful but in general the bombings had been ineffective. In 65 raids, the Gare Maritime, the southern section of the city around Fort le Roule and the Arsenal (Port Militaire), had been heavily damaged. Thirty-six percent of the city was destroyed.

The Americans launched their attack on the city, against 21,000 to 30,000 Germans manning its defenses. These were the remnants of the 91st, 243rd and 709th Divisions, the 14th and 235th Antiaircraft Battalions, the 16th Artillery Battalion, the 258th Searchlight Battalion, the 1st Parachute Training Regiment, naval and air force personnel. Also, there were two battalions (144th and 604th) composed of Russian and Ukrainian volunteers who had joined the German army when their homeland was occupied. They were not diehard units as a German officer remarked, "You can't expect Russians to fight tenaciously for Germany against Americans on French soil." To strengthen their fighting spirit their German comrades had emphasized that if captured they would be shot by the Americans as turncoats or turned over to the Russians for retribution.

To simplify the narrative of the battle for Cherbourg in which twelve American battalions were involved simultaneously along a 7 kilometers frontline, we will study the actions geographically and chronologically, moving from east to west.

On June 25, the 1st Battalion, US 12th Regiment advanced north from their positions at Tourlainville (5 kilometers east of Cherbourg) against the German beach defenses at Pointe des Greves. (See the Tourlainville narrative for the battles of that day in the Tourlainville area). The German defenses were along the beach at the juncture of the outer harbor jetty and the land.

The Americans descended the steep slopes to the southeast and crossed the flat open fields of the narrow coastal plain. It was still light at 9 p.m. as they came within range of the three pillboxes (numbers 207, 208 and 209) and the protective machine gun nests. Between the cultivated fields and German positions was a barren field completely void of protective cover except for the east-west railway line (since removed) and an earth embankment running north from the American lines to the beach, a hundred meters west of the fortifications. German mortars were ranged on the earthworks prohibiting its use as an avenue for outflanking the German positions. The railway that cut through the embankment was under machine gun fire, making the sprint across its opening a very unattractive exercise. The Americans took up positions along the coastal road facing across the open no-man's land. The three storied farmhouse became an artillery observation post. From here the spotter could readily study the German positions 150 meters to the north. Before charging across the field, artillery was to "soften" the defender's resoluteness. At 11:23 p.m., the barrage landed squarely on the positions. An ammunition dump went up with a roar. Adjacent barracks and a mess hall turned to flame. At 11:46 p.m. Able and Charlie Companies jumped off. The flaming buildings and German flares illuminated the attacker's route. The machine guns from inside the undamaged concrete pillboxes laced the field with a web of death. Although the Americans moved closer they were still too far away to thrust demolition's into the fire embrasures or down the ventilation ducts. The firing subsided, the flares died out and both sides waited for daybreak under the eerie glow of the smoldering buildings.

(In Cherbourg throughout the night, German demolition teams were razing the harbor installation of Fort des Flammands, the Gare

Maritimes and the buildings adjacent to the docks. The ports capture was imminent, only its destruction could further deny its use by the allies.)

With the visibility of dawn American tanks moved forward to support the planned infantry assault. A few rounds of high explosive shells hit the casements. Before the American assault could proceed a white flat fluttered from a machine gun nest. It was 5:50 a.m. Three hundred and fifty Germans were led off to the prisoner cages at UTAH Beach.

American engineers moved in immediately to de-mine the beach and make it available for ship unloading operations. As a precaution, the German guns were made inoperative to prevent re-manning the positions.

On June 25, while the 1st Battalion fought north of Tourlainville, the 12th Regiment's other battalions advanced west against the defenders in outposts defending the city's eastern limits. Moving along the axis of parallel highways D901 and D116 by 8 p.m. the 2nd and 3rd Battalions abreast crossed the railway lines. The 3rd on the north flank moved along the Boulevard Maritime and Rue Carnot. At Rue Jules Ferry, K Company came under fire from the antiaircraft battery in Strongpoint 252 on Terre-Plein des Meilles and Fort des Flamads (Resistance Nest 210), both to the north a few hundred meters. Moving off the boulevard, the battalions continued moving west along the undefended Rue Carnot and Rue General Leclerc as far as the Rue de la Bretonniere. This was the boundary line between the 4th and 79th Divisions. The 313th Regiment (79th Division) was to clear the eastern half of the port as far as the Avant Port and the Bassin de Commerce.

On June 25, on the left flank of the 12th Regiment (4th Division) the 313th Regiment (79th Division) moved against Cherbourg from the southeast. The 1st and 2nd Battalion moved out from Hameau Gringor (3 kilometers southeast), advancing into the city's outskirts via the Rue du Bois (highway D121). By late afternoon the 2nd Battalion's lead scouts had passed through Cite Vaur but stopped at the level railway crossing. On their left flank, the guns firing from the embrasures on the north face of Mont du Roule, were making the Rue du Bois too hazardous.

With darkness covering their movements, the regiment entered the city and began clearing the buildings between Rue du Bois and the Rue Vauban.

By 8 a.m. the next morning (June 26) and the 313th Regiment had cleared up to the Boulevard Maritime where it halted. The house to house fighting was sporadic. The shelling and bombing had reduced many of the buildings leaving them impractical for organized defense. The Germans depended largely on their prepared defenses consisting of several strongpoints and a considerable number of resistance nests.

On the morning of June 25, the 314th Regiment (79th Division) was south of the city, with its left flank on highway N13 at Hau Lucet. Between the regiment and the houses of Cherbourg stood Fort du Roule atop 115-meter high Mont du Roule. On its west face, a tortuous twisting road leads to the fort from highway N13. Its slope and the five sharp bends in the ascending road prohibited a flank attack. The north and northeastern sides of the hill are steep and a difficult approach. The hill's southern slope, facing the Americans was the best and only approach.

The 19th century fort, modernized by the Germans, presented a formidable bastion. Primarily built for defense against seaborne assault the hill had been tunneled and gun embrasures dotted its north face with seaward aimed coastal guns. These were on the lower levels and did not effect the Americans on the south side. On the crown of the hill were the landward defense positions facing down the ridge over which any attack would have come. Strongpoint 255 as it was identified by the Germans consisted of automatic weapons and mortars in concrete pillboxes. Behind the fort's conventional walls were machine gun positions and rifle pits. Several hundred meters down the southeast slope was an antitank ditch 200 meters beyond a stream.

The strongpoint had been heavily bombed by medium bombers on June 22. The next day it was bombed again. Recognized as being the most formidable position in the Cherbourg defense picture, it received a lot of attention by the allied air force.

Considerable emphasis was placed on its early capture. The fort's positioning offered an excellent observation post for fire controlling the coastal guns on the north side at the lower levels. Moving into Cherbourg under sight of these guns would be an unnecessary waste of lives. The port would be useless, nor could traffic move until the hill positions were cleared.

On June 25 at 8 a.m., P47 fighter-bombers bombed the fort. Shortly thereafter the 2nd and 3rd Battalions launched their attack from along the D410 (Quievastre road). The 3rd Battalion on the left flank ran into trouble at the first draw. As it descended the slope, withering fire tore into their ranks from across the draw where the Germans were well dug in along the east-west trail on the far side of the stream. Reeling under the surprise the two battalions opened up with all they had on the German positions. Slowly the German counterfire diminished and disappeared. The defenders had all been killed. No one withdrew to the fort 700 meters behind.

Easy and Fox Companies (2nd Battalion) resumed the attack. Clearing out positions in their path and capturing a German motor pool the companies pivoted left and advanced northwest up the ridge against the fort. Nearing the German main position the companies drew heavy fire causing the attack to peter out. Support artillery fire from Octeville (2 kilometers west) smashed into the American forward platoons. Alone Corporal John D. Kelly (Easy Company) crawled forward and placed a pole charge at the base of a pillbox. The explosion was ineffective. He returned to his lines, grabbed a new charge and again wormed his way forward to place it under the pillbox. A third and final attempt accomplished his mission, he blew in the door and then tossed in handgrenades. The pillbox surrendered. (For his action Corporal Kelly received the Congressional Medal of Honor posthumously, as he died of wounds in November, 1944.)

While the 2nd Battalion was inching its way up the last 200 meters, on its left flank, the 3rd Battalion was meeting the same kind of devastating firepower from the fort's defenses. K Company leading came under direct fire from an 88mm gun and several heavy machine guns. Single handed, 1st Lieutenant Carlos C. Ogden, advanced with a grenade launcher, grenades and a rifle. Although wounded he was able to position himself to get a shot from his grenade launcher into the 88's pit. Though wounded again and the gun destroyed he sought out the two machine gun nests that were holding up the advance. A few well placed handgrenades knocked them out. (Lieutenant Ogden was awarded the Congressional Medal of Honor on April 2, 1945). The American advance against the fort resumed. By 10 p.m. the top level had been cleared.

Although the fort had been captured, the two lower levels were still to be subdued. This task was given to the 2nd Battalion, which spent the night (June 25-26) resting and preparing for the daylight job. German fire from the embrasures hampered movement by other regiments around the city's periphery.

Throughout the following day various methods were used to clear the Germans. American antitank guns along the Rue du Maupas fired up into the openings with limited results. Demolition charges were lowered down ventilator shafts and triggered. Although the air deep inside the tunnels and corridors was poisoned, sufficient air came in through the openings on the rocky face to keep the German gun crews alive and firing. TNT was lowered down the face from the Fort and triggered in front of the gun embrasures. A demolition team led by Staff Sergeant Paul A. Hurst of Easy Company cut a path along the precipitous face until close enough to enable them to inject pole charges. One by one the gun tunnels were subdued by a combination of several methods. Resistance came to an end by early evening when several hundred prisoners filed out.

Today, one can climb the winding road, which passes along the fort's walls, crosses a draw bridge and enters the courtyard through a porte-culus. Areas of the fort are restricted but the outstanding museum is open to the public. In the courtyard stands a German half track truck. Above, on the ramparts, is a row of German guns representative of those in the battle of Cherbourg. The panoramic view is ideal for studying the battle scene.

The Museum of War and Liberation depicting the history of Cherbourg from the Middle Ages is housed in the mid 19th Century Citadel. The Normandy campaign and the battle for Cherbourg is extensively covered with relief maps, photographs, weapons, uniforms, flags and propaganda literature. A photograph of 1st Lieutenant Carlos C. Ogden, a hero in the battle for the fort, is displayed. A room is devoted to the activities of the French forces throughout the war.

On June 26, while the 2nd Battalion (314th Regiment) cleared the lower levels of Fort Roule, the 1st and 3rd Battalions slipped past the west side of the fort, entering the city via the Avenue de Paris (N13). Small arms and antitank fire from Resistance Nest 288 across the Bassin du Commerce threw flank fire into their advance delaying movement until the 39th Regiment cleared it out. By mid afternoon the battalions were up to the Gare Maritime. The two wharves flanking the Darse Transatlantique were Strongpoint No. 213 consisting of machine guns in steel turrets, two antitank guns in concrete pillboxes, interconnecting dugouts, barbed wire and an antitank ditch. The positions were overrun after being blasted by mortars, antitank guns and automatic weapons.

Several blocks west, on the Place de Republic, the Germans in the city hall were surrounded. Completing the capture of Octeville and St. Sauveur, the 39th 2nd Battalion had moved up Rue Emile Zola to Place Henry Greville. Fanning out the companies advanced to the harbor. Resistance from the city hall drew the battalion tight around its perimeter. Well fortified and amply defended, the building held out all day. In the evening four hundred men and their commander, a colonel, surrendered to Lieutenant Colonel Frank L. Gunn (2nd Battalion Commander) after assurances were given by the Americans that French snipers would not shoot at his captive men.

The 47th Regiment (9th Division) was actually the first US unit to penetrate into Cherbourg's suburbs on its western side June 25. At Equeurdeville, the old fort on Haut Bourgeois was attacked after being bombed and shelled. The garrison of 89 men surrendered in fifteen minutes, to Easy Company (2nd Battalion). Although ominous and a good defense position it was really an observation and control bunker for a coastal battery of 155s dug in on its northern slope. The company occupied the gun pits and waited until the next day to continue its advance. In Equendreville there is a V-1 rocket site bunker, its launch pad aimed at London. To locate the site ask "Ou est le vay-un construction?" On the same day, following the 2nd Battalion to the south, the 1st and 3rd Battalions had captured the forts at Hameau du Tot and Reboute des Fourches respectively.

The following day, June 26, the three battalions tightened the ring around the thick walled Arsenal and Port Militaire. The 3rd Battalion north of the Rue Roger Salengro (D3), was first held up by the mined cemetery. Circumventing the hallowed ground on its north side, the battalion and the 1st Battalion on its left came under withering fire from 20mm antiaircraft cannons perched on the roof tops. Tanks and tank destroyers were called in and battled the roof top guns as well as the concrete pillboxes Nos. 260, 266 and 264 blocking the path to the Arsenal's south side. On the northwest end of the American line, the 2nd Battalion fought to the railway lines immediately west of the Arsenal's walls. The Arsenal comprised three Strongpoints (Nos. 217, 264 and 267). Gun pits and pillboxes bristled along its perimeter. A partial moat held the American attackers from its thick high walls. On its ramparts, depressed antiaircraft guns, antitank guns and machine guns awaited the attackers.

Although smoke and haze shrouded the objective, an extensive bombardment was planned for the morning of June 27, to soften-up the defenders before the infantry launched their attack. A psychological warfare unit broadcast an ultimatum over their loud speakers. An American platoon approached the bastion on its southwest side to test the German reactions. White flags appeared and Colonel George W. Smythe (47th Regiment Commander) accepted the surrender of General Sattler, deputy commander, and the 400 men under his immediate control. The Arsenal's surrender, 10 a.m., June 27 was the end of organized resistance in the city. Most remembered by the veterans was the "liberation" of 50 sides of beef and 300 sides of pork, providing 7th Corps with their first fresh meat in a month.

The port of Cherbourg has an inner (Petite Rade) and outer (Grande Rade) harbor separated from each other by the Jettee du Homet and the Jettee Hersent. The former juts out from the Arsenal. Along its length were Resistance Nests Nos. 216, 263, 215, 262 and 214 running from west to east. The three outer jetties forming a breakwater to the English Channel were also manned strongpoints. From Fort de Querqueville (Resistance Nest No. 221) each jetty fort served as a resistance nest. (Ft. de Charaignac, No. 220; Ft. de l'Quest, No. 219; Ft. Central, No. 231 with four 94mm guns; Ft. de l'Est, No. 212; Ft. de Ile Pelee, No. 241). After the capitulation of the Arsenal, the resistance nests along the jetties held steadfast throughout June 27 and 28. Dive bombers and tank destroyers plummeted bombs and shells on the Germans until one by one the defenders were either blasted out or killed.

The capture of Cherbourg liberated supplies esteemed by the Americans, the beef and pork from the Arsenal and the wines and spirits found in the caves at Octeville and Fort du Roule. All three assaulting divisions shared in the booty. The battle for the city had yielded over 10,000 prisoners.

Although the allied timetable had expected the prize to fall by D+15, not D+21, the Germans were sorely disappointed by its early capture. German defense policy was to deny the use of port facilities to the allies and thereby stall or inhibit the landing of the allies greatest asset, material superiority. Consequently, General von Schlieben was held in disgrace by his early surrender.

Although the Americans were in possession of the valuable and essential harbor, its use was still denied. German demolition experts had been thorough. The city's heating and electric systems were completely destroyed. In the Dorse Transatlantique, 20,000 cubic meters of masonry had been dumped and two ships sunk across the mouth of the basin. Demolition of the harbor had been complete. Buildings and rubble were booby trapped the waters were unnavigatable and frogmen began the dangerous task of clearing the many and varied devices left in the waters. Only after their job was well advanced could the sunken ships be removed and the inner port become serviceable.

It was not until July 16 that ships could enter the port. Still unable to unload at the wharves, the cargoes were ferried in via DUKWS. Fashionable Nouvelle Plage became a huge ramp across which the DUKWs would convert from boats to trucks and carry their loads inland to a truck roadhead. To aid the engineers in their clearing operations and the unloading the port remained open around the clock. In spite of the possible attacks by German E boats and aircraft, the facilities were brightly illuminated throughout the night. On the first day of use (July 16) 15,000 tons of equipment and supplies were unloaded. A short time later its cargo handling capacity increased to a level doubling that of the Port of New York in 1939.

This well exceeded the anticipation of the allies, who had believed it capable of only supporting fourteen divisions. Until the capture of Antwerp and the clearing of its estuary (November 24), the majority of supplies for the fast moving front lines had to be hauled from Cherbourg.

The essential fuel requirements of the mobile army were met by PLUTO (pipeline under the ocean) across the English Channel from the Isle of Wight to Cherbourg. The submerged PLUTO began functioning on August 12, 1944. Its terminal was at the west end of the Grande Rade where the westbound highway D901 skirts along the shoreline of Hameau de-la-Mer. PLUTO's four lines produced a continuous flow of fuel night and day throughout the campaign, until Antwerp became a useful facility. From Hameau de-la-Mer PLUTO became an on-the-ground pipeline, twisting like a giant snake to the road fork at le Pont (6 kilometers south, the junction of D904 and D800). In the field east between the highway and the railroad the pipeline split with lines running south to the American supply depots and others running southeast to the British army supply dumps. As the armies advanced, the pipelines were extended and further split to feed the broad front.

In early August, General Eisenhower's chief logistician for the entire US forces, Lieutenant General J.C.H. Lee, moved the Communication Zone Headquarters from London to Cherbourg and Valognes.

On August 19th the armed citizens of Paris rose against their oppressors. The American forces, although not far away, had planned to bypass the city in their pursuit of the then broken German army. On August 20th General Charles de Gaulle flew from Algiers to Maupertus Airfield (11 kilometers east) in the two motored Lodestar, "France". While the plane was refueled, General de Gaulle drove to the Cherbourg prefecture to refresh himself and make a speech on its steps. Returning to Maupertus he continued his flight to General Eisenhower's headquarters, "Shellburst" at Tournieres, where he attempted unsuccessfully to change the allied plan.

In April, 1945 Germans once again marched through the Cherbourg streets. The German garrison of Alderney Island (British Channel Islands), long since bypassed and cut off by the rapid mobile war that was then being fought in Germany, surrendered.

There are two monuments at the city hall. One commemorates Sergeant Finlay as the first American into Cherbourg and the second remembers the city's civilians deported to Germany 1940-1944.

Picture 8: Cherbourg - Looking North
August 13, 1947

Napoleon designed the port and its defenses to be the Gibraltar of the English Channel. It was captured by Major General Erwin Rommel June 19, 1940. In anticipation of the 1944 invasion and to deny the port's use by the Allies, Rommel had the defenses expanded around the circumference. Fort Roule, mid-photo, is a dominating honeycombed mountain with little accessibility. Although the city and port were captured June 26 (D-day +19) German demolition of the port facilities denied its use for several months thereafter.

7.17 Querqueville

(6 kilometers west of Cherbourg via D901)

North of the village lies the Cherbourg-Querqueville airfield, in 1944 a strongpoint ringed with four resistance nests. One kilometer directly west was a four gun 170mm battery.

With the fall of Cherbourg the US 9th Division regrouped before driving west to clear the Cap-de-la-Hague Peninsula. On June 27 the 47th Regiment started its move westward from Cherbourg towards Hainneville (2 kilometers southeast). Not until the next day could the regiment detach itself completely from the port city as it awaited the arrival of its replacement the 8th Regiment (4th Division) before vacating the city. Patrols moved north-west along D901 to Querqueville. Captain William L. Gledhill of Headquarters, 9th Engineer Command accompanied the infantry surveying the airfield for its potential use by the air force. His unit penetrated the airfield defenses but came under heavy fire. Creeping forward, Gledhill came to within 7 meters of the pillbox dominating the field. Although alone, he called to the Germans demanding their surrender. After several hours of negotiations he succeeded in talking 265 Germans into surrendering and dissuaded them from destroying the hangars, fuel storage and auxiliary installations.

While the battle and discussions at the airfield were in progress, P-47 fighter-bombers attacked the battery with limited success.

The 1st Battalion (47th Regiment) occupied the area during the following day and evening. The defenders had withdrawn west to their Gruchy-Vauville defense line.

On June 29, the 850th Battalion (9th Engineer Command) moved into the airfield and began the task of improving and extending the existing airstrip to a 1200-meter runway. The initial clearing of the 3600 mines of various types and sizes caused more casualties than the battle. A D-7 bulldozer hit an antitank mine and was destroyed. Although the Advanced Landing Ground (A-23) became operational shortly thereafter, it was later extended to 1,500 meters, its present length. The airfield continued to operate until the end of the war.

7.18 Gruchy

(13 kilometers northwest of Cherbourg via D901, 2 kilometers to D45, the coast road. Go 7.5 kilometers to Gruchy)

Following the capture of Cherbourg by the US 7th Corps, the 9th Division was ordered west to clear up the remaining Germans holding fortified positions in the Cap-de-la-Hague area.

The Germans had established a defense line Gruchy-Greville-Beaumont-Hague across the neck of the Cap-de-la-Hague Peninsula. Although the exact strength of the defending forces was unknown it was determined that two battle groups, remnants of the 919th and 922nd Regiments, commanded by Lieutenant Colonels Keil and Mueller, held the peninsula . Although German morale was low their available firepower of three light, two medium batteries and four heavy caliber guns was still a formidable opponent. Two of the "heavies" were railway guns, which had dueled with the navy during the battle for Cherbourg. These long range guns, although located at Laye and Goury, (11 kilometers west) could easily revolve on their turntables to fire eastward into the US lines.

The strongest portion of the Gruchy-Beaumont line was the ridge from Greville (1 kilometer southwest) to Gruchy. This sector, Strongpoint Westbeck, was fortified with concrete shelters, turreted machine guns, mortars and antitank guns dug into the slopes. Firing trenches and antitank ditches defended the forward approaches, with a secondary entrenchment line several hundred meters to the rear.

On June 27, P-47 fighter-bombers blasted the Gruchy positions with limited effectiveness. The next day the 47th Regiment, Colonel George W. Smythe commanding, moved west from Cherbourg and occupied Querqueville (7 kilometers east) at 9 p.m. Acqueville (5 kilometers east) fell to the regiment's 2nd Battalion on June 29. While the battalion cleared the resistance along the coast to the north of Acqueville, the 3rd Battalion moved west and occupied the ridge road D402, 2 kilometers southeast of Gruchy by mid afternoon without opposition.

Five hundred meters ahead of the American positions on a ridge across the stream in the hamlet au Fevre, was a fortified position. Companies L and K (3rd Battalion) advanced across the stream and up the slope. The positions were undefended and forty Germans surrendered. The companies continued west but came under heavy artillery fire as they attempted to cross the Greville-Urville road (D45). A German resistance nest straddled the four point junction on D45, 1 kilometer southeast of Gruchy. American light and medium artillery battalions pounded the fortified position, followed up by the companies advancing into the road junction. It took two hours to subdue the resistance, which netted 250 prisoners. It was then 10 p.m., June 29, and the last resistance pocket before the main defense line had been taken. During the night of June 29-30 the 3rd Battalion moved up the stream, 600 meters east of Gruchy. On the battalion's left flank, the 2nd Battalion came abreast for the attack against Gruchy and Greville respectively.

The Friday morning of June 30 brought rain and poor flying weather. The air strikes were canceled but effective artillery fire plummeted down on the German positions from 8:05 to 8:15. The 2nd Battalion moving against Greville occupied outlying trenches abandoned during the bombardment. F Company fought its way into the village, clearing it by 9 a.m.

The 3rd Battalion advanced up the slope from the stream to Gruchy but was harassed by mortar and machine gun fire. 2nd Battalion fire support from Greville aided the advance and by noon Gruchy was occupied. Serious fire continued to come from the German positions on the ridge west and south of Gruchy. The 2nd and 3rd Battalions spent the afternoon flushing the Germans from the ridge. By 5 p.m. their mission was accomplished.

The actions of the 47th Regiment and those of the 60th Regiment at Beaumont-Hague that day broke the organized German defense line. Except for localized delaying skirmishes clearing the Cap-de-la-Hague forces became a mop-up operation. The American forces quickly pursued their advantage. At 2:30 a.m. July 1, Colonel Keil, senior German commander of the Cap de la Hague forces surrendered to the 47th Regiment near Digulleville (5 kilometers west). At 3 p.m. July 1, the 9th Division reported that all resistance had ceased. Six thousand prisoners were taken as well as two 250mm railway guns, four 155mm howitzers, five 88mm self propelled guns, two 47mm guns and ten 20mm guns.

With the Contentin Peninsula completely cleared, the 4th and 9th Divisions moved south for new operations.

Chapter 8 The Battles for Mont Castre

(20 kilometers west of Carentan on D903)

On June 18 the American forces reached the west coast of the Contentin Peninsula at Barneville-sur-Mer. Throughout the remainder of the month the US 7th Corps directed its efforts north to the clearing of the peninsula and the capture of Cherbourg. The US 8th Corps positioned itself along the southern flank. The Germans facing the 8th Corps did not attempt to contest the drive against Cherbourg but instead prepared their defenses anticipating a southerly drive by the 8th Corps. Between June 19 and July 3 the German defenses west of the marshes, (Marais de Gorges), became formidable. The 8th Corps line arced westward 24 kilometers to Portbail, on the west coast of the peninsula .

Meanwhile the US 1st Army drew up plans for an offensive in which the 8th Corps would drive south 36 kilometers to Coustances. In conjunction with southern drives by the army's other corps the American forces would have an east-west line from Caumont to Coustances. The marshes of the Vire, Taute and Douve Rivers would be behind them as they then assembled on the dry hard ground of the Normandy bocage.

The terrain features and the narrowness of the 8th Corps front was advantageous to the German defenders.

The crossroads town of la Haye-du-Puits, straddling the major north-south highway, was an early objective of the corps' offensive. Hills encircled the town while surrounding moat like marshes further limited the avenues of attack from the northwest and northeast. Once over the hills and through la Haye-du-Puits the front became squeezed between the marsh, Marais de Gorges, and the Ay River flats at Lessay.

The western half of the German 84 Corps, commanded by General Lieutenant Dietrich von Choltitz, faced the US 8th Corps. Von Choltitz was transferred from the Italian front on June 18, taking over the corps after the "death-by-fighter-bomber" of General Erich Marcks on June 12. Later when transferred to Paris he circumvented Hitler's request to destroy the city. Facing the American front lines was Group Koenig consisting of the remnants of the mauled 91st, 243rd and 265th Divisions who held the flanks with their European "volunteers" in the middle. Behind, 2 kilometers, lay the main line of resistance, the Mahlmann Line consisting of parts of the 243rd, the 353rd Divisions and a combat group of the 77th Division. The reserve 2nd SS Panzer Division was in St-Lo (44 kilometers south).

Strong artillery supported the two defense lines. The 243rd Divisional artillery, two cannon companies, five antitank companies, a tank destroyer battalion, howitzers, rocket launchers, antiaircraft guns and a miscellaneous assortment of captured guns and tanks presented a formidable defense to the attackers.

The US 8th Corps was commanded by Major General Troy H. Middleton. Its three divisions were the 79th on the west, the 82nd Airborne in the center and the 90th Division on the east. The southerly advance would cause a convergence of the 79th and 90th Divisions south of la Haye-du-Puits at which time the 82nd Airborne would be pinched out and re-outfitted in England in preparation for their next airborne operation.

The elevated terrain provided the defenders excellent artillery observation posts. US artillery and air attacks were planned to knock them out before the land attack was launched. A heavy storm prior to the attack canceled the air strikes and grounded the artillery spotter aircraft.

At 5:15 a.m., July 3, the artillery opened up with its 15 minute pre H-hour bombardment.

8.1 Les Sablons

(A hamlet 12 kilometers west of Carentan on D903, 0.5 kilometers before the St. Jores, D24 intersection)

The 8th Corps line from Baupte (3 kilometers east) arced westward to Portbail (24 kilometers west on the coast) passing a kilometer to the north of the hamlet crossroads of les Sablons. Facing across the sloping fields from Coigny (1.5 kilometers northeast) the 358th Regiment (90th Division) awaited H-hour. American patrols in the days prior to the offensive had encountered strong resistance in the les Sablons area. This had generated a cautiousness in the infantrymen about pre-registered crisscrossed fields of fire.

At 5:30 a.m., July 3, the 358th Regiment attacked as planned, on schedule. The downpour and lack of air support diminished the ardor of the assault companies as they advanced from their jump off line along the Coigny-Baupte road (D233) 1.5 kilometers northeast of les Sablons. German self propelled guns threw fire into the flank of one of the battalions causing it to stop and dig in for the remainder of the day. A more forceful battalion was successful, advancing down the wooded slopes almost reaching the hamlet. German automatic fire and artillery shelling stopped the battalion's advance short of the objective. The regiment's commander, Colonel Richard C. Partridge, had the battalion disengage and withdraw so the American artillery could "demolish the place".

The American artillery did a thorough job of destroying the German defenses including the half dozen buildings harboring the defenders. Into the smoldering hamlet entered the American infantrymen. It was noon hour. The riflemen had been in the ruins only 15 minutes when two German half- tracks and a self-propelled gun appeared from behind a nearby hedgerow. The riflemen fled and twelve engineers clearing the mines and booby traps hid amongst the rubble. Colonel Partridge was quick to grapple with the potentially dangerous situation. He threw in his reserve battalion, brought forward several tanks and positioned a platoon of tank destroyers north of the hamlet to throw flank fire into any German forces attempting to enter les Sablons from the west. The American infantry line was bolstered with three assault guns and three platoons of the regiment's antitank company to be ready in the event the German armor attempted a breakthrough.

Before blanketing the German armor, in the hamlet, with additional shellfire the hiding engineers had to be withdrawn. This was not accomplished until late afternoon, after which a coordinated "shoot" by tanks and artillery fell again on the devastated hamlet. A follow-up advance by the infantry took les Sablons and the crossroads, a few hundred meters west in the early evening.

Although in US hands, the hold was tenuous. That night German harassing shellfire made organizing and preparing for the next day's actions very difficult.

On July 4 the regiment attacked southwest from les Sablons towards Beau-Coudray (3 kilometers). German artillery fire although not voluminous was devastatingly accurate. The high rate of casualties, on that day ,so depleted the 358th Regiment that Major General Eugene M. Landrum, 90th Division Commander, had to commit his reserve regiment (357th) for the battle of Beau-Coudray.

8.2 Beau-Coudray

(12 kilometers west of Carentan via D903 to D24 south 2 kilometers to the intersection of D140)

On July 3, the US 8th Corps from its positions 5 kilometers north of the Beau-Coudray – la Haye-du-Puits line, launched its offensive southward. At 5:30 a.m., the 358th Regiment (90th Infantry Division) from its forward foxholes on the Coigny-Baupte road (D223, 5 kilometers northeast of Beau-Coudray attacked les Sablons (3 kilometers northeast). The severity of the fighting so depleted the regiment's ranks that with the capture of les Sablons the 357th Regiment had to take over the attack against Beau-Coudray.

On July 5, Colonel George H. Barth's 357th Regiment was 1.5 kilometers north of the Beau-Coudray intersection of D140 and D24, in the hamlet of les Belles-Croix straddling D24. To the east of the asphalt road was the flooded marsh, Marais de Gorges, dry pasture lands today but impassable in 1944. Flanking the road's west side were the pastoral eastern slopes of Mont Castre. Situated 500 meters north of the intersection on a knoll stands the ruins of an ancient castle. It served as a strongpoint in the German's main line of defense. Its approaches were covered by fire positions on Mont Castre's slopes.

The 2nd Battalion led the advance down the narrow asphalt corridor, supported by artillery and tanks. A German self propelled gun positioned along the road shoulder was overrun. German fire on the road forced the American infantry into the hedgerowed fields. The battalion advanced to within a kilometer of the Beau-Coudray hamlet before being stopped by the intense resistance of the defenders.

The following day, July 6, mist and smoke shells enabled one company to slip past the castle ruins and occupy the hamlet. Two more companies slipped into Beau-Coudray and advanced several hundred meters south, halfway to le Plessis. By evening the regiment was in a favorable position to drive south to secure its objectives in the St. Germain-Gorges area. Three companies were in and south of Beau-Coudray, two companies were immediately north, strung out along the road back to les Belles-Croix and a sixth company was in les Belles-Croix awaiting commitment. The antitank guns were a precautionary maneuver to foil a possible counterattack. The regiment's reserve battalion was shifted to Mont Castre leaving only a company for defense back-up.

Colonel Barth's gains threatened to outflank the German positions to the west. At 11:15 p.m. (July 6) the Germans attacked the American positions south of Beau-Coudray and the corridor. Artillery and mortar fire fell on the foxholes and positions along their right flank. German infantry and tanks followed. The battle of that rainy, black night changed the American picture drastically. One rifle company south of Beau-Coudray withdrew to positions north, along the corridor, forcing a company in the corridor to withdraw to les Belles-Croix. By morning, July 7, two inactive companies were in les Belles-Croix. Two along the corridor were hard pressed but not in danger of being overrun and the two companies in and south of Beau-Coudray were cut off surrounded by their attackers.

A rifle company and two platoons of medium tanks attempted to break the German ring around the isolated companies. Although suffering heavy casualties the relief force was only able to reach the last hedge on Beau-Coudray's northern edge when a small German counterattack struck from the west. All the American officers and non-commissioned officers were either killed or wounded. The infantry and tanks withdrew into the secure position of the corridor. German artillery and mortars pounded the positions along the road stopping the American attempts to re-group, re-organize and re-attack.

That evening radio communication with the surrounded companies ceased. A messenger from the "pocket", managing to regain the American lines by way of the marsh, reported that one of the two beleaguered companies had been forced to surrender when its command post was overrun.

The following morning, July 8, the sounds of battle from the Beau-Coudray vicinity stopped. Six survivors, having escaped through the marsh, reported that the remaining company holding the fields several hundred meters south of Beau-Coudray had been killed or captured. Colonel Barth cancelled plans for relieving or extracting the decimated companies. Few of those men that managed to escape capture by hiding as the German infantry swept through the hedgerows returned to their lines. From their regained ground, German snipers scanned the marshes for the escaping survivors plodding their way north in the chest-deep waters.

The battle for Beau-Coudray was renewed on July 10, when Colonel Barth's regiment again tried to extend their corridor into the intersection and hamlet. The American ranks already grossly depleted of officers and non-commissioned officers were broken by concentrated German machine gun, mortar and artillery fire.

American gains on Mont Castre (3 kilometers west) throughout this period forced the Germans to withdraw from the hill during the night of July 10-11. The Americans occupied the high ground west of Beau-Coudray making the German positions in the hamlet and adjacent fields untenable.

On July 12, the much bloodied and depleted 357th Regiment entered and passed through the hamlet encountering only a few rearguards left to delay the advance.

As the battle lines moved south in July and August the demand for front line air support required the construction of forward airfields.

In the latter days of July, the 826th Battalion, 9th Engineer Command, constructed one such airfield at Gorges, 3 kilometers southeast of Beau-Coudray. Designated A-26, the airfield had a 2,000-meter runway with hardstands for medium bombers. The airfield was on the south side of Gorges between the road GC97 running southwest from the Gorges village center and the road running southeast to Gonfreville.

8.3 Poterie Ridge

(16 kilometers west of Carentan on D903 to Lithaire.)

The ridge parallels the north side of D903 starting at la Poterie (0.5 kilometers north of Lithaire west to St. Catherine 1.0 kilometers north of La Haye du Puits).

The 82nd Airborne Division held the middle of the 8th Corps line pushing southward. On the 82nd Division's eastern flank, in close liaison was the 90th Division. However, to the west the division was separated from the 79th Division by the flooded Prairies Marecageueses marsh. The 82nd Airborne Division was in the Bois de Limors, 11 kilometers north of the Poterie Ridge. Their start line was from Varenguebec (on D137) southeast 5 kilometers to Pretot (on D24).

The plans of the 8th Corps offensive of July 3 called for the division to capture Hill 131 (4 kilometers north of la Haye-du-Puits just east of D900), link up with the 79th Division and secure highway D900, also capture Poterie Ridge and secure that portion of the la Haye-du-Puits to Carentan highway (D903).

Major General Matthew B. Ridgway, the division's commander, planned a southwesterly sweep from its positions along the Varenguebec-Pretot line. The terrain over which the airborne troopers would advance was sparsely settled with a few hamlets, void of good roads but with a few sunken rural tracks, through the hedgerowed lowlands.

Before the American artillery opened its bombardment at 5:30 a.m., July 3, a reinforced company of the 505th Regiment, guided by a French patriot moved southwest from Varenguebec along the track to the hamlet of la Dupinerie (1.3 kilometers southwest of Varenguebec). The trail skirts the northern slope of Hill 131. The move outflanked the German positions on the hill. The light of dawn revealed the situation to the surprised Germans who hurriedly withdrew up the hill. The regiment followed up the advantage quickly and by midmorning the northern half of the hill was in American hands. The southern half of Hill 131 was captured simultaneously by similar rapid thrusts of the 507th and 508th Regiments. Pressing west, a battalion of the 505th Regiment reached D900, a division objective by 3 p.m. The battalion, followed by the regiment proceeded south along the highway (D900) until reaching the western slopes of Hill 95 at Ste. Catherine (1 kilometer north of la Haye-du-Puits railroad overpass). The following evening, July 4. The regiment's western flank made contact with the 79th Division.

The Poterie Ridge is 4.5 kilometers long running east from D900. Along its southern slopes passes D903, the la Haye-du-Puits to Carentan Highway. A triplet of hills evenly spaced along the length afforded the German defenses good visibility and fire control positions. The higher ground of Mont Castre, 3 kilometers to the southeast, provided additional covering fire further strengthening the positions along the ridge, especially at its eastern end.

On July 3rd, at 5:30 a.m., the 325th Glider Infantry Regiment, commanded by Colonel Harry L. Lewis attacked westward from their positions around Pretot (9 kilometers northeast of la Haye-du-Puits 1.5 kilometers north of D903 on D24), along the axis of the la Poterie road, D67.

After a slow start, the assault battalions moved rapidly until nearing the D368 road where a tank hit a mine, three floundered in the mud and concentrated artillery and mortar fire rained down from the German positions on Mont Castre, to the south. The ridge's eastern extremity marked by the village of la Poterie was still 1.5 kilometers ahead. Pressing the attack the regiment made some gains and by 1 p.m. was within 600 meters of the village. Here the advance stalled. The tactics to capture the ridge shifted to its northern slopes with the 507th and 508th Regiments. A night attack, July 4-5 by the 325th Regiment was successful. By dawn, July 5, the eastern end of the ridge was in American hands.

The 100-meter high hill, one kilometer southwest of la Poterie was attacked from the north in the late evening of July 4 by a battalion of the 507th Regiment. Unsuccessful in their first attempt the battalion commander split his force and renewed his attack from the east and west simultaneously. About 7 a.m., July 5, the battalion's two forces rejoined on the ridge. The Germans had withdrawn.

The middle hill of the hill triplet has a chateau on its eastern slope. On the evening of July 4 a battalion of the 507th Regiment captured the northern slope and the chateau. Light resistance indicated the Germans had withdrawn. A company sized patrol descended the southern slope and dug in. Dawn revealed that the Americans were in a German bivouac area. A fight followed that rapidly brought in the remainder of the battalion from the hill's crest. Not until late afternoon, July 5, was the hill secured and the American positions consolidated.

The most westerly of the three hills topping the ridge is Hill 95. A secondary road, D136 winds up the north face slope through the hamlet of la Fliche, near the top. On July 4, noontime, a battalion of the 508th Regiment, following an artillery barrage on the hamlet and hilltop, attacked from the east, west and north, with three companies. Although successful, the seizure of the hill was short lived. An immediate German counterattack forced the Americans to withdraw 800 meters north to the east-west Neufmesnil road (D67). In the late hours of the day (July 4) the battalion re-assaulted the hill, battling throughout the night. Dawn of July 5 found the crest once more in the American's hands. The morning and afternoon were spent securing the hill's southern slope.

Although the three hills and the ridge's eastern end were in the paratroopers hands by the afternoon of July 5, it was not until the afternoon of July 7 that the ridge and its slopes bordering D903 were consolidated. Total losses for the four days of fighting had been 500 Germans killed and 772 captured. American casualties were of the same magnitude. Of the most severely wounded, the 325th Regiment alone lost over 300 men.

These were the last battles fought by the 82nd Airborne Division in France. Since the early hours of D-Day the division had been in continuous frontline duty. Fifty percent of its strength was either buried or in hospitals. The US 8th Infantry Division, freshly arrived replaced the 82nd along D903. The paratroopers returned to England for replacements, refitting and reorganizing. In September they were once again dropped into action in Holland in Operation MARKET GARDEN.

8.4 Mont Castre

(16 kilometers west of Carentan, bordering D903 and D140 to the south and west respectively)

The ridge of Mont Castre is five kilometers long running east-west, south of route D903. Its western half is barren. The ruins of a crushing mill, an old castle and a church stand on its northern slope. Midway on D903 between the villages of la Rue du Bocage and Litharie, a dirt road winds up the ridge's north face. Past the crushing mill, the right hand turn leads to the castle on a wooded rise and the church on its south side. The eastern half is thickly wooded. The Foret de Mont Castre is laced with trails, sunken roads and hedgerows. Once the site of a Roman encampment, in 1944 the high point (122 meters) was a German observation post. From the pinnacle one can view the complete width of the Contentin Peninsula. Up until its capture by the Americans in early July, the Germans could readily observe, on a clear day, the allied ships unloading on UTAH Beach, twenty-four kilometers to the northeast. This dominating ridge across the 90th Division's line of advance commanded the approach flatlands. No roads climbed the ridge, only a maze of tangled alleyways and cow paths. German observation was excellent, the American's had none. Any plan to pass along the corridor to its east (Beau-Coudray on D24) would leave the hill threatening the American flank and supply route. Possession of Mont Castre was a prerequisite to the 90th Division's advance on Periers.

Holding the ridge, on July 1, were two battalions of the German 265th Division, the remnants of the 77th Division and a battalion of the 353rd Division.

General Eugene M. Landrum's (90th Division) plan was to attack from its Pretot (D24)-Baupte (D903) line (5 kilometers northeast), two regiments abreast. The 358th Infantry Regiment, on the left, was to force its way through the Beau-Coudray corridor (3 kilometers east of Mont Castre's highpoint) while the 359th Infantry Regiment, under Colonel Clark K. Fales, on the right was to assault and capture the predominate ridge. With the two regiments in possession of Mont Castre and the Beau-Coudray corridor, the division's 357th Regiment would pass through to the initial 8th Corps objective.

To aid the assault regiments across the lowlands, a massive array of artillery firepower was arranged. Heavy weapons of the reserve regiment, tanks, tank destroyers, battalion artillery, corps artillery and the 4th Division's artillery were included. The 9th Division's artillery was alerted to be available for fire missions as requested. With this drenching fusillade on Mont Castre the Germans were expected to keep under cover as the Americans advanced.

On July 3, 5:30 a.m., the division's attack was launched in a driving rain storm. German resistance was stiff and by darkness the American advance was only two kilometers closer than when they had started. 600 casualties lay in the fields and first aid posts.

At daybreak, the following morning (July 4) a ten minute barrage by the American artillery preceded the jump-off. A German counter barrage delayed the planned start and caused the attackers to expect a German counterattack. The appearance of three German armored cars substantiated the front line infantrymen's fears who pulled back, loosing what little ground had been gained. Although no German counterattacks materialized, the day was spent in readiness. At dusk the advance got rolling again and kept going over four kilometers of the lowlands to the foot of Mont Castre along D140. The effect of the American artillery on the hill was being felt. Without reserves and replacements the German casualties weakened their defense. To the north, across D903, the 82nd Airborne Division on the Poterie Ridge was menacing the German positions in the barren fields on Mont Castre's western end. The severity of the situation forced the German High Command to release the 15th Parachute Regiment for commitment in the defense of the Mont Castre line. Throughout the night of July 4 -5, the German regiment moved in strengthening the ridge's defense.

Throughout July 5, it was a battle to secure a toehold on the northeast slope. A battalion of the US 358th Regiment (reserve) was brought in to the foray. German artillery and tanks supported their many small local counterattacks along the narrow trails and entangled hedgerows. Few gains were made but important lessons were learned that proved effective in the engagements over the next few days.

On July 6, Colonel Fales redirected one of his battalions to the western end of the ridge. This wide envelopment movement resulted in the capture of the old castle. With this gain and the general broadening of the Mont Castre action area the German holding force on the ridge was forced to widen its line or be outflanked on the west. The German maneuvers thinned out their defense lines. American artillery and the air force pounded the weakening lines. By nightfall Fale's four battalions had ascended the northern slopes and were in possession of the 122 meter pinnacle.

The four days of fighting had been costly. The division's two regiments had lost 2,000 men for the seven kilometer advance. The front line rifle companies were so depleted that their hold on the ridge was tenuous. A cohesive unified line was not possible. Pockets of infantrymen reinforced with engineers, now riflemen, held all around defensive positions against German marauder units. The terrain difficulties made supply, reinforcements and evacuation difficult. Trucks crossing the lowlands came under fire. What did get through was difficult to move up the slopes because of the mined sunken trails and ambushes by small German units. Ammunition, food, water and medicines were dwindling. Reinforcements became confused, lost their way, came under attack, dug in and formed a new pocket of resistance. Casualties and prisoners couldn't be removed as the depleted platoons were unable to provide escorts or guards. The German defenders had spent four years preparing themselves for such a battle. Their knowledge of its trails and terrain intricacies compensated for their numerical deficiencies.

Throughout the dark night of July 6-7 rain soaked the battlefield. German counterattacks attempted to recapture Point 122. Unsuccessful in the dark hours, the Germans maintained their pressure throughout July7- 9. The stalemate that had developed was the result of the American supply and reinforcement problem as well as the tenacious fighting qualities of the defenders. The Germans threw attack after attack against the American positions on the northeast corner. From the tower of the chateau's stable at the ridge's western end an officer of the 82nd Airborne Division set up an exposed observation post from where he directed support fire for the division's mortars against the German counterattacks.

On the afternoon of July 10, a company of 358th Regiment supported by six tanks crossed the top of Mont Castre reaching the woods on its southern slope. As they left the concealment of the woods to descend the slope German self-propelled guns using flat trajectory shells picked off the tanks forcing the supporting infantry to withdraw into the woods. The actions of Colonel Jack W.Beakle, Jr.

and Captain John W. Marsh (killed) were recognized by being awarded the Distinguished Service Cross. Only Colonel Beakle and twenty-four men of the company made it back to the forest.

Throughout the night (July 10-11) the Germans made an orderly withdrawal, abandoning Mont Castre, leaving a rearguard to delay the foreseeable American descent at dawn. The following day, the 358th Regiment moved down the slope against little opposition. A German machine gun nest was knocked out by Pfc. Theodore G. Wagner who crawled up to its position and tossed in handgrenades. He was awarded the Distinguished Service Cross.

Three days later the 90th Division reached the Seves River (8 kilometers southeast). Twelve days of fighting and a gain of twelve kilometers had cost the 8th Corps, 10,000 casualties, with 4,000 to the 90th Division alone. German regimental histories also record this as one of their bloodiest battlefields.

8.5 Hill 121

(26 kilometers west of Carentan on D903 through la Haye du Puits to D127 and north 2.5 kilometers to St. Nicolas de Pierrepont. Hill 121 is 1.5 kilometers to the east).

Within the plan of the 8th Corp's drive to Coustances the 79th Division, on the corps' western flank, was to clear its zone along the coast from the Portbail and the Ollande River (8 kilometers northwest) to St. Germain sur Ay and the Ay River (9 kilometers south). Half way along and astride the drive's axis stood the natural defense barrier of the Montgardon Ridge. Flanking the division's route, close to the start line stood Hill 121. In American hands it would provide excellent observation for the battles of la Haye-du-Puits and the Montgardon Ridge.

On July 2 the US 79th Division held the neck of land between the marshes of the Prairies Marecageuses marsh and the ocean. It's front line ran along the south side of the l'Ollande River between St. Lo d'Ourville (8 kilometers west) and Neuville-en-Beaumont (3 kilometers north).

The terrain over which the offensive would cross was low lying with boxed fields enclosed by tall hedgerows, and numerous north-south roads along the axis of attack.

Defending were the remnants of the German 243rd Division. Southwest of la Haye-du-Puits a battalion of the German 353rd Division was spread out along the Montgardon Ridge.

Major General Ira T. Wyche's (79th Division) plan was to advance with two regiments abreast. The 314th Regiment on the east against Hill 121 and the 315th Regiment, to the west, against the ridge.

On schedule the corps launched its offensive at the crack of dawn, July 3. Colonel Warren A. Robinson's 314th Infantry Regiment held the portion of the corps' line stretching east from Canville-la-Rocque(5 kilometers northwest) to the north-south railroad flanking the western limit of the Prairies Marecageuses marsh. From Neuville-en-Beaumont (3 kilometers northeast) two rifle companies, flanking the highway (D127) to la Haye-du-Puits, lead the regiment's advance southward. Half a kilometers south of Neuville-en-Beaumont, at the crossroad north of St.

Sauveur-de-Pierrepont, the company on the east side of the road came under heavy machine gun and mortar fire from German positions along the railroad embankment several hundred meters on the American's left flank. The American's had arrived at the outer line of resistance defending la Haye-du-Puits. PFC William Thurston charged the embankment, alone, clearing out a machine gun nest. For his action he was awarded the Distinguished Service Cross. This local penetration of the defense positions along the railroad embankment opened the route into St. Sauveur-de-Pierrepont. The first patrol of a dozen men spearheaded the battalion's assault on the hill. Darkness, the hedgerows and lack of radios kept Colonel Robinson ignorant of the action on the hill. A second battalion was sent up the slopes to support the one already locked in combat. Dawn revealed the hill was only held by a few German resistance nests that were overrun during the morning of July 4.

The division's artillery immediately set up observation posts overlooking la Haye-du-Puits and the Montgardon Ridge. To the southeast, along highway D900 the 79th Division's left flank linked up with the 82nd Airborne Division's right flank near Neufmesnil (2 kilometers southeast).

In late July, after the front lines had moved south, a battalion of the 9th Engineer Command established a 1300 meter grass strip, Advanced Landing Ground, A-25, near Bolleville. A search of the records has revealed little more. Local inquiries of Bolleville's older citizens may pinpoint its location. There is evidence the airstrip was in the northeast field adjacent to where the railroad overpasses D127.

8.6 Hill 84

(24 kilometers west of Carentan on D903 to la Haye-du-Puits and southwest on D136, 2.5 kilometers. The road ascends Hill 84).

In Phase I of Major General Troy H. Middleton's 8th Corps' drive to capture Coustances the 79th and 90th Divisions were to pass la Haye-du-Puits on its west and east sides respectfully. Having been bypassed the town would fall without a fight. Success meant the Americans had to capture the high ground east and southwest of the town.

The Montgardon Ridge, with its high point, Hill 84, lay to the southwest of la Haye-du-Puits and blocked the route of Major General Ira T. Wyche's 79th Division's route to Lessay (7 kilometers south) on the Ay River.

On July 3, the division's 315th Infantry Regiment (Colonel Bernard B. McMahon) was positioned along the l'Ollande River, 10 kilometers to the northwest. The hedgerowed lowlands between the Americans and the ridge was defended by remnants of the German 243rd Division. The ridge, the German main line of resistance, the "Mahlmann Line", was held by a battalion of the 353rd Division.

On July 3, 5:30 a.m., the regiment launched its attack as part of the overall corps offensive. With two battalions abreast and the third in reserve to the right rear, the regiment made good progress in the morning until three German armored vehicles, on the west flank, attacked. Bypassed by the American advance, the German attack caused confusion amongst the American follow-up infantry. Artillery and antitank guns responded quickly, destroying the intruders. Continuing their advance, by nightfall the 315th was still 8 kilometers short of Hill 84.

The following day, the gains brought the regiment up to the St. Remy-des-Landes road (D67, 5 kilometers northwest). Two days of rain had made the lowlands an unmanageable quagmire for the American tanks and armored vehicles. The rain had grounded the tactical air force and the artillery spotter aircraft.

Up to that time German resistance had been strong but not aggressive. In the evening a determined German counterattack was launched to extricate the remnants of the 243rd Division. Reasonably successful the beleaguered German infantry was able to withdraw onto the Montgardon Ridge including 64 American prisoners. To the northeast, 4 kilometers, American artillery observers on Hill 121 directed a strong artillery barrage into the German lines that stopped the counterattack.

General Wyche recognizing that the 315th's advance had been stopped short of the ridge line quickly ordered the neighboring regiment to bypass the ridge. Hoping to outflank Hill 84 by a drive down highway D900, General Wyche ordered the314th Regiment to seize la-Haye-du-Puits and press down D900. The attack on the town on July 5 morning, was stopped by the Germans' strong defensive positions along the northern edge of the town.

By midmorning it was apparent that the plan would not be successful. The 313th Regiment, in reserve, was ordered to move past the west end of the ridge by skirting the coastal shore through Bretteville-sur-Ay (4 kilometers west). In the late afternoon, July 5, as the lead companies were but a few hundred meters from the west end of the ridge, approaching Bretteville-sur-Ay, the Germans fired an artillery barrage followed by two infantry counterattacks. Only darkness, German confusion and the marshy terrain saved the Americans who were thrown back four or five kilometers. A threat developed to the 315th's flank. The Germans missed the opportunity of exploiting their advantage.

Before the German counterattack, General Wyche had reservations about the 313th's gains and ordered the 315th to renew its attack on Hill 84. Supported by tanks and tank destroyers, the 315th was more successful and secured a foothold on the northern slope of Hill 84, late July 5.

The following morning witnessed the further consolidation of these gains when the 314th Regiment side slipped around the west side of la Haye-du-Puits and battled up the eastern slope of Hill 84. Throughout the remainder of the day the 314th and 315th Regiments fought their way up the slopes and over the top of the hill. On the ridge's west end German minefields, barbed wire and machine guns stopped the 313th from advancing. However, the gains by the other regiments on Hill 84, by dawn of July 7 had made la Haye-du-Puits an untenable situation for the German defenders.

Still, however, the Germans in the few remaining ridge positions and in the town held on. American attempts to talk the Germans into surrendering were only greeted by devastating counterfire.

In the afternoon of July 7, elements of the 2nd SS Panzer Division counterattacked the Americans on the ridge. The strength of their artillery supported attack almost succeeded in regaining Hill 84's crest and slopes. The German effort petered out by midnight. The American casualties for that day on the hill were 1,000 killed and wounded. Since the start of the offensive on July 3, the 79th Division had had 2,000 casualties. Weakened and facing strong German resistance, the 79th's intermediate goal, the Ay River (7 kilometers south) appeared illusive.

On July 8 and 9, the Germans maintained strong pressure on the American positions. Although la Haye-du-Puits fell on July 9th, the 8th Corps' southerly movement had been stopped.

On July 10, German pressure decreased and the 79th Division got their offensive rolling again. Moving down the southern ridge slopes Angoville-sur-Ay fell the following day and the Ay River was reached on July 14.

8.7 La Haye-du-Puits

(24 kilometers west of Carentan)

The 8th Corp's offensive plan of July 3 envisioned the capture of la Haye-du-Puits without a shot being fired. The capture of the surrounding hills and a linkup of the 79th and 90th Divisions south of the town would cause the Germans to abandon their defense positions in the important crossroads town.

On July 3 when the American offensive commenced the town was held by 150 men, remnants of the 353rd Division's Pioneer Battalion. Shelled sporadically previously the road junction through which supplies and reinforcements would move was severely bombed and shelled on July 9. 75% of the town was destroyed.

Gains by the 8th Corps on July 3 and 4 brought the 82nd Airborne Division onto the hills to the northeast and the 79th Division to the northwest and west by July 5.

To the southwest the 315th Regiment (79th Division) was stopped short of the Montgardon Ridge. Major General Ira Wyche ordered his 314th Regiment to take la Haye-du-Puits and outflank the ridge from the east.

During the morning of July 5, an American company entering from the north down D900 fought its way into the railroad yard in the northeast outskirts. The cratered roads and minefields tended to isolate the company in the railroad yard although support fire was supplied by a second company to the north. Recognizing the value of the town and its intersecting roads, the Germans fought the invaders tenaciously. Mortars and shellfire blanketed the Americans in the railroad yard. The company was driven back.

Further gains to the west and southwest outflanked the town by July 7. Still the defenders stuck to their posts. With a prisoner's aid an American patrol attempted to persuade the Germans to surrender, unsuccessfully. Vicious counterfire stopped their movement forward at the first houses on the northern edge of town.

Surrounded and under siege the Germans refused to surrender. Machine guns, mortars and small arms behind minefields covered with barbed wire were their defense. An American battalion with artillery and armor support was assigned the task of taking the town. In the late afternoon, July 8, the battalion's three companies moved in from the north. The fields adjacent and north of the railroad were densely mined. Strung over the fields, 30 centimeters (2-feet) high was a checkerboard of barbed wire forcing the G.I.'s to high step and be visible to machine gunners whose hidden locations and deadly fire crisscrossed the fields. Costly gains were made as engineers taped de-mined lanes and armored bulldozers cut open cleared avenues of approach. By evening the infantry were clearing the railway station area on the town's northwest outskirts. Throughout the night (July 8-9), with the scene illuminated by the burning buildings, the infantrymen waged a house to house battle. By noon, July 9, German resistance had been quelled. Only 40 prisoners shuffled off to the prison cages. Units of the freshly committed US 8th Infantry Division took over the town and prepared to drive south flanked by the 90th (east) and 79th (west) Divisions.

Chapter 9 OMAHA Beach

(16 kilometers northeast of Bayeux via N13-E46 13 kilometers to the Formigny road, D517, north 3 kilometers to St. Laurent, west 3 kilometers on D514 to Vierville.)

Wars leave names indelibly impressed into the psyche of our lexicon. Half a century later successive generations hear of these places without thought to their significance. To the British they are Dunkirk, El Alamein and Arnhem. To Canadians Dieppe and Vimy Ridge (WW I) recognize catastrophe and success. To Americans, Iwo Jima, Tarawa and Omaha Beach symbolize costly, bloody triumphs against diehard enemies. "Bloody Omaha" is the image of killers, untouchable in concrete bunkers, slaughtering America's youth helpless on an open beach. OMAHA Beach is sacred, hallowed ground bloodied by men who came three thousand miles to free Europe and subdue Hitler's nazis.

Lest we be distracted by the new summer homes and restaurants aligned along the beach. Hollywood's "The Longest Day" and "Saving Private Ryan" show us the grim reality, how death stalked several thousand Americans in the water and on the sands June 6, 1944. After death they moved but a few kilometers to their eternal rest on the bluff overlooking this consecrated ground.

The allied armies struck across five beaches on D-Day. The combined casualties on the other beaches did not equal those here. UTAH, the second American beach, seldom referenced, had only 95 casualties. Its beach commander, Brigadier General Teddy Roosevelt, was awarded the Medal of Honor for his quick thinking to secure their objectives with minimum casualties.

OMAHA Beach is a seven-kilometer (4 miles) long concave arc. The 35-meter (100-foot) bluffs gave the Germans, in long established positions, the high ground from which they dominated every square foot of the beach. Two thirds of the eastern end of beach was shingle making vehicle traffic impossible. At the western end a 2-3 meter sea wall ran the length of the promenade. A significant obstacle for mobile equipment. Five valleys (called draws) led from the beach up to the higher ground. The westerly one at Vierville was paved but the other four were undeveloped tracks. The draws were wooded and defended by paired "resistance nests" (Wiederstandsnest). Six more resistance nests on the bluffs between the draws and three inland at the towns created a formidable defense. Along the beach were eight large caliber guns in concrete casements, thirty-five antitank guns in pillboxes and eighty machine gun nests. Communication trenches interconnected the defenses.

On the sandy beach were three lines of log obstacles, 7 meters apart, tipped with contact mines and shells. Closer to shore were metal hedgehogs tipped with explosives (similar to 4 meter tidily winks) to tear open the hulls of landing craft. At high tide the obstacles were beneath the water and difficult to see. From the beach to the foot of the bluff were antitank ditches, minefields and barbed wire, thickest around the draw entrances. Scattered liberally over the slopes were thousands of antipersonnel mines designed to explode under foot or pop up and explode at waist level.

The Germans anticipated the allies would invade at high tide, less ground fire exposure time. Their casements were angled to fire along the high tide line. Sidewalls on the gun casements protected the embrasure from naval fire. The allied planners chose low tide with tanks accompanying the infantry facing only light machine gun fire until reaching the high tide line when the tanks could fire into the enemy casements through the embrasures. The air force and battleship fire were to reduce German artillery fire from inland. As the tide rose, engineers would clear wider entrance corridors through the water obstacles for the landing craft.

Off the coast lay 1,213 naval combat vessels, 4,126 landing ships, 736 ancillary craft and 864 merchant ships manned by 195,701 men. In the air 11,590 aircraft and gliders were committed to the invasion.

Two battleships, three cruisers and eight destroyers lay in close support of OMAHA. Following a two-hour bombardment by the navy and air force the assault force of thirty companies went in at 6:30 a.m. in four waves.

The OMAHA assault plan was flawless. H-Hour was set for 6:30 a.m.

6:25 a.m. 64 amphibious dual drive tanks would swim in and be in position at the waters edge.

6:30 a.m. 16 Landing Craft Tank (LCT) would off load tanks on the beach.

6:31 a.m. Assault troops land and cross the beach. Five waves follow at 6-minute intervals.

6:33 a.m. Underwater demolition engineers land.

7:00 a.m. 16 paths, 50 meters wide are opened for follow-up troops and supplies.

8:00 a.m. Heavy equipment i.e. artillery, tanks, bulldozers, etc. enter through the opened lanes.

10:30 a.m. Half tracks, cranes, large artillery land.

Each assault boat was a self-reliant 31-man platoon that could accomplish its tasks without dependence on men and equipment from other landing craft. That is, with each boat there were officers, teams of riflemen, wire cutters, Browning Automatic Rifles, mortars, bazookas, flame throwers, demolitions and a medic. A full company required six landing craft.

What went wrong on Omaha? With the same intricate and coordinated planning, having a vast armada of warships, an inexhaustible uncontested air force, an infinite number of troops in unlimited water transports how could one beach be so different?

Because:

1. There were more German forces holding the beach than Americans attacking. Initially, the German 716th Infantry Division was spread out along the full length of the invasion coastline. In May the 352nd Infantry Division took over the western half of the 716th defenses. Three battalions up front with three in reserve, close to the coast, tripled the force defending Omaha. One of the reserve battalions was exercising in the area June 5 and 6. This large force, with its firepower in well-prepared protected positions behind rows of obstacles and minefields was the most significant cause for the high casualties. Knowledge of 352nd's presence was received too late to be acted upon.

2. Between Bayeux and Isigny were eight more 352nd Division battalions, not four as expected, of fair quality troops giving the beach defenses strength and depth.

3. The pre-bombardment was ineffective. The 329 bombers with the highest level approval cautiously delayed their 13,000-bomb release a few seconds missing the beach defenses by five kilometers. Smoke from brush fires along the bluffs obscured the beach from accurate naval fire. Up to a few hundred yards from the beach the soldiers were euphoric in believing nothing could have survived the bombardment. It was a surprise and shock when they learned harshly the enemy fortification had not been neutralized.

4. Amphibious armor did not materialize as the tanks were swamped and sank by the 2-meter waves. The 1st Division launched 32 tanks. Twenty-seven sank, two swam in and three came in on landing craft.

5. The stormy weather and a strong eastward current led to inaccurate landings and poor gunnery by the mosquito fleet. The twelve-mile ride in caused 50% of the units to touch down a kilometer off plan. Training had oriented the men to expect and see specific visual objectives. Beaching with unfamiliar landmarks and separated from their units forced on the spot improvisations further handicapped by the high casualties amongst the officers.

6. The assault waves lost more men and radios than expected reducing air-ground coordination support.

7. The US 1st Infantry Division was experienced and more aggressive. This was the 29th Division's first action. The landing craft were launched from transport ships 12 miles from the beaches. The soldiers were drenched from the cold spray. The rolling boats brought on seasickness. The men were more heavily burdened than in their training exercises. They were tightly packed together. The chilled, cramped, seasick men were not in top condition for what awaited them when the ramps dropped.

8. The plan to frontally assault the heavily fortified beach exits was faulty and a repeat of the erroneous Dieppe (August, 1942, disastrous Canadian French coast raid) mindset.

9. There was no use made of British specialty engineering tanks to aid in obstacle clearing and providing infantry protection. Off loaded tanks had to wait at waters edge for engineers to clear lanes through the obstacles.

The Canadian Dieppe raid demonstrated the impossibility of capturing a French port by frontal assault. The allies therefore brought two prefabricated ports from England. "Port Churchill" was built at Arromanches, 20 kilometers east, and "Port St. Laurent" off OMAHA. 10,000 men and 132 tugs were involved in floating 213 breakwaters, 6,000 ton Phoenixes, across the channel to be partially submerged in an arc out from the beaches forming an artificial port providing deep water sheltered anchorage. Floating roadways connected the supply ships to the land allowing 24-hour unloading independent of the tides. 6,500 vehicles and 14,000 tons of supplies were being unloaded weekly when the storm of the century, June 19 to 23, destroyed Port St. Laurent as it neared completion. 800 craft were driven up on the beach producing a massive iron scrap yard up to and across the coastal road. The port at OMAHA was abandoned. Other methods were improvised to off load the ships arriving directly from the US

9.1 Vierville-sur-Mer

The town was captured the afternoon of June 6, not by troops coming up the draw road that directly connects the town to the beach but by units that had landed 1,300 meters to the east. They had fought their way across the 275-meter beach, and the 185-meter shelf, up the 35-meter bluffs, then fought westward through every hedgerow 800 meters to the town occupied by seasoned German troops. B Company (5th Ranger Battalion) and C Company (116th Regiment) had a hard fight through Vierville along D514 to the road intersection 300 meters west of the draw road intersection. Depleted sections of A, B and C Companies (2nd Ranger Battalion) reinforced the position before nightfall. Two platoons of B Company (116th Regiment) moved south from the Vierville intersection 500 meters to the Chateau de Vaumicel where they met strong resistance. A Company (5th Ranger Battalion) slipped through the German lines to continue west to relieve the rangers at Pointe du Hoc. By nightfall the American perimeter 500 meters west and south of the town was very thin but holding against the German pressure. During the following days small groups of German snipers infiltrated back into the war damaged buildings to pick off individual soldiers coming into the main intersection from the beach. When located, the snipers lost the opportunity to surrender.

The first American rape of a local civilian in Normandy occurred here on June 14. Four American soldiers of the 240th Port Company (494th Port Battalion) accosted two Polish farm girls pulling a milk cart towards a herd of cows. The soldiers pushed the cart into the field then asked for a drink of milk. As Aniela Skrzyniarz milked one of the cows her sister Zofia went to the adjoining field to round up more cows. The soldiers had been drinking the local Calvados apple cider. Private Clarence Whitfield threatened Aniela with a rifle shot before she submitted. Zofia being raped in the adjoining field jumped up and ran when hearing Whitfield's shot. She ran home to find Aniela's husband. Returning in a jeep with three officers of the 3704th Quartermaster Truck Company and Aniela's husband they found Aniela and Whitfield struggling. The husband struck Whitfield before being taken to his battalion commander.

A General Court Martial was convened at the 11th Port US Army Headquarters in the Vierville Chateau, June 20. (On D514, west of town intersection, south side, plaque on gate pillar). Whitfield was judged guilty and sentenced to be hanged. The Judge Advocate General in Britain confirmed the court findings July 24. A gallows was erected in the kitchen garden of the chateau at Canisy, seven kilometers southwest of St. Lo. Whitfield was brought in August 13 to help dig the pit below the gallows. The following day guards were posted at the shell holes in the surrounding walls. Monsieur Aimable Lehoux was the only civilian witness. Whitfield went to his death smoking a cigar.

Vierville has a private museum housed in a wartime Nissen hut used for troop entertainment. Open April to the end of September.

South of the intersection, in the churchyard there is a plaque to the 81st Chemical Mortar Battalion. Going north from the intersection towards the beach there is a monument to the 29th Infantry Division and a 5th Ranger Battalion plaque.

Picture 9: Omaha Vierville Draw – Looking East
June 14, 1948

The valley road "The Vierville Draw" or code named D1 is at the top. Six German strongpoints defended the beach in this area. The movies "The Longest Day" and "Saving Private Ryan" depict the battle on these sands. C Company Rangers landed under the cliff immediately west of the draw. Their battle along the bluff greatly reduced the firepower on A Company, 116th Regiment assaulting the beach. Further west to the right is Pointe Percee from where a German officer observing the battle erroneously misjudged the American successes and redirected German reinforcements to another area. The German defenses around Vierville draw are visible and accessible.

9.2 OMAHA Beach – Western Beachhead

(North from Vierville-sur-Mer to the beach road intersection)

The road descending the draw was paved in 1944. This most westerly road off the beach was designated as Exit D1. Concrete pillboxes on the valley slopes were surrounded with barbed wire covered minefields. The emplacements were sighted to provide machine gun cover fire to each other. Anti-personnel mines throughout the slopes made attack difficult. Not until 2 p.m. that afternoon was the exit valley cleared.

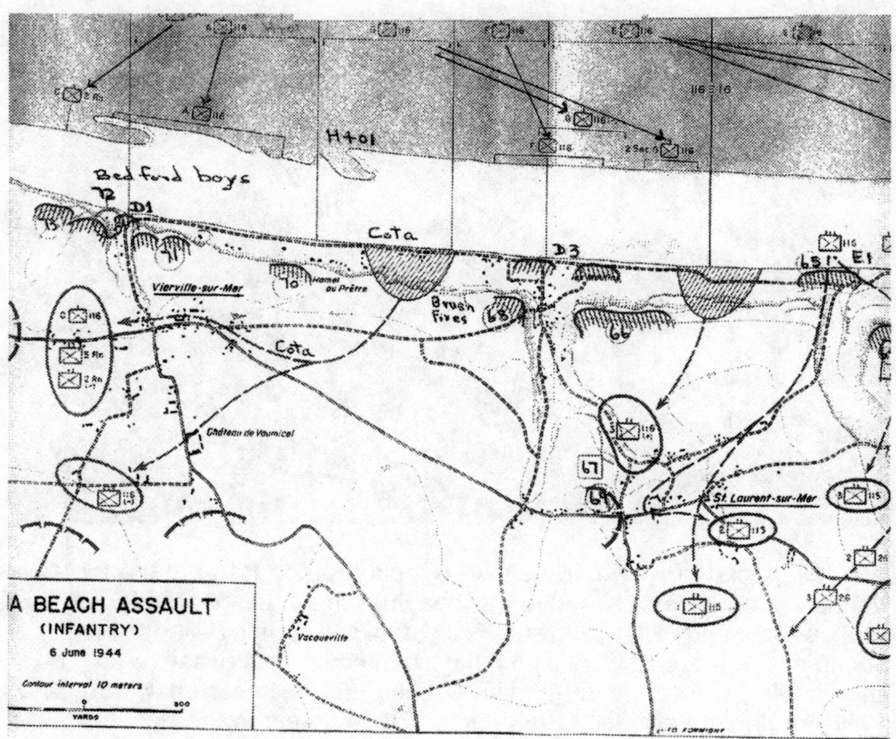

Map 1: Omaha Beach West End

Pointe et Raz de la Percee

(Visible 2 kilometers west of OMAHA Beach from the beach coast road.)

Aerial reconnaissance and the French underground confirmed there were no artillery batteries on Pointe de la Percee but there were machine gun and mortar nests within range of OMAHA Beach and the incoming landing craft. Neutralizing these threats was assigned to C Company, 2nd Ranger Battalion landing on "Charlie Beach"

Two platoons (64 men) in two landing craft landed 300 meters west of the Vierville draw at 6:45 a.m. Coming in, an antitank gun bracketed Captain Ralph E. Goranson's craft killing twelve of his men. Machine gun nests on the beach and on the slope of the bluff took casualties as the ramps dropped. The second craft under Lieutenant Sid Solomon lost 15 men. More fell as the rangers scurried across the shallows to the base of the 35-meter (100-foot) high cliffs. Only 30 of the original 64 remained to seize their objectives along the cliff top. First Lieutenant William D. Moody and two men went further west three 300 meters where a crevice in the cliff face gave them a chance to climb to the top using their bayonets for successive hand holds. Undaunted that they were in a minefield they dropped rope lines down to the beach. In spite of machine gun fire Moody and a ranger then crawled east along the cliff edge until they were above C Company. Moody shouted down directions to the ropes. All the rangers were on the top by 7:30. By good luck a landing craft of B Company, 116th Regiment had gone astray and landed on the beach below the rangers. They joined the rangers doubling their force.

Lieutenant Sid Solomon's platoon of 37 men had only nine left. The landscape was a maze of communication trenches interconnecting the machine gun and mortar nests leading to the Vierville draw. Overlooking the area a hundred meters back from the cliff edge was the ruins of a house assumed to be fortified. With the ruins as an objective and knowing mines were covering the approaches the rangers moved forward through the German trenches. A bullet through the eye killed the second platoon leader, Bill Moody, as he sat next to Sid Solomons in a shell hole. The rangers quick on the trigger surprised the defenders as they moved towards the fortified ruins. This the first close hand to hand fighting on OMAHA Beach carried the battle for the rangers. The ruins, not fortified, were occupied (visible today). Several machine gun nests and an 80mm mortar pit were taken. Inside the mortar pit photographs of the area were posted around the 360-degree circumference with the elevations premarked to allow the mortar crew to fire blind around their perimeter. German reinforcements continued to enter the battle from the Vierville draw communication trench. It was not until late afternoon that the area was completely secured. The 116th Infantry section had only suffered two losses of their original 31 men. The rangers had lost 53 men and Germans 69. This small, day long battle however had distracted Wiederstandsnest (Resistance Nests) Nos. 73 and 72 (per the German fortification map) from firing onto the beach and into the Vierville draw.

Captain Goranson sent a squad west to Pointe et Raz de la Percee to eliminate German artillery observers whom throughout the day had directed inland batteries shelling the beachfront and telephoning their encouraging eyewitness accounts to headquarters. The German officer, Colonel Goth, out on the point was so optimistic in his 8-9 a.m. reports that the German 7th Army declined accepting a transfer of the 346th Infantry Division from the 15th Army. Further information at 11:00 from Goth convinced Generalleutnant Dietrich Kraiss, Commander of the 352nd Division, that he was dealing with an inferior force on OMAHA and diverted his reserves eastward to counter the British advances from GOLD Beach towards Bayeux. There was justification for Kraiss' evaluation. At noon, Lieutenant General Bradley at his headquarters on the heavy cruiser Augusta contemplated withdrawing from OMAHA to divert the force to the US UTAH Beach and the British GOLD Beach.

Along this narrow "Charlie" (codename) beach is the remains of a Mulberry, part of the portable port floated across the channel from England, now incorporated into a fishing pier with a small stone marker and plaque commemorating the D-Day landing of the 58th Armored Field Artillery Battalion.

Vierville Draw (Exit D1) to les Moulins (Exit D3)

The beach assaulted stretches from here eastward to the cliffs seven kilometers (4 miles) in the distance. The greatly improved coast road only covers a third of the distance. The eastern two thirds is readily viewed from the American Cemetery elevation from where paths lead to the beach and several intact German resistance nests.

The Exit D1 here and Exit E3, 4.5 kilometers (2 miles), were the most strongly defended. Across the valley here was a concrete wall. On the top of the bluffs dominating the draw and beach were three concrete/trenches resistance nests. Atop the beach seawall (still present) was a 75mm gun, in a concrete emplacement, aimed to fire along the beach. Two hundred meters out began the four rows of wood and steel obstacles tipped with mines, exposed at low tide but efficiently destructive on boats and humans on the rising tide that morning. At the high water mark was a wood and masonry seawall that varied in height from 2-3 meters as it ran the length of the beach next to the road.

The H-Hour assault was carried out initially by 16 tanks of B Company, 743rd Tank Battalion. Although amphibious they did not swim in but stayed on their LCTs (Landing Craft Tank) to the beach. During the run in German artillery fire sank one LCT. Eight tanks sank including all officers but one. The remaining eight commenced firing from the water's edge.

A few minutes later the seven LCVPs (Landing Craft Vehicle Personnel) of A Company, 116th Infantry Regiment and three LCMs (Landing Craft Mechanized) of the 146th Special Engineer Task Force came in. Today the National Guard Monument for the 116th Regiment (Virginia National Guard), previously the famous Stonewall Brigade of the Confederate States Army, stands shadowing their landing point.

There was little opposition until the landing craft ramps dropped. The water depth varied from waist deep to over a man's head. As if on signal the ramps dropping brought German automatic fire into the landing craft. The infantry filing out plan became chaotic. Men were crumbling and dying in the boats. Over the sides they jumped seeking shelter under the water. Drowning became the issue. Water soaked and weighted with guns and ammo they struggled out of their equipment. Those that made it to the beach were caught in the machine gun crossfire and a rapidly rising ride. They returned to the beach obstacles or stayed submerged in the water. B Company was landing. More men, more death, and very few places to seek shelter from the intense machine gunfire. Men on the beach burrowed into the sand and stayed put until the tide enveloped them. Within 10 minutes A Company had become inert, leaderless, and incapable of action. Almost all the officers were dead. As the men moved closer to the seawall they became larger targets. On one boat all 30 men were killed before getting to the sea wall. Personal survival from bullets or drowning was the objective of every man. Bodies floating in with the tide became the shields as their buddies pushed them ahead towards the sea wall.

The men of A Company were all pals. They came from Bedford, Virginia, a town of 3,000 people that lost 23 men here that morning. Two pairs of brothers died. A third pair, twins, one was killed the other wounded. The situation along the length of OMAHA mirrored Vierville. Men died by the hundreds. The living were stunned and in shock.

All along the beach the enemy had taken its toll. The German resistance nests at the mouth of each draw with more firepower created proportionally more casualties. The flotsam of the rising tide was boat debris, discarded equipment, flotation belts, bodies, and pieces of the dismembered dead.

Slowly, throughout the morning engineers cleared paths through the obstacles opening the routes for more men and equipment. Navy destroyers came into the shallows for close fire support. Bulldozers arrived clearing paths through the minefields, pushing aside obstacles and barbed wire. With the infantrymen's equipment came mine detectors, bangalore torpedoes, heavy machine guns and light artillery. As German machine gun nests were overpowered the fire onto the beach diminished. The concrete wall blocking the draw was blown up. Bradley on the USS Augusta ordered the twelve 16 inch guns to fire on the resistance nests. The large shells, slow enough to be visible, sounding like express trains, targeted the concrete pillboxes.

By 2 p.m. the Germans firing onto the beach (codename Dog Green) had been eliminated. Those Germans in positions along the draw's slopes were then under attack from the beach, Vierville, and the top of the eastern slope. Not until mid-afternoon was the road cleared to Vierville.

Casualties on the beach averaged one per every 2 meters (6 feet). It was difficult to step between the dead and wounded. The bodies floated in and out with the tide. Fresh troops drew apprehensive as their craft passed through the human remains. Millions of green and blue jellyfish are remembered by the veterans of that morning, floating in the red bloodied waters.

Absolute numbers for casualties are inaccurate however the generally accepted number is 2,000 killed, wounded and missing.

Hamel-au-Petre

East of Exit D1, on the right, stands a stone marker commemorating the first US cemetery in France in WW II. The cemetery was opened for a brief period for internment of the D-Day casualties. The St. Laurent Cemetery overlooking OMAHA was commenced as soon as the Germans withdrew. A steady stream of jeeps transported the D-Day remains from the temporary beach cemetery up the St. Laurent Draw (D-3) to the cemetery.

This area of the beach was code named Dog White. Prior to the German occupation in 1940 the beach road serviced ninety summer homes located between the road and bluff. All but seven were razed to open lines of fire. The remaining were fortified with concrete machine gun emplacements in the basements. One building still remained as a home and store from where Michael Hardelay, a 31 year old lawyer, was able to observe the developing fortifications which he passed along to the allies through the French underground.

As successive assault waves approached and saw the casualties and chaos on Dog Green beach they shifted east to areas less dangerous. This stretch, Dog White, was assaulted by C Company of the 5th Ranger Battalion who originally planned to land at Exit D1 and move west to relieve the rangers on Pointe du Hoc. At 7:30 a.m. Brigadier General Norman "Dutch" Cota the 29th Division Assistant Commander and Colonel D. W. Canham the 116th Regiment Commander also landed here as did an Army-Navy Special Engineer Task Force. The engineers cleared a gap through the beach obstacles with 40% casualties. At the seawall Cota said "rangers lead the way". This phrase has carried forward and is now today's official Ranger motto when saluting a superior officer. The rangers blew gaps in the barbed wire covering the beach road, crossed the 200 meters to the base of the bluff. Grass fires along the bluff in this area concealed their action as they worked their way to the top. By 8:30 they had overrun the German trenches and rifle pits along the crest.

Andre Farine, of the French Resistance living near Grandchamp, identified 300 German resistance nests and numerous minefields in the OMAHA area. From this intelligence the Americans were able to use four of the five unmanned paths across the plateau above the beach. This information reduced losses and sped up their movement from the beach inland.

In the afternoon the battle here had moved inland. A mile out to sea was dotted with scores of tanks and trucks, their crews trapped and drowned in watery graves, destroyed landing craft sunken or blown on their sides, jeeps embedded in the sand. On the beach were the burned hulks of mobile equipment, bulldozers without tracks, cranes tipped over, half tracks spilling out their headquarter contents of typewriters, file cabinets, tables and chairs. Communication wire, like black spaghetti draped itself over and through the debris. LSTs and LCVPs damaged and abandoned were stacked on the beach by the record-breaking 7-meter (20-foot) rising ride. Here and there amongst the scrap were neat piles of shells, rifles, machine guns and telephone wire. A few supplies had managed to arrive safely. The carnage defied imagination.

Atop the bluff a tent hospital had sprung up. Also, a guarded barbed wire enclosure for the accumulating prisoners.

<u>les Moulins</u> – the easterly end of the coast road.

Here the road turns south up through the draw to St. Laurent-sur-Mer. This was designated as Exit D3 and the beach west and east of the draw was codenamed Dog Red and Easy Green respectively. Four lines of water obstacles were in the high and low tide area. A machine gun/riflemen trench surrounded with barbed wire ran parallel and adjacent to the beach A fortified, large three story villa at the edge dominating the beach was incorporated into the trench line. The beach itself was shingle i.e. small round stones that spun under the treads of tracked vehicles. A hundred meters behind the road ran a five meter wide, four meter deep zigzagging antitank ditch running the full width of the draw broken in two places to allow the defenders access to the beach edge trenches. Concrete blocks and walls throughout the flat area acted as tank obstacles and defenders shields. Topping the two bluff crests were Resistance Nests 68 and 66, firing trenches surrounded by barbed wire and minefields. The flat ground and slope east of the exit road was mined.

The grass along the west side bluff was burning and producing westerly blowing smoke. Sixteen tanks of A Company, 743rd Tank Battalion in four LCTs preceded the infantry. Regardless, F Company (116th Regiment) took severe losses on Dog Red beach in front of the fortified villa. The second wave twenty minutes later had similar experiences. On Easy Green beach, just east of the draw road, G Company made it to the low seawall successfully but took heavy losses crossing the flat ground. 116th Regiment Companies L, I, K and sections of G and F landed 800 meters east of the draw, climbed the bluff and moved to St. Laurent by noon.

At the fortified villa, the 2nd Battalion (116th Regiment) Commander, Major Sidney V. Bingham, set up his command post and organized the successful taking of the exit defenses (awarded the Distinguished Service Cross).

A few hours later Major General Charles Gerhardt (29th Division) set up his headquarters at the mouth of the draw and Major General Clarence Huebner (1st Division) established his headquarters in the draw in the large home, at the second bend on the east side of the road.

Lieutenant General Omar Bradley (1st Army Group Commander) and Major General Leonard Gerow (5th Corps Commander) met in the home June 7. Bradley had disembarked at the next exit (E1) and hitchhiked over.

There is a memorial with commemorative plaques to the 1st and 29th Division combat teams at Exit D3 at the junction of Dog Red and Easy Green beaches. On the pillbox is a memorial to the 6th Engineer Special Brigade.

Draw D3 and St. Laurent-sur-Mer

Ascending the draw at the second curve on the east is the large home that was 1st Division headquarters for a short period. The crest of the bluff opposite, on the west side, was Resistance Nest 67 (taken by Russell Stover, K/116th) consisting of firing trenches covering the adjacent pathway east and north to the beach. The draw road, developed by the Americans, was only a farm path June 6. As the 116th Regiment companies moved across the plateau east of the draw towards St. Laurent, they received flank fire from this resistance nest. Two platoons descended from the plateau, moved past the large home, crossed the road and climbed the slope to silence the nest.

That evening the three companies (116th Regiment) held the draw and the buildings on the north side of St. Laurent. The town was taken by the 115th Regiment. The road D514 between St. Laurent and Colleville-sur-Mer (2.5 kilometers east) became the front line. German Resistance Nest 69 at the St. Laurent crossroads stopped westward movement. The land between St. Laurent and Vierville (3 kilometers west) was still in German hands.

Two days later, when the area was clear, in the fields southeast and adjacent to St. Laurent Emergency Landing Strip (A-12C) for medical evacuation of the wounded was developed. A meter deep dry ditch bisected the field. As no culverts were available the bulldozers contoured the ditch into the runway leaving a slight depression in the runway. The ELS was started on D+2 and completed the following day. This became the first American airfield in France and developed to become the most important. Over the first six weeks of operation it averaged 100 C-47 cargo planes per day not including a damaged B17 that landed, was repaired and took off to England a few days after the airfield was completed. By D-Day + 90 days there were 48 American and 45 British airfields in Normandy.

Picture 10: Omaha Beach and Bluffs - Looking West
February 22, 1949

The plateau is 150 feet above sea level. It is several hundred yards from the high tide line to the foot of the sloping bluffs. The beach obstructions were removed shortly after D-day. Five valleys (identified as D1, D3, E1, E3 and F1 not shown) run through the plateau down to the beach. German concrete pillboxes still abound along the bluffs and along the valley walls. The heaviest fighting with the highest casualties occurred when our troops landed at the mouth of these fortified valleys. The development of the US Normandy Cemetery can be seen in the center.

9.3 The US Cemetery and the Eastern Beachhead

St. Laurent US Cemetery

Travel east from St. Laurent-sur-Mer on D514 1.5 kilometers towards Colleville-sur-Mer. There is signage to the cemetery located 0.8 kilometers north.

The cemetery land, donated by the people of France, is a magnificent memorial to the fallen providing a vantage point to view the eastern half of the D-Day assault beaches not readily toured by car.

The 172-acre site was chosen because of its historical importance overlooking OMAHA Beach. The cemetery receives 1.3 million visitors annually.

Construction commenced June 8. After the war re-internments from temporary wartime Normandy cemeteries were made here and in the St. James Cemetery (Brittany). The cemetery contains 9,386 burials, 307 of who are unknown. Over 14,000 remains were returned to the United States.

Medal of Honor recipients' headstones are lettered in gold, for example, Brigadier General Theodore Roosevelt (Plot D, Row 28, Grave 45), July 12, 1944. His youngest brother Quentin, a World War I pilot, killed in France, July 14, 1918, has been re-interned next to him. A father and son, Colonel Ollie Reed (E-20-19) and Ollie Reed, Junior, lie next to each other. Thirty-two pairs of brothers and four women: (Red Cross nurse and WACS) Mary Bankston, Pfc., D-20-19; Dolores Brown, Sgt., F-13-19; Mary Barlow, Pfc, A-19-30; and nurse Elizabeth Richardson, A-21-5, are buried here.

Just inside the entrance, right side, is buried a time capsule containing sealed reports of the landings to be opened June 4, 2044.

Behind the semi-circle colonnade memorial is the "Garden of the Missing", a wall listing the names of 1,557 missing with no known graves.

Overlooking the beach are several orientation tables describing the D-Day actions on the beach. A path leads down to the shore creating the opportunity to stand at the water's edge and face the German defenses as did a battalion of the 16th Regiment on D-Day morning.

The cemetery is situated between the beach Exit E1, 500 meters west and Exit E3, 700 meters east. Directly ahead, is beach Easy Red and to the east are Fox Green and Fox Red beaches, the latter running under the cliff face. On the crest of this bluff were three significant resistance nests firing into the draws and onto the beach. Many entrenched Germans along this ridge took American lives now buried a few meters away.

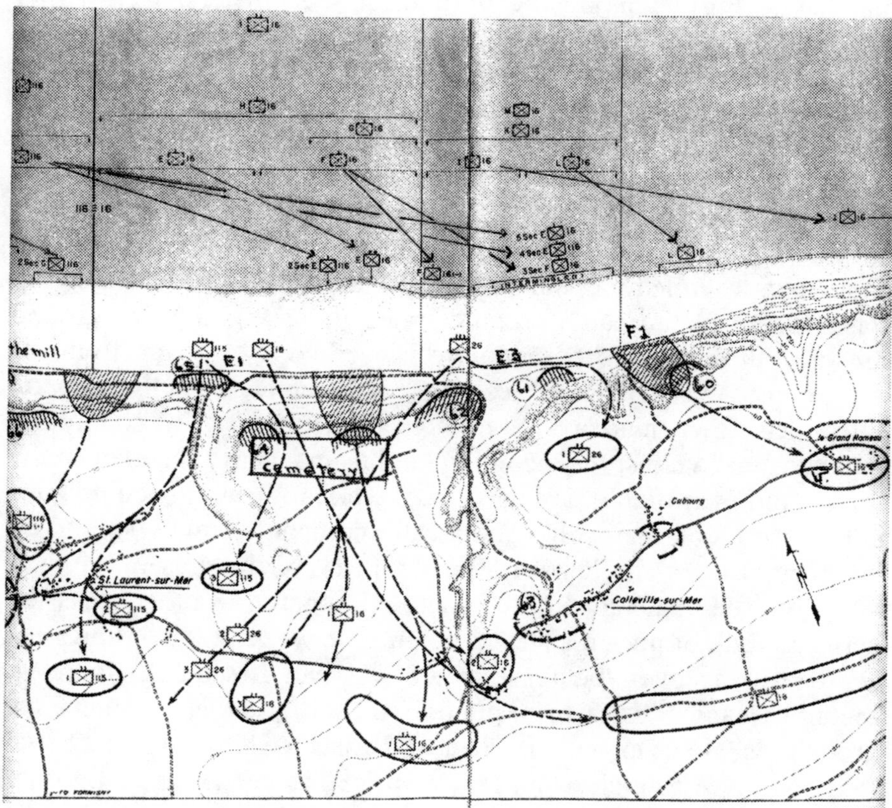

Map 2: Omaha Beach East End

<u>Easy Red Beach and Exit E1 Draw</u>

The E1 draw was merely an undeveloped path and a stream, the Ruquet River. Ascending, the valley narrows. The overhanging trees created a tunnel.

The defenses here as at the other exits were formidable. In the water were rows of stakes and hedgehogs. Shingle between the water and land was an additional obstacle to rubber tired and tracked vehicles coming in on LCTs and LCMs. Across the valley mouth ran a 600-meter zigzag antitank ditch 6 meters wide. Resistance Nest 65 consisting of trenches surrounding a concrete pillbox lay at the foot of the western slope. High up, 50 meters on the eastern shoulder, Resistance Nest 64 with a 76mm howitzer and machine gun emplacement fired down on the attackers approaching Nest 65 across the draw. Further along the bluff crest, 500 meters, were firing trenches to stop a thrust up the slope should the attackers cross the beach and flat ground.

The first assault wave intended to land in front of Exit E1, however, the east running tide carried most of the boats 1,200 meters (3/4 of a mile) further east. G Company (16th Regiment) and tanks of the 741st Tank Battalion did land on target between Exits E1 and E3 on the beach below the cemetery bluff. The company lost a third of its men between leaving the boats and the shoreline. The follow-up waves suffered the same casualty rate. Crossing the flat ground strewn with mines and barbed wire proved costly. Firing from the bluff's crest and the Exit E3 resistance nests created deadly crossfire as the men slowly maneuvered through the obstacles. The enemy fire from the bluff against the incoming landing craft gave the men on the flat ground identifiable targets. The American heavy machine guns and mortars took their toll. The assault company slowly worked up the slope along a single path 50 meters east of the present winding path from the cemetery to the beach. Compared to other areas the Germans did not put up a strong defense between the two draws. G Company was over the crest by 0830. 2nd Lieutenant John M. Spauling leading a 23-man platoon moved west along the crest through four fields to get to the rear of Resistance Nest 64 firing down on Exit E1. Although caught by surprise the defenders stubbornly resisted for several hours. Several died and 21 were captured. The Americans had no casualties.

The path up the slope was heavily used that morning. Troops along the beach embankment funneled themselves to this relatively safe corridor. Colonel George Taylor, Commander of the 16th Infantry Regiment set up his headquarters along the path below the crest. Colonel Taylor is remembered for cajoling his troops to move off the beach by shouting to his stagnated force, "Two kinds of people are staying on this beach, the dead and those who are going to die – now let's get the hell out of here".

On June 7 engineers graded a road from the beach, up to the cemetery that ran diagonally from the flats near Exit E1 to the mid-point of the crest between E1 and E3.

Fifth Corps headquarters was established on the E1 draw road June 7. The road was under construction when Lieutenant General Omar Bradley landed on Easy Red beach. Not finding Major General Leonard Gerow at his headquarters, Bradley hitched a ride over to 1st Division headquarters in the D3 draw. Passing through St. Laurent he was encouraged to see engineering bulldozers clearing the Emergency Landing Strip to handle the wounded.

There were two Roosevelts, father and son, on the D-Day beaches in the assault waves. Brigadier General Teddy Roosevelt, Assistant Commander, 4th Infantry Division on UTAH beach, and Captain Quentin Roosevelt, 25, 1st Division, here on Easy Red beach. Brigadier Roosevelt, son of President Teddy Roosevelt, was the oldest and most senior officer to land in the assault waves. He died of a heart attack July 12.

On the German bunker, part way up the west side slope, facing the beach, is a 2nd Infantry Division memorial and a Provisional Engineers Special Brigade plaque. The bunker was in the Resistance Nest 65 complex.

Fox Green Beach and Exit E3 Draw

The area can be viewed from the cemetery. A path leads down to the Fox Green beach or from Colleville a road descends the E3 draw to the beach.

The landings here were very costly in human life in the same magnitude as at Vierville draw. Defenses as at the other exits were strong. A 7-meter wide and 600-meter long zigzag antitank ditch 50 meters from the water edge protected the draw's opening. The western shoulder of the bluff, Resistance Nest 62, stretched from the bottom to the top of the slope. (Recently cleared and re-exposed for visitors). Along the base of the eastern bluff lay Resistance Nest 61. Mines and barbed wire were abundant. The pathway up the draw became a tunnel of foliage as the path ascended and narrowed. Engineers started the present road D-Day afternoon. All the draws and additional routes engineered became supply roads for many months.

The incoming tide and easterly current disrupted the timetable and landing sequence. Boats that were to land 2 kilometers to the west came in with boats that should have been one kilometer west. Those that should have landed here were further east. The mixed companies from different regiments and divisions had a smooth run in until the ramps dropped and machine gun crisscross fire caught the troops disembarking. E and F Companies of the 16th and 116th Regiments took severe casualties getting to the shingle. Of three boats (93 men) only 60 made it to dry land. In another boat, the men stepped into neck deep water, lost 17 of the 31 men within five minutes. In one boat section of 31 men, only seven made it ashore. Just two officers in F Company survived. Along the beach a third of the forces'strength was lost before reaching the waters' edge. E Company (16th Regiment) lost 105 men in the water or on the tidal flats. The 116th Regiment, E Company far from its planned landing, came in with four boats. Three of the sections lost 30 men immediately upon leaving the landing craft. The company commander Captain Laurence A. Madill, twice wounded while helping his men in the water, received a fatal third shot but cried "Senior noncom, take the men off the beach" before dying.

The situation at 10 a.m. was so desperate the 1st Division Commander, Major General Clarence Huebner ordered the destroyers to move in close to shore and shell the resistance nests with point blank fire regardless of American casualties. The bombardment slowly turned the tide of battle. The navy shells exploded mines, destroyed barbed wire, creating paths and shell holes for cover. The German fire onto the beach diminished. Successive waves took fewer casualties arriving in planned sequence with the needed equipment. A half-track on the shingle with its 50-caliber machine gun firing into a cement pillbox embrasure effectively ricocheted the bullets inside silencing the 88mm gun.

The Germans' resistance was overcome by noon. Troops moved up the draw and across the plateaus. Engineers cleared the mines. In Colleville and along the D514 road to St. Laurent the Germans were reforming their land front.

The E3 draw was opened for vehicle traffic at 4 p.m. Three hours later the first US tanks and tank destroyers ascended the road. On the pillbox, in Resistance Nest 62, is a monument to the 5th Engineer Special Brigade who landed at 8 a.m. and while under fire cleared paths through the beach obstacles. Later, still under fire they started opening the E3 draw road for vehicular traffic.

A second monument, an obelisk and seat, up the slope is a 1st Infantry Division (Big Red One) memorial on which are inscribed the names of the division's men who died June 6 to July 24.

In Colleville, the 16th Regiment waged a house to house battle all afternoon. The regiment, depleted from the grueling beach assault, needed reinforcements to face the fresh Germans that had now entered the battle. Colleville was the German's eastern anchor to their newly formed defense line. The American advances south and east soon diminished the village's significance. By dusk only a few German holdouts remained. As a rearguard they fought under orders with no tactical value. The following dawn finalized their fight.

Anne Marie Broexkz, 19 years old, then a kindergarten teacher in Bayeux, pedaled back to her home between Colleville and the beach June 6 morning amid the din of the battle. She married PFC Leo Leroux and opened and auto driving school in Bayeux.

The Colleville church tower, a German observation post, was destroyed by three direct hits D-Day morning.

Fox Red Beach and Exit F1

Seven hundred meters east of the Exit E3 draw a footpath ascended the 50-meter slope then forked to the villages of Cabourg and le Grand Hameau. The beach east of the path becomes a cliff with a narrow band of shingle. Two-thirds up and adjacent to the path was Resistance Nest 60 containing a 75mm howitzer, not under concrete, and numerous machine gun nests interconnected by deep communication trenches. Mines and barbed wire covered the 75 meters between the high water mark and the base of the cliff.

L Company, 16th Regiment, landed east of the path along the base of the cliff at 7 a.m. Of the company's six LCVP, one had floundered off shore losing 8 men. Shellfire fell amongst the landing craft caused light casualties. An empty craft was destroyed as it prepared to return to the troop ship. The low tide left 200 meters of exposed beach to cross. Machine guns trained on the flats exacted more casualties. Reduced to 125 men it was, however, one of only eight companies across OMAHA that were still organized to operate as a company after crossing the tidal beach. The company commander was killed before their assault on the pathway (Exit F1) commenced. 1st Lieutenant Robert B. Cutler, Jr. took command. Two tanks to the west gave fire support as three sections climbed the path. The heavy brush of the slope hid their ascent from the Germans in the resistance nest to their left. At the top two sections faced south while one section prepared to attack the nest from the rear. I Company reinforced L Company. Naval and tank fire was called in on the Germans. Men of I and K Companies were in place along the path. The support fire was lifted and the attack launched from below. Handgrenades and satchel charges subdued the resistance. Thirty-one prisoners, half of them wounded, were moved off to a prison cage. The area was cleared by 9 a.m. The 3rd Battalion moved off southeast to le Grand Hameau (1.5 kilometers) that it occupied and secured D-Day night. The 26th Regiment secured the plateau around the top of F-1 draw with its 1st Battalion that night. Engineering bulldozers commenced work immediately readying the "path" for vehicular traffic June 7.

On the beach, at the foot of the Exit F1 "path" is a memorial to the 2nd Armored Division (Hell on Wheels) and the 749th Armored Battalion.

The area north of Colleville became an active airfield (Terminal A-22C) July 18. The channel storm of June 19-22 showed how vulnerable the supply sea link could be. The 816th Engineering Command Battalion commenced construction June 30 of an airfield that could accommodate heavy supply planes. The ground had to be firm, hard packed, and the 1,200-meter runway be of heavy gauge pierced steel plank. Once started the ground was found to have soft spots and PSP (pierced steel plank) from England was in short supply. The obstacles were overcome bringing the strip into use later than anticipated. The aircraft hardstand also of SMT (square meshed track) was 700 meters by 200 meters.

9.4 Pointe-du-Hoc

(6 kilometers west of OMAHA Beach, on D514. Or, 22 kilometers northwest of Bayeux via N13 to Longueville, 18 kilometers. North on D125, 5 kilometers to D514, then west 2 kilometers)

The American Monuments Commission maintains Pointe-du-Hoc. The battle site retains its character of 1944 although the addition of grass and erosion around the craters has diminished its starkness.

Pre-invasion allied intelligence had assessed the presence of a six 155mm gun battery with a 17 kilometer range housed inside concrete bunkers which threatened the invasion fleet, OMAHA Beach, 6 kilometers east, and UTAH Beach, 14 kilometers to the northwest. The battery had to be neutralized as quickly as possible in the early hours of the invasion. The battery was bombed April 15, May 22 and June 4. Post war analysis indicates there were only two unfinished casements capable of accommodating 122 mm guns which had been diverted to Cherbourg harbor defenses. Telephone poles, under camouflage netting disguised the non lethal battery.. Andre Farine, the café owner in Letanville (3 kilometers southwest), in seeking wood for baking would visit M. Fouche's farm overlooking the Pointe du Hoc battery site and secure intelligence he transmitted to England. He discovered the German ruse but the ships had sailed under radio silence. His own observations and what he gleaned from the labor building the Atlantic Wall while eating in his café saved many lives. He was awarded the Croix de Guerre.

The 8th Air Force bombers cautiously held their bomb loads a few seconds longer to avoid hitting the assault wave. The bombs landed harmlessly inland. At 6 a.m. the battleships Arkansas and Texas commenced their bombardment. Before lifting their shelling a half-hour later they had fired 600 12 to 14 inch shells. The 10,000 tons of explosives equaled the destructive power of the atomic bomb on Hiroshima. One battleship shell exploded inside an empty bunker collapsing the rear wall.

The plan called for the 2nd Ranger Battalion (Companies D, E and F) to land east and west of the Pointe at 6:30 a.m. The rangers, using British LCPs (Landing Craft Personnel) manned by British coxswain had one of their 10 boats swamped shortly after leaving the mother ship. The company commander and platoon were rescued but returned to England. A 20mm cannon shell fired from the cliff top sank one of the four DUKWS (amphibious truck). In error the coxswains had headed for Pointe de la Percee, 5 kilometers east. Colonel James Earl Rudder seeing the error ordered a course change that brought the 9 landing craft, 3 DUKWs and one supply boat (a second had swamped) back to Pointe-du-Hoc along a route paralleling the coastline. A German machine gun nest on the cliff edge 300 meters east of the Pointe raked the passing attack force. All the craft landed east of the point forty minutes late and long after the USS Texas bombardment had lifted. (The delay caused the reinforcement 5th Ranger Battalion to believe the rangers on the Pointe had not been successful and diverted to OMAHA Beach.) The Germans rushed to the cliff edge firing and throwing hand grenades down on the invaders. Two navy destroyers, the HMS Talybout and the USS Satterlee moved in close firing their machine guns and antiaircraft pompom guns into the German ranks. From the landing craft grappling hooks with rope ladders attached were fired to the top of the 35-meter high cliffs. Many of the ladders heavy with seawater fell short. On each hook a burning fuse terrorized the Germans attempting to cut the attached rope. From one of the DUKWs a ladder borrowed from the London Fire Department rose to overview the cliff top. Sergeant Bill Stivinson with his machine gun climbed the ladder. The DUKWs unsteadiness on the rocky beach combined with Stivinson's weight caused the ladder to sway back and forth 45 degrees. Each time the sway brought Stivinson past the cliff top he fired on the Germans along the edge.

Within five minutes a number of rangers had climbed to the top. In another ten minutes the remaining 120 of Rudder's 225 men were slithering over the edge and into the welcome protective shell craters. The platoons moved off to seize their pre-assigned bunkers ignoring the machine guns and four barrel 50mm fire from the large strongpoint to the west. Determining they had captured empty bunkers containing only telephone poles the rangers moved south to D514. Although the bunkers had been taken the battery area was still not cleared. The enemy would unpredictably appear from their elaborate tunnel structures, fire a burst from an automatic weapon or throw a grenade then disappear. The machine gun east of the Pointe that had harassed the landing craft now poured fire over the heads of the rangers in the shell holes. The navy and army fire control team had been knocked out with a short shell and the radios damaged. A visual Morse code blink light signaled the USS Satterlee to knock out the machine gun nest. A few rounds tumbled the nest and occupants down the cliff face onto the beach. No one survived.

Colonel Rudder himself wounded set up his battalion headquarters in a large shell hole near the still active German strongpoint and observation post. It was overcome when fuel was poured into the exhaust ventilators and ignited consuming the oxygen and asphyxiating many of the occupants.

The intact battery bunker nearest the point became the medic's aid station. The Germans had pulled back south of D514. The rangers set up defenses. Sergeant Leonard Lomell and Jack Kuhn followed a dirt road south (now the entrance driveway). Two hundred and fifty meters south of D514, in an orchard, they found six 122mm howitzers and ammunition unmanned. This was a mobile battery in training and unrelated to the Pointe du Hoc position.

The German gun crews had cautiously pulled away from their ammo dump. The Americans blew up the ammo, destroyed several guns and incapacitated the remaining gunsites. For their aggressive actions Lommell received the Distinguished Service Cross and Kuhn the Silver Star.

By 9 a.m., in less than two hours, the rangers had achieved their objectives. Only 50 of the original 200 were still standing. A request for reinforcements was minimally answered. Three misdropped 101st Airborne Division paratroopers found their way into Rudder's lines. 20 rangers from the 5th Battalion were ferried over from OMAHA Beach. The Germans counterattacked from the west, twice in the afternoon and three times that evening. Rudders force of 90 men were squeezed back to a 200-meter defense arc around the point. The next day 23 more returned on the landing craft ferrying wounded to OMAHA. German attacks persisted. The defending German 1st Battalion, 914th Regiment, 352nd Division was tough and experienced. Throughout June 7 a sizeable force of troops from OMAHA Beach moved west along the axis of D514 arriving in the St. Pierre-du-Mont hamlet (1 kilometer southeast) by evening.

Colonel Rudder's force was relieved at noon, June 8, by the 2nd and 3rd Battalions of the 116th Regiment, elements of the 5th Ranger

Battalion, and two companies of the 743rd Tank Battalion. The tanks came up the access road to today's parking lot positioning themselves between the Germans to the west and Rudder's men on the northern tip.

Within hours of its capture the orchard that contained the six-gun battery became FUSAGH (1st US Army Group Headquarters) under Lieutenant General Omar Bradley. The exact location is the thinned out orchard northeast and adjacent to Criqueville. Construction on Advanced Landing Grounds, A-1, Ste. Pierre-du-Mont (1 kilometer east) and A-2 Criqueville (2 kilometers south) commenced on June 9th and 10th respectively by the 9th Engineer Command. Both fields became active within a few days for fighter support and wounded evacuation.

Today the observation post on the cliff edge is intact with a minor structural addition. An obelisk memorial to the 2nd Ranger Battalions stands on the fortification complex. Several bunkers are but giant blocks of concrete blown apart in the barrage. A few of the communication trenches are visible. Underground, the ammunition pushcart railroad still exists including a large turntable.

Colonel Rudder was awarded the Distinguished Service Cross. He returned several times to anniversary events before passing away.

General visited the site in 1963 in preparation for the 1964 20th Anniversary events.

"The Longest Day" movie was filmed here. Tommy Sands was filmed throwing a satchel charge into the observation post through the seaward side slit.

As a small unit action site Pointe-du-Hoc is exemplary of success in the face of bad luck and adversity. Although the effort appeared fruitless it must be recognized that the Germans engaged here were unavailable to reinforce the defenses at OMAHA.

Picture 11: Pointe du Hoc - Looking South Today

The guns housed in cement casements were a major threat to the invasion forces off Omaha and Utah Beaches. Bombing had not destroyed these positions. Companies D, E and F of Colonel James Rudder's 2nd Ranger Battalion landed at the base of the cliffs at 7:00 AM. Hand grenades and machine gun bullets thwarted the Rangers climbing roper to the top. Of the 225 in the assault only 120 made it to the plateau. The casements were empty with only camouflaged telephone poles as decoys. The Rangers moved south to the coast road intersection discovering a six howitzer field battery. Sergeants Leonard Lommel and Jack Kuhn using thermite grenades demolished the firing and sighting mechanisms. German counterattacks compressed the Rangers back within 50 feet of the cliff face which they held until relieved by Omaha landed forces on D-day +2.

Chapter 10 UTAH-OMAHA Link-up

Two thirds of the width of the base of the Contentin Peninsula, where it joins the mainland, is below sea level at high tide. In Napoleon's time this unique topography had been incorporated into a plan to make the peninsula an island and Cherbourg on its northern shore a fortress port comparable to Britain's Gibraltar. Although the plan had never been realized, the defense potential of this geographical feature was fully appreciated by the Germans and the allies in 1944.

French engineers constructed dikes and canals to stop the sea from flooding the land on each tide. La Barquette Lock was built 125 years ago to regulate the rate of fresh water flow into the Bay of the Seine at low tide and the amount of seawater flooding at high tide.

The allied planners recognized that if they could seize and control the lock early in the invasion time table they could transform the low pasture land into a shallow salt lake stretching two thirds across the peninsula. With this accomplished, German reinforcements moving north into the peninsula to counterattack the American beachhead would have to funnel across the few narrow causeways traversing "the lake" under the eyes of the American artillery and air force. A blueprint of the lock was secured through the French underground.

A plan was developed and integrated into the invasion plan. U .S. paratroopers would seize the lock early D-Day morning, before it could be destroyed by a German demolition team. Its destruction would produce erratic and uncontrolled tidal flooding. It was expected that the Germans, recognizing its value, would fight tenaciously to hold it.

What the allied planners failed to realize was that the Douve River flow was not large and the twice daily tide flow would only flood during a short period at maximum tide. To create the desired salt lake would require more time than the mobility of the invasion plans or the rapid German counter measures would allow.

Applying similar logic the defenders reasoned that flooding would hamper allied invasion forces on the Contentin Peninsula moving south to attack across narrow, easily defended causeways. Therefore, both the defenders and the attackers believed that flooding the river valley was to their advantage. The allied aim had been achieved by the defenders.

The Germans started flooding the marshes with salt tidewater in 1942, completing the project by the fall of 1943, by which time the area was covered with three to four feet of saltwater.

Allied reconnaissance had identified the flooded Douve River but not recognized the flooding of its northern tributary, the Merderet River. The tall marsh grasses had camouflaged the water's presence and its depth. Today the broad river valleys are dry returned to their pre-war status as rich pastoral grazing lands interlaced with drainage ditches.

The plan called for seizing control of the causeways crossing the Douve River valley to prohibit German reinforcements from entering the UTAH Beachhead during the lodgment and buildup period.

OMAHA Beachhead forces, after developing its lodgment area, moved westward to link up with the forces from UTAH Beach who had advanced south across the Douve River valley and east to meet the OMAHA Beach forces. The narrow 10-kilometer corridor between Carentan and Isigny would be widened by the American forces pushing southward at the same time as they advanced towards their link-up.

In the meantime, the German efforts would be to keep the Americans from joining. Two south to north flowing rivers, the Taute and Vire, passed through the narrow Carentan-Isigny corridor further complicating the field tactics of both armies. The four years of occupation benefited the Germans with familiarity, defense positions and frequent battle exercises of numerous invasion scenarios.

10.1 La Barquette Lock

(la Barquette Lock is 2.5 kilometers directly north of Carentan. From Carentan take route N13 north 3 kilometers across the Carentan causeway over the broad Douve River valley. Turn east on D913, the road to Vierville and Ste. Marie-du-Mont. After passing over the Liberte Expressway (0.5 kilometers), take the next right, turn (south) to Bse de Addeville passing through the hamlet to the "T" junction. Turn right (west). The lock is 200 meters on the left (south side) across the pasture.) The lock and buildings are readily visible east of the Liberte Expressway as the highway crosses the Douve River lowlands.

The assignment of capturing and holding the lock was given to the 501st Regiment (101st US Airborne Division) under the command of Colonel H.R. "Skeets" Johnson. Following the successful completion of their first objective elements were to hold the lock while the regiment seized the four bridges on the Carentan causeway (1.5 kilometers to the west) and the elevated railway crossing the Douve River 1 kilometer west of the highway causeway.

In the early hours of D-Day the regiment parachuted into the area north of la Barquette Lock. Multiple factors caused the majority of the paratroopers to parachute into unfamiliar terrain. The regiment missed their Drop Zone D and were scattered over a broad area. Throughout the dark hours the paratroopers determined their locations and moved to their rendezvous point. By dawn, Colonel Johnson had collected only 150 men of his original 800. The others were either lost, linked up with other units or casualties. The reduced force proceeded south on its assignment. The Douve River and the smaller Madelaine River converge west of the lock. To control the river, it had been excavated to become the Carentan Canal. The lock controls the canal.

Johnson's force secured the north side of the lock without opposition. They could see German firepits and hutments 50 meters to the south beyond the lock. Four rifle platoons crossed the lock and after a brief skirmish established a defense perimeter on the south side. Having achieved its initial objective a force was directed to move west along the north edge of the marsh to seize the road causeway and its four bridges. (The Liberte Expressway passes between the lock and the causeway today). Determined German resistance between the lock and the causeway stopped the American advance. During the morning Colonel Johnson returned to Bse Addeville for reinforcements. At noon as the returning force was passing through the road "T" junction northeast of the lock, it came under 88 artillery and machine gun fire from the high ground around Ste. Come-du-Mont, 2.5 kilometers to the northwest. Lieutenant Farrell, the navy liaison officer, called in counterfire from the heavy cruiser USS Quincy, silencing the German guns.

The scattering and misdroppping of the two US Airborne Divisions (82nd and 101st) had created a serious situation. The paratroopers that had rendezvoused into sizable forces were deployed into key areas such as the beach exits and roads entering the battle zone. La Barquette Lock's position, although isolated, was the important southern flank. Three companies were holding an objective planned for three battalions. The force formed a defense perimeter along the canal banks. Throughout the remainder of D-Day concerted but unsuccessful westward thrusts to reach the causeway were attempted.

Around the lock the four rifle platoons with machine guns, created a hundred meter defense zone. The German defenders of the lock had been unenthusiastic. No German died defending the position on D-Day. That evening Major R.J. Allen brought in additional paratroopers from Bse Addeville.

Lack of reinforcements, supplies, and ammunition became serious to Johnson's force by the second day, June 7. A morning air force supply drop landed in German lines. At noon the position was almost bombed by the air force. The pilot veered off at the last moment after spotting the yellow identification flare.

Throughout the morning and afternoon 88mm artillery fire from Carentan, mortar fire from Ste. Come-du-Mont, and snipers along the northern perimeter caused increasing casualties making movement difficult.

At 2 p.m., German troops (1st Battalion of the 6th German Parachute Regiment) were observed approaching from the northeast. In anticipation of a German attack, Johnson established a six-machine gun strongpoint at the "T" junction in the north ditch immediately east of the road junction deploying riflemen in the field between the road and the river (became known as "Hell's Corner"). At 4 p.m. the

Americans opened fire on the Germans from 350 meters. They fell back seeking protective cover in the uneven water-soaked terrain. Artillery and mortar fire called in by the attackers blanketed the American position. Colonel Johnson, realizing the tenuous position he held and lacking enough ammunition for an extended battle, decided to try a bluff on his opponents. With an interpreter (Private L. E. Runge) and a trooper (Technician W. F. Lenz) Johnson crossed into no-mans land between the two forces and demanded the Germans surrender or be annihilated by the US firepower. The rouse worked! After a brief firefight, 350 Germans crossed the no-mans land into American captivity. Their casualties in the earlier skirmish had been 150 dead or seriously wounded. The American losses were 10 killed and 33 wounded. As the prisoners were marching along the road to the Peneme farm 0.5 kilometers east, an 88mm shell landed amongst them, killing 20 and wounding 12. Major Francis Carrell, the US surgeon was hard pressed for medical supplies. Shirts and farm linens became bandages, blood plasma was only available for the desperate cases.

In the late afternoon, German harassment fire decreased and successful supply drops temporarily eased the suffering until a US infantry detachment from the beach relieved the position.

Related stories are Brevands, 2.5 kilometers east and the Carentan causeway, 1.5 kilometers to the west.

Picture 12: la Barquette Lock - Looking North
August 13, 1947

German control of back flooding the lowlands behind Utah Beach and the Douve and Merderet River valleys was accomplished by opening and closing the lock gates at the appropriate times over a two year period. Colonel "Skeets" Johnson, commander of the 501st Regiment of the 101st Airborne Division, attacked from the north early D-day morning with 150 men. The Germans withdrew south several hundred feet to prepared positions. US Navy counter fire against two German 88s in Carentan silenced the Germans. On D-day +1 German paratroopers of the 1st Battalion, 6th Parachute Regiment attacked from the top right towards the T-junction. Although out-manned, the Americans bluffed the Germans into surrendering. In error, German artillery killed many of their comrades as the POWs were being marched into captivity. Today, the Libertte' Expressway across these lowlands near Carentan passes very close to the lock.

10.2 Brevands

(The hamlet of Brevands is 4.5 kilometers northeast of Carentan. It is reached by driving east from Carentan on route N13, 4.5 kilometers to the intersection of route D89. Proceed north on D89, through the hamlet of Catz, 2.5 kilometers to the D444 intersection. The road to the left is west, tree lined, and passes the Brevands church, half a kilometer from the intersection. Continue west 1 kilometer to the village of le Moulin, where two wooden bridges span the Carentan Canal.

To link up the UTAH and OMAHA Beachheads, three natural barriers had to be captured, secured and crossed. They were the flooded Douve River valley, the Carentan Canal and the Vire River. All three areas were marshlands affording good defensive positions to the Germans.

Only one highway, N13, crossed the area and interconnected the two beachheads. German resistance along this highway and its straddling towns was expected to be strong. Demolished bridges, rubble strewn roads and German artillery shelling the highway would further delay the union of the UTAH and OMAHA forces.

To overcome the limitations of the highway linkup, the allied invasion planners saw advantages to crossing the Carentan Canal via the le Moulin bridges. American troops could then pass through Brevands and Catz to bypass heavily defended Carentan.

The Germans had been aroused by the noise of the C-47 transports passing from west to east over their positions. Although the majority of the airplanes flew well to the north, a few strayed southwards over le Moulin and Brevands. Brevands contained Strongpoint No. 98, a heavy machine gun emplacement under the command of Captain Ernst During (352nd Infantry Division). As the planes passed over at 150 meters, he jumped out of bed and hurriedly dressed. Rushing to the window he was just in time to see two American pathfinders disentangle themselves from their parachutes. He fired his Schmeisser submachine gun but they faded into the night. A logged phone call to his superior recorded this incident as one of the first confirmed reports of paratroop landings. Later the same day During noticed he had put his boots on the wrong feet.

Paratroopers were assigned the task of capturing or destroying the bridges in the pre-dawn hours of D-Day. They were to be taken by a rapid, surprise thrust and establish a foothold at le Moulin.

The 3rd Battalion of the 506th Infantry Regiment (101st Airborne Division) landed in the vicinity of Angoville-au-Plain, 2.5 kilometers northwest. The German defenders had recognized the area as being particularly suitable for paratroop landings and had planned accordingly. Buildings in the region had been oil soaked. At the first signs of the airborne attack the buildings were ignited and flares triggered. In the brightly illuminated fields, the parachutists dropped, to be greeted by machine gun fire from well -sited and carefully camouflaged positions in the hedgerows. This was Drop Zone D. Fortunately many planes dropped their "sticks" to the north and west, thereby saving many lives.

Those landing in Drop Zone D were decimated. The battalion commanding officer Lieutenant Colonel Robert Wolverton and the executive officer Major George Grant, were killed. All the company captains were either killed or captured. Captain Charles Shettle, a staff officer, assumed command, collected two officers and twelve men and headed for the bridges. His meager battalion grew to 33 as they reached the north end of the objective at 4:30 a.m. His orders were: if the bridges were intact, cross over and gain a foothold on the south side. If the Germans were rushing reinforcements across, destroy them.

The two wooden bridges were 300 meters apart. Both crossed the Carentan Canal to le Moulin. The westerly bridge was a walkway, the easterly bridge was wider and sturdier for farm vehicle traffic. Two-meter high embankments or berms lined both sides of the canal acting as levies against exceptionally high tides. The German tactic of flooding the neighboring low lands had made the area a morass of mud, sand, water, and marsh grasses. The higher ground across the canal afforded the Germans in le Moulin, le Port, and Brevands hard ground for their artillery and good observation over the berms. The paratroopers close to the berm were relatively safe. Those back 20 meters were visible to the Germans. Helmets silhouetted over the berms received snipers attention immediately.

Captain Shettle, at the north end of the footbridge, spotted a dual purpose 88mm gun on the Brevands hillside. Private Donald Zahn crossed the bridge to reconnoiter the gun position and its defenses.

Shettle was joined by Sergeant George Montilo and ten men. The Germans, aware of their intrusion, attacked the dozen Americans who retreated back to their line hand swinging along the bridge's understructure. The bridge was prepared for demolition. Zahn and Montilo were awarded Distinguished Service Crosses for their actions.

Lost radios and generally poor communications stopped Shettle from reliably updating his headquarters about his situation and status. No word was bad news. It was assumed the 3rd Battalion had been too decimated to achieve its objective. Fighter-bombers were ordered to destroy the bridges. Bombing and strafing were successful but the Americans had "friendly fire" casualties. Only when the chaplain, T. S. McGee exposed himself with the yellow identification panels did the fighter-bombers turn away. Several Americans were killed including one of the pilots who clipped the vehicle bridge.

The Carentan Canal separated the 709th Infantry Division, defending the area to the north, and the 352nd Infantry Division defending the area to the east. To attack Shettle's force located in 709th territory, the 352nd Infantry Division requested corps approval. Corps, instead of directing an attack across the Canal, ordered a battalion of the 6th Parachute Regiment (a reserve unit) to attack. Units of the regiment had been in combat on D-Day. The 1st Battalion moving from Carentan to Ste. Marie-du-Mont had been cut-off by the rapid advances of the airborne and seaborne forces on D-Day. To regain their lines the battalion had moved south from Ste. Marie-du -Mont along the same paths used by Shettle's force on D-Day morning to reach the le Moulin bridge. The German battalion split to attack both Captain Shettle's force and Colonel Johnson's force at la Barquette Lock, 3 kilometers west.

At 2 p.m., June 7, after the air force erroneously bombed Shettle's position and the Americans were reorganizing themselves and tending their casualties, the German battalion units attacked from the north. In spite of the bombing and cross-fire from the opposite canal bank, the Americans held capturing 250 attackers. Of the original 800 man German force that had left Carentan the previous morning, six hundred had been captured, 175 killed. Only 25 returned to their own lines.

Captain Shettle's force held their positions until the evening of June 8 when they were relieved by elements of the 327th Glider Infantry Regiment who had disembarked on UTAH Beach.

At 1:45 a.m., June 10, C Company crossed the canal by boat and established a bridgehead. An artillery and mortar barrage on the German positions followed, which allowed the full regiment to cross in strength by 6 a.m. Brevands fell soon after and the regiment, including the 1st Battalion of the 401st Regiment, moved south along the road to Catz and route N13.

Related stories are la Barquette Lock (3 kilometers west) and Auville-sur-le-Vey (6 kilometers southeast).

10.3 Vierville to Dead Man's Corner (D913)

(The village of Vierville is 8 kilometers north of Carentan on the route to UTAH Beach. Proceed north from Carentan on N13 across the Douve River valley lowlands to the junction of D913 running northeast to Ste. Marie-du-Mont. Vierville is 5 kilometers along the road. In Vierville turn left (north) on the Hiesville road and proceed 1.2 kilometers to the hamlet of Culoville.)

The distance traveled from Carentan to Culoville is one of the most bloodied roads in the annals of the 101st Airborne Divisions actions in Normandy.

Northeast of Vierville, 7 kilometers, was UTAH Beach. Twenty-five kilometers due east was OMAHA Beach. The allies establishment plan called for a link up of the UTAH and OMAHA beachheads as quickly as possible. The road D913 from UTAH Beachhead to N13 and Carentan was an essential transport and supply route to be seized in the early hours of the invasion.

The bridges crossing the Douve River, on the southern edge of the UTAH Beachhead sector, were to be captured by units of the 101st Airborne Division on D-Day. The Germans had dammed the river at la Barquette Lock and back flooded the entire low-lying valley. American movement south from the beachhead had to funnel across the few bridges and the roads which had become elevated causeways over the Douve marsh.

To achieve a rapid, surprise seizure of these crossing points, airborne troops parachuted into the sector in the early pre-dawn hours of D-Day, ahead of the seaborne invasion forces.

The fields to the north of Culoville were Drop Zone C, where the men of the 1st and 2nd Battalions of the 506th Regiment were to land. Anti-air landing preparation of flares, oil soaked buildings, machine gun nests and pre-registered mortar fire portended severe casualties. Antiaircraft fire and the pilots' evasive maneuvers shifted their flight paths. Consequently only eight of the eighty-five airplanes dropped their paratroopers into Drop Zone C. Twenty-six plane loads landed around Ste. Marie-du-Mont. The majority of misdrops were 4 kilometers to the north. The farthest from target were three plane loads that landed 45 kilometers to the northwest.

The scattering saved many lives, however the time required assembling into organized fighting units delayed moving on their objectives.

Major General Maxwell Taylor, 101st Airborne Division Commander, had not heard from his southern flank units throughout D-Day. He sent the 1st (227 men) and 2nd (300 men) Battalions of the 506th Regiment south from Culoville to determine if the southern units had taken their objectives, otherwise the two battalions would undertake the tasks.

Colonel Robert F. Sink moved out of Culoville, June 6 at 4:30 a.m. German sniper fire from the hedgerows and farm buildings made the dirt road into Vierville untenable. Leaving a few decoy paratroopers on the road to draw and identify the location of the German fire, Lieutenant Colonel William L. Turner deployed men into the fields and advanced on Vierville on the broad front. Ground mist and the Germans' well-prepared positions hampered the American movements.

Four hours later, 8:30 a.m., Vierville was in American hands. General Taylor joined Colonels Sink and Turner in their command post at the village church. Before sending his battalions to their objectives Colonel Sink and Major H. H. Hannah, engaged a jeep, a driver, and headed southwest out of Vierville down the road (D913) to the Beaumont hamlet on a reconnaissance. One and a half kilometers along the road nearing Beaumont they passed a German horse park. They shot the guard and sped on through a German regiment resting in the ditches. They careened on a few hundred meters to the Beaumont junction where German artillery blocked their path. A quick U turn and back they sped through the gauntlet. The officers firing their .45 automatics and the driver shooting his carbine from his lap. Both sides had been equally surprised and the firing had been wild. The jeep and its occupants pulled back into Vierville unscathed.

Sink directed the 1st Battalion, under Colonel Turner, down the road to Beaumont. The 2nd Battalion still in Culoville was directed to pass through Vierville on to Angoville au Plain to the southwest. The 1st Battalion vacated Vierville before the 2nd Battalion entered The village was unoccupied for a short period. The Germans seized the opportunity to reoccupy the village and establish defenses in the houses including chipping out firing slots in the stone garden walls.

The 2nd Battalion entering from the Culoville road became trapped in withering crossfire. 1st Battalion tanks on the road to Beaumont returned to Vierville and supported the 2nd Battalion in clearing the village. The armored supported paratroopers fought doggedly for three hours to clear Vierville for the second time.

The 2nd Battalion with tanks, leaving a small holding force in Vierville, proceeded across the fields to Angoville au Plain. Germans holding the hedgerows on the southern edge of the village again delayed the 2nd Battalion's advance to its objective. The tanks moved in and broke the hedgerow defenses. This force became the essential reinforcements required by Colonel Ballard's force at les Droueries (separate Chapter 10.4). By moving southwest parallel to the Beaumont road, (D913) the 2nd Battalion directly assisted the 1st Battalion's actions on the road by outflanking the Germans defending the road.

The 1st Battalion was battling along the Beaumont road. German snipers and machine guns in the orchards, behind hedgerows and from the paralleling ridge to the north harassed the American flanks. With the support of medium tanks (A Company of the 746th Tank Battalion) the battalion fought into Beaumont by noon but were stopped by two German counterattacks. On D-Day a German parachute battalion had left Carentan to reinforce the batteries at Ste. Marie-du-Mont. The German regiment commander, Lieutenant Colonel von der Heydte, from his command post in Ste. Come-du-Mont, dispatched a recon company to locate his lost battalion. Colonel Sink's force at Beaumont was now engaged against the German recon company.

The "lost" German battalion was 2 kilometers south preparing to attack Colonel Johnson's force, holding the Douve River crossing at la Barquette Lock. The German battalion realizing it was cut off by American advances attempted to reenter their own lines at Carentan by crossing the marsh at la Barquette Lock. The battalion was unaware von der Heydte was in Ste. Come-du-Mont and they could regain their lines by proceeding west to the Cherbourg highway through minimal American forces.

Baker Company on the southern edge of Beaumont bore the brunt of the German attacks. In repelling the second attack the Americans followed up their advantage and pursued the Germans down the road 1 kilometer to the road junction to Ste. Come-du-Mont.

Two German parachute battalions well dug in, held the fields between the junction and Ste. Come-du-Mont. German attacks on Baker Company at the crossroads forced the company back. Colonel Turner, driving forward with armored support, was shot through the temple standing in his tank turret.

Major Foster who took over the battalion on the death of Colonel Turner, was severely wounded. The company recoiled to the Beaumont hamlet where Captain Patch took charge. The company was so small that they were able to cluster in a single courtyard.

Two fields north of the Beaumont hamlet stood a large German occupied fortified farm that threatened the American position in Beaumont. The greatly reduced Baker Company remnants attempted throughout D-Day afternoon to dislodge the Germans. Hand to hand fighting with bayonets and grenades ensued. Unsuccessful, the few remaining Americans pulled back into their defenses amongst the Beaumont farm buildings.

Colonel Sink returned to Vierville where he met Dog Company of 94 men supported by a platoon of medium tanks. A General Grant tank took the lead and with the paratroopers trotting along in the ditches, entered Beaumont and passed on through towards the N13 junction. The tank raked the hedgerows with machine gun fire. The Germans pulled back and let the column pass. Miraculously, at the D913 Ste. Come-du-Mont road junction the company slipped through between the movement in and out of the area by German forces reinforcing the defenders of les Droueries, half a kilometer east

Able Company and a tank moved into the crossroads behind Dog Company. The Germans had returned and the route open to Dog Company was now closed to Able.

Ahead, Dog Company entered the N13 junction. A German antitank shell hit the General Grant tank as it left the secondary road and wheeled on to the Cherbourg highway. The crew was incinerated and the dead tank commander remained grotesquely sitting upright in the turret. For several days the burned hulk, including its dead commander, stood at the intersection. The troops nicknamed it "Dead Man's Corner", the name it still bears today. Machine gun fire from the hedgerows opened up on the Americans. Their advance stopped and they now fought to hold their gains.

An American eight-truck convoy, lost, entered the scene from the north along the Cherbourg (N13) highway. Unknowingly, it had passed through German-held Ste. Come-du-Mont! (Colonel von der Heydte's post war explantation was that his headquarters staff were in the church and his troops were in the town's peripheral buildings and hedgerows. Although in German hands there were very few of his men along the N13 highway/main street.)

As a result of these advances, several companies were now spread out along the ditches from the N13 junction back 2 kilometers to Beaumont. The narrow line, although an arrow directed at the Carentan causeway and its important bridges, was exposed and over extended. At 11 p.m. the companies pulled back to Beaumont to organiz0e and prepare for an assault on Ste. Come-du-Mont the next day.

The following day (D+2), elements of four American battalions converged on the D913 junction east of Ste. Come-du-Mont. The 1st Battalion in Beaumont took three hours of intensive fighting with artillery support to move along the road vacated the previous evening, to reoccupy the jump-off positions for the attack on Ste. Come-du-Mont. The massive American buildup from UTAH Beach squeezed the German forces westward to their only escape route, the north-south elevated railroad line into Carentan.

Related stories are Ste. Marie-du-Mont, les Drouriers, la Barquette Lock, Ste. Come-du-Mont and Dead Man's Corner.

10.4 Les Droueries

(The hamlet of les Droueries is 4 kilometers northeast of Carentan at the base of the Contentin Peninsula . After passing over the Douve River valley via the Carentan causeway take D913 at the first junction (Dead Man's Corner), towards Ste. Marie-du-Mont. One kilometer from Dead Man's Corner a narrow road crosses D913. To the left the road leads to Ste. Come-du-Mont, to the right it divides leading to Bse. Addeville and Angoville au Plain. Proceed along the Angoville road 0.7 kilometers to the next junction called les Droueries. Paralleling the Angoville au Plain road is a second road to the same village but 150 meters to the southeast. Where these two roads enter les Droueries the battle for the hamlet was waged. The actions here relate to the Vierville to Dead Man's Corner story (10.3). Although parallel actions with common objectives they were not coordinated as a unified effort).

Allied invasion strategy called for the landing of parachute troops inland from the UTAH Beach. The troops were to destroy threatening gun batteries and to capture and hold important intersections, bridges and causeways. To the south of les Droueries, one kilometer, lies the Douve River, which in 1944 had been back flooded by the German's control of la Barquette Lock creating a broad shallow Douve River marsh isolating the Contentin Peninsula from the mainland. The Americans had to seize the four north-south crossing points quickly in the early phase of the invasion. The task in this area was assigned to the 2nd Battalion (501st Regiment) and the 3rd Battalion (506th Regiment) of the 101st Airborne Division.

The battalions were to parachute into Drop Zone D, the fields between les Droueries and Angoville au Plain in the predawn hours of D-Day.

The 2nd Battalion of the 501st Regiment, under the command of Lieutenant Colonel Robert A. Ballard, had trained to rendezvous to a green electric light and the clang of a bronze bell. In the night parachute drop the two troopers carrying the rendezvous "beacons" vanished. The drop zone became illuminated by German flares. Snipers in the hedgerows and mortar fire into the area further delayed the battalion from assembling. Colonel Ballard had landed in the planned field. By 3:30 a.m. he had collected one radio (his own), four machine guns, a bazooka, a 60 millimeter mortar and 100 men. He planned to move westward immediately to Ste. Come-du-Mont, which straddled his main route to the Carentan causeway and the Douve River bridges.

Intelligence had indicated that Ste. Come-du-Mont was held by a German platoon. The mortar and machine gun fire his force was receiving from the area led him to believe otherwise. Whatever the German strength in Ste. Come-du-Mont he had first to eliminate the strong German infantry force in les Droueries before he could move westward.

At 5:30 a.m. as dawn broke, his incomplete battalion assembled in the field southeast of Angoville au Plain organized into companies Dog, Easy, and Fox and proceeded along the two parallel farm tracks from Angoville au Plain to the farm buildings, at les Droueries. Easy Company was on the north track with Fox Company on the south. Dog Company followed behind Fox. Each company had a compliment of thirty men.

Easy Company entered the T junction but was stopped by machine gun fire. The Americans dug in along the first hedgerow.

Parallel to the south Fox Company was also stopped abruptly. The Germans at the les Droueries end of the two farm tracks had tunneled through the separating hedgerow into the roadside ditch at ten points in its bank. With automatic weapons the Germans would fire from their ditch positions. As the Americans worked their way closer along the ditches, over their dead and wounded comrades to within grenade throwing distance, the Germans would crawl back into the field through the tunnel. In a rifle pit from behind the hedgerow they would snipe at the lead paratroopers then return to the ditch side position. This tactic stopped the two company advances. Colonel Ballard swung his reserve Dog Company into the field separating the two tracks. German mortars, pre-registered on the field, zeroed in and blasted the company attempting to move up to the hedgerow directly opposite and across the road from the German positions. The forces were stalemated. The American casualties mounted until 8 a.m., when Lieutenant W. W. Wood and twenty men of the 506th Regiment arrived at Colonel Ballard's command post.

Lieutenant Wood led his force north and west in a flank attack on the north T junction, already being pressured by Easy Company. Wood's force entered the farm buildings at the junction but was immediately attacked by Germans who moved laterally along their side of the hedgerows to the buildings. Hand to hand fighting ensued forcing the attackers to retreat.

Leaving half of Easy and Fox Companies at les Droueries as a holding force, Colonel Ballard withdrew his depleted force under orders to occupy Bse. Addeville one kilometer to the south.

Reinforced with forty-five men, at 2:45 p.m. Colonel Ballard attempted to move into Bse. Addeville from the Douve marsh. Machine gun fire from the les Droueries vicinity stopped his attempted side-slipping.

Germans (6th Parachute Regiment) from Ste. Come-du-Mont had reinforced their comrades holding the hedgerows around les Droueries. From the edge of the marsh Ballards men deployed as companies and moved against the same T junction as the morning attack, except this time from a more southerly position. Moving up to the hedgerows across the road from the German positions, the paratroopers were stopped.

Throughout that evening and night groups of paratroopers backtracked to their drop zone in search of men and ammunition for the next day's battle.

The following morning, Wednesday, June 7 at 6:30, Colonel Ballards force made strong probing attacks without success. Four German machine guns sited down the ditches killed and wounded the advancing Americans.

US artillery fire came to their aid and successfully destroyed the German headquarters in a farmhouse 120 meters away. The next salvo landed 120 meters short on Fox Company killing five and wounding eight men. Artillery fire was halted, attacks were stopped and Colonel Ballard went to Angoville to discuss a new plan with the divisional artillery commander, General Anthony C. McAuliffe. The general gained prominence in December '44 for his classic reply "nuts" to the German request that he surrender Bastogne during the Battle of the Bulge.

During the afternoon a German flank force of twenty men attempted to enter the American lines from the Douve marsh. Thirteen were killed and seven captured.

Colonel Ballard returned from Angoville with four Sherman tanks and orders to clear the area by dusk. To weaken the German defenses the dominating armor bombarded the hedgerows with 50 rounds of 75mm shellfire interspersed with machine gun bursts.

Easy Company attacked the north junction and Dog Company came in from the south against the southern junction. The tanks spread out to offer the infantry maximum protection as well as covering the strongest known resistance points. The infantry moved in close to the German firing pits along the ditch. At arms length they gunned down the defenders. With the ferocity of the hand to hand combat only a few wounded prisoners were captured. By 7:30 that evening the crossroads and les Droueries were secured. The American casualties were four men killed and six wounded.

Related stories are Vierville to Dead Man's Corner, Dead Man's Corner, Ste. Come-du-Mont.

10.5 Ste. Come-du-Mont

(Four kilometers north of Carentan on N13)

The Douve River meanders from west to east through the low pasturelands two kilometers south of Ste. Come-du-Mont. The highway N13 is an elevated causeway over the lowlands. Backflooding of the river through German manipulation of la Barquette Lock had created a wide marsh crossed by the causeway. The allies' strategy necessitated the American forces from UTAH and OMAHA Beaches to link up as quickly as possible. Seizing the towns along N13 was a primary objective.

Ste. Come-du-Mont straddled N13, the major north-south paved highway and dominated the American's line of advance along D913 (.5 kilometers) to the east. (Note: The Liberte Expressway of recent construction obscures the relationship of the two roads N13 and D913 and their significance in 1944.) The town slightly elevated with its lofty church belfry afforded the Germans excellent observation for supporting artillery fire. The reality of possibly retreating south on N13 to Carentan further increased the Germans tenacity.

When the first paratroopers dropped on the Contentin Peninsula in the early hours of D-Day the village and surrounding area was garrisoned by the 3rd Battalion, 1058th Regiment of the 91st Anti-Air Landing Division, specifically trained to handle an airborne invasion.

By dawn, as reports of allied paratroop landings and beach assaults clearly indicated the invasion had begun, elements of the 6th German Parachute Regiment, under the command of Lieutenant Colonel Freidrick August von der Heydte, rushed from Periers (20 kilometers southwest) through Carentan to Ste. Come-du-Mont. The force was to kill or capture the American paratroopers that had landed in the Ste. Come-du-Mont, Ste. Mere-Eglise area. Colonel von der Heydte directed the 1st Battalion, under Major Rolf Mager, east to Ste. Marie-du-Mont to reinforce two German batteries. He climbed the church belfry in Ste. Come-du-Mont. Peering through binoculars he studied the invasion fleet. The scene off UTAH Beach stunned him. The invasion fleet was much greater than his High Command had anticipated. The number of ships and the troops they contained, including powerful naval support, all under an umbrella of fighters, fighter -bombers, medium and heavy bombers, staggered his imagination. He decided to keep the route south to Carentan open for his probable withdrawal.

By noon battle actions had developed at les Droueries and la Barquette Lock both just a short distance away, though surprisingly unnoticed by the colonel's observer posted in the church steeple. The magnitude of the armada to the northeast dominated his attention.

The colonel's artillery men and mortar platoons came to the aid of their defending comrades and concentrated much harassment fire on the American advance. This combined with the dug in positions of von der Heydte's troops stopped the paratroopers attempting to seize the causeway. The cruiser USS. Quincy directed her attention on the German 88's in support of the paratroopers and greatly diminished the German artillery's effectiveness.

On Wednesday afternoon June 7, (D+1), units of 1st Battalion, 506th Regiment (101st Airborne Division) attacked Ste. Come-du-Mont from the east. The battalion had fought their way along D913 from Vierville through Beaumont to the road intersection half a kilometer east of Ste. Come-du-Mont. However, von der Heydte had anticipated the American thrust and had prepared defenses. The German paratroopers were dug in behind every hedgerow, camouflaged and armed with automatic weapons.

The hedgerows were thick stone, earth and root berms topped with high bushes and trees. Their two to three meter height created road corridors which in some areas where the trees branched over the road became tunnels of vegetation. The drainage ditches were a meter deep. The German soldiers had dug tunnels through the base of the hedgerow berm from the field to the road ditch. From the ditch they would fire at the Americans then crawl back through the hedgerow secure from the counterfire. The procedure was repeated frequently. As the advancing paratroopers crawled along the ditch the Germans would fire through the tunnel as the GI helmet came into view. This tactic combined with their excellent weaponry thwarted the American progress. The American were halted. They withdrew from the intersection back to the hamlet of Beaumont.

Von der Heydte's regiment was deployed to numerous "hot spots". The Americans approaching Ste. Come-du-Mont by June 8 were facing two companies of German paratroopers and a battalion of infantry.

The American plan for June 8 called for a four battalion attack northwest from the Beaumont-les Droueries line, to seize the area from Ste. Come-du-Mont to the Carentan causeway that included the highway.

A bombardment by the navy and army of 2500 shells on fifteen targets in the "triangle" preceded Colonel Robert F. Sink's four-battalion advance.

The "jump-off" was at 4:45 a.m. Poor coordination between the infantry and its artillery diminished the firepower's effectiveness. The plan of advance had been hastily organized and passed down the line verbally. The small hedgerowed fields tended to channel units and misdirect them from their goals. The convergence of the four battalions each with its three or four companies into the narrowing area, squeezed out units creating changes in the plan as it proceeded. The height and density of the hedgerows concealed the church belfry. The D913 road passing to the southwest funneled units away from their allotted task to the west. German artillery effectively forced many of the Americans to dig deeper and stay put in their foxholes.

The 1st and 2nd Battalions of the 506th Regiment were dug in east of Ste. Come-du-Mont. A detail of clerks, cooks and wiremen from the regiment's headquarters company had entered the village but withdrew under attack. Colonel Julian Ewell's 3rd Battalion of the 502nd Regiment had moved southwest to Dead Man's Corner and the 1st Battalion of the 401st Glider Infantry Regiment had been temporarily pinched out of the action. The attack was a limited success.

As a result of the American pressure in the mid-afternoon the defenders vacated the village by moving west to la Croix from where they could regain their lines in Carentan via the railway embankment leading south across the Douve marsh. Others took the highway route south and ran into Colonel Ewell's battalion at Dead Man's Corner.

At 4 p.m. a patrol from the 1st Battalion (506th Regiment) entered Ste. Come-du-Mont without a shot being fired. The Germans had withdrawn and were then fighting at Dead Man's Corner. The German units that withdrew to Carentan via the la Croix railway line established themselves in positions along the Carentan causeway the next day, and once again stopped the planned seizure of its bridges.

The village of Ste. Come-du-Mont almost completely destroyed in the bombardment of June 8, has since been rebuilt. This arduous task is in itself mute evidence of the bitter struggle, which destroyed and damaged many buildings. Ploughing has leveled the cratered fields, while time has restored the damaged and shredded trees to their natural beauty. Declevities along the hedgerows are due to the collapse of gun pits and foxholes. The road D913 and the lane to Ste. Come-du-Mont are now paved. Some of the battle described took place where D913 passes over the Liberte Expressway.

Related stories are Vierville to Dead Man's Corner and Dead Man's Corner.

10.6 Dead Man's Corner

(3 kilometers north of Carentan, on N13, at the intersection of D913, the Ste. Marie-du-Mont Road)

The name comes from an incident on June 7 when an American tank was destroyed at this intersection..

The elevated Route Nationale 13 between Carentan and Dead Man's Corner is lush grazing pasture land. By control of la Barquette Lock (2 kilometers east, but out of sight behind the new Liberte Expressway) the Germans controlled the flow of the Douve River valley and the intake of the twice-a-day tides. By June 1944, the Douve River valley had become a marsh causing north-south traffic to funnel along N13 or walk the elevated railroad line visible 1 kilometer to the west. The four small bridges (large culverts) stabilized the water level on both sides of the two-lane causeway.

Units of the US 101st Airborne Division paratroopers were to land into their specified Drop Zone, 2 kilometers northeast of Dead Man's Corner, then via D913 and N13 move south and destroy the four causeway bridges thereby stopping German reinforcements entering the UTAH Beach lodgment area during the American buildup period. Misdropping and scattering of the airborne troops upset their timetable so the bridges were not destroyed. On D-Day the American forces only came to within 1 kilometer of the northern bridge located on the southern edge of the hamlet, Pont-du-Douve, that straddles the causeway road.

Although the French Resistance had cut many German communication telephone lines the evening of June 5 and the dark morning hours of June 6, German Lieutenant Colonel Freidrick von der Heydte received orders at his Periers (18 kilometers southwest of Carentan) headquarters at 6 a.m. to move his 6th Parachute Regiment northward rapidly to meet the invasion. Lieutenant Colonel von der Heydte crossed the causeway around noon (June 6), passed through the N13/D913 intersection, setting up his headquarters in Ste. Come-du-Mont (1 kilometer north on N13). From the church steeple he was awestruck by the magnitude of the invasion fleet visible off UTAH Beach (12 kilometers northeast). The Colonel deployed his 2nd Battalion, under Hauptman Priekshat, (300 men) northward 8 kilometers on N13 to Fauville and his 1st Battalion northeast 6 kilometers to Ste. Marie-du- Mont. This battalion was quickly cut off by advances of the US 8th Regiment coming from UTAH Beach. The German battalion fled southward and surrendered the following day to Colonel Howard Johnson's (501st Parachute Regiment, 101st Airborne Division) small force at la Barquette Lock.

Lieutenant Colonel van der Heydte (see footnote) deployed the 3rd Battalion, 1058th Regiment into the fields and hedgerows east of N13 from Dead Man's Corner to Ste. Come-du-Mont. Recognizing the sizable American forces, he wanted to keep the N13 causeway open for possible withdrawal. The "Corner" became a focal point for the American advance and German reinforcements or withdrawal.

On D-Day, Colonel Johnson's men captured la Barquette Lock and several footbridges across the Douve River east of the lock. American patrols moving along the north edge of the flooded valley towards the northern most bridge at the Pont-du-Douve hamlet were stopped by German 88mm artillery fire from Ste. Come-du-Mont and Carentan. The Germans in Pont-du-Douve were well entrenched with two heavy machine guns and an antitank gun. Against these defenses and artillery support fire the Americans made little progress.

On D+1 (June 7 late afternoon, Dog Company of the 2nd Battalion (506th Regiment) entered the junction from D913. (Eleven months later Colonel Robert Sink's 506th Regiment occupied Hitler's Bavarian Berghof in Berchtesgarden.) The column was lead by a platoon of medium tanks. The lead General Grant tank, as it pivoted southbound onto N13, received a direct hit from a German antitank gun in Pont-du-Douve. (Some veterans believe it was a panzerfaust rocket fired from a west-side hedgerow.) The crew was incinerated and the dead commander remained sitting grotesquely upright in the burned tank for several days. The GI's referred to it as "the corner where the dead man's in the tank." The corner's name is still a local identification.

A little later, an American eight-truck quartermaster supply convoy arrived at the "Corner" from the direction of Ste. Come-du-Mont. Having disembarked on UTAH Beach, the convoy proceeded west joining N13 at les Forges (6 kilometers north). The convoy turned south, passed through German held Ste. Come-du-Mont, arriving at the "Corner" oblivious that they had passed safely through a German headquarters town. Dog Company and the eight trucks, being exposed and over extended, under Colonel

Sink's orders withdrew, at 11 p.m., eastward along D913 2 kilometers to the Beaumont hamlet.

On D+2 (June 8) at 4:45 a.m. an American four battalion attack was launched from the northeast against Ste. Come-du-Mont and Dead Man's Corner. At 8 a.m., Colonel Julian Ewell's 3rd Battalion, 501st Regiment reoccupied the intersection. He saw the German paratroopers withdrawing westward from Ste. Come-du-Mont towards la Croix (1 kilometer west of the "Corner") from where they could retreat south to Carentan along the elevated railroad. Colonel Ewell decided to move his force down N13 towards Carentan. As his force approached the roadside hamlet Pont-du-Douve, small arms fire, two machine guns, an antitank gun, and an 88mm gun in Carentan laid down a curtain of death between the hamlet and the "Corner". Colonel Ewell's men pulled back to the "Corner" where they were attacked by German paratroopers coming from Ste. Come-du-Mont attempting to retreat along N13 to their line at Pont-du-Douve. The Germans came through the fields and hedgerows on both sides of the highway. To the west 150 meters, two hedgerows away, the enemy occupied the hill and fired into the Americans holding the "Corner". The present building at the "Corner" has been repaired. (The dominant home was used as a German casualty dressing station.) The American paratroopers attacked and cleared the hill, then spread out behind the east-west hedgerow, crowning the hill, anchoring their line in the apple orchard storage barns.

Between 9:30 a.m. and 4 p.m. six concerted attacks were made against their line. At 2:30 p.m. the strongest attack, in the field immediately east of the highway and house was nearly successful. The timely arrival of three tanks coming westward along D913 strengthened the weakened positions and saved the day.

A short time later the 1st Battalion of the 401st Glider Infantry Regiment entered the battle scene. The Germans had given up the southward N13 withdrawal plan and were retreating west through la Croix to the railroad line and then south to Carentan. Two battalions pursued the Germans. Although contact was broken, the Germans were quite visible scurrying along the sloping west side of the protective railroad embankment.

Bordering the second field north and west of the "Corner" is a narrow hedged track leading to la Croix. The ditches of this east-west road were the German start positions for their attack on the Americans holding the hill. Able Company (506th Regiment) pursuing the retreating Germans captured forty supply wagons under the canopy of trees. The wagons contained guns, ammo and a sizable German cash payroll. The road was littered with dead Germans and dead horses. In the field immediately southwest of the "Corner" and adjacent to the N13 highway, several dozen German paratroopers were found dead in their sleeping bags, killed by an airburst concussion from a naval shell.

As the fighting moved on, the farmers returned to their fields. Engineers removed unexploded ordinance and casually threw many miscellaneous military relics into the hedgerows to be out of the way of the farm equipment. After securing the owners' permission to roam his property, a metal detector unearths the relics of the 55+ years.

Footnote:

Lieutenant Colonel Friedrich August Freiherr von der Hedyte, was the Commander of the 6th Parachute Regiment of the 91st Anti-Air Landing Division. Prior to the Japanese bombing of Pearl Harbor and the United States declaration of war on Germany, von der Hedyte had been a law professor at New York's Columbia University. He was conscious of the great American industrial power, untouchable by the distance between the two continents.

Lieutenant Colonel von der Hedyte's high quality troops faced the American material superiority on the afternoon of June 7 when American C-47 cargo planes dropped re-supplies to the 82nd and 101st Airborne Division's troops. Without defined frontlines the supply canisters also fell behind the German lines. Falling into German hands were guns, ammunition, medical kits and unfamiliar but much appreciated delights such as Carnation Milk, Nescafe Instant Coffee, Camel cigarettes, and toilet paper packets! How could they win against such an untouchable supply stream?

Picture 13: Deadman's Corner- Looking North
June 14, 1948

The road entering from the right is from Utah Beach, 4 miles northeast. On D-day, resistance along the road and adjacent fields were costly to Colonel Robert Sink's 506th Regiment of the 101st Airborne Division. German Colonel van der Heydte, commander of the 6th Parachute Regiment was headquartered in Ste. Come du Mont half a mile north of the intersection. Fighting around the important corner lasted several days until the Germans were forced to withdraw westward, their only line of retreat. From here the Americans pushed south to Caretan and north to Ste. Mere Eglise opening up the advance from the Utah beachhead.

10.7 Carentan

(The town of Carentan is located at the base of the Contentin Peninsula on route N13 midway between Cherbourg and Bayeux.)

UTAH and OMAHA Beachheads, 25 kilometers apart, were established June 6. During the following week forces from both sectors moved towards each other to effect a linkup.

From OMAHA the 175th Regiment (29th Infantry Division) had moved south to N13, then driven westward occupying Isigny on the morning of June 9 and the Vire River bridge at Auville-sur-le-Vey that evening. As the Vire River bridge was to be the demarcation line between the two forces the 175th stopped and awaited the arrival of units from the UTAH Beachhead.

Carentan was therefore to be captured by the 101st Airborne Division holding the north side of the Douve River. The division's objectives were to seize the town, link up with the OMAHA forces at Auville-sur-le-Vey and reopen route N13.

The division's plan was a two-prong pincer. The 327th Glider Infantry holding the Douve River bridge at Brevands northeast of Carentan, was to move south and approach Carentan from the east. Part of the force was to move eastwards to join the 175th Regiment at Auville-sur-le-Vey.

Another regiment simultaneously would attack south from the north side of the Douve River along N13, pass south and west of Carentan and seize Hill 30 southwest of the town. The two prongs forming the attack would meet on Hill 30, encircling the town and severing the German escape route.

The execution of this plan resulted in four distinct and separate action areas: The Carentan causeway leading in from the north, The Vire-Taute Canal bridges on the eastern edge of Carentan, Hill 30 south of town, and the seizing of Carentan.

The battle for the Carentan causeway commenced at Dead Man's Corner 3 kilometers north of Carentan on N13.

Carentan was being held by the severely weakened survivors of three German battalions. The 795th Georgian Battalion (Russian volunteers and conscripts) had retreated from Isigny and held the east side of the town along the Vire River. The battalion had placed itself under the command of the German 6th Parachute Regiment whose two battalions held the northwest section of the town bordering the N13 highway crossing the Douve River Valley. The two German parachute battalions had been fighting the US 101st Division since D-Day morning. With staggering losses they had pulled back from the north end of the causeway. The 1st Battalion with an original compliment of 700 men had been beaten and captured at la Barquette Lock and Brevands. Only 25 men had crossed the marshes and regained their lines. The 2nd Battalion although stronger had received severe losses in defending Ste. Come-du-Mont (3.5 kilometers north) and in their retreat via the railway embankment back to Carentan.

The decimated battalions had no armor, their artillery had been knocked out by allied fighter-bombers, and German air support was nil. A reserve supply of mortar shells was of a smaller caliber than their mortar's firing tubes. Wrapping blankets around the shells to increase their diameter created a few inaccurate but deadly rounds.

The allied air force dominating the skies bombed and strafed German truck convoys attempting to re-supply the beleaguered German paratroopers. As a last resort the Luftwaffe made their first air drop in the Normandy campaign. Under the cover of darkness on the night of June 11-12, JU-52 transports dropped 18 tons of ammunition to the German defenders.

The German 6th Parachute Regiment was considered by the allies as one of the finest and toughest German units in Normandy commanded by Lieutenant Colonel Freidrich-August Freiherr Baron von der Heydte. Colonel von der Heydte with his regiment had fought in North Africa and had covered the Afrika Korps long retreat from El Alamein to Tunisia. Again in Normandy Field Marshal Rommel was relying on the unit and its commander. The regiment's advanced headquarters was located in the Ingouf farm facing north across the Douve River valley and a position of significance in the battle for the causeway.

The importance of Carentan was emphasized in a directive from Hitler stating that the town was to be held to the last man.

Napoleon's engineers had attempted to make Carentan an island fortress by utilizing the channel tides and the low land to the north and east of the town. The Napoleonic works are still evident as bays in a modern canal system draining the tidal flats.

Applying similar techniques, German engineers manipulated the locks to coincide with the tide schedules and successfully flood the Douve River and its tributary the Merderet River. The overflowing rivers flooded the low lying pasture land creating marshes as obstacles to the allies mobility forcing movement to be directed across the few elevated causeways that traversed the marshes.

In 1944 to the Americans at Dead Man's Corner looking southward, the highway was just a ribbon of asphalt across a "lake". Drainage in the intervening years has returned the lake into pastures interspersed with drainage ditches. The roadway was straight, level and stood about 2.5 meters above the water's surface. The lake was 2 kilometers wide and stretched from the Bay of the Seine on the east westward 12 kilometers. Between the causeway and the railway embankment, 1 kilometer west, are hummocks of solid ground, which hid German snipers and machine gunners. The causeway embankment on the west side is steep and drops off sharply. The east embankment is wider and gently sloped but still lacked sufficient protection for "digging in". The few stunted poplars afforded little cover and the exposed causeway made the Americans "sitting ducks". Four bridges along the causeway spanned the Douve River channel and its tributaries.

Although the causeway and the destruction of its bridges was a D-Day objective of the US 101st Airborne Division it was not until the morning of June 8 (D+2) that an effective sized force came within striking distance. At 8 a.m. Colonel Julian Ewell's 3rd Battalion (Regiment) occupied Dead Man's Corner and pressed south along the highway to the hamlet of Pont-du-Douve at the north end of the causeway 50 meters from the first bridge. The German defenders of the hamlet with an anti-tank gun, two machine guns and small arms stopped the American battalion forcing them to retreat to Dead Man's Corner.

Developments throughout the remainder of that day and the following morning made the German resistance nest in Pont-du-Douve untenable. In the early afternoon on June 9 they abandoned the hamlet blowing up the 2nd bridge as they moved south across the causeway.

A little later in the afternoon an American patrol scouting by boat moved along the east side embankment as far as the 3rd bridge and confirmed that the Germans had withdrawn and that bridge No. 2 was demolished and resting in the river's channel.

Lieutenant Colonel Robert G. Cole's 3rd Battalion (502nd Regiment) was assigned the task of crossing the causeway and taking up a position on Hill 30 to the south of Carentan. The original invasion plans had called for demolition of the causeway bridges to stop German reinforcements from entering the UTAH Beachhead, but now the bridges had to be held for the flow of American reinforcements moving south.

American aerial reconnaissance indicated that the railroad embankment to the west was impossible to cross as a result of a direct hit. The causeway was the only practical approach to Carentan. As the light reconnaissance aircraft had not drawn enemy fire from the town optimism prevailed that the objective was lightly defended.

In the darkness of the first minutes of June 10 the battalion's intelligence officer, Lieutenant Ralph B. Behauf, leading a reconnaissance party of ten men crossed the length of the causeway mapping all they viewed. Using a small boat they crossed the flood waters. At the second and fourth bridges a beach obstacle called a Belgian Gate had been erected by the Germans. It was 4-5 meters wide, 2 meters high, too heavy to manhandle and was anchored with steel cables, a formidable obstacle. The German demolition charge destroying the second bridge had twisted its gate open. The fourth bridge gate however was intact with a 35 centimeter opening through which Behauf's party filed and continued an additional 50 meters along the east embankment. German flares illuminated the scene as machine guns on the road shoulders ahead and from the Ingouf farm to the west raked their position. Noting the machine gun positions for artillery spotting, the patrol withdrew as dawn increased the precariousness of their position.

From 8 a.m. until noon the artillery of the 65th Armored Regiment, the field artillery battalion and the 907th Glider Field Artillery Battalion pounded the fields and orchards in and around the Ingouf farm.

At noon in column of companies, Cole's battalion moved south from Pont-du-Douve along the causeway. An improvised footbridge was thrown across the number. two bridge gap. The bloodiest "minor battle" in US military history was about to start for a hamlet misspelled on their maps.

In 1944 after crossing bridge No. 1, there was a sharp turn to the left after which the causeway proceeded directly into Carentan. The bend has since been straightened and as a result the highway now passes to the east of the old No. 1 and No. 2 bridges. Their foundations still stand and are readily visible.

In the vanguard of the American column an officer moved ahead with a flag of truce to the gate at bridge No. 4. He presented a letter in German from General Maxwell Taylor (Commander of the 101st Division) demanding the Germans surrender. Colonel von der Heydte returned his reply in English. "What would you do in my place?"

As the battalion moved along the causeway's embankments a sniper in a hummock west of bridge No. 2 managed to score additional casualties. Wriggling along one of the few earth dikes still above water level, Staff Sergeant A. L. Zeroski and Private C. A. Williams hurled two grenades into the snipers slit trench.

A similar elevated dike running west across the lake from bridge No. 3 was occupied by several American machine gun teams who set up an almost constant fusillade into the Ingouf farm.

By 5 o'clock the whole battalion was strung out along the causeway. Retreat was only possible back across the one-at-a-time footbridge spanning the remnants of bridge No. 2. With little recourse the battalion continued, and man by man squeezed through the bent bars in the gate blocking bridge No. 4. From the farm German bullets whined as they ricocheted off the gate's steel work. American dead on the embankments forced movement along the exposed roadway. In the lead after squeezing through the Belgian gate, Lieutenant Behauf's section received heavy small arms fire from the Ingouf farm and the neighboring fields. American artillery again relentlessly pounded the farm hamlet from 4 to 11:30 p.m. with little effect. The majority of the rounds were 200 meters "long" landing in the orchard and on the crossroads beyond the farm.

That evening two German dive-bombers attacked the bridge No. 3 area dropping canisters of antipersonnel bombs and machine gunning the exposed infantry. There were thirty more casualties to an already decimated battalion whose Item Company had lost 63 out of 85 men.

Throughout the late hours of June 10 and the predawn hours of June 11 the headquarters and two companies squeezed through No. 4

bridge gate. By 4 a.m. 265 men were through temporarily huddled in the drainage ditches and behind the highway embankment. The men that squeezed through found themselves in a very small bridgehead being racked by automatic fire from the south and west. (Today commercial buildings and a parking lot cover the 1944 field on the southwest corner where N13 and the Ingouf road intersect.) George Company moved southward along the east side embankment. Their point was only 100 meters south of the gate. Ahead 250 meters at the culvert over which the secondary road travels eastward, a German machine gun and a Schmeisser fired directly into their leading platoon. Five hundred meters further down the highway a house bordering the east side shoulder sheltered a machine gun and several snipers. American mortars and small arms subdued the two resistance nests but not before the company had sustained serious losses. (Commercial development on both sides of N13 have destroyed and covered over much of this hallowed ground.)

The other companies once through the gate attempted to move westward across the fields to the Ingouf farm. (After crossing the causeway take the first road on the right. The Ingouf farm is half a kilometer on the right before the railroad overpass.) German machine guns hidden in the first hedgerow stopped their advances. The Americans huddled in the ditches and along the Madelaine River bank crossed by the fourth bridge.

The Ingouf farm road bends to the left 50 meters from the highway. Twenty meters from the bend in the field directly in line with the straight portion of the farm road was a solidly built elevated German machine gun nest. Twenty meters beyond it was a V shaped defense trench. From the second floor windows of the farm machine guns further amplified the rain of death that crisscrossed into that 50-meter bridgehead south of No. 4 bridge.

From 5:30 to 6:00 a.m. American artillery pounded the farm and hedgerows with air burst and delayed action shells. At 6:15 the artillery changed to smoke shells and then, when they had obscured the target area completely reverted to explosive shells that shot "long" and fell along the railway line 500 meters southwest of the farm.

Colonel Cole ordered a bayonet charge. The first and only one so ordered by an American officer in World War II. His whistle heralded the charge from the east side protected embankment position, across the N13 highway and into the two fields flanking the road to the Ingouf farm. However, instead of the three companies only 25 men followed. Ignorance of the plan, fear and casualties had decreased his force. These brave few charged across the two bullet swept fields flanking the farm road. More men soon joined the advance. Two men raced up the elevated machine gun nest on the road's north side, tossed in grenades and continued towards the distant hedgerow atop a hillock across the road from the farm buildings. The rifle pits and machine gun emplacements cut into this excavation pile adjacent to the Napoleonic canal were cleared with bayonets and grenades. The main body of US paratroopers charging across the field south of the farm road took heavy casualties from the machine guns in the first hedge. A drainage ditch crossing the field afforded some protection and a brief respite before moving on and clearing the hedgerow. The charge carried and the Americans occupied the hedgerow and farm beyond. Under attack the Germans withdrew through the orchard west of the farm. Several Americans continued past the farm along the road and stationed themselves along the flank of the German withdrawal route through the orchard. With their automatic weapons they killed many retreating Germans in the orchard. German dead in and out of their foxholes lay throughout the farmyard and the adjacent fields.

Colonel Cole now occupying Colonel von der Heydte's headquarters in the farmhouse called in the 1st Battalion (502nd Regiment) under Lieutenant Colonel Patrick J. Cassidy to reinforce their positions around the farm. The reinforcements crossing No. 4 bridge and the fields came under mortar and machine gun fire causing additional casualties.

In the mid morning the Germans counterattacked the American positions in the farm through the orchard and at the crossroads 150 meters to the west past the railroad overpass. Two American machine guns behind the farmhouse under the command of Sergeant Harrison Summers (the "Sergeant York" of WWII awarded the Distinguished Service Cross. See St. Martin-de-Varreville battle site, 2.5) fired across the field into the orchard and at the hedgerow to the south stopping the attack.

The American paratroopers behind the brick wall in the northeast corner of the crossroads sustained severe casualties but stopped the attack across the crossroads. Of the 30 Americans holding the positions at the stone wall and along the Napoleonic canal, only 6 could stand after the engagement. At the intersection in the ditch on the southwest corner an American casualty lay across a dead German sitting upright behind his machine gun.

Shortly after noon the German attack was renewed and some ground at the stone fence was lost, but covering fire from one of the two machine guns behind the farm helped the defenders to hold their positions. Major General Maxwell Taylor, the 101st Division's commander, came forward to the farmhouse headquarters where he outlined the plan for the follow-through action to capture Carentan.

Colonel Cole was awarded the Congressional Medal of Honor, posthumously, for his actions and leadership in this battle. On September 18 at Best, Holland, a sniper from a house 100 meters away shot him in the temple killing him instantly.

The farm owner, Mr. Ingouf, and his family had been evacuated prior to the battle and the present owner's took over the renamed "Madelaine" farm in 1953. The farmhouse and north barn have been repaired and the south barn has been rebuilt. The fields around are uneven as a result of the shell craters and the orchard is rather sparsely treed. The hedgerows at the far side of the fields facing across the crossroads from where the German attacked have gaps as a result of shellfire.

In the late morning a lull passed across the battlefield as the Americans attempted to secure a truce affording time to clear the casualties from their lines. The regimental surgeon, Major Douglas T. Davidson entered the German lines but was refused an interview with Colonel von der Heydte. He returned to the American lines and the battle continued.

At noon Colonel Cassidy moved C Company from reserve on the causeway south down the highway and into their front line position at a cabbage patch 50 meters south of the easterly running side road. In 1944 the field west of the highway and bounded by a parallel hedgerow was not developed as it is today. The cabbage patch was a small four sided field bounded on the south and west by hedgerows which are still present. With C Company in the cabbage patch and along its hedgerows, A Company was moved in behind for support. Their line ran east-west along the secondary road. Their west flank was the hedgerow to the west of the highway.

At 1 p.m. a coordinated attack by the Germans against the American positions along the highway and in the farm was launched.

C Company in the cabbage patch was attacked from the west by Germans moving along the lateral hedgerows. A spearhead coming from Carentan along the highway and in the fields on both sides caused the Americans severe casualties. For the next six hours the Germans maintained the pressure and tried to overrun the bridgehead. The pileup of German dead along the hedgerows and ditches to within 10 meters of C Company decreased the momentum of their own attack. The ferocity of the battle created a high demand for ammunition supplies. To the soldiers on both sides ammunition was passed forward from man to man until it reached the forward fighting units. By 6 p.m. with 80% casualties the Americans prepared to withdraw across the causeway. To cover themselves all regimental guns fired a 5 minute close support bombardment into the front line positions. Some Americans were killed by their own shellfire but the German attack was stopped and broken. The German paratroopers withdrew into Carentan. The Sunday battle for the bridgehead was over.

In the predawn hours on June 12 the 1st and 2nd Battalions of the 506th Regiment (101st Airborne Division) moved out from the farmhouse and highway N13 positions south across the fields to the west of Carentan against little German resistance.

While the two day battle for the causeway and its bridgehead was in progress a second American force was battling for Carentan in its eastern outskirts.

The 327th Glider Infantry crossed the Douve River near its mouth at Brevands 3.5 kilometers northeast of Carentan at 1:45 a.m. on June 10. Proceeding through Brevands they took its secondary road south and joined the Carentan highway N13. A Company of the 401st Regiment, attached to the 327th Regiment, turned eastward and made contact with the OMAHA Beachhead forces at Auville-sur-le-Vey. The main body of the regiment moved west along the N13 highway towards Carentan.

By 6 p.m. the regiment was within 500 meters of the Vire-Taute canal bridge east of Carentan but came under intense mortar and machine gun fire from the houses and hedgerows on the canal's bank. Coordinated attacks by the Americans along the north and south sides of the highway were successful and by midnight they had moved up to the hedgerow bordering the east bank.

The railway bridge a hundred meters south was destroyed but the highway bridge was intact. German strength in Carentan covering the bridge and the canal exacted high casualties on the Americans attempting to cross. Colonel Joseph H. Harper, Commander of the 327th Regiment, attempted to outflank the German position by sending two companies down stream (north) 1.5 kilometers. Repairing a footbridge they crossed (June 11, 10 a.m.) onto the island formed by the splitting of the canal as it passes to the northeast of Carentan. The main stream called the Bassin a Flot is bordered by a wooded stretch on the west and east banks.

G Company (327th Glider Infantry Regiment) on the west bank and A Company (401st Glider Infantry Regiment) on the east bank advanced several hundred meters through the woods towards Carentan. At 1 kilometer from the town's outskirts the companies were stopped by German mortar and machine gun fire from the houses facing the Bassin a Flot. American counter artillery bombarded the houses and although German fire decreased it maintained sufficient strength to hold back any further American advances from that direction.

That evening and during the night Carentan was set ablaze by American artillery and naval guns. The German delaying tactics did not stop the 101st Airborne Division's plan to encircle Carentan.

From the east bank of the Vire-Taute canal the 501st Regiment side slipped around the 327th Regiment, crossed the canal and passed south of Carentan then advanced on Hill 30 1 kilometer south of Carentan on the Periers road, D917, where they planned to link up with the 506th Regiment moving south from the Ingouf farm.

In Carentan Colonel von der Heydte, on June 11, recognized the precariousness of the German's position. The Ingouf farm had been lost and a lasting American bridgehead established. From the Vire-Taute canal the Americans could fire directly into the town. From the wooded embankments of the Bassin a Flot, northeast, two companies were threatening his defenses. The German paratroopers were decimated and exhausted.

The casualty rate was so high that in an old cider store on the edge of Carentan the German regimental Doctor Ross, with two captured American surgeons, treated 1,000 Germans, Georgians, Americans and civilians in a twenty-four hour period.

The remnants of the 795th Georgian Battalion were no longer capable of defensive fighting. Major General Ostendorff's 17th SS Grenadier Division arrived and prepared to counterattack from the southwest rather than expend his forces by reinforcing the Carentan defenses.

Von der Heydte withdrew his "Georgians" in the morning and positioned them in the hills southwest of the town. In the late afternoon after his unsuccessful six hour counterattack along the causeway highway he recognized his regiment would be encircled and annihilated. At dusk the German parachutists disengaged and withdrew from the towns' ruins leaving a delaying rearguard. The American bombardment that followed fell on a weakly defended town.

Von der Heydte's withdrawal was considered a blunder for which he would have been court marshaled but for his past exemplary record in Africa with Rommel. As a result of his regiment's withdrawal the Americans easily occupied Carentan the following day. Engineers with bulldozers pushed back the rubble and opened the N13 highway as a supply route. The 17th SS Grenadier Division's attack on June 13 faced a strong and readily supportable American force.

The continuing battle for Carentan evolved around Hill 30, a 30-meter elevation south of Carentan on highway D971 to Periers. The picturesque hill has become the site of a fashionable housing development comprising four two story, semi-detached homes forming a crescent centered around two tall oak trees. A white house facing the highway marks the entrance to the crescent. The two story single dwelling home in the northeast corner of the crescent was there in 1944.

The hill was occupied in the early hours of June 12 by the 506th and 501st Regiments who had encircled Carentan from the north and east respectively. Little German resistance had been met in this maneuver but Colonel Sink (506th Regiment) inadvertently positioned his command post group south of Hill 30 in the hamlet of la Billonnerie. Dawn of June 12 made it apparent he was surrounded "in a sea of Germans". The regiment's 1st Battalion attacked south from the hill into la Billonnerie's houses and barns. Heavy fighting followed before Colonel Sink's group could be extracted.

June 12 was spent clearing Carentan and probing south and west of Hill 30. The 2nd Battalion (506th Regiment) at dawn thrust north from Hill 30 into Carentan as G Company (327th Glider Regiment) attacked from Bassin a Flot. By mid morning the town was cleared of German resistance.

The loss of Carentan in the morning was the second serious event of the day to the Germans in Normandy. As Carentan was being cleared General Erich Marks, 84 Corps Commander, was strafed and killed by US fighter-bombers near Caumont.

On that day the Germans opened the missile age by launching the first V-1 rocket against London. It was an unmanned, air breathing, flying bomb that created much havoc and destruction. The launching sites were located around Cherbourg and Calais. The urgency to capture the launch sites became a priority.

On June 12 the 506th Regiment moved westward along the Baupte road (D903) and after repulsing a minor German counterattack reached Douville 2 kilometers from their start point. The Germans parachutists and panzer troops well entrenched held the American at bay for the remainder of the day.

On the Periers road (D971) the Regiment was not as successful. Passing through la Billonnerie the American paratroopers encountered stiff resistance just two fields south of the last group of barns on the east side of the road. From the third hedgerow German machine guns traversed the field and road arresting the advance.

Referring to the map one can readily see that the two roads, D903 and D971 entering Carentan from the south, join and point like an arrow at the town. Using the two roads and the fields in between the 17th SS Panzer Grenadier Division attacked the American positions on June 13 at 6:30 a.m.

The German force consisted of elements of the 37th and 38th Panzer Grenadier Regiments, the 17th Tank Battalion and the remnants of von der Heydte's 6th Parachute Regiment. The attack caught the US 506th Regiment at Douville off balance as it was just about to launch an attack. The Germans carried through and occupied the two road intersections just 500 meters from Carentan. An unsubstantiated German post battle report claims that a unit reached the Carentan railroad station.

Elements of the US 2nd Armored Division's Combat Command A arrived in Carentan at 10:30 a.m. and counterattacked along the

Baupte road three hours later with infantry support of the 502nd. Simultaneously another task force counterattacked down the Periers road. The 14th Armored Field Artillery Battalion added its support by laying a barrage on selected targets along the route of advance.

By the evening the front lines had moved 2.5 kilometers south and west of Carentan. In the fields apexed by the two roads lay 500 German dead.

On the following day the front lines were further advanced 3 kilometers on the Periers road and to Baupte on D903 7 kilometers. Gains along the Carentan front were so successful that the junction of the UTAH-OMAHA Beachheads was considered complete.

On the same day, June 14, the 826th Battalion of the 9th Engineer Command arrived in Carentan and commenced construction of the Advanced Landing Ground (ALG) A-10 near the town. The field became operational on June 19 and was completed two days later. Throughout June 22 and 23 sporadic German 88mm shellfire blasted the airfield wounding an engineer but going little damage. On June 23 the 50th Fighter Group occupied the strip. The dust situation became so critical that water-sprinkling procedures had to be adopted. Ingeniously the engineers made such a device from salvaged pontoons from the Rhino ferries being used to carry supplies across the channel.

On July 27 the 840th Battalion moved into the village of Meautis 4 kilometers southwest of Carentan and commenced construction of ALG A-17 with a 1,200-meter runway.

After the fall of Cherbourg on June 27, the way was open for receiving supplies directly from the United States. Only the condition of the port and the railway line leading south prohibited the immediate utilization of the tremendous load handling capacity of this great port. A milestone was reached on July 12 when the railway line from Cherbourg to Carentan was opened and supplies directly from the American east coast were able to move rapidly to the battle lines.

A monument in front of the Carentan town hall commemorates the actions of the 101st Airborne Division and the consolidation of the UTAH-OMAHA Beachheads. The 82nd Airborne Division is commemorated with a summer flower display. The Musee de la Liberte is on N13 400 meters past the town hall. There is a commemorative marker at the junction of N13 and the Ingouf farm road to the 502nd Regiment's actions.

Related stories are Dead Man's Corner, la Barquette Lock, Brevands and Auville-sur-de-Vey.

Picture 14: Carentan Causeway - Looking North
August 13, 1947

To link the Omaha and Utah forces the capture of Caretan was essential. Its northern side buildings are seen to the bottom. The low land was under three feet of water in June 1944. Colonel Robert Cole's 3rd Battalion of the 502nd Regiment moved south from Deadman's Corner, seen at the top right, on D-day +4. The German 6th Parachute Regiment had withdrawn along the elevated railroad line, seen on the left side, and deployed at the farm and along the road connecting the highway and the railroad. Snipers hidden in the marshes flanking the highway picked off Cole's men moving south. By dawn the following day Cole and 265 men were at the south end of the causeway. They launched a bayonet attack westward along the connecting road axis clearing out the farm and orchards and then moved to the railroad overpass. The few remaining German paratroopers withdrew into Caretan.

10.8 la Cambe

(24 kilometers west of Bayeux on N13)

On June 6 the US 5th Army Corps successfully assaulted OMAHA Beach establishing a beachhead 7 kilometers wide to a depth of 2 kilometers. On the eastern half of the corps front the 1st Division advanced south to gain depth and east to link up with the British advancing from GOLD Beach.

The 29th Division, the western half of the corps, advanced south on the flank of the 1st Division and westward to capture Isigny and join with the American forces from UTAH Beach at Auville-sur-le-Vey.

The 175th Infantry Regiment disembarked on OMAHA Beach (at les Moulins) June 7, at 4:30 p.m. They moved westward to Gruchy, a hamlet overlooking the beach. The 747th Tank Battalion (minus C Company) with infantry and armor moved out at 9:30 p.m. They proceeded south through Engelesqueville-le-Percee, arriving at the N13 highway 3 kilometers east of la Cambe. The advance tank echelon reached the eastern outskirts of la Cambe at 3 a.m. on June 8 but was stopped by antitank fire. A concerted tank attack at 5:30 a.m. destroyed the five defending antitank guns with the loss of one tank. Tank supported infantry moved into the village, which fell during the morning.

The American battalions moved through the village towards their westerly objective, Isigny. As the column was passing through it was mistakenly strafed by allied aircraft inflicting 20 casualties.

The American force proceeding westward faced stiff resistance 2 kilometers west of la Cambe at the St. Germain-du-Pert crossroads and along the narrow track south into the hamlet. A German force supported by a few mobile 88mm guns disabled six tanks.

Two kilometers further along N13 and to the north one kilometer at Cardonville, the 2nd Battalion (175th Regiment) ran into fierce resistance at the German strongpoint defending the radar station. With fire support from the twelve 6 inch guns of the British cruiser HMS Glasgow the strongpoint was reduced and taken by the later evening.

The following morning a party of engineers arrived on the site and drafted the plan for an airstrip. In the afternoon additional personnel (816th Battalion, 9th Engineer Command) arrived and the plans were put into action. Thirteen Germans hiding in the bunkers surrendered and several hundred horses, complete with saddles and bridles, were "liberated". The Cardonville Rearmament and Refueling strip (A-3) became operational at 6:30 a.m. on June 13. Over 500 missions were flown from this strip in the first six days until officially taken over by the 368th Fighter Group on June 19. The landing strip was between the Cardonville hamlet and the N13 highway.

Three kilometers northeast of la Cambe in the hamlet of Deux Jumeaux was another landing strip. Advanced Landing Ground, A-4, was started on June 15 by detachments of the 816th Battalion. This strip is immediately north of Deux Jumeaux, east and adjacent to the Englesqueville road (D125). There is a memorial plaque to the 367th Fighter Group.

The original invasion plan had anticipated more intervention by the German Luftwaffe throughout the campaign and therefore the strips were to receive fighters to counter the German marauders. As a result of the limited activity of the Luftwaffe the strips were lengthened to accommodate fighter-bombers increasing tactical support to the ground troops.

There is a large German cemetery one kilometer west of La Cambe on the south side of N13.

Initially the Americans established the war time temporary cemetery for American and German casualties. Throughout 1945 and 1946 the American bodies were either returned to the United States or re-interned in the St. Laurent Cemetery overlooking OMAHA Beach. Re-internments from the OMAHA sands of June 6 marked the first burials in the St. Laurent Cemetery.

Upon completion of the American transferals there remained only 8,000 German graves. In 1948 German re-internments from temporary wartime sites commenced and continue today. The cemetery contains over 21,000 German burials.

10.9 Grandcamp-les-Bains

Grandcamp-les-Bains is a resort and fishing town 10 kilometers west of OMAHA Beach. (From Bayeux take N13 west 3 kilometers to la Cambe. Take D113 north 5 kilometers.)

The Grandcamp and neighboring Maisy citizens were very active in the French Resistance. The Mayor, M. Gouye, and the Resistance Sector Chief, Jean Marion, worked tirelessly in collecting German defense information for the allied invasion planners. For example, Jean Marion informed London that an artillery gun recently mounted on the sea wall could only traverse left. On June 6 morning the destroyer USS Herndon positioned itself east of the gun firing into its blind spot. A shell penetrated the German ammo compartment obliterating the gun and its crew.

Too late on June 5 after the invasion fleet had sailed in radio silence, Jean Marion discovered and transmitted two very significant pieces of information. Southwest of Grandcamp a 25-gun antiaircraft battery had moved in. These guns would take their toll of the paratrooper transport planes exiting the area in the predawn D-Day hours. Also the gun battery supposedly housed in the casements at Pointe du Hoc (4 kilometers east of Grandcamp-les-Bains) was actually a kilometer to the south in open field positions. The following day's assault by US rangers upon Pointe du Hoc to seize a battery removed was therefore needless.

The transmission of the intelligence information to England was difficult. The resistance transmitter of Andre Farine in his Letanville cafe was continually threatened by German detection. Carrier pigeons did not always get through. Off-duty German soldiers were paid bounties for shooting pigeons carrying messages.

On June 6 the American 116th and 16th Regiments assaulted OMAHA Beach. Throughout that day and the following day the regiments fought for a toe-hold in France. By noon on June 8 the 2nd and 3rd Battalions (116th Regiment), elements of the 5th Ranger Battalion, and two companies of the 743rd Tank Battalion were at Pointe du Hoc, 4 kilometers to the east. These units had left Vierville at OMAHA Beach in the early morning hours and advanced west along the coastal highway relieving the beleaguered rangers at Pointe du Hoc at noon.

Without a pause the Americans pressed onward towards Grandcamp-les-Bains. The Germans holding the town were from the 3rd Battalion, 726th Regiment (attached to the 352nd Division). Two strongpoints defended the town as well as minefields between the western outskirts down to the river valley. One strongpoint of machine guns was housed in a pillbox on the northwest corner of the town on the edge of the beach. The second Strongpoint (No. 79 on German maps) was situated on the northeast edge of town in the fields across the road from the church. The strongpoint stretched 400 meters along the shore edge and inland to the coastal road. In addition to the small arms and automatic weapons it contained mortars and a 47mm gun. The position was well situated to repel a seaborne assault and dominated the valley to the east crossed by the coast road. The Germans had closed the sluice gate at the river's mouth. The low-lying land quickly flooded. The American advance had to channel along the road over the marsh. The 5th Rangers were first to arrive at the bridge. The German strongpoint from the higher ground poured machine gun and mortar fire into the leading platoon checking its advance. The British cruiser HMS Glasgow turned her guns on Strongpoint 79 and between 3 and 4 p.m. fired 113 shells into the position. The fusillade lifted, C Company tanks (743rd Tank Battalion) crossed the bridge. A tank triggered a mine and was disabled. The 3rd Battalion (116th Regiment) followed. King Company deployed to the north of the road while Love Company skirted the south side. The companies advanced up the slope and entered the strongpoint position. Hand to hand combat was needed to suppress the resistance.

Item Company pressed through the town while sniper fire continued to harass. A platoon under 2nd Lieutenant Norvin Nathan passed through and captured the pillbox on the western beach. By dark all resistance had been eliminated. The battle is remembered by many veterans as more bitter than D-Day.

Within hours of its capture Grandcamp-les-Bains became the site of the 1st United States Army Group Headquarters (FUSAGH) under Lieutenant General Omar N. Bradley. The beaches became a minor port and several airfields were established nearby. General Bradley's headquarters exact location is at Cricqueville (3 kilometers southeast) in the two thinned-out orchards adjacent to the village on its northeast corner.

On June 12 General Eisenhower, along with General George C. Marshall, Admiral Ernest J. King, and Lieutenant General Henry (Hap) H. Arnold, landed on OMAHA Beach and drove to Bradley's Grandchamp headquarters (actually in Cricqueville) to lunch on C and K rations.

As the front lines advanced General Bradley moved forward with Tactical Headquarters facilities and staff but it was not until after the fall of Paris on August 25 that the complete headquarters moved out of the Grandcamp-les-Bains area. Throughout the intervening months the most senior allied statesmen, politicians and commanders visited General Bradley here.

On June 14 General Charles de Gaulle made a one-day whirlwind visit to Bayeux, Isigny and Grandcamp-les-Bains. He was enthusiastically welcomed by the freshly liberated populace. His reception at Bayeux and Isigny delayed his planned arrival at the Grandcamp-les-Bains town hall. By 5:30 p.m. Mayor Gouye and the awaiting citizens had just about despaired of his arrival when in roared the general's jeep. After his third rousing speech of the day, followed by the singing of the Marseillaise, his group drove off to Courseulles-sur-Mer (Canadian JUNO Beach) where they re-embarked for England.

In Grandcamp-les-Bains the Musee des Rangers commemorates their actions at Pointe du Hoc.

One kilometer southwest of Grandcamp-les-Bains is the rebuilt village of Maisy. In the fields south of the village and west of the road the Germans had located two batteries consisting of five 155mm guns in open pits and four 100mm guns in casements. These two positions, Strongpoints 80 and 86 on German defense maps, encompassed an area 1 kilometer square. Although naval shellfire had torn Maisy apart the two batteries were still active on June 7.

On June 8 while the 3rd Battalion (116 Regiment) was sweeping the coastal road and battling for Grandcamp-les-Bains the 1st Battalion with Able Company of the 743rd Tank Battalion proceeded directly to Maisy through Jucoville. Meeting little opposition the force moved against Maisy and the batteries' positions from the east. German artillery and mortar fire stopped the advance. Throughout the night June 8-9 the Americans reorganized the received fuel supplies for the tanks. The following morning the American 58th Armored Field Artillery Battalion and destroyers off the coast pounded the German positions. A successful attack followed with the 3rd Battalion from the east and the 1st Battalion from the north. After completing their mission the American battalions moved southwest towards Isigny mopping up the Germans in their shoreline pillboxes.

Three kilometers southwest of Maisy is the coastal fishing hamlet of Gefosse-Fontenay. On June 8 the "Cossacs" of the Eastern Battalion, 439th Regiment, 352nd German Division watched as a bullet riddled American landing craft drifted onto their beach with the incoming tide. Aboard were six dead American naval officers, including a "beachmaster" responsible for the organization of a sector of UTAH Beach. He was slumped across a water soaked briefcase containing coded documents. Their "find" was rushed to 84th Corps Headquarters in St. Lo for translation and decoding.

Within a few hours the Germans knew the allied invasion plan. The U .S. 7th Corps was to push westwards from UTAH Beach, cut off the Contentin Peninsula, establish a defense line on its southern flank, and swing its main strength north to capture Cherbourg. The 5th and 7th Corps were to effect a link-up of the OMAHA and UTAH Beachheads at Carentan as soon as possible. The American 5th Corps from OMAHA Beach was to link up with the British 30th Corps from GOLD Beach at Bayeux. There would then be a continuous beachhead from the Orne River to the west coast of the Contentin Peninsula. This indicated that the allied landings were not a diversion but a major effort. Excerpts were rushed to the effected divisions, to Field Marshal Rommel in Roche-Guyon and to Field Marshal von Runstedt at Saint Germain. Orders were issued and deployments were made to utilize the information and upset the allied plan but all in vain. German strength was too weak to capitalize on their knowledge. The German Luftwaffe had been shot out of the sky. What reinforcements were available from other sectors were delayed and badly mauled by the allied fighter-bombers. The best the Germans could do was slow down the allied timetable and watch the great might roll steadily forward on with its plan. Hitler doubted the documents authenticity. "Probably a clever rouse to mislead us. No army would have such a significant document near the front lines subject to capture and exploitation."

Two kilometers southeast of Grandcamp-les-Bains is the hamlet of Letanville. The café proprietor, Andre Farine, listening to the conversations of the laborers working on defenses in the area was able to secure important information for the allied invasion planners in England. Under the guise of securing wood for his baking ovens he could study the German battery at Pointe du Hoc. He would then send his findings to London from his concealed transmitter.

On the evening of June 5, Farine heard over his receiver the code phrase he had been awaiting "It is hot in Suez". Splitting his force of forty fellow resistance men into eight groups they set off for Fontaine (1 kilometer south of Isigny) and cut the important telephone cable from Cherbourg to Germany at eight points. For his gallant efforts and exploits he was awarded the Croix de Guerre.

Within a short distance of Grandcamp-les-Bains three landing strips were developed by the 9th Engineer Command in the first few days of the invasion.

At St. Pierre-du-Mont 4 kilometers east on June 9, construction of landing strip A-1 was started by the 834th Battalion. It became operational on June 13 as a refueling and rearmament strip. On June 25 it was taken over by the 366th Fighter Group.

At Criqueville en Bessin 3 kilometers southeast on June 10, the 1500 meter Advanced Landing Ground, , was started. From June 14-25 it was operated as a refueling and rearmament strip until a tactical fighter squadron moved in from England.

At Cardonville, 5 kilometers south, the 816th Battalion commenced construction of a refueling and rearmament strip A-3 on June 9. It was completed on June 13 and functioned in this capacity until June 19 when the 368th Fighter Group moved in.

Related to actions at Grandcamp-les-Bains is the battle of Pointe du Hoc and the capture of Isigny.

Picture 15: Gefosse Fontenay - Looking North
June 14, 1948

A Hamlet southwest of Grandcamp-les-Bains

On D-day +2 German troops boarded a bullet riddled American landing craft that drifted onto this beach. Aboard were six dead naval officers, one slumped across his water soaked briefcase containing the invasion plans and the follow-up ninety-day timetable. Copies were sent to German headquarters; however, skepticism treated the information cautiously. Although this information confirmed there was no other invasion planned in the Calais area no German divisions were shifted into this area to strengthen the German positions.

10.10 Isigny

(The town of Isigny is 11 kilometers east of Carentan on the Bayeux-Cherbourg highway, N13.)

To the south of the town, 2 kilometers, is the hamlet of Fontaine. Through here in 1944 ran the German telecommunications cable from Cherbourg to Germany. Upon receiving a coded signal from London on the evening of June 5, Andre Farine of the French Resistance living at Letanville near Grandcamp-les-Bains, moved with a force of forty men into Fontaine. In the darkness of the last hours of the day his force divided into eight groups of five men who removed eight sections of the telephone cable. Several hours later the allied armies swarmed across the five invasion beaches as German communication units tried to locate the broken cable and restore their lines of communication.

Once ashore and a foothold established the American forces on UTAH and OMAHA Beachheads pressed forward to link up their sectors. Isigny and Carentan were vital road centers for German communications and the key to a junction of the beachheads.

From OMAHA Beach to the east the American 175th Regiment and 747th Tank Battalion (29th Division) advanced westward clearing la Cambe on June 8. While the 175th was destroying German opposition along the N13 highway, the 116th Regiment to the north was sweeping the coastal region. The advances of the two regiments isolated the remnants of the German 914th Infantry Regiment and artillery. Under pressure from the north and east and threatened by being "pocketed" by the fall of Isigny, the German troops holding the coastal region northeast of Isigny escaped through Isigny during the night of June 8-9 as the American forces were entering the eastern outskirts.

Throughout June 8 from 8 a.m. to 8 p.m. the town was shelled and bombed by the allies. The center was obliterated. Only 40% of the town still stood. Miraculously the Aure River bridge had not been damaged or destroyed by the retreating Germans.

At 3 a.m. on June 9 American tanks entered the town supported by infantry of the 3rd Battalion (175th Regiment). The town was aflame. There was little organized resistance except for snipers. At 8 a.m. a strong German counterattack was repulsed. Two hundred prisoners were taken including naval, marine and air force personnel.

From the town center the tanks turned south down D5 towards Pont Benard and Fontaine. King Company of the 175th Regiment moved westward to capture the Vire River bridge at Auville-sur-le-Vey.

With Isigny captured the American engineers opened the locks of the Aure River to the north previously closed by the Germans to flood the low lying land to the east. The stench of the marshes is still remembered today.

A monument at Place de Gaulle in the rebuilt town center commemorates the general's visit on the afternoon of June 14. General Charles de Gaulle on his first visit to the liberated French soil landed at Courseulles-sur-Mer, (Canadian JUNO Beach), June 14, and drove to Bayeux. A message was sent ahead to Isigny at 2 p.m. that the general would be visiting shortly. The cure, Abbe Lecoq, the mayor and deputy mayor accompanied by many of the citizens greeted the general's party on the eastern outskirts when they arrived at 4:45 p.m. The parish priest climbed aboard the general's jeep and escorted the group into town where they were enthusiastically received by the townsfolk. The crowds thronged at the crossroads of Grand and Rue de la Mairie. Rubble lay for 300 meters in all directions. The front lines were only 5 kilometers south. The general made a brief speech, lead the citizens in the Marseillaise and then departed for Grandcamp-les-Bains.

Four and a half kilometers north of Isigny is the coastal fishing hamlet Gefosse-Fontenay. On June 8th a bullet riddled landing craft with dead American officers and the invasion plan was washed up on the beach. For further details refer to the story of Grandcamp-les-Bains (Battle Site 10.9).

Related stories are Auville-sur-le-Vey, la Cambe and Grandcamp-les-Bains.

10.11 Auville-sur-le-Vey

(Auville-sur-le-Vey is a village 7 kilometers east of Carentan on the Bayeux highway, N13. The action described centered around the Vire River bridge 100 meters to the east.)

After establishing the UTAH and OMAHA Beachheads the American forces moved towards each other to effect a linkup at Auville-sur-le-Vey.

On the morning of June 9 Isigny was captured by American infantry with tank support. The force had moved westward from OMAHA Beach. Once captured and secured, King Company (175th Regiment, 29th Infantry Division) accompanied by a platoon of tanks moved west toward the Vire River bridge at Auville-sur-le-Vey. Six hundred meters east of the bridge the N13 highway crossed a railroad. The adjacent station was German Strongpoint 94, a machine gun nest. This afforded brief opposition. Overcoming the strongpoint, King Company moved on to its objective.

The bridge Pont-le-Vey crosses the Vire River a hundred meters east of Auville-sur-le-Vey. On the river's west bank a hundred meters south of the bridge, at the mouth of a drainage ditch, was a machine gun and mortar pit. Amongst the hedges and trees bordering the village's eastern boundary and in the copse of trees to the neighboring south were automatic weapons and riflemen. The German strength, although not formidable, held the high ground with open fields of fire into the American ranks on the east bank. The only concealment for the US infantrymen was a barn, a row of trees north of the highway, and a deep drainage ditch to the south.

It was almost noon when the Americans arrived at Pont-le-Vey to discover it had been destroyed by the retreating Germans. Machine gun and mortar fire from the west bank splattered onto the highway scattering the company into the trees, the barn and the drainage ditch.

The 29th Reconnaissance Squadron came forward in the afternoon. At 6 p.m. the squadron's tank guns and armored car machine guns provided covering fire as King Company left the line of trees and barn north of the highway, crossed the open field and forded the fifteen meter wide Vire River. The demolished bridge and elevated roadway protected the company's left flank from the German fire positions to the south and southwest. Pressing into the village the Americans took full advantage of the compactness of its buildings to skirt around behind the German defenders facing east along the tree line. The defenders either surrendered or died. The American casualties numbered three dead and nine wounded.

Auville-sur-le-Vey became the front line that night as Chaarlie Company of the 254th Engineers Combat Battalion placed a Bailey bridge over the river.

On June 10 four days after the invasion commenced, at 3 p.m., Able Company of the 1st Battalion of the 401st Glider Infantry Regiment from the UTAH Beachhead entered King Company lines on the western outskirts of Auville-sur-le-Vey, 200 meters from the village crossroads where the highway crosses a stream. Although the UTAH-OMAHA linkup was tenuous, contact had been made and developments during the next few days consolidated the position.

For several weeks after, until the southerly movement of the Americans pushed the Germans out of artillery range, N13 and its bridge were prime targets for the German gunners. The Carentan to Isigny road was a well traversed traffic artery between the 7th and 5th Corps. On June 12 German forces were but 3 kilometers to the south when General Dwight D. Eisenhower, against the advice of his driver, ordered him to "step-on-it", and crossed the bridge unscathed.

Four kilometers south of Auville-sur-le-Vey on the east bank of the Vire River is the hamlet of St. Lambert. On July 8 the 832nd Battalion of the 9th Engineer Command commenced construction of Advanced Landing Ground A-11 which was completed and released to the 1st Army on July 21. Harassment fire killed one man and wounded two other battalion members during its construction.

Related stories are Isigny (east), Carentan (west) and Brevands (northwest). The latter story describes the actions of the UTAH Beachhead units in effecting the linkup at Auville-sur-le-Vey.

Chapter 11 Carentan-**Periers Isthmus**

On June 12 regiments of the US 101st Airborne Division encircled Carentan from the northwest and took up positions to the south. On the following day a German counterattack by the 17th SS. Panzer Grenadier Division unsuccessfully attempted to recapture the town. Although the US 7th and 5th Corps had joined the UTAH and OMAHA Beachheads, their sparse numbers and consequent weakness south of Carentan made the union tenuous. Throughout the remaining days of June the Americans fought hard to push the front lines south and away from the only highway (N13) joining the two beachheads. The highway and its bridge across the Vire-Taute Canal, at Auville-sur-le-Vey, 7 kilometers east of Carentan, was under constant harassment fire from German artillery 4 kilometers southwest. The Americans ever mindful of further German counterattacks, could not afford to decrease their vigil when deploying their reserves.

The Germans recognized that if they lost the sector southwest of Carentan the Americans could move mobile forces down the highway, D971, to Periers (18 kilometers) then turn west towards Lessay and outflank the German forces facing the US 8th Corps with an end run. To maintain their defense positions and to withstand the American pressure, German reinforcements were secured from neighboring divisions' reserves not engaged.

Running southwest from Carentan, D971, passes along an 8 kilometer isthmus of dry land to Sainteny. The Germans, when they controlled the locks of the Douve and Taute Rivers had back flooded the valleys and marshes to create a natural isthmus of land 2 kilometers at its widest point. South 7 kilometers at Sainteny the isthmus broadens.

Major General J. Lawton Collins' (7th Corps Commander) plan was to attack south with the 83rd Division to Sainteny. The narrowness of the "neck" limited the troops that could be used at the "point". Once south and through the restriction the 4th and 9th Divisions could move into the battle area and fan out on the flanks of the 83rd Division.

Facing the Americans in the narrow funneled corridor were hardened troops of the 6th Parachute Regiment, the 17th SS Panzer Grenadier Division and 2nd SS Panzer Division.

By July 4 hard fought gains had been made by the Americans along D971 to the D29 junction 4 kilometers south of Carentan. Throughout the next eleven days the battles in the area produced tremendous casualties but removed the threat of German counterattacks on Carentan and eased the German harassment shellfire on the N13 highway and its important Vire-Taute Canal Bridge.

The 1st US Army Group's Commander, Lieutenant General Omar N. Bradley, encompassed the broader strategy, which further emphasized the need to advance out of the marshes and into maneuvering space. He wished to mass forces on a narrow front and launch a powerful attack cutting through German defenses. Wheeling west he would then cut off and encircle the German division facing Major General Troy H. Middleton's 8th Corps west of the 7th Corps. Before launching such an operation General Bradley wanted two German strongpoints southwest (St. Germain-sur-Seves) and southeast (le Varde) of Sainteny occupied to ensure a continuous uninterrupted operational momentum. A more desirable start line, not in swamps and marshes, was essential.

11.1 Junction D971 – D29

(4 kilometers southwest of Carentan on D971.)

On July 4 the American front line had pushed south from Carentan to this intersection. Their attack on July 4 encompassing the hamlets of le Varimesnil, la Moisentrie (0.5 kilometers west) and le Mesnil (2 kilometers southeast) claimed 1,500 American casualties, 6 Germans were captured and 200 meters were gained. The vicious fighting and resulting high casualties caused General Collins to change his plan from a one division front to include the 4th Division on the west side of highway D971. By July 7, after three days of fighting, casualties were 3,500 dead and wounded. The German 6th Parachute Regiment's Commander, Lieutenant Colonel Freidrich von der Heydte, returned the captured American medical personnel. In his accompanying note he recognized the medical personnel were needed. Should the situation be reversed he hoped the division's commander, Major General Robert C. Macon, would return the consideration.

After four days of battle, gains had been made. The 12th Regiment (4th Division) on the west of D971 advanced two kilometers reaching the junction of D197, 2.5 kilometers northeast of Sainteny. The 330th Regiment (83rd Division) had advanced southeast on D29 5 kilometers to St. Andre-de-Bohon. The villages and hamlets in the path of the advance were completely destroyed by shellfire, bombing and the house to house fighting.

Two kilometers west of the D971-D29 junction is the village of Meautis. On July 27 the 840th Battalion of the 9th Engineer Command moved into the area and commenced construction of an Advanced Landing Ground, A-17, including a 1,400-meter runway for fighter-bombers.

Related stories are Sainteny and le Port.

11.2 Sainteny

(8.5kilometers southwest of Carentan on D971 east of les Forges)

On July 8 the 22nd Regiment (4th Division) was 2.5 kilometers north of the town on the west side of D971. The 8th Regiment was to their west. The 12th Regiment rested in reserve. The American advance from the D29 junction (one kilometer) had come to a standstill. A major break in the stalemate occurred on July 10 when the Germans, leaving their excellent defense positions, attacked. No longer hidden in the foliage of the hedgerows, but "naked" in the fields, American firepower dealt a devastating blow on the attackers. Artillery, mortars and machine guns laced the fields. Fifty prisoners were taken and 480 Germans buried.

The Americans followed their advantage with an attack against the weakened and depleted German defenses. By July 15 the 4th Division which had moved past Sainteny 3 kilometers along D971 to Raids. In its ten days of combat the division had 2,300 casualties.

On the east side of the highway the 331st Regiment (83rd Division) occupied the gutted town of Sainteny on July 9. The town, one of the hardest hit in the Carentan sector, had half of its homes destroyed and the dairy industry had been dealt a harsh blow when it counted 2,000 slaughtered cattle.

Related story Junction D971 - D29.

11.3 le Port

(4 kilometers south of Carentan on D971 to D29, then turn left and drive 5 kilometers to le Port)

From the junction of D971 and D29 on July 4 the 83rd Division attacked south towards the Taute River and its crossing points at le Port and la Brechellene (1.5 kilometers southwest).

The terrain was not conducive to attack. D29 was paved but the connecting roads were mere wagon tracks. Rain had soaked the fields and the ditches were flooded. Vehicle traffic was almost impossible and infantry movement was slow. The following four days the 331st Regiment battled determined German resistance in the fields bordering D29. As they came closer to le Port and its causeway over the Taute River, German resistance increased. German tanks dug in as pillboxes with infantry and machine guns defending had to be knocked out by bazooka teams. Superb German camouflage concealed the targets from American artillery and fighter-bombers.

The causeway across to Tribehou was undefended. However, the Germans held the fields west of the le Port intersection also denying the Americans the la Brechellene causeway 1.5 kilometers to the southwest crossing the Taute River to le Varde. German combat units consisting of one tank and thirty supporting infantry counterattacked the American positions along the D29 road.

By July 14 the Tribehou causeway had been crossed. The next day a halt was called by General Collins to relieve the mauled division. The point regiment (331st) had lost five commanders in the first week. The divisions casualties numbered 5,000.

Related story Junction D971 - D29, la Varde Causeway

11.4 la Varde Causeway

(4 kilometers south of Carentan on D971 to D29, then turn left and drive 5 kilometers to le Port, turn right and drive 1.5 kilometers to la Brechellene)

From the intersection at la Brechellene the road D57 crosses the marshy Taute River valley to the hamlet of la Varde, 2 kilometers across the causeway.

The seizing of the le Port - Tribehou causeway to the north on July 14, and the subsequent collapse of German resistance on the west side of the Taute River, set the stage for the battle to seize the la Brechellene - la Varde causeway.

Although the Germans did not have a strong defense in la Varde, the terrain with unrestricted visibility greatly enhanced the German defenses. Five well camouflaged and sited machine gun nests supported by a reinforced company held the east bank of the river valley. From the American positions at la Brechellene the causeway runs directly south to the east bank. German self propelled artillery in and around Marchesieux 2 kilometers beyond la Varde, combined with the long range visibility across the open fields, further strengthened the defenses and presented a serious obstacle to the battalions of the decimated 83rd Division.

Separating the opposing forces was the river, 5 meters wide and 1 meter deep, the valley itself was a kilometer and a half of soft mud flats. Crossing the valley was the two lane asphalt road slightly elevated above the marsh, flanked by two rows of evenly spaced trees.

At the US jump off point in la Brechellene, overshadowing the road intersection and nestled into the trees and hedges, was a chateau used previously as a German headquarters. The Americans utilized it as an artillery observation post and a headquarters. The small bridge in the causeway spanning the river had been demolished by the retreating Germans. The mud flats could not support vehicles. Eight amphibious "Alligators" arrived too late to be of use. It was an infantryman's battle of slithering and crawling through the muck and mire until the dry hard ground on the eastern bank would cease to camouflage their movement. Their sheltered foxholes filled with water and fearful of counterattack, these wallowing fighters hesitated to take the necessary time to clear their mud clogged and jammed weapons.

In the late afternoon on July 17 a reconnaissance party of the 330th Regiment made a sally towards la Varde from Tribehou to the northeast. A machine gun raked across their path, stopping the advance.

At 6 p.m. a company of the 331st Regiment made a diversionary attack from the northwest but halted after receiving thirteen casualties.

The main attack commenced at 6:30 p.m. by a battalion of Colonel York's 331st Regiment. Avoiding the road and its crossfire, the men crossed the marshes on the prefabricated footbridges laid as they advanced. By dusk a small bridgehead was established on the la Varde bank. German fire pre-sited on the bridge, stopped attempts by American engineers to establish a temporary span across the demolished section. Lacking ammunition, supplies, and replacements the division's commander, Major General Robert C. Macon, permitted the battalion to withdraw during the early hours the following morning.

Under the cover of the semi-light of dawn on July 19, with smoke shells and flank fire support by the 330th Regiment (to the German's north and east), the 331st Regiment re-attacked across the length of the causeway. There was light resistance and a bridgehead was secured.

Engineers quickly laid a Bailey bridge across the demolished section, taking the precaution of preparing it for demolition so it could be destroyed in the event of a successful German counterattack. A German shell exploding nearby detonated the demolitions and destroyed the bridge. Without tanks in the bridgehead the infantry's position was precarious. A small counterattack that afternoon forced the Americans to once again pull back across the Taute valley to their own lines.

Thus ended attempts to assault la Varde. A battalion commander was missing and the companies involved suffered 50% casualties.

On July 27 the 2nd Battalion of the 331st Regiment (83rd Division) moved across the causeway in conjunction with the follow through of the July 25 Operation COBRA. The Germans fearful of encirclement had withdrawn leaving the fields strewn with mines.

Related stories are Junction D971 - D29 and le Port.

11.5 St. Germain-sur-Seves

(13 kilometers southwest of Carentan on D971 and 1 kilometer north on D301)

Since July 5-12 the US 90th Division had been fighting at Beaucoudray 7 kilometers to the northwest. The division was seriously weakened as a result of the costly battle to dislodge the German forces holding a narrow front flanked by Mont Castre to the west and Marais de Gorges (marsh) to the east. Once through the funnel they passed south towards Periers, continually opposed by determined and fanatical resistance. With the 357th Regiment on its east flank and the 359th Regiment on its west, the division advanced on a 3 kilometer front. Simultaneously the US 4th and 83rd Divisions were fighting down the D971 highway from Carentan southwest towards Periers.

By July 20 the 90th Division had reached the banks of the Seves River opposite St. Germain-sur-Seves.

Heavy rains throughout June had swollen the Seves River and one of its tributaries east of the village, creating an island village 3 kilometers long and 1 kilometer wide.

Lieutenant General Omar N. Bradley's (Commander of the US 1st Army Group) plans for Operation COBRA required the reduction of this strongpoint. Capturing the island village would place the division in an advantageous position to seize Periers and cut the St. Lo - Lessay highway. This east-west road provided the Germans an excellent supply route along the full length of their northern defense line. Allied fighter-bombers controlled it by day but throughout the seven hours of night time, German supply columns moved relatively unmolested.

Access onto the island was across the paved road (D140) on its southwestern end and a muddy lane fording the marsh at the north end. The island was hedgerowed and defended by a reduced German battalion with several assault guns and light tanks. The marsh was treeless and without cover of any consequence.

The 358th Regiment commanded by Lieutenant Colonel C. E. Clarke, Jr. moved into position west of the river. The regiment was burdened with fresh green replacements. A planned night assault was discarded when the inexperience of the force was considered.

Saturday morning , July 22, was rainy and overcast. Fighter-bomber attacks were called off and artillery spotter aircraft were grounded. 8th Corps Artillery blasted the island but without observers did not target specific defense positions. As the American artillery fire heralded the infantry attack, German counter battery fire was directed on the American start line across the marsh. Heavy casualties and confusion resulted.

Three hours behind schedule an American battalion advanced across the muddy ford. A two hundred meter toehold was punched into the German defenses with the American infantry suffering 50% casualties. The four hundred still able to fight repelled a minor German counterattack. German artillery pounded the ford crossing, stopping the flow of reinforcements and ammunition supplies.

Darkness brought insecurity to some of the green troops so they slipped back quietly across the marsh to their division lines. Officers not recognizing the new men of their units were powerless to stop the withdrawals.

Dawn brought forth a two pronged German pincer against the bridgehead. Supported by thirty infantrymen, four armored vehicles approached from the flanks. The Americans compressed their line and pulled back behind the D301 road bordering the marsh into two hedgerowed fields at the east end of the ford. German machine gun fire rattled across the ford cutting off the only retreat route. A shell landed amongst a bunched group of soldiers inflicting heavy casualties. Handkerchiefs fluttered and the surrender began.

The battle was lost and over. The American casualties were 100 killed, 500 wounded, and 200 captured.

Developments of Operation COBRA in late July caused the Germans to withdraw from St. Germain-sur-Seves, leaving the area strewn with many types of mines and booby traps.

This widespread and prevalent tactic combined with American caution, delayed the 7th and 8th Corps in their pursuit of the withdrawing Germans.

As the American's increased their gains additional airfields were established. In late July the 826th Battalion of the 9th Engineer Command moved into Gorges 4 kilometers northwest of St. Germain-sur-Seves, where Advanced Landing Ground A-26 was constructed with a 2,000-meter runway and hardstands for medium bombers.

Chapter 12 Vire-Taute Isthmus

By early July the American forces were embroiled in battles for difficult terrain whose geographical features benefited the defenders. To the far west around La Haye du Puits and Mont Castre the 8th Corps, although progressing, was fighting against determined resourceful defenders. South of Carentan, squeezed into a narrow funnel, the 7th Corps was also incurring high casualties with little gains.

Lieutenant General Omar N. Bradley, Commander of the 1st US Army, planned a decisive breakout by puncturing the German defense line at a point favorable to immediate development by his mobile and armored divisions. The success of this operation would depend, in part, on the acquisition of a number of strategic positions. One of these was the southward movement of the 8th, 7th, and 19th Corps to the St. Lo-Lessay (D900) highway.

The constant pressure by the Americans had forced the Germans to spread their reserves and reinforcements across the front in piecemeal actions. At no time were the Germans able to concentrate a significantly strong enough force to launch a strategic counterattack.

Recognizing that the slugging matches of the 7th and 8th Corps were not going to gain D900 quickly, General Bradley shifted his attention to the Vire-Taute isthmus. The isthmus base line stretched east-west along the N13 between Carentan and Auville-sur-le-Vey and southward 15 kilometers between the Vire River on the east and the Taute River on the west. As both rivers flowed north to the sea through Auville-sur-le-Vey and Carentan respectively a narrow north-south land corridor was created by the Germans defensively back flooding the rivers and turning the adjacent low lands into wide marsh lands.

Major General Charles H. Corbetts' 30th Division (19th Corps) straddled the Vire River. East of the 30th Division, the 29th Division had fought its way south to within 3.5 kilometers of St. Lo's northern outskirts. The two mauled German divisions (352nd and 3rd Parachute) had fought with aggressive and successful defense tactics since June 6 thwarting the American plans for a quick capture of St. Lo.

The Vire-Taute isthmus was untried and awaiting development. The 120th Regiment north of the Vire et Taute Canal straddling N174 had not advanced as successfully as its neighboring 117th Regiment east of the Vire River.

A divisional simultaneous double thrust attack was planned. The 120th Regiment was to cross the canal causeway from the north as the 117th Regiment moved west crossing the Vire River at Airel-le-Pont, St. Fromond (11 kilometers south of Isigny). Both regiments were up to their start line positions.

General Corlett's intelligence officers predicted stiff resistance. Intelligence had not uncovered the fact that the German defenders has shifted westward in the last weeks of June to meet the threats of the 7th and 8th Corps. The holding force on the isthmus were the 500 soldiers of Kamfgruppe Heinz and a panzer grenadier unit. Although numerically small the Germans had been on the isthmus for several weeks constructing well sited defense positions on high ground and across water barriers. To overcome these foreseeable obstacles American air power and artillery was to "soften" the front line defenses. As the infantry advanced a rolling barrage would overcome pockets of resistance. On the day of attack bad weather grounded the fighter-bombers and the artillery spotter aircraft. Regardless the attacks proceeded.

12.1 Montmartin-en-Graignes

(8 kilometers southeast of Carentan. From Carentan drive east on N13 3 kilometers to N174, south 5 kilometers to D305, east 1 kilometer)

Three and a half weeks before Montmartin-en-Graignes was to serve as the 120th Regiment's (30th Division) start line for the July 7 offensive across the Vire and Taute Canal, there were noteworthy actions around the village.

On June 10 the OMAHA and UTAH Beachheads were joined at Auville-sur-le-Vey at the Vire River bridge on N13. The American defense line approximated the width of the highway. It was a very tenuous union. To gain depth and remove the threat of the Germans reoccupying the highway and cutting the thin thread on June 12, Easy and Charlie Companies (175th Regiment, 29th Division) drove south of Isigny to a position east of Montmartin-en-Graignes on the east side of the Vire River. Their objectives were to reconnoiter and capture the two bridges crossing the Vire et Taute Canal south and southwest of Montmartin-en-Graignes. In their cross-country trek from Isigny they had avoided German Strongpoint 95 at the railroad bridge crossing the river 2 kilometers north of Montmartin-en-Graignes. This Paris to Cherbourg railline had been a major German supply route to the Contentin Peninsula. Similar to other important bridges it was guarded against French Resistance activities and possible commando raids.

Easy company, accompanied by Brigadier General Norman Cota and initially by the regiment's commander Colonel Paul R. Goode, crossed the 150 meter wide river and marsh a kilometer south of the railroad bridge at 7 a.m. The assault boats drew some distant machine gun fire but casualties were light.

Note: General Cota, played by Robert Mitchum, in the movie "The Longest Day" has been immortalized for his aggressive leadership on OMAHA Beach, D-Day morning, that saved many American lives.

At the same time half a kilometer south at the loop in the river, Charlie Company crossed in assault boats under light distant automatic fire. Both companies were to rendezvous at Montmartin-en-Graignes.

Easy Company approached the village from the north passing between the village and the Chateau des Vignes. The company joined the road D444 exiting to the west from the village. At the junction of D444 and D305 on the northwest corner of the village, a German ambush trapped the company. In this sunken road lined by the tall steep impenetrable hedgerow, two walls of machine gun fire engulfed their numbers. The enemy ambush force was not large. Two of the Americans crawled through a drainage pipe under a hedgerow bringing them to a position behind the Germans who were machine gunning randomly through the bushes. The Germans fell. The Easy Company survivors took the brief lull to retreat eastward. They scattered. Some headed back to the river. Thirty rallied around General Cota at the chateau. At 10:40 a.m. 50 men of Charlie Company who had met a similar fate as they neared the eastern outskirts of the village joined the chateau group. At 11 a.m. the enlarged force attempted to reach the canal bridge on N174 by side slipping east and south of the village. About 400 meters southeast of the village the force ran head on into prepared defense positions. Cota called for American artillery fire which turned out to be ineffective. The force withdrew to circle around north and west of Montmartin-en-Graignes. By 4 p.m. the force had fallen back to the sunken road, the site of the mornings ambush. German fire once more took its toll. Cota's force withdrew to a position 500 meters northwest of the village. At 6 p.m. 60 men of the Regiment (101st Airborne Division) part of a two-regiment pincer movement on Carentan chanced into the American position.

Simultaneously to the north, a battalion of the 327th Glider Infantry Regiment was battling its way south from Auville-sur-le-Vey to support Easy and Charles Companies actions. German defenses all along the east-west railroad embankment were impenetrable wall.

Cota's force, now 150 men strong, attacked the lightly defended village.

While General Cota's force was bedded down in Montmartin, Colonel Goode on the east bank of the river took charge of George Company. Upon crossing the river in the dark the company moved south past Montmartin-en-Graignes, 2 kilometers to the Vire River bridge at the hamlet of la Raye. In the fields immediately north of the hamlet the Americans attacked a German bivouac area. A sharp short firefight followed with high German casualties. After recovering from the surprise attack, the Germans rallied and moved to outflank the American company that had moved to the hillock, Point 35, a few hundred meters west of la Raye. The fight lasted a few hours until darkness started giving way to dawn. Low on ammunition, the Americans who were able divided into groups, making their way back to the river. Wounded, Colonel Goode was captured fighting a rearguard action. Only 30 men made it back to the American lines. (Colonel Goode's outstanding leadership as the senior officer at the POW camp has been recognized with a commemorative plaque at the National POW Memorial Museum in Andersonville, Georgia).

Although Cota's force heard the sounds of battle a kilometer to their south, exact positioning and the nature of the activity was uncertain, as there was no communication between the two American units.

The withdrawal of George Company left Cota's force low on supplies and dangerously isolated. Division headquarters ordered them to withdraw. Throughout June 13 the force battled its way northeast across the fields to the Vire River. At midnight the remnants, 110 men, crossed and regained their lines.

Throughout the remaining days of June the 327th Glider Infantry Regiment fought southward, took the railway line, and carried on to the marshes of the Vire et Taute Canal.

Two and a half kilometers east of Montmartin-en-Graignes on the east bank of the Vire River, is the hamlet of St. Lambert. Here on July 8, the 832nd Battalion of the 9th Engineer Command commenced construction of Advanced Landing Ground A-11. It was turned over to the 1st US Army Group on July 21.

Related stories are Auville-sur-le-Vey, Isigny, and Vire-Taute Canal.

12.2 Vire et Taute Canal

(10 kilometers southeast of Carentan. From Carentan east on N13 3 kilometers to N174, south 8 kilometers to the canal)

The canal connects the Vire River 3 kilometers to the east with the Taute River, 5 kilometers to the west. This seven meter wide excavated water course serves to drain the low-lying valley. Its banks are sloped and is shallow enough in places to ford. Two causeways cross the canal and the adjacent marsh, N174 and D89, 4 kilometers west at Port des Planques. The two canal bridges had been destroyed by German demolition teams. Although the highway N174 was usable and would allow tanks to advance in support of the proposed infantry attack, the blown bridge was at the German end of the causeway. The tanks unable to proceed were vulnerable to German antitank fire as they awaited engineers positioning a bridge. The narrowness of the roadway blocked by vehicles delayed moving the bridge sections to the point. The toe hold on the south bank had to be made by artillery supported infantry.

Two kilometers south of the canal bridge the town of St. Jean-de-Daye, a road junction, straddled D174. The 30th Division, commanded by Major General Lelland S. Hobbs, planned a two pronged assault against St. Jean-de-Daye. The 117th Regiment on the east bank of the Vire River was to attack westward at Airel, followed shortly thereafter by the 120th Regiment's assault across the canal from the north. The two forces proceeding along their line of assault roads would meet at the junction of N174 and D8, 1.5 kilometers south of St. Jean-de-Daye.

On July 7, 1:45 p.m., two battalions abreast, Colonel Hammond D. Birk's 120th Regiment moved south from their start line on the north end of the causeway. The plan called for infantry in the marshes, engineers and vehicles on the road. The wide dry shoulders of the roadway were more attractive to the infantry than the soggy muddy marshes, and it was not until German mortar and artillery fire splattered the leading platoons that the infantry abandoned the exposed road and slid into the marshes to continue their southward advance.

Although bad weather had canceled the air strikes and grounded the artillery spotter aircraft, the reduced fire support was very effective. The German positions facing across the causeway had been destroyed, resulting in very low American casualties. Once across the canal and through the first two shell pocked fields, German resistance stiffened. Dug in behind their hedgerows they took a heavy toll of the inexperienced regiment.

German mortar and 88mm fire zeroed on the bridge and causeway, hampered the bridge construction, delaying the armor entering the bridgehead. Not until General Hobbs ordered the engineers to disregard the shelling was the bridge set in place.

Colonel William S. Biddle's 113th Cavalry Group moved along the causeway to enter the bridgehead. Rain, harassment fire, and road conditions combined to produce a bottle neck and traffic jam at the bridge and road junction several hundred meters south. Not until late evening did the cavalry manage to disengage itself from the traffic and move westward along D289.

To ease the flow of traffic and congestion resulting from the returning wounded meeting the arriving reinforcements on the narrow bridge, a second bridge was created by bulldozing and filling in the canal adjacent to the bridge. This job was completed by midnight July 7, relieving the bottle neck condition.

The day's advances from the north and east were considerable. By late afternoon units of the pincers had joined north of the N174-D8 intersection.

The light resistance encountered encouraged the senior commanders. In a rapid succession of orders the 19th Corps Commander, Major General Charles H. Corlett, was assigned the 3rd Armored Division for development and a drive south 12 kilometers to the high ground west of St. Lo.

The Vire et Taute Canal is now little more than a stream. Four houses flank the highway bridge. A large new red clay and stone house-barn identifies the corner where the cavalry cleared itself of the bridgehead's congestion and moved west to extend the day's gains. In 1944 the marsh and river valleys were flooded as a German defense measure, however, during the interim years the waters have receded and their beds have become lush pastureland, which is now hardly discernible from the dry higher ground. The growth of the shrubs, hedges, and marsh grass misrepresent the scene when the causeway, elevated above the marsh, was exposed to clear visibility and lines of fire.

St. Jean-de-Daye 2 kilometers south is a new town with broad streets and modern buildings. Paradoxically, the "rebirth" draws attention to its "death" in 1944.

Operation COBRA, the breakout west of St. Lo and its subsequent developments in late July, demanded more front line air force bases. An air reconnaissance team of Major Q. P. Gerhart and Lieutenant Colonel B. J. Ashwell on July 30 flew over the area in a borrowed L-5 and spotted a site near St. Jean-de-Daye for an Advanced Landing Ground. The 852nd Battalion (9th Engineer Command) moved in and constructed Advanced Landing Ground, A-18, for fighter-bombers with a 1200-meter runway and 500-meter earth extension for "over-shoots". The ALG was to the northeast between the town and the low lying pasture land, a marsh in 1944.

Related stories are Montmartin-en-Graignes, Airel and le Dezert.

12.3 Airel

(15 kilometers southeast of Carentan. From Carentan, east on N13, 3 kilometers to N174. South 11 kilometers through St. Jean-de-Daye to D8, east 3 kilometers to the Vire River bridge)

As part of the plan for the 30th Division to gain a bridgehead on the isthmus between the Vire and Taute Rivers, the 117th Regiment was to attack across the Vire River at Airel, in conjunction with a similar effort by the 120th Regiment from the north across the Vire et Taute Canal. The link up of the two prongs was to be the N174-D8 intersection.

At Airel the Vire River is about 4 meters deep, 20 meters wide with steep 3-meter banks. From the village of Airel on its east bank a slightly damaged stone bridge spanned the waterway to the village of Pont du St. Fromond on the German held west side.

Colonel Henry E. Kelly's regiment was to launch their attack at first light July 7. Throughout the early hours of that day the regiment moved to their crossing points several hundred meters north of Airel. It was drizzling. Air support had been called off but artillery pounded the German positions blowing gaps in the river banks about to be assaulted.

At 4:30 a.m. the first wave crossed in rubber assault boats equipped with scaling ladders to climb the foreboding bank. The thirty-two boats crossed without drawing fire. Quickly the boats returned and took on the second wave. German artillery and mortar fire pounded the east bank and the river. The second and third waves not as fortunate as the first drew casualties.

Engineers a few meters north of the stone bridge were attempting to lay a duckboard footbridge. Mortar fire rained down upon them causing fifty percent casualties. Doggedly they persevered and by 6 a.m. the footbridge was competed. The boats were pulled out as reinforcements now trotted into Pont du St. Fromond across the footbridge.

As the assault troops fought in the hamlet, engineers removed the mines from the stone bridge and laid treadway on the mortar-shell pocked surface. At 9 a.m. the first Sherman tank mounting a bulldozer blade crossed into the hamlet. Quickly it cleared a path through the rubbled street (D8) opening it to the traffic that was to follow.

Throughout the morning the toehold was enlarged. By noon two pontoon footbridges and a pontoon-vehicle bridge were functioning in addition to the more stable stone bridge being used by the armor. The regiment was across and pressing west along D8 to the N174 highway and the rendezvous intersection.

In the early afternoon when the congestion at the bridges was becoming critical, a German shell hit a half track towing a supply trailer crossing the pontoon bridge. The armored truck slithered nose first into the river. A pontoon was punctured, the roadway twisted, and the connecting links bent. Removing the half-track and trailer and replacing the pontoon was not completed until midnight.

By that time the days gains had been formidable. The 120th and 117th Regiments had joined north of the planned intersection, the 113th Cavalry Group was protecting the western flank. Resistance had been lighter than anticipated. The day's fighting had cost the division three hundred casualties.

The surprising success of the day, as measured by gains with a minimum number of casualties, clearly indicated to the 1st Army's Commander, Lieutenant General Omar Bradley, that the 19th Corps had found a soft spot in the German lines that needed to be exploited quickly and forcefully. That evening the alerted 3rd Armored Division was placed under General Corlett's command. Within a few minutes he had its commander, Major General Reroy H. Watson, on the phone ordering him to get his armor into the bridgehead and drive directly southwest 12 kilometers to the ridge northwest of St. Lo.

The division was the large "old type", not yet reorganized into the smaller triangular groupings. To become a more manageable contingent it was split into two Combat Commands, A and B.

Orders followed swiftly. By 6:30 p.m. July 7, Combat Command B (CCB) under the command of Brigadier General John J. Bohn, was in motion moving towards the Airel crossing. By 10:30 p.m. 45 vehicles per hour were crossing the stone bridge.

CCB, consisting of 6,000 men, 800 vehicles, and 300 trailers was 40 kilometers long. The CCB under shellfire and pursuing the same roads and bridges as the 30th Division's fresh battalions, also entering the bridgehead, crossed the stone bridge during the night of July 7-8 without the aid of radio, lighting or the loss of human life.

Only the light of day on July 8 revealed the congestion in the bridgehead. The gains to the south of D8 had been very shallow. As CCB flowed into the 30th Divisions bridgehead the compactness pushed the tanks into the fields bordering the secondary east-west road. Infantry, fatigued from the day's fighting, grouped to avoid being crushed by the medley of vehicles overrunning their encampments. Artillery units unable to relocate quickly saw guns damaged by the ungainly tanks elbowing their way into the fields.

Standing on the original stone bridge today and looking alternately at the villages of Airel and le Pont St. Fromond the battles direction is clear. Airel, the American start line, was not shelled and remains an aging village. le Pont St. Fromond, the assault's objective received a devastating pounding; its uncluttered spacious central square evidences its rebirth. The collapsed river banks are apparent although bushes camouflage the shell holes. A few of Airel's older inhabitants remember the pontoon bridge locations, seen when they returned to their homes after the bridgehead was secured.

A kilometer west of le Pont St. Fromond, the secondary road D377 passes through St. Fromond in a southwesterly direction for 4 kilometers to join highway N174.

The D8-D377 junction is clustered by a group of houses and a road sign to Cavigny.

Twenty-five meters north of St. Fromond the Germans established a roadblock facing north supported by antitank and automatic weapons.

In the early morning hours on July 8, CCB tanks having just entered the bridgehead approached the roadblock in their search for a tank park. The lead tank was knocked out, the remainder blocked. A sharp battle resulted in which the Germans counterattacked up the road with armor, driving the Americans back to D8. The Americans recovered, regrouped and repulsed the German efforts, then followed their advantage to the northern limits of St. Fromond. The Germans lost four Mark IV tanks (2nd SS Panzer Division) against the loss of one Sherman.

The remainder of the day was spent unsnarling the congestion and confusion in the bridgehead and extending the lines south. By midnight the 119th Regiment was 3 kilometers south to the outskirts of Cavigny. Task Force "X" (CCB) faced the junction of D377 and

D546, and the 3rd Battalion of the 117th Regiment held la Perrine straddling N174.

On July 9 armored units of CCB deployed in the fields bordering the St. Fromond road (D377) moved off towards their objective les Hauts Vents, 6 kilometers to the southwest. The previous days experience at the roadblock had shown the tankers how effectively a single antitank gun could stop a complete column. Moving from field to field the hedgerows were either blasted away or bulldozed through. The nature of the terrain and the day's rainstorms, decreased visibility and greatly reduced the anticipated progress although the plan demanded speed.

A kilometer and a half south of St. Fromond the tanks pivoted west. Paralleling D546 they went on to the junction at N174. German resistance had been light resulting in a few casualties.

As the battle lines moved south throughout July and August more air fields were required for ground support. In early August, Advanced Landing Ground, A-18, was constructed near St. Jean-de-Daye, 3 kilometers to the northwest.

Related stories are St. Jean-de-Daye and le Dezert.

12.4 le Dezert, la Caplainerie and Hill 32

(12 kilometers southeast of Carentan. From Carentan east on N13 3 kilometers to N174. South 11 kilometers, through St. Jean-de-Daye to D8, west 2 kilometers)

On July 7 the US 120th Regiment fought its way across the Vire et Taute Canal 5 kilometers northeast of le Dezert. The American supply and communications line along N174 was vulnerable to German shellfire.

To provide and sustain close range artillery support the Germans positioned in the le Dezert area three battalions of 105mm guns, a battalion of 150mm, and a miscellaneous collection of other calibers. American artillery and fighter-bombers providing counter battery fire to quell the effectiveness of the German's barrage severely damaged the town. The battles in and around le Dezert in the following days destroyed 75% of the town.

July 8 saw the southerly movement of the American forces fighting tenaciously to enlarge their bridgehead and by midnight the 3rd Battalion, 120th Regiment, was 500 meters north of the town. The 2nd Battalion passed east of the town in their southerly push.

The 3rd Battalion was hit by a two company, three tank counterattack. A company of the 743rd Tank Battalion and division artillery joined the battle, which was fought across the fields and orchards climbing the slopes of Point 38. The attack was repulsed and the Americans secured their gains.

The following morning the battalion attempted to sweep down the hill and occupy the town. Their attempts were countered by equally strong movements by the Germans to retake the hill. At 4 p.m. the US 9th Division extended its sector to include le Dezert. The 3rd Battalion moved to the east of D8 and the 2nd Battalion, 39th Infantry Regiment took over Point 38.

Throughout July 10 the 39th Regiment's, 2nd Battalion from the north, and 1st Battalion from the northeast fought their way into the town and established their line perpendicular to D8 outwards 700 meters on both sides. The western flank of the 2nd Battalion front lines ran along the secondary road 1 kilometer from le Dezert to D445 (la Caplainerie road).

By midnight American strength in the bridgehead was formidable and greatly underestimated by the Germans preparing to counterattack. Two infantry divisions, an oversized armored division, a cavalry group, corps artillery, and a close support air force faced the Panzer Lehr Division and the remnants of a decimated battle group.

Disregarding what German intelligence thought was in the bridgehead their choice of action was limited. The 19th Corps successes of July 7-10 were threatening St. Lo, their major east-west supply highway D900 and outflanking their defense line stretching west to the Contentin coast. All German divisions were in front line positions with little or no reserves readily available. The serious American threat had to be eliminated by the annihilation of the US bridgehead. The only German force capable of achieving this objective was the Panzer Lehr Division to the east facing the British. It was withdrawn from the line and transferred into the Vire-Taute Isthmus sector where it arrived piecemeal throughout July 9 and 10. The Seventh Army commander and the division's commander were sufficiently optimistic of their chances of destroying the bridgehead as to plan a follow through drive into Carentan.

General Fritz Bayerlein's division was considered the finest the German's had in the west and possibly the best Germany had ever produced. Formed in early 1944, it was equipped with the latest and most modern armored vehicles. The officers and non-commissioned officers were teachers and demonstrators from armor schools.

The first months fighting with the British had inflicted 30% casualties and of the remaining 10,000 men, 20% were not transferred to the American sector but left to bolster the British front.

The Panzer Lehr's attack was three pronged, synchronized for the early hours of July 11. Two prongs attacking north from the Pont Hebert sector and the 3rd prong launched from le Hommet-d' Arthenay (2 kilometers southwest of le Dezert on D8) would dissect the bridgehead, meet at St. Jean-de-Daye, and destroy the Americans.

General Bayerlein was not totally convinced his under-strength force was large enough to accomplish the complete task. He did not know the size of the US 3rd Armored Division and was unaware that the 9th Infantry Division as well as the 30th Division were in the bridgehead.

The German 901st Panzer Grenadier Regiment launched its attack at 1 a.m. July 11. Driving along D8 from le Hommet d'Arthenay, it split at the D445 crossroads. The 2nd Battalion, with an additional eleven tanks, struck north towards la Caplainerie while the 1st Battalion enlarged by the addition of two companies of antitank guns, moved against le Dezert. The German armor, hitting the American infantry line in darkness, was successful. A hole was punched through the lines wherever the German armor could use the roads. Coming out of le Dezert a column drove east along D545 towards le Perrine on N174. Three hundred meters out of le Dezert the three German tanks, now five hundred meters behind the US front line, hit A Company of Major Hoyt K. Lorance's, 899th Tank Destroyer Battalion. An American tank destroyer and the German lead tank were destroyed. Damaged and aflame the two remaining tanks withdrew.

With daylight came the inevitable, American fighter-bombers and artillery spotter aircraft. On the German reinforcement roads a curtain of death was drawn across as artillery shellfire pounded specific points preventing any movement across that stretch of inferno. A column of 40 tanks idled under the trees of D8 waiting for the barrage to shift so they could move out of le Hommet d'Arthenay. Aerial reconnaissance sited their location, the artillery elevated their fire slightly and the column struggled to get off the road away from its own destruction. Fighter bombers roared in and destroyed thirteen tanks.

By 4 o'clock that afternoon the German breakthrough had been completely stopped and isolated pockets were being cleared. The American infantry took the next five hours to recover the ground lost and by 9 p.m. had regained their positions of the previous night.

The 2nd Battalion (Panzer Lehr Division) that had driven north towards la Caplainerie on D445 also recorded initial successes. Fortuitously their road of advance was a gap in the American line between the 47th and 39th Regiments. Once through the relatively light resistance they arrived at the la Caplainerie hamlet and road junction. Splitting, a column moved eastwards along D389, climbed the hill and occupied Point 38. The remainder continued north along D445 towards le Mesnil-Veneron. Elements of these columns were now 2 kilometers behind the American lines. Recovering and reorganizing American counter actions materialized as dawn broke. The 1st Battalion, 47th Regiment, with four tank destroyers attacked, battled its way down the road from le Mesnil-Veneron and regained the la Caplainerie crossroads, thus cutting off the column's line of retreat on D389.

That column was already heavily engaged with A Company and its tank destroyers. The US gunners were very successfully ferreting and destroying their opposition along the road as far as the hamlet of la Scellerie. Three Mark Vs and a half track were billowing smoke and flames as a result.

At the intersection a Mark V rounded the corner turning off D445 onto D389 running into tank destroyers of C Company, 899th Tank Destroyer Battalion. Two rapid-fire shots sent the German tank and the soldiers it was ferrying sky-bound with a thunderous roar.

In the afternoon a sharp battle occurred at the crossroads when a company of German reinforcements equipped with Panther Mark Vs, attempted to move through the junction. F Company of the 32nd Armored Regiment (3rd Armored Division) were in the fields flanking the road and two tank destroyers of Charlie Company (899th Tank Destroyer Battalion) were holding the road. The German armor moved towards the junction from the south. The American Shermans opened fire but saw their shells bounce off the reinforced armor of the Mark Vs. They switched to high explosives for concussion and tread damage. It was similarly ineffective. At 120 meters the lead Panther engaged in a duel with one of the M-10 tank destroyers. Although damaged, it hit the M-10 killing and wounding its crew. The second tank destroyer (TD) opened fire destroying the tank. Challenging the second tank to a duel the tank destroyer directed its fire against the treads and bogie wheels. It took ten rapid fire rounds before the tank, loosing its drive and steering system, churned out of control and slithered into the ditch becoming entangled in the hedgerow. The crews had "baled out" and were captured by infantrymen in the nearby farmhouse.

Throughout the area the battles continued in a similar manner. As the American artillery was pounding the roads, German armor attempted to move across the fields. The tank destroyers waited camouflaged in the hedgerows, picking the tanks off as they lumbered across the open fields. Air strikes knocked out any formations and the armor and tank destroyers attended to the few that managed to penetrate or were pocketed within their sealed line of retreat. American infantry hunted down the German infantry that had accompanied the armor in its initial breakthrough.

As in the le Dezert area the penetration was sealed and the American lines of the previous evening were reoccupied at 9 p.m.

The attacking regiment had 50% casualties and combined with the similar rebuff southeast around le Haut Vents and the Vire River the division had lost 50-75 tanks, 25% of its effective strength, and was no longer capable of a large scale counterattack with its resources in the isthmus area.

Although incapable of another attack, the defense line established by the reserve battalions and the forces as they retreated from le Dezert and la Caplainerrie were formidable.

The following day on July 12, the 39th and 47th Regiments battled their way down D8 and D445 field by field. Their advance was intermittently knocked off balance by small local German counterattacks of infantry-armor teams that made coordinated advances difficult as different sections of the advancing line were under attack and being defensive. During the four days from July 12-16, slow but steady progress was made and by midnight July 16 the two regiments had pushed their lines 4 kilometers south.

Operation COBRA, the breakout west of St. Lo and its subsequent developments in late July demanded more front line air force bases. An air reconnaissance team of Major Q. P. Gerhart and Lieutenant Colonel B. J. Ashwell on July 30 flew over the area in a borrowed L-5 and spotted a site near St. Jean-de-Daye for an Advanced Landing Ground. The 852nd Battalion (9th Engineer Command) moved in and constructed ALG A-18 for fighter-bombers with a 1200-meter runway and 500-meter earth extension for "overshoots".

Immediately south of le Dezert bordered by the two roads exiting the town is Hill 32, a significant factor in the 120th Regiment's southern thrust July 8.

Hill 32

July 8 midnight saw the Americans holding a line anchored at le Dezert (on D8) and la Perrine (on N174) and 1.5 kilometers north of Point 32. Armored support German counterattacks were anticipated. American artillery was alerted and prepared to lay down a dense carpet of fire at any point along the line. Still the aggressor, the US infantry prepared to move against southerly objectives the following morning aware of the German buildup in their area.

The 2nd Battalion (120th Regiment) holding the line 1500 meters north of Point 32 was positioned somewhat ahead of its flank support. On its west the 1st and 3rd Battalions were in positions to le Dezert and to the east the 3rd Battalion

(117th Regiment) edged up to its 2nd Battalion in le Perrine (N174).

Before the 2nd Battalion (120th Regiment) could jump off at 7 a.m. German fire rattled down its flanks. Although intense, casualties were not heavy and the anticipated German attack did not materialize. The battalion did get moving three hours later. Behind and slightly to the west the 1st Battalion followed providing depth to the advancing line. Ahead the 743rd Tank Battalion moved in support of the infantry.

Point 32 on the 120th's line of advance was its first objective. As the American infantry and tanks approached German resistance was more concerted with considerable artillery support. The German shellfire was not aimed primarily at the leading companies but generally into the triangle defined by D8 and N174 to their juncture. The regiment's command post, slightly to the rear, was receiving Lieutenant General George S. Patton Jr. (3rd Army), Major General Manton Eddy (9th Division) and Major General Leroy Watson (3rd Armored Division) when German artillery fire commenced falling in its vicinity.

At 2:30 p.m. the full force of the Engineering Battalion, (2nd SS Panzer Division) counterattack hit the Americans on the northern slopes of Point 32. B Company (2nd Battalion, 120th Regiment) had crossed D389 and was ascending the slope with its east platoon entering the hamlet of Quesnel. On its western end the A Company's tanks (743rd Battalion) had crossed D389 and were climbing up the farm track leading to the top of the hill. Ahead they could see two German Mark IV's maneuvering on the hillside. Not realizing these were decoys pulling them into a trap, the Americans proceeded up the hill to within 200 meters of the road fork when German armor and infantry struck their column head on and simultaneously from the flanks. With sirens screaming, German tanks lumbered out of the forks and ploughed down on the Americans. Close quarter and hand to hand combat ensued for the following fifteen minutes until 3 o'clock when the Americans withdrew, abandoning their nine serviceable tanks, three additional damaged tanks, and one destroyed bulldozer.

During the next half hour the German attack swept past the flanks of the leading 2nd Battalion (120th Regiment), cutting it off and driving head long into its "back stop", the 1st Battalion. Four battalions of German artillery were supporting the attack in an unusual show of coordination and concentration.

The battle reached its peak between 4 and 5 o'clock. The 2nd Battalion pulled back 400 yards, formed a defense perimeter and held back the assaults. The 743rd's tanks stayed in the fields shooting up all vulnerable targets in sight. The 1st Battalion advanced closer to the 2nd Battalion and provided covering fire.

Throughout the period the division's artillery fired 13,000 rounds into the sector as well as concentrating on the reinforcement roads. The hamlet and all its buildings on and around the hill were destroyed or damaged. At one time eighteen artillery battalions, including those attached to corps headquarters were involved. This tremendous counter bombardment is officially credited with stopping the German counterattack.

By 6:30 p.m. the attackers were forced to withdraw leaving behind five Mark IV tanks and 123 prisoners.

On July 10, as part of the general southerly move of the division towards le Hauts Vents crossroads, on the dominating hill 3 kilometers away, the 2nd Battalion cleared the hill and by midnight were positioned amongst the buildings and fields on its south and west slopes.

On July 11th a strong German counterattack drove along D8 into le Dezert (2 kilometers north). Point 32 did not come under attack but was used as an observation post for directing artillery fire on the German armor.

Related stories are Hauts Vent (3 kilometers south), Vire-Taute Canal (5 kilometers north) and Airel (6 kilometers northeast).

12.5 Les Hauts Vents

(16 kilometers southeast of Carentan. From Carentan east on N13 three kilometers to N174. South 16 kilometers to D92. West 1 kilometer. Or from St. Lo north on N174 6 kilometers to Pont-Hebert. West on D92 1 kilometer)

The crossroads of "high winds" is on the north end of a ridge running south between the Vire (east) and Terrette Rivers (1.5 kilometers west). The crown of the ridge at the crossroads is 91 meters above sea level and frequently referred to as Hill 91. The hill overlooks the lowlands north to Carentan, dominates the highway (N174) to St. Lo, and commands the Vire River bridge at Pont-Hebert. Apple orchards cover its northern and eastern slopes.

Two derelict war torn stone barns overshadow the northeast corner of the five-road intersection. Tall trees border the west side and looking west down D92, at the foot of the hill across the Terrette River can be seen the Chateau Esglandes. Two iron gates hanging on tilted cement posts, flanked by 2-meter high hedgerows, face the intersection on its northwest corner. The building that stood to the rear of the chateau has since been destroyed. The successful establishment of a firm bridgehead on the Vire-Taute Isthmus by the 30th Division on July 7 indicated a weak point in the German defense lines had been found. Major General Charles H. Corlett, commanding the 19th Corps, recognizing the prize to be gained with a fast powerful force, moved Combat Command B (CCB/3rd Armored Division) across the Airel bridge during the night of June 7-8. Its objective was the ridge northeast of St. Lo crowned by the les Hauts Vents crossroads.

On the German side Field Marshal Erwin Rommel realized that the American's gains were critical and if the penetration was exploited it would be difficult to continue their stand in Normandy. As a temporary measure nearby units were shifted into the gap until the arrival of the Panzer Lehr Division. A strong counterattack was being planned for the annihilation of the bridgehead.

Generals Corlett (19th Corps) and Hobbs (30th Division) were already receiving reports of German armored columns moving into the bridgehead area. The rain of July 7-8 had restricted fighter-bomber sorties, however observers in light observation aircraft were witnessing a large buildup of German armor.

Task Force "Y" (Combat Command B) was to the east of N174, 3.5 kilometers northeast of les Hauts Vents at the junction of the two secondary roads D546 and D377, just north of Cavigny. Bulldozing and blasting their way through the hedgerows and fields were delaying their speed considerably. German harassment fire and the mud produced by two days of rain further aggravated the situation. CCB's Commander, Brigadier General John J. Bohn, took part in getting Colonel Graeme G. Park's Task Force "Y" moving by 1 p.m. July 9. Moving his tanks out of the fields and into the narrow sunken road D546 the force moved towards N174. Several German antitank positions were put out of action, casualties were light and progress increased.

I Company (33rd Armored Regiment of TF "Y") leading surged ahead onto N174 at 4 p.m. and turned north instead of south. To the west a German counterattack was also pushing north. American infantrymen of the 117th Regiment were holding positions facing south down D174. Knowing German armor was to the west and that a counterattack was in progress, the American antitank gunners on N174 were prepared to repel any German armored thrust from the south. Four hundred meters along the road from the D546 junction on the southern outskirts of the Rauline hamlet, the American gunners began to fire at the eight American tanks that in error had turned north. They had heard the rumble of the oncoming tanks and waited for their silhouettes to appear over the top of the small rise in the road. While awaiting their arrival, radio men reconfirmed that there was no American armor in the area. It was believed that fifty German tanks were proceeding along the highway from the south. At a distance of a kilometer a rapid fire fight developed as the tank's 75mm cannons and machine guns raked the American positions. Tank destroyers retaliated and knocked out the two lead tanks including the company commander's. By now the closeness of the fighting units revealed identity. Realizing their error of direction the six remaining tanks tended their casualties then turned and proceeded back down the road to Hauts Vents.

Passing by the D546 junction they proceeded ahead half a kilometer to D377 which branches to the southwest, leading up the hill to les Hauts Vents. Behind them, TF"Y" had been halted at the

D546-N174 junction by orders from General Hobbs. German counterattacks of the day and intelligence of new German armor arrivals indicated a need for strong defensive positions. In vain General Bohn tried to recall the six tanks. Peculiarly their transmitters worked well but not their receivers.

Climbing D377, a road 2 kilometers in length, the six tanks arrived at the les Hauts Vents crossroads at dusk. The rain and fog of the past three days had lifted. American fighter aircraft, fulfilling an earlier request for a fire mission on the crossroads, spotted the tanks. Again believing these to be a part of the 2nd SS Panzer Division, they strafed the armor doing little damage other than knocking off the radio antennae. Somewhat dismayed by their fellow soldiers and airmen's activities of the day, the tankers established a defense perimeter in an adjoining field and awaited the arrival of TF"Y", unaware there was a halt order holding the force at the N174 junction.

Gains throughout the day for the 30th Division had not been spectacular. To the north 2 kilometers German counterattacks in the vicinity of Hill 32 had been repulsed. To the northeast the CCB was a kilometer ahead of its frontlines and still 2 kilometers from its objective. Between N174 and the Vire River, two battalions (119th Regiment) were well south of Cavigny to a point 2.5 kilometers north of the bridge at Pont-Hebert.

July 10 morning, the six tanks roared into life, pivoted north, descended the hill via the road D377, and re-entered CCB lines at the N174-D546 junction from where their foray the previous afternoon had started.

Rain showers predicted a day of battles without air support and observation aircraft.

At 6 a.m. Task Force "X" (TF"X") with Combat Command B, 3rd Armored Division, passing through TF"Y" took over the point of the attack and turning off N174 onto D377, commenced the steep climb up the hill just vacated by the six tanks of I Company.

German small arms and antitank fire from their positions on the hill slowed the advance. In the narrow sunken road, bordered by the ever present hedgerows, a damaged lead tank became a plug until removed by recovery vehicles. TF"X" deployed in the east side fields and continued their uphill climb on a broader front with appreciably more success. Seven hundred meters from the top at the steepest part a concentrated German artillery and mortar barrage fell on the tanks.

On the hill road where American infantry (3rd Battalion, 120th Regiment) were supporting TF"X"'s advance, the barrage struck them in the hamlet of le Rocher.

The shellfire was originating from Belle-Lande, the village on N174 half a kilometer north of Pont-Hebert and only a kilometer from TF"X"'s lead tanks. Further movements up the hill slope awaited the 119th Regiment who was straddling N174, attempting to seize the 88mm and mortar positions entrenched north of Belle-Lande. In spite of the American artillery barrage that engulfed the positions, the Germans held out with determination.

In the morning the battle up the hill had been fought against resolute resistance. In the afternoon elements of the very powerful Panzer Lehr Division occupied the ridge and a 4 kilometer sector of the front to the northwest.

The 3rd Battalion and TF "X" on the slopes dug in and prepared for a possible German attack. At 1:30 a.m. (July 11) there were reports from the companies in the fields flanking D377 and le Rocher of German tanks and infantry moving down the hill against their positions. For the next six hours a confused fight raged. American and German tanks, armored cars and infantry, punched holes in each others lines, became enmeshed, took prisoners and lost prisoners. The battalion's command post in the village was only saved from capture by hand to hand combat.

The Panzer Lehr's (units of three battalions) 902nd Panzer Grenadier Regiment thrust down D377 was stopped at le Rocher. By midmorning (July 11) German pressure slackened and they dug themselves in on the ridge leaving behind five Mark IV tanks, four armored cars, and sixty prisoners. An American follow-up attack was stopped.

At 3:30 p.m. a simultaneous attack by all three units around the hill was launched. The 119th Regiment (two battalions) towards Belle-Lande and Pont Hebert, the 120th Regiment (one battalion) up D377 from le Rocher and in between, Task Force "Z" (plus three companies of TF"X") along the eastern slope. American and German artillery was liberally used on defenders and attackers. Tanks of TF"Z" occupied the le Hauts Vents crossroads at 5:30 p.m. Infantry and armor poured over the crest and dug in against strong German pressure. A threatened armor counterattack was smashed by American artillery fire before it got started. When darkness fell the

American lines were half a kilometer south of the crossroads along D77, where the cart track descends the west side of the ridge through the orchards. The track defined the American front line.

The German attacks and counterattacks of the day were part of a two pronged drive by the Panzer Lehr Division to roll back the American bridgehead on the isthmus. Simultaneously, 3 kilometers to the northwest, two battalions (with tank support) of the 901st Panzer Grenadier Regiment attacked le Dezert and le Caplaninerie but were stopped and driven back.

The ridge and those occupying it were greatly exposed to fire from the east and west flanks. Until the two bridges crossing the Terrette River at the Chateau Esglandes and Armigny were captured there was a threat of a west flank counterattack. July 12-15 witnessed the very slow advance of the Americans towards the St. Lo-Lessay highway (D900), along the ridge road and its slopes. By mid July a point had been reached for observing the highway and directing artillery fire on registered targets.

Three days later St. Lo fell to the corps' 29th Division east of the Vire River setting the stage for Operation COBRA.

Related stories are Airel and le Dezert.

Chapter 13 OMAHA to St. Lo

The operations of June 7 and 8 were a continuation of reaching the D-Day objectives on OMAHA Beach. Although the allied air force commanded and dominated the skies the ground forces were under-strength. The beaches were still exposed to German artillery and small resistance pockets continued to harass the beachhead. Troop landings on the 6th had met the plan but two of the eight regiments had been so decimated in the assault that they were hardly capable of functioning as regiments. By dawn on the 7th five divisions were ashore but the supply shortage was grave. Tanks, transport and artillery had not landed per plan due to the beach obstacles not being cleared away fast enough and the delays in opening the beach exits because of the German defense effectiveness.

Regardless, the Americans had to move inland, create space for buildup and be prepared for the German armored counterattack. From their broad front and thin depth foothold on OMAHA, the Americans were to move west (link up with the UTAH Beach troops), east (link up with the British who had landed on GOLD Beach) and south towards St. Lo.

13.1 Etreham

(8 kilometers northwest of Bayeux . Drive west from Bayeux via N13 7 kilometers to D206. Drive north 2 kilometers).

The hamlet is nestled in the Aure River Valley. The river is blanketed by trees and bushes. The raised bridge crosses a very flat river bed.

A kilometer to the northeast is the 60-meter high Mont Cauvin with its ridge stretching north to Port-en-Bessin and flanking the east side of D206. The hill, an obvious high point feature of the area today is clear of trees and under cultivation as it was in 1944. The openness of the fields to the north between Mont Cauvin and the small fishing port of Port-en-Bessin were potentially excellent landing zones for an allied glider armada. Foreseeing this the hill and fields were heavily staked with antiglider posts interconnected by trip wires and triggered explosives (nick named "Rommel's Asparagus").

Midnight on D-Day saw the US 16th Infantry Regiment (1st Division) holding the eastern perimeter of the OMAHA Beachhead at le Grand Hameau (3 kilometers northwest). Far short of its D-Day objectives the regiment the next day (June 7th) was to move east to Huppain, a distance of 3 kilometers and there link up with the British troops moving west from GOLD Beach. This action and the movements southeast to capture Etreham were assigned to the 1st and 2nd Battalions of the 16th Infantry Regiment with the 2nd Battalion (26th Regiment) in reserve.

The German forces holding the area, although mauled and shocked by the magnitude of the power thrown against them the previous day, were still an organized opposition. The Huppain area was held by the 1st Battalion of the German 726th Infantry Regiment. The river valley around Etreham was still strongly held by elements of the 916th Regiment.

On D-Day the 1st Battalion of the 352nd Division's Artillery Regiment was located in the Etreham area. The twenty guns of its four batteries were sited to fire on the eastern half of OMAHA Beach. Their observation post for fire control was dug into the cliff face at Ste Honorine-des-Pertes (3.5 kilometers north). The battalion's commander, Major Werner Pluskrat, had his command post in the chateau at the Ferme de Russy, 1 kilometer west of Etreham on the south side of the Aure River.

On schedule the US 1st Division started rolling on June 7. From le Grand Hameau, the 3rd Battalion of the 16th Infantry Regiment with Baker Company of the 745th Tank Battalion moved straight down the coastal road , D514, occupying Huppain with little opposition. Major Pluskrat's remaining guns were destroyed by counter battery fire of the US 62nd Armored Field Artillery Battalion.

Simultaneously, the 1st Battalion of the 26th Regiment moved south from le Grand Hameau along D97 2 kilometers to the hamlet of Russy, where it arrived at 5 p.m. Proceeding east the battalion cut across the orchard covered slopes to the le Marais hamlet just a kilometer northwest of Etreham and a kilometer west of Mont Cauvin.

As the Americans moved east during the day, the British 50th Division had advanced westward to effect a link-up at Port-en-Bessin and along the Drome River. By midnight, June 7, the British were holding a line from Bayeux to the east at Longues. Five kilometers separated the two allied divisions. Between them were the German 30th Mobile Brigade and elements of the 726th Regiment.

Pressing to effect a link-up on June 8, the 3rd Battalion (16th Regiment) moved south from Huppain along the ridge and occupied Mont Cauvin. The 1st Battalion (26th Regiment) entered Etreham via D206 from the north at noon encountering only snipers. Approaching the bridge along the two roads that converge at the bridge, the lead patrols came under fire from prepared positions on the far side of the river. The remainder of the day witnessed severe fighting as the Germans determined to hold open the narrow corridor between the British and Americans put up stubborn resistance.

One and a half kilometers to the west of Etreham at the hamlet of Beaumont, the 2nd Battalion (26th Regiment) successfully crossed the Aure River, continuing south to the highway N13 at Mosles. Outflanked, the Germans at the Etreham bridge withdrew allowing the corridor's walls to close and entrap their comrades.

Later in the summer, Port-en-Bessin became a receiving port for fuel and oil tankers direct from America. The life blood of a mobile army was pumped from the carriers through pipelines to fuel dumps advancing with the armies. One such large fuel dump was situated on the slopes of Mont Cauvin. From there two fuel pipelines ran south and southwest to other US supply dumps.

There is a commemorative plaque to the 1st Infantry Division, near the Etreham bridge, recognizing the sacrifices made to cross the Aure River valley.

Two and a half kilometers east of Etreham at the junction of D100 was General Eisenhower's guest quarters, SHAEF (Supreme Headquarters Allied Expeditionary Force) Visitor's Camp. When the General's SHAEF Advanced Command Post, code named "SHELLBURST" moved to France August 7 it was located 20 kilometers southwest near Tournieres. To accommodate the numerous visitors from the US and the UK a visitors tent camp was established in the field adjacent to the south side of the D123-D100 junction and bordered on the south side by the banks of the Aure River. The camp was on the boundary of US 1st and British 2nd Armies. The port Port-en-Bessin (2 kilometers north) and nearby US and RAF airfields made the location convenient but far enough from SHELLBURST to control the interference by visitors and politicos. There is no marker identifying the site's historical significance.

13.2 Ste. Anne

(A hamlet bordering N13 3 kilometers west of Bayeux)

The 3rd Battalion of the 26th Regiment (1st Infantry Division) after landing on OMAHA Beach, D-Day bivouacked on the high ground southeast of St. Laurent-sur-mer. The following day they were held up by German resistance at Formigy. On the eighth the battalion bypassed the resistance, joined N13 and moved southeast down the highway arriving at the smoking ruins of Tour-en-Bessin (1.5 kilometers west of Ste. Anne) at 6 p.m. At midnight with 6 tanks (C Company, 745th Tank Battalion) heading the column and infantry columns on both sides of the road, the force moved against Ste. Anne. German resistance from snipers and strongpoints were brushed aside by the tanks firing on anything looking suspicious. The column arrived in the hamlet at 1.30a.m. (June 9). Enemy patrols retreated towards Bayeux.

The coastal port town Port-en-Bessin is 6 kilometers north. American forces from OMAHA Beach were moving east to link up with the British forces moving west from GOLD Beach. An enemy corridor had been created between the allied forces coming together in the area north of N13 to the coast at Port-en-Bessin.

The British 47th Marine Commandos entered Port-en-Bessin June 8, 8 a.m. They moved south against the northern edge of the corridor. The 2nd Battalion at Tour-en-Bessin and the 3rd Battalion in Ste. Anne were sealing the German escape route. The remnants of the German 1st Battalion (726th Infantry Regiment) had been reinforced on June 7 and 8 by units of the 517th Battalion of the 30th Mobile Brigade. Now entrapment and loss of the force was a possibility. The Americans in Ste. Anne had dug in and awaited the anticipated counterattack. L Company along the north edge, I Company on the east and K Company on the south side. From the north down the 3 meter wide track into the hamlet retreating Germans blundered into L Company. It was 3 a.m., dark, raining and poor visibility. The German force of miscellaneous supply vehicles, bicycles and infantry opened up at close range. A fire fight with hand to hand combat developed. Both sides had been surprised. The tanks were useless at such short range. American artillery was called in (including naval guns off the coast) to bombard the area northeast and east of the hamlet. Two German trucks transporting US prisoners were hit. L Company's casualties were very high. By 6:30 a.m. the 3rd Battalion had beaten back the attack, secured the area and captured 125 prisoners. The Germans were astounded by the artillery firepower and its accuracy.

Simultaneously the German force had attacked the British 56th Brigade, 2 kilometers east, in Vaucelles, successfully. They retook the village reopening the southbound road over which the mobile units escaped the corridor in the dark and dawn hours of June 9.

The significance of the Ste. Anne battle was that the rapid deployment of the 3rd Battalion (26th Regiment) east on the N13 highway threatened the German corridor, forcing a withdrawal. The US and British forces consolidated their front so their efforts could be directed southward. The D-Day objectives had been achieved and an inviting gap for a German armored counterattack to the coast had been eliminated.

Tour-en-Bessin (1.5 kilometers west of Ste. Anne) was the site of Advanced Landing Ground A-13 for the American 9th Air Force. On July 9 in a L-5 reconnaissance two-seater flown by Major Q.P. Gerhart and accompanied by 21st Army Group liaison officer Lieutenant Colonel B. J. Ashwell (Royal Engineers) a suitable location for the ALG was identified immediately northeast of the village. The ALG had two 1600-meter runways and two 13-meter wide taxiways made of interlocking pierce steel planks (PSP). Additionally it had 75 hardstands of square mesh track (SMT) for medium bombers. Construction started July 12 by the 883rd Aviation Engineering Battalion (9th Engineer Command). Four days later the 846th Battalion was added, then a company each from the 819th and 826th Battalions. The landing ground was completed in two weeks.

As all the temporary wartime airfields have been returned to agriculture, inquiry of the local inhabitants may turn up evidence of its presence. There is a memorial to the 846th Aviation Engineering Battalion in the vicinity. This is an apple orchard district. The PSP and SMT may now be gates and fences.

13.3 Formigny and Engranville

(14 kilometers west of Bayeux on N13 to the Formigny road (D517) then turn north 0.5 kilometers).

On June 7th the road (D517) north to St. Laurent-sur-Mer and OMAHA Beach was the separation line between the US 1st Division advancing east and south and the US 29th Division advancing west and south to increase the 5thCorps lodgment area.

The 3rd Battalion of the 26th Infantry Regiment (1st Division) moved from their overnight bivouac area, on the elevated ground 2 kilometers northeast of Formigny in the morning (June 7th). The battalion advanced through the hedgerowed fields adjacent to D517, on its eastern side. One kilometer north of Formigny, the German (elements of the 916th Regiment) machine guns nests, camouflaged in the hedgerows, poured murderous fire into the advancing Americans. They were stopped with no further progress that day. A German intelligence officer reported this battle as an example of the American soldiers reticence to attack across open terrain compared to their tenaciousness as riflemen in house to house fighting.

Although a battalion was stalled at Formigny the 1st Battalion, 18th Regiment (1st Division) east of Formigny moved rapidly southward on June 7, crossed the N13 highway and moved against the hamlet of Engranville on the high ground 1 kilometer south of N13. Aided by 5 tanks of the 741st Tank Battalion the force had only skirmished with isolated pockets of resistance. Near Engranville they ambushed cyclists from the 352nd Division. At 2 p.m. the tanks shelled the hamlet in support of C Company's attack. Fighting continued until evening when the enemy platoon retreated down to the Aure River, 400 meters south. The capture of Engranville threatened the German defenders to the north at Formigny.

At Formigny, on June 8, the stalemate of the previous day was broken.

At midnight (June 7) from Engranville (southeast), came tanks and elements of the B Company, 1st Battalion (18th Regiment). The enemy was driven out of the village leaving 10 dead and 15 prisoners. On the village's north side, the machine guns facing the 3rd Battalion (26th Regiment) continued to hold out until late morning.

At 1 p.m. the 3rd Battalion of the 115th Regiment (29th Division) entered Formigny from the northwest (Vierville-sur-Mer road, D30). The area was completely secured.

Four kilometers west on N13 turn right (north) on D127 to Deux-Jumeaux. The field on the east side of D127 immediately north was Advanced Landing Ground A-4, a 1,500-meter runway paralleling the road for fighter-bombers of the 9th Tactical Air Force. Originally planned to be 1,200 meters for fighters, the absence of the Luftwaffe gave reason and opportunity for adding bomb loads to the fighters to maximize their ground support roll. A-4 built by the 816th Aviation Engineer Battalion of the 9th Engineer Command was started on June 14 and finished a few days later. The airfield runways were built in the US and brought to the site via England. The aircraft wheels and windmill propellers churned up dust, stones and vegetation. Rain would turn a runway into an unusable muddy quagmire. To overcome these obstacles, portable runways were developed called square mesh track (SMT) and/or pierced steel plank (PSP). The SMT was rolled out across the field and staked to hold it flat. The PSP arrived stacked on pallets. The individual planks interlocked along their four edges to each other and then were staked to the ground. As the war moved on, the airfields were moved forward but much of the SMT and PSP remained to be used for gates and fences enclosing the wartime gaps in the hedgerows.

Also near Formigny is an airfield site north on D517 to St. Laurent-sur-Mer in the field north of the village, east of the road, down to the beach. This was an "Emergency Landing Strip (A-12C) for medical evacuation of the wounded. A dry ditch a meter deep crossed the field. As no culverts were available the bulldozers contoured the ditch into the runway by scraping back the ditch sides to a gradual slope leaving a slight depression in the runway. The ELS was started on D+2 and completed the following day. This became the first American airfield in France and developed into the most important. Over the first six weeks of operation it averaged 100 C-47cargo planes per day not including a damaged B17 that landed, was repaired and took off to England a few days after the airfield was completed. By D-Day + 90 there were 48 American and 45 British airfields in Normandy.

Related battle sites are Trevieres and Colombieres.

13.4 Trevieres

(14 kilometers west of Bayeux on N13 to the Trevieres road (D30) then turn south. Drive 2 kilometers and stop at the bridge crossing the Aure River before the town.)

The US 2nd Division, under the command of Major General Walter M. Robertson, landed across OMAHA Beach June 7 and 8. The division (part of 5th Corps) was inserted into a 4.5-kilometer front between the US 29th and 1st Divisions. Their mortars and machine guns, essential for hedgerow combat were still being unloaded from the freighters. Trevieres was the division's first battle of the war.

On June 7th, Engranville (1.5 kilometers north of the Aure River bridge had been taken by a battalion of the 1st Division's 18th Infantry Regiment. The following day the battalion shifted east to accommodate the 2nd Division's arrival into line. The Engranville area was taken over by the 9th Regiment. The 38th Regiment, due north of the Trevieres bridge, was given Trevieres as its objective. During the afternoon and evening of June 8 the 2nd and 3rd Battalions (38th Regiment) fought the hidden Germans dug into the east-west hedgerows paralleling the river. The attack on Trevieres was timed for early morning June 9 from the hedgerows overlooking the Aure River valley. To gain their start line, artillery fire was called upon frequently to augment the regiment's lack of mortars, machine guns, communication equipment, transport and inexperience. Their training exercises in England, through penetrable hedges had not prepared the Americans for the French hedgerows six to ten feet high growing on dense foundation of stones, earth and intertwined thousand year old roots. These were impenetrable by man and/or tanks. As a tank clawed its way up and over a hedgerow it's thin skinned underbelly was vulnerable to antitank fire from across the field. The tanks were confined to the roads where the destruction of the lead tank could block a column for hours.

Each field was a self contained isolated battlefield defended by a strong well positioned enemy with rehearsed tactics developed intensively over a two year period. To the men of the 2nd Division this was learning as you go without the essential equipment.

The 9th Regiment passing southward east of Trevieres received intense flanking fire from heavy machine guns in the fields east of the town.

The American attack down the sloping sides of the valley adjacent to the bridge, through the river, across the valley and up into the village was pressed all day (June 9). Posthumously, Captain O.S. Weathers, K Company, was awarded the Distinguished Service Cross for his leadership and bravery getting his men across the River. The artillery battalions fired 3,652 shells into the village.

The regiment's 3rd Battalion crossed the Aure River west of Trevieres (hamlet l'Etard), attempting to outflank and take the village from the southwest. That evening a prisoner informed his captors that the 916th Regiment was withdrawing. Only the obstinate rearguard opposed the Americans. The German 352nd Division Commander Generalleutnant Dietrich Kraiss recognized the tenuous position of his troops in Trevieres now bypassed on the east and west.

Following a heavy bombardment, June 10, starting at 7 a.m., the battalion moved in and cleared the town in two hours. With the town secured the 246th Engineer Combat Battalion brought in a double wide Bailey bridge to span the Aure River. The north-south road D30 through Trevieres became an important supply route.

During the three day bombardment 22 civilians were killed.

There is a 2nd Division memorial in the town.

Related battle sites are Formigny and Engranville to the north and Blay and la Mine south.

13.5 Colombieres

(14 kilometers west of Bayeux on N13 to the Trevieres road D30. South to Trevieres. West on D29 6 kilometers to Colombieres.)

There is no road connecting Colombieres to Canchy 3 kilometers to the north. The rich agricultural land today was a marsh in 1944 created by the Germans back flooding the l'Aure and l'Esque Rivers between Colombieres and Canchy. Regardless of the presence of the non-traversable marsh the 115th Regiment (29th Infantry Division) had Colombieres their objective when it arrived at Canchy June 8. The l'Aure River was the division's east-west front line. Roads to the east and west of the 115th Regiment did cross the marsh but not here. German defenses at Colombieres were expected to be formidable.

On the night of June 9-10 2nd Lieutenant K. C. Miller of Easy Company lead a patrol out of Canchy across the marsh and into the partially destroyed town, Colombieres. The holding garrison was caught off guard. A quick short fire fight followed killing and wounding 40 Germans and the capture of another dozen.

Miller's actions saved numerous lives as the regiment crossed the marsh to pass through the town that morning. Snipers along the marshes' southern bank took their toll. The pathway into the town had to be kept open. The American's rapid advance bypassed pockets of resistance and left their flanks open to counterattacks. In Colombieres German snipers crept back into town in the night hours to harass the troop lines passing southward.

Lieutenant General Courtney H. Hodges, Commander US 1st Army, established his headquarters here July 1 in an apple orchard near the town.

At Castilly 4 kilometers southwest the 9th Engineer Command established their headquarters in the chateau June 24. The command was responsible for building 48 American landing fields for transports, medium bombers, fighter-bombers and fighters throughout the Normandy campaign.

Related battle sites are Trevieres and le Carrefour.

13.6 La Mine and Tournieres

(la Mine is 13 kilometers southwest of Bayeux on D5. Tournieres is 6 kilometers further west on D15).

These are the sites of General Eisenhower's Advanced Command Post code named SHELLBURST, and the landing strip he frequently used Advanced Landing Ground, A-9.

La Mine was the command post of the German 352nd Division until June 10 when it moved to le Mesnil-Rouxelin north of St. Lo. The 9th Regiment (2nd Infantry Division) overran the area in its rapid southern advancement reaching highway D572 (6 kilometers south) that night.

Howard Gillingham a veteran (2nd Armored Division) who landed across OMAHA Beach on June 10 settled here after the war. He married, had four children and opened the Café de Paris.

North of the la Mine crossroads, 1 kilometer, is the village of le Molay. One kilometer north of the le Molay railroad crossing in the field to the right (east) was the site of Advanced Landing Ground A-9. The 834th Aviation Engineering Battalion commenced construction on June 19, 10 days after the area was taken. It was finished in eleven days at which time it was expanded to a Tactical Air Depot with hardened taxiways, hardstands, an ammo and bomb depot, and fuel tanks. The runway was 1,500 meters of steel-meshed track paralleled by a grass crash strip. The airfield area bordered the D5 road to the la Poterie hamlet (2 kilometers) and northeast across the fields 2 kilometers.

ALG A-9 was used by General Eisenhower in July for his numerous trips from England to meet with his field commanders. When he moved to SHELLBURST August 7 he, his commanders and visitors used the airfield until September 8 when his command post was moved to Julloville

<u>Tournieres</u>

(From the le Molay church take route D190 west 4 kilometers to Tournieres.)

One kilometer west of the Tournieres crossroads on D15 a secondary road to the left leads to a marker identifying SHELLBURST was "near this site". Three hundred meters further towards le Percas on the left is an iron gate. Through the gate, a hundred meters ahead can be seen several tall trees. General Eisenhower's command post was immediately beyond the trees. Visitors would arrive at the gate and walk 200 meters to the General's reception tent that faced south towards the gate.

The camp consisted of two large wooden cocoa-matted floored office tents, one for the general's receptions and one for his staff. There were four sleeping caravans and numerous small accommodation tents. Visitors stayed at SHELLBURST Visitors Camp near Port-en-Bessin on the coast. The field immediately east of the tents was a light liaison aircraft landing strip.

The small size, few vehicles, etc. in a terrain of hundreds of similar camps of an advancing army created security. The fighters stationed at ALG A-9 kept a watchful eye assuring the command post had no Luftwaffe intruders.

During the SHELLBURST period momentous events occurred on the battlefields that brought France's political leadership into focus. British Foreign Secretary Anthony Eden and General Charles de Gaulle met here on August 21 to discuss France's leadership and could American troops be sent in to liberate Paris. Numerous press conferences held here released the news of front line events. The announcements of Lieutenant General George Patton as US 3rd Army Commander and Lieutenant General Courtney Hodges, US 1st Army Commander, were made here August 16. The appointments had been made much earlier but publicity was purposefully delayed for security and strategic reasons.

Two and a half kilometers southeast of SHELLBURST at la Carbonnierie was Advanced Landing Ground A-5 called Chipelle. The 820th Aviation Engineering Battalion commenced construction June 20. Construction involved a great deal of clearing and grading. The soil was poor so excavation and back-filling was necessary the length of the runway. Further complications developed when a spring was uncovered in the runway. Twice the Luftwaffe strafed the engineers wounding two. The field was completed July 4.

Related battle site is Fosse Soucy.

13.7 le Carrefours

(20 kilometers west of Bayeux. Take D5 13 kilometers to la Mine. Continue west on D15 five kilometers to the D29 intersection at l'Epinay-Tesson. North on D29 500 meters to Cartigny-l'Epinay. Take the left fork D113, drive one kilometer to the le Carrefours crossroads.)

On June 10, 2:30 a.m. the 2nd Battalion/115th Regiment (29th Infantry Division) entered the Carrefour intersection from the north (D113). The battalion had left Canchy (10 kilometers northeast) early morning the previous day, crossed the l'Aure River marsh to Colombieres, moved west and cleared the Calette woods (6 kilometers north). A hard battle was fought in Vouilly against German snipers and bicycle troops armed with automatic weapons. From Vouilly the battalion was misdirected east three kilometers but then returned to their southern route D113 arriving at Carrefour in the early hours of June 10 exhausted. The night was dark and overcast. Reconnoitering was difficult. The men moved to the right off the road through a gate into two hedgerowed fields. They had marched 24 kilometers (15 miles) with few rations. They immediately fell asleep along the hedgerows. A German task force (352nd Division) retreating south along the same road surrounded the fields, fired off illumination flares then opened up with all they had including three tracked assault guns. The battalion commander, Lieutenant Colonel William Warfield, with his headquarters staff in a home next to the road, rushed out but was cut down by machine guns. American bazooka teams took out two of the tracked guns. G.I.s shooting wildly shot their buddies by mistake. The battalion fled the fields wherever possible. German bayonets glittered in the light from the descending flares. In twenty minutes it was all over. The Germans withdrew to continue their retreat south leaving the two self-propelled 88's with their mangled crews on the road. Of the battalion's 600 men, 50 were killed and a hundred wounded or taken prisoner.

As dawn brightened the landscape the survivors reunited several kilometers north. By mid-afternoon the new CO, Lieutenant Colonel Arthur Sheppe, with the addition of a hundred replacements reformed the battalion. Sheppe sent a medical detachment, in ambulances, ahead to remove the bodies and evidence of the massacre. When the battalion, a short time later, passed down the road and through the crossroads in the daylight there were no reminders of the event twelve hours prior. The forces moved south on their objective Ste. Marguerite-d'Elle (4 kilometers) which fell in the late afternoon.

At Castilly, 3 kilometers north, the 9th Engineer Command established their headquarters in the chateau June 24. The command was responsible for building 48 American landing fields for transports, medium bombers, fighter-bombers and fighters throughout the Normandy campaign.

Related battle sites are Colombieres and Tournieres.

13.8 Cerisy Forest

(Take D572 southwest from Bayeux 16 kilometers to the Balleroy D13 road. Continue on D572 highway through the Cerisy Forest.)

The forest was a wood supply source to two opposing armies, a battlefield and an army group headquarters.

For two years prior to the invasion a German division labored here cutting and stripping trees. The logs were moved north on horse drawn carts for the beachhead defenses. The shorter logs were implanted into the sandy beaches, tipped with mines, to demolish incoming landing craft. The longer logs were mounted vertically in open fields becoming antigliderlanding obstacles called “Rommel’s Asparagus”.

The foliages’ natural camouflage made the forest a hidden staging area for German infantry and armor. On June 7, 200 bombers with tank destroying 1,000 lb. bombs devastated the woods. Again on June 9 as the 2nd Infantry Division’s regiments moved south towards the forest’s northern boundary a second heavy bombing took place. Artillery fire added to the softening up. On June 10 the 9th Regiment passed through the eastern edge of the woods along the north-south road D10, arriving at Balleroy that evening with little opposition. Six men had been wounded. To the west the 38th Regiment did not fair as well. Their days trek from Trevieres (12 kilometers north) had met only minimal rearguard delays until arriving at Cerisy-la-Foret at 9 p.m. Organized defense by the 352nd Division’s 916th Engineering Battalion slowed the advance. The road D34 from the village of Cerisy-la-Foret to the intersection of D572, la Malbreche, was not taken until the following day after subduing strong resistance around the crossroads. The woods west of the intersection saw the heaviest fighting. Interrogation of the ninety German prisoners clearly indicated a disintegrating enemy, lacking supplies and leadership. These factors explained the comparative ease of taking the forest in contrast to intelligence estimates of a strong holding force.

The forest was taken over by the British August 1 as the front lines shifted to accommodate new divisions. The British forestry engineers removed many more trees to supply the moving army’s need for construction lumber. General Montgomery moved his headquarters to the forest from Creully (12 kilometers east of Bayeux) August 1.

Two kilometers east of Cerisy-la-Foret at la Carbonnierie was Advanced Landing Ground A-5 called Chipelle. The 820th Aviation Engineering Battalion commenced construction June 20. Construction involved a great deal of clearing and grading. The soil was poor so excavation and back-filling was necessary the length of the runway. Further complications developed when a spring was uncovered in the runway. Twice the Luftwaffe strafed the engineers wounding two. The field was completed July 4.

Related battle site is Tournieres.

13.9 Hill 108 (Villers Fossard)

(19 kilometers southeast of Carentan. From Carentan east on N13 three kilometers to N174, south 23 kilometers through Pont-Herbert to D54, east three kilometers to the intersection of D91. Hill 108's summit is to the southeast of the intersection.

Or

From St. Lo go north on N174 one kilometer to la Houssaye. Turn east on D91 and go three kilometers to the intersection of D54, the Villers Fossard road. Hill 108's summit is the southeast corner of the intersection.)

The hedgerows on the hill diminished its observation value. On the American maps it appeared significant. Within two days it became "Purple Heart Hill".

It was taken by the 1st Battalion of the 175th Regiment (29th Division) June 17 in a battle that saw its regimental commander Lieutenant Colonel Alexander George seriously wounded by a hand grenade exploding in his face. George had replaced the wounded, captured Lieutenant Colonel Paul R. Goode three days before. Lieutenant Colonel William Purnell was made temporary regimental commander.

At 8:30 the following morning German artillery and mortars blasted the American positions on the hill. Shortly thereafter Kampfgruppe Bohm, 2 battalions of the 943rd Regiment (353rd Division) fresh from Brittany, attacked up the northern slope. Dazed from the bombardment the Americans faced a fresh determined assault where only a hedgerow separated the adversaries. The battalion commander Lieutenant Colonel Roger Whiteford was wounded. American support artillery was unavailable because of radio difficulties. The persistent attacks throughout the day seriously threatened the American position that would likely fall that night. Fortunately, a radio link with the American howitzers was established in the evening. The artillery blasted the German reinforcements moving up the hill. Throughout the night the shelling continued forcing a German withdrawal. The battalion had lost 40% of its strength. 250 men were dead or wounded. Only 12 officers and 308 men walked away from their positions when relieved by the 3rd

Battalion. The battalion was awarded a Distinguished Unit Citation and the Croix de Guerre.

Related sites are Hill 122 and St. Lo.

Chapter 14 The Battle for St. Lo

Terrain features i.e., flooded rivers, marshes and hedgerowed fields limited the buildup of supplies and reinforcements in the UTAH and OMAHA Beachheads. The German defensive flooding broadened the wet lowlands and narrowed the land into limited offensive corridors. The geography benefited the occupiers, who over a four year period had rehearsed and honed their defensive tactics to a high effectiveness.

Lieutenant General Omar Bradley, 1st US Army Commander, envisioned a massive buildup of men and material followed by a breakout with his mobile army. The land west of St. Lo favored mobility. First, however, the front line west of St. Lo had to move south of the restrictive marshes and hedgerows. The east west front had to be straight with no exposed flanks.

St. Lo was a major road hub. Eight roads lead into the city that also straddled the north/south Vire River. Its seizure would cut the German lines of communication and psychologically discourage the defenders. The German front line west to the coast would become vulnerable.

The 1st US Army had hardened to their roll in the "Battle of the Hedgerows." In the area the size of a football field there could be three or four hedgerowed fields and two sunken roads. Four square kilometers contained 350 hedgerowed fields. The Germans lay in wait behind every hedgerow with their machine guns aligned from hidden camouflaged pits to crisscross the open fields. From the sunken roads mortars lobed shells into the field and the American hedgerow front line. Tanks and antitank guns defended the lanes from the American tanks that when de-tracked or destroyed blocked the roads. The American infantrymen were fatigued and scared. The repetitiousness of the hedgerow battles, the constant losses with inexperienced replacements, who died before their names were known, wore the men down.

The task of taking the rubble of St. Lo, for it had been bombed every day from June 6th to 14th, was given to the 19th Corps with the 2nd Division (of the 5th Corps) attached. The taking of St. Lo, July 7-29, took a heavy toll. 11,000 men were either killed or wounded.

Many were never seen again. The hills and ridges north and northeast proved to be a formidable defense.

14.1 Hill 192

(Hill 192 is 6 kilometers east of St. Lo. Take D974, the St. Lo-Bayeux highway, east 8 kilometers to D192. Go north 1 kilometer to St. Georges d'Elle.)

The D192 road just traveled skirts the eastern slope of Hill 192. From its vantage point the Germans had a commanding view of the countryside specifically the advancing line of the 2nd Infantry Division as it approached the Elle River two kilometers east June 12.

Hill 192, the Martinville Ridge (three kilometers southwest) and hills north of St. Lo gave the Germans a natural defensive barrier overlooking the advance lines of all the three American divisions descending on the smoking ruins of St. Lo. In American hands the hills overlooking St. Lo would quickly facilitate the city's capture.

At 8 a.m. June 16, the 2nd Infantry Division attacked with its three regiments (9th, 23rd and 38th) on an eight-kilometer front. The 38th Regiment, on the western flank was to capture Hill 192. The hedgerow fighting was slow and costly. By midnight the road running west from the St. Georges-d'Elle crossroads to St. Andre-de l'Epine for two kilometers had become no man's land. The 38th Regiment was 700 meters north of Hill 192. The 23rd Regiment occupied the hedgerowed fields and orchards north and adjacent to St. Georges-d'Elle.

The tenacious defenders, 3rd Battalion 9th Parachute Regiment and the 1st Battalion 3rd Parachute Regiment of the German 3rd Parachute Division, held their line throughout June. The 2nd Division took 1200 casualties and gained little. St. Georges-d'Elle changed hands several times before the 23rd Regiment consolidated its position in the buildings on the village's south side. The buildings beside D192 to the St. Lo-Bayeux highway were German strongpoints with automatic weapons. The northern slope of Hill 192 descending to the St. Georges-d'Elle St. Andre-de-l'Epine road was dotted with German resistance nests that defended each other with crisscrossed lines of fire. Tunneling in and under the hedgerows allowed the Germans to live in protected foxholes beneath their hedgerow firing positions. The small fields and numerous farm tracks benefited German antitank guns against the American armor. Artillery and mortar fire from St. Lo fell on the American lines.

Roadblocks, minefields and the liberal use of barbed wire further frustrated the Americans.

July 11th dawned cloudy with haze. Air support for the day's attack was canceled. The American front line troops had pulled back several fields to avoid being shelled by short falls of their own artillery. Shortfalls were not the result of poor gunnery, but of the wear on the rifling in the artillery gun barrels that caused the propellant force to vary from shell to shell. The only answer was to continually use new gun barrels. As had happened in the past and would be repeated again and again, the Germans probing revealed the pullback so they moved into the vacated positions. The American artillery bombardment fell on the German empty positions. At 6 a.m. two battalions of the 38th and 23rd Regiment advanced having to fight for the ground voluntarily vacated a few hours before. Within an hour the first wave of six American tanks had been knocked out or had to withdraw. The rolling artillery barrage placed 45 tons of explosive on Hill 192's slope between the east-west road and the pinnacle.

The hamlet of Cloville 2.5 kilometers west of St. Georges-d'Elle on the east-west road was in the line of advance for Easy Company of the 38th Regiment. A draw runs north 400 meters from Cloville to a ridge, a German strongpoint, manned by half a company that had survived the bombardment. Nicknamed "Kraut Corner" the defenders with clear lines of fire and pre-registered mortars impeded the American advance. Under strong small arms covering fire a 10-man platoon broke through the defenses from the east. Resistance stopped after a fierce fire fight. Only 15 prisoners were taken. Three die hard defenders would not give up. A tank dozer buried them alive under dirt scraped from their own defense berms.

By noon the 38th Regiment had taken Hill 192 and proceeded to follow up the German withdrawal down the southern slope reaching the St. Lo-Bayeux highway at la Calvaire late afternoon.

The 23rd Regiment advanced south from St. Georges-d'Elle down D192. In June the 23rd Regiment troops attacking from the northeast had sustained heavy casualties in the area. Three hundred meters south of St. Georges-d'Elle the gully had been named "Purple Heart Draw" by the survivors. Again it would take another terrible toll on lives. Too steep to descend four tanks lined up on the north edge to support a platoon attack across the draw. The platoon met disaster at the bottom. Mortars and artillery fire zeroed in on pre-registered lines of fire combined with machine guns along the southern slope and houses adjacent to the St. Georges-d'Elle road rained death into the draw. Two tanks silenced the fire from the houses. The enemy could not be subdued until advances to the west outflanked the positions causing the Germans to withdraw southward. By that evening the 23rd Regiment was within 400 meters of the St. Lo-Bayeux highway.

Four kilometers northwest of St. Georges-d'Elle, at Couvains was Advanced Landing Ground A-19, built by the 818th Aviation Engineering Battalion. The ALG was for fighter-bombers with a 1300-meter runway of pierced steel plank. As the steel plank was left behind when the front line advanced the fencing in the area bears mute evidence of its former use. The field was half a kilometer due west of the town.

Related battle sites are Martinville Ridge, Hill 108, Hill 122 and St. Lo.

Picture 16: Hedgerow Country Today

The battles for St. Lo were fought in the bocage area of Normandy. In the area of a football field there were 100 small farmed fields surrounded by impenetrable 1000-year-old hedges growing on thick foundations of stone, rock, earth and roots. Tree limbs meet covering the dirt farm track. German covered foxholes were established during the occupation. Burrowing through the hedgerow foundations, defenders could fire down the road and scurry back through their tunnel to the safety of their foxholes in the field. Mortar air burst shells impacting in the overhanging branches scattered deadly shrapnel into the advancing Americans.

14.2 Martinville Ridge

(Due east of St. Lo. Take D972, the St. Lo-Bayeux highway, east 6 kilometers to le Calvaire and the D59 intersection. Turn north, drive half a kilometer to the ridge road, D195, that parallels the D972 highway.)

East of the ridge road, D195 - D59 junction, one kilometer, lies Hill 192 the objective of the 2nd Infantry Division. Running westward is the Martinville Ridge with the village of Martinville three kilometers west overlooking St. Lo. Martinville was a grouping of a dozen farming homes scattered around the slopes of a valley in which several roads converged. The hedgerowed fields flanking the ridge road witnessed hard sustained fighting causing severe casualties to both armies.

The hills north of St. Lo were strongly defended by the Germans. American advances were slow with many casualties. Major General Charles H. Gerhardt's, 29th Infantry Division Commander, tactic was to pass south and east of the resistance and take St. Lo from the east causing the Germans to withdraw from their northern defenses or be encircled. He left the 115th Regiment straddling the la Luzerne road, D6, and shifted his two other regiments (116th and 175th) eastward with their axis of attack south down the road D59 through St. Andre-de-l'Epine. The neighboring 38th Regiment (2nd Infantry Division) would move south against Hill 192 while the 116th would take St. Andre-de-l'Epine, then move west along the ridge road to Martinville. A pre dawn German attack northward towards Belle Fontaine against the 115th Regiment disrupted communications and the timetable for the 116th's advance southwards.

Late morning July 11th, the 116th Regiment (Colonel Charles D. W. Canham) moved out of their front lines a kilometer north of St. Andre-de-l"Epine. A rolling barrage preceded them down the road and across the numerous hedgerowed fields. Progress was good. At St. Andre-de-l'Epine resistance stiffened. A SP (self-propelled gun) on D59 (to la Calvaire) just south of the hamlet stopped the advance. The sunken dirt track road leading southwest from St. Andre-de-l'Epine to Martinville was mined. In five hours only five fields were taken. The capture of Hill 192 to the east, by the 38th Regiment eliminated flank fire. The 1st and 2nd Battalions of the

116th Regiment moved through the fields adjacent to the sunken dirt track towards Martinville. By midnight the 2nd Battalion was on the ridge road two kilometers east of Martinville and the 3rd Battalion was flanking the valley road, D972, half a kilometer west of la Calvaire. The Americans were on the slope facing south and advancing along the ridge road. The Germans south of D974 on the high ground, Hill 101 at Barre-de-Semilly, had a clear line of sight. Automatic weapons, mortars and artillery peppered the ridge and its slope down to the highway. On July 11th German flank fire took out 500 men of the 116th Regiment. Captured American documents allowed the Germans to counter Gerhardt's attack plan. Regardless the American infantry pressed on and gained ground.

On the second day, July 12th, Colonel Ollie W. Reed unsuccessfully attempted to move his reorganized 175th Regiment into the 116th Regiment's positions to re-energize the attack's momentum. Again, German fire fell on the American positions immobilizing the division and causing 500 more casualties.

The division's high losses caused Gerhardt to reconsider his plan. He gave the regiments one more day to reach the objectives.

In the pre dawn hours of July 13th the 175th Regiment took up positions on the slope overlooking the D972 highway. The tank advance west along D972 with aerial support did not materialize. The attack fell apart. The 116th made ready to push the one kilometer along the ridge into Martinville. The German artillery fire from Hill 122 to the west was suppressed but still the Americans could not take Martinville. Major General Charles H. Conleh, the 19th Corps Commander, pressured the 35th Infantry Division to take Hill 122.

On July 15th, Major Sidney V. Bingham sideslipped his 2nd Battalion (116th Regiment) down the Martinville Ridge slope to the highway (D972) a kilometer east of St. Lo (300 meters east of la Fresnelliere). His battalion was 700 meters ahead of the American front line. German mortar and shellfire bombarded the separating gap. Bingham's battalion was totally isolated and under the gun sights of the Germans on three sides. In the dark morning hours of July 17th Major Thomas D. Howie lead his 3rd Battalion through the mist and fire-swept slopes to re-enforce the Bingham's battalion before daybreak. Major Howie had taken command of the battalion only three days before. (Before the war Howie was an English literature teacher and football coach at Virginia's Staunton Military Academy.)

He moved out of the battalions' position along D972 to reconnoiter into St. Lo. Just 200 meters east of the la Fresnelliere crossroads he turned around to check that his men had their heads down when a mortar shell fragment tore through his back and lungs. He died in two minutes. Captain William H. Puntenny took over. The Americans dug in under direct German mortar fire. That afternoon German tanks and infantry using the highway from St. Lo attacked the two isolated battalions. American dive-bombers blasted the attackers. Artillery fire created a protective defensive wall.

Up on the ridge Martinville fell to the 1st Battalion (116th Regiment) on July 18th.

The 116th and 175th Regiment held their positions as Major General Gerhardt devised a plan to have Task Force "Cota" take St. Lo from the north.

Three kilometers north of St. Andre-de-l'Epine, at Couvains was Advanced Landing Field A-19, built by the 818th Aviation Engineering Battalion. The field was half a kilometer due west of the town. The ALG was built with a 1300-meter pierced steel plank runway for fighter-bombers. As the front line advanced and the airfield was abandoned. The steel plank runways became local fences filling in the hedgerow gaps caused by shelling and tank dozers.

Related battle sites are Hill 192, Hill 122 and St. Lo.

14.3 Hill 122

(Three kilometers north of St. Lo. From St. Lo take N174, the Pont-Hebert, St. Jean-de-Day road to the northern suburb St. Georges-Montocq. D191 to Villers-Fossard branches off to the right. The road ascends Hill 122 over the next one and a half kilometers.)

Hills surround the north and eastern perimeter of St. Lo. Their seizure would position the Americans overlooking the city making its defense untenable and forcing the Germans to retreat. Major General Charles Corrlett's plan to seize St. Lo from the east had proven costly, slow and unsuccessful. The task of taking Hill 122 and the slopes down to St. Georges-Monocq was assigned to Colonel Butler B. Miltonberger's 134th Regiment (35th Infantry Division) July 15.

Hill 122 with its flat top plateau was held by elements of the German 352nd Division reinforced with units of the 226th Division and the 30th Mobile Brigade. Their troops were trained and experienced in hedgerow defense techniques. Hill 122 was the linchpin to the German defense of St. Lo. Its outer defenses stretched to the north four kilometers through the fields and surrounding hedgerows. Experienced defenders in depth faced the Americans. The dominating position overlooked the advancing Americans to the west. On July 15 the 137th Regiment five kilometers west had sustained 117 casualties from Hill 122 positions and been stopped in its tracks.

The American 35th Infantry Division had only recently landed in Normandy. Its training in the English hedgerows of Cornwall had not equipped it for those of Normandy. As the 134th Regiment advanced southward to Hill 122 July 10-14 the men recognized the vigorous defense by their opponents.

The axis of Colonel Miltonberger's attack on Hill 122 was the road D191, then a dirt track, from a line two kilometers north. The 134th Regiment moved through the fields on both sides of the road following behind a rolling barrage. Deep covered foxholes behind the hedgerows allowed the Germans to survive the bombardment then man their firing positions camouflaged in the hedges and crisscross their lines of fire across the field cutting down the advancing Americans. Progress was slow and casualties high. All the battles were small unit actions that succeeded although uncoordinated. By noon (July 14), Emelie, 500 meters north of Hill 122, was in American hands. That evening a task force of the 134th Regiment Infantry, tanks of the 737th Tank Battalion, a company of the 60th Engineer Battalion, and a platoon of the 654th Tank Destroyer Battalion made the final push to the hill's crest. The summer evenings are long in Normandy's July. The rolling barrage in twilight was supportive. By midnight the force was overlooking St. Lo.

A few hours later, as expected the Germans counterattacked. The Americans gave up some ground but dug in to their engineered prepared defense positions. On July 16 a more powerful counterattack caused the Americans to fall back to Emelie. Their counterattack carried the day. What ground had been lost was regained and by that evening the hill was securely in US hands.

With the hills in American hands the defense of St. Lo became small rearguard actions.

Northeast of Emelie at the hamlet of Bourg d'Enfer was a very large radar site. The concrete bunkers are still visible.

Two and a half kilometers northeast of Hill 122 at la Forge on D6 at the intersection of D448 is a chateau. An American story substantiated by a captured German officer is that before the invasion the chateau was the Luftwaffe headquarters for the radar station at Bourg d'Enfer 700 meters west. Its wine cellar was well stocked by the occupying Germans. On the night of July 10 an American patrol, knowing the chateau was occupied, entered through a basement access. Discovering the wines they proceeded to "load up" but were interrupted by the occupants seeking replenishment. A quick short fire fight followed with the Americans retreating bottles in one hand and weapons in the other. In the following days the chateau was either in German hands or in no man's land. Patrols from both sides at agreed upon schedules would raid the wine cellar without molesting each other. An overzealous American officer set up an ambush for the German patrol thereby ending the gentlemen's agreement. A retreating German officer left a note inviting the new occupants to enjoy the wine cellar as they had over the occupation years.

Related battle sites are Hill 108, Martinville Ridge and St. Lo.

14.4 St. Lo

(35 kilometers southwest of Bayeux on D972)

General of Artillery Erich Marcks, Commander of the German 84th Corps, holding the Normandy area, had his headquarters in the suburban Chateau de Chiffrevast. An underground bunker was built against allied bombs. The telephone lines to Cherbourg and the German divisions on the Contentin Peninsula were cut by the French Resistance the late evening of June 5 resulting in delayed information coming in and response orders going out.

Throughout the occupation Adolph Frank, living in St. Lo and former schoolmaster, was head of the French Resistance "Century" unit who collected intelligence of the German defenses that was forwarded to England.

General Marcks was strafed and killed in early June and replaced by Lieutenant General Dietrich von Choltitz who transferred from Italy. He moved the Corps headquarters from St. Lo on June 16. (von Choltitz later became renown as commander of the Paris garrison who defied Hitler's orders to destroy Paris as the allies approached in late August. Von Choltitz was captured at his Hotel Meurice headquarters opposite the Louvre Museum.)

Allied bombing of this major road junction commenced June 5, at 5 p.m. The bombers returned three hours later. The population fled to the countryside or into the cave behind the hospital. St. Lo was bombed every day until June 14. As the armies grew near it was shelled. A thousand civilians perished. The heap of smoking rubble was known as "the capital of ruins". German cameras captured the scene and propagandists carried the message to the French populace "this is what liberation means".

Between July 3 and July 17 the Americans had 40,000 casualties getting to the town's outskirts.

The 29th Division's tactic to capture the town was to seize the high ground north and east causing the Germans to vacate St. Lo hoping for a minimum of fighting in the town itself. By occupying the town and the Vire River bridge on its western edge, Lieutenant General Omar Bradley wanted his flank protected for Operation COBRA, his major southward thrust west of St. Lo.

The capture of St. Lo was assigned to Task Force C headed by General Norman D. Cota. (Brigadier Cota had played a significant roll in getting his men off OMAHA Beach D-Day morning. Robert Mitchum played his part in the movie "The Longest Day".) His Task Force C consisted of tanks, tank destroyers, engineers and the 1st Battalion (15th Regiment). Cota's force moved on St. Lo down the St. Lo-Isigny road (D11). The road came under heavy shellfire from German artillery located south of the town. The bridge at Moulin Berot, on the northern outskirts, was targeted. There was very little cover, a steep vertical bank to the right and an abrupt fall off on the left. The last two kilometers before entering the town was a very hot spot. The first troops and tanks entered St. Lo, July 18, at 6 p.m. The northeast corner of town was relatively untouched by bombs and shells. The first obstacle was the German strongpoint in the cemetery. The fusillade from the American armored cars, tanks and tank destroyers quickly cleared the resistance. Snipers from the high windows surrounding the neighboring square and streets slowed the advance. Like exuberant cowboys the troops rode through the streets in their half tracks, armored cars and tanks shooting at any suspicious German hideout. The 1st Battalion headquarters was in the "Café-Restaurant" on the northwest corner of the junction of D11 and the Bayeux road, D972 (Rue du Neufbourg). Colonel Ed McDaniels mounted the blue and gray 29th Division flag on the café in full view of the Germans on the ridge to the south. In response shellfire and airbursts fell on the intersection. The battalion was forced to evacuate its headquarters from the café to the Famille Blanchet mausoleum in the cemetery. The portico and heavy door were shrapnel shields from the shells exploding in the cemetery's trees. The ground floor chapel, 4 by 5 meters, led down a narrow stairway to the crypt with a sarcophagus in the middle and a table on the far wall. Wine bottles and bread on the table evidenced the Germans use of the sheltered mausoleum just a few hours before. The mausoleum, to the right of the entrance gate, still intact, shows the shrapnel sprang on its granite structure. The stone cross over the portico was broken by German shellfire after the Americans took over the mausoleum. The regimental headquarters was in a distillery at the foot of the hill as the D11 road enters the town.

Within a few hours key points throughout the town were secured. The enemy had retreated two kilometers south from where they poured artillery and mortar fire on the occupiers. German 88s shot off the spires of the Notre Dame Cathedral to deny the Americans an observation post. Methodically the Germans rearguard was eliminated. An ineffective counterattack on the south side in the late evening was repulsed. Shelling, Luftwaffe bombing and strafing on July19 added to the ruins by collapsing buildings in the northeast corner. Germans retreating from the north attempted to regain their lines through St. Lo's western suburbs. These skirmishes continued for several days.

Until US forces pushed the Germans off the southern hills St. Lo was a perilous place. Clearing out snipers and artillery observers continued for a week. Major Howie's body (see the Martinville battle site) was placed in front of the Ste. Croix Church as a symbol of the effort and losses in the bitter struggle for St. Lo.

There is a plague to Major Howie on the side wall of the church as well as a granite memorial on the Rue de Vire. At the old prison a "French Resistance" memorial commemorates the member's activities and those that died during the German occupation. A memorial to the civilians killed because of the German occupation is on the site of the destroyed hospital. There is a new memorial hospital.

Related battle sites are Martinville Ridge and Hill 122.

Chapter 15 Operation COBRA

(An area 7 kilometers west of St. Lo along the D900 highway to Periers).

COBRA was a plan developed by the 1st US Army's Commander Lieutenant General Omar N. Bradley. Its success and development concluded the battle of Normandy within a month and set the massive mobile allied armies into high gear towards the German borders. Planned originally as a breakthrough to outflank and encircle German forces facing the US 8th Corps at the base of the Contentin Peninsula it developed into a breakout that encircled the complete German army in Normandy.

Bradley's plan was to blast a hole through the German lines. The area chosen was the German line south of D900 from Hebecrevon to le Mesnil-Eury, seven kilometers, and southward 2.5 kilometers. The operation commenced July 24 with a preceding bombing by 1800 heavy bombers, 396 medium bombers, 350 fighter-bombers, and 500 fighters. 5,000 tons of bombs were to obliterate all opposition in 18 square kilometers. Surprise was essential. The civilians could not be forewarned.

The breakout between the Vire River immediately to the east, and the ocean 20 kilometers west, was characterized by larger fields on rolling hills and scattered small woods. The hedgerows and marshes were of the past. The numerous roads were paved with major highways running south to Brittany and France's interior.

Major General Lawton Collins' 7th Corps was to launch the attack with six divisions, punch through the devastated enemy line, protect his flanks with two divisions and pour his four armored and motorized infantry divisions through the gap.

Holding the zone to be obliterated were remnants of the Panzer Lehr Division, a regiment of the 275th Division and elements of the 2nd SS Panzer Division.

On July 24 a.m. the American front line troops pulled back 900 meters as a precaution to avoid accidental short bombs. The 1:00 p.m. bombing plan although canceled due to cloud cover did not stop 335 bombers dropping 550 tons of explosives and 135 tons of fragmentation bombs on the American lines. Twenty-five men died and 131 were wounded in the 30th Division. With COBRA postponed until the following day the Americans moved back to reoccupy their previous line along the road. The Germans had moved up and gained the ground voluntarily given up as a cautionary move. There were more casualties before the positions were reoccupied by nightfall.

July 25, the COBRA Operation recommenced at 11 a.m. The 8th Air Force bombardiers aware of the previous day's mishaps held their bomb loads a moment longer. A good portion landed south of the intended target area. 35 heavy and 42 medium bombers dropped their ordinance short killing 111 and wounding 490. Newsmen, spectators and General Lesley J. McNair were killed. General McNair, a close personal friend of General Eisenhower, was the decoy commander for the 1st US Army Group headquartered in England. The Germans still anticipated a Dover to Calais crossing with McNair's army. He was only an observer at COBRA. For security reasons his death and funeral a few days later were classified Top Secret so the second invasion subterfuge could be maintained.

The erroneous bombing and canceled attack of the 24th mislead the Germans. The Panzer Lehr Division Commander Lieutenant General Fritz Bayerlein thought his men had repulsed an American attack. He misunderstood that the afternoon and evening battles after the bombing were to regain the voluntarily given ground. His confidence ran high. He reinforced his front line troops. The following day turned pastureland into a moonscape. In addition to the air force the American artillery had stockpiled 140,000 shells in support of the breakthrough. German tanks were flipped over and buried with crews and infantry. Communication became non-existent as phone wires were cut and radio antennas were blown away. The parachute regiment disappeared, three battalion command posts were destroyed. A third of the 3,500 men in the zone were dead, missing or wounded. The remainder were shell shocked and dazed. Only 10 tanks survived. A local resident could not recognize the familiar features of his property. At the corps and army level the German generals foresaw the catastrophe ahead.

Bradley launched his breakthrough with fifteen divisions and 750 tanks against nine remnant divisions and 115 tanks.

15.1 la Chapelle-en-Juger

(8 kilometers west of St. Lo. Take D972 from St. Lo, the Coutances highway two kilometers to D900, the road to Periers. Five hundred meters at the la Clergerie crossroads turn left onto D149 the road to la Chapelle-en-Juger, 6 kilometers.)

La Chapelle-en-Juger was a significant intersection of six roads. Before the COBRA bombardment there were roadblocks across all the incoming roads. The village was significant and well defended. A day later, the village priest thought he was in another world.

In the afternoon of July 25 a German regiment of the 275th Division moved north from Canisy (6 kilometers) to reinforce the area. By the end of the day only 200 men had survived.

The American 8th Regiment (4th Infantry Division) moving south at the center of the 7th Corps attack line were to the north and east of the village by nightfall. They had been short bombed and had to be reorganized. Their momentum bypassed pockets of German resistance north and south of their start line D900. Coming in from the north along the sunken road D89 the lead battalion faced off against two tanks with infantry support. There was strong resistance and stiff fighting until the stalemate was broken by the arrival of Sherman tanks. American softening-up shellfire into the village's northeast corner broke the German defense but stalled the regiment's advance. German reinforcements, a regiment of the 353rd Division, attempted to enter the village from the west the same afternoon but were intercepted by the 47th Regiment (9th Division). The Germans planned to establish a new defense line between la Chappelle-en-Juger and Hebecrevon (4 kilometers east). They had yet to comprehend the magnitude of the breakout.

The 8th Regiment occupied the village during the night July 25-26 however the crossroads was not secured until the morning.

The 4th Division continued south, overran the Panzer Lehr artillery positions. By late July 26 afternoon the division was three kilometers south of la Chapelle-en-Juger, one kilometer east of Marigny. By late evening they had cut the St. Lo-Coustances D972 highway having advanced seven kilometers from their start line.

The German Marigny War Cemetery is three kilometers southwest. Go south on D89 two kilometers, west 500 meters on D341. Signage "Deutsche Kriegsgraberfursorge."

Related battle sites Hebercrevon and Marigny.

15.2 Marigny Road

(10 kilometers west of St. Lo. Take D972 two kilometers west from St. Lo to D900, the road to Periers. Proceed on D900, nine kilometers to the intersection of D29 at hamlet Hotel-Calin. Turn left, south on D29)

This is one kilometer from the western end of the bomb zone that stretched to the east six kilometers along D900. The American 9th, 4th and 30th Infantry Divisions were 500 meters north paralleling the highway. Six roads lead southward from the American front lines. D29 and D77 (east four kilometers) are the widest roads. These roads were the breakout lines of advance. To minimize deep cratering of the roads and fields the bombs were all less than 500 pounds, large enough to destroy tanks and personnel but not create insurmountable obstacles.

The infantry was to clear the immediate area, move out on the flanks and open up the safe roads for the rapid deployment of the armored divisions.

The 9th Infantry Division jumped off July 25, 11a.m., crossed D900 and moved down D29. The 60th Regiment fanned out westward into areas that had not been in the bombardment plan. Resistance was stiff as the German survivors fought for their lives and fresh reinforcements from the west tried to regain the lost ground and plug the seven kilometer hole in their line. Progress was slow. By evening the 47th Regiment took Montreuil, two kilometers from the start line.

On July 26 a German counterattack came up the D29 road from Marigny. The 2nd SS Panzer Division sent in a company of tanks supported by an infantry company. The American battalion holding the road with armor support held their ground stopping the Germans cold. The infantry moved west through the fields and orchards creating a deep flank defense at the same time giving space for the armored thrust down the Marigny road. The German 353rd Division attempted to cut through the American flank position to retake la Chappelle-en-Juger. The American infantry lines were two kilometers west of D29 facing westward on a two-kilometer front.

With the German counterattack stopped, Combat Command B of the 3rd Armored Division advanced south towards Marigny through the fields west of the road. The 1st Infantry Division paralleled east of D29. Both divisions met determined resistance. Roadblocks, defended hedgerows and bomb craters slowed the advance with high casualties. The defenses around the high ground at l'Aubrie were particularly strong. Several Mark IV tanks, a 75mm antitank gun, two companies of the 2nd SS Panzer Division and troops of the 353rd Division blocked the road and the fields to the east and west. The Americans were halted. An air strike was called in breaking the resistance. (There is a German Cemetery 500 meters east of the l"Aubrie crossroads. For details see the next page.) The battle continued as the Germans withdrew down the slope to la Barberie. By nightfall armored elements were in Marigny's northern outskirts. Armor moved west from the la Barberie crossroads taking the road that bypasses the town on the west. With darkness the infantry and armor stopped.

The following morning the 18th Regiment (1st Division) cleared the town and continued south on D29, crossed D972, taking the high ground that overlooked Marigny.

From Marigny the 3rd Armored Division's Combat Command B moved southwest out of Marigny, joined D972 proceeding towards Coustance.

There is a German Military Cemetery two kilometers north of Marigny on D29 to l'Aubrie then east 500 meters. The Deutsche Kriegsgraberfursorge has 11,169 internments.

Marigny was the site of an American temporary wartime cemetery. 61% of the burials were repatriated to the United States. The remaining 39% are in the OMAHA Beach (Normandy) Cemetery and the St. James (Brittany) Cemetery. The cemetery was across the road from the present German cemetery.

Related battle sites le Neufbourg, Chapelle-en-Juger, and Hebercrevon.

Picture 17: Marigy - Looking North
July 3, 1948

On July 25 (D-day +49) General Omar Bradley launched Operation Cobra with 15 divisions and 750 tanks from their positions a few miles north of Marigy (top center). The 2nd SS Panzer Division rushed north to the town. The American forces counterattacked from the fields to the right and left of the road being used by the panzers. The enemies' resistance was strong. Two days later the American 3rd Armored Division reached the intersection sending half its strength west to Coustances while the remainder continued south at full speed. This north-south road was the principle thrust line for the famous Patton Breakout.

15.3 le Neufbourg

(15 kilometers southwest of St. Lo on D972, to Coutances. The le Neufbourg hamlet bordering the highway is at the intersection of D102 to le Lorey, 1.5 kilometers north)

The Operation COBRA breakout was initially envisioned by its planners as an end run to turn west and encircle the German 84th Corps facing the US 8th Corps at the base of the Contentin Peninsula . The US 1st Infantry Division with Combat Command B (3rd Armored Division) at Marigny (4 kilometers east) moved onto D972 from the north heading west to capture Coutances. The Germans boxed in on the east by the 1st Division and being pressured on the north needed the three southerly escape routes that passed through Coutances. A ridge east of Coutances, paralleling D972, two kilometers to its north has three prominences near the villages of Camprond, Cambernon and Montuchon. In German hands they would hold up the US 1st Division and allow more Germans to escape through Coutances. In American hands the elevations would seal the fate of the 84th Corps by assuring the town's capture. A hill northwest of Coutances dominated the remaining coastal escape road. Aerial reconnaissance confirmed the Germans were escaping through the town July 26. The 1st Division had 13 kilometers to cover to make its objective. The Germans were in confusion. Those retreating westward from the 1st Division met those retreating southward form the 8th Corps. Although the highway was undefended the hedgerowed fields on either side had many squad and platoon sized battles that upset the American timetable.

Here at le Neufbourg a lone German Panther tank stopped the Combat Command B tanks rapid advance on D972. The 2nd SS Panzer Division's 2nd Regiment was moving from the northwest towards Marigny on July 26 to fill the gap created by the destruction of the Panzer Lehr Division. Tank 424 commanded by SS Unterscharfuhrer (Sergeant) Ernst Barkman broke down with a carburetor problem near le Lorey. The other tanks continued. Within an hour four fighter-bombers pounced on the lone, stranded and exposed Panther. With the engine hatches open for repair, in a matter of minutes the engine compartment was riddled and smoking. Misreading the oily smoke as total destruction the planes moved on to other targets of opportunity. By dawn, however, tank 424 had been repaired and was moving along D102 from le Lorey to D972. Germans fleeing the Americans were scrambling past Barkman's monstrous tank hidden in the sunken road. Entering D972 from the north side, flanked by tall berms and hedgerows, Barkman pulled into the junction under a large oak tree. Coming towards him, several hundred meters east on D972, were the lead tanks of Combat Command B. The Panther's 75mm gun flashed. The first Sherman blew up. Barkman poured shell after shell into the armored column. Jeeps, half tracks, ammo carriers and fuel tankers became twisted masses in a burning inferno. Smoke hid the intersection. Two Shermans came along the road's north side shoulder. Two hits on the Panther's thick armor plating were ineffective. Within minutes Barkman's counterfire had the two Shermans aflame. Dive-bombers were called in. Their bombs were close but not close enough. Barkman's gunner fired on anything moving. With a tread off and a wounded driver, the tank pulled into the hamlet. With quick repair Panther 424 escaped leaving nine smoking Shermans along D972. The next day he took out six more American tanks. He was awarded the Knight's Cross on August 27. On August 1, Panther 424 parked, too close to a burning tank. It caught fire igniting its fuel and ammunition. The crew escaped and fought to the war's end.

Related battle site is Marigny.

15.4 Hebecrevon-Canisy Road

(Five kilometers west of St. Lo. Take D972 two kilometers west from St. Lo to D900, the road to Periers. Proceed on D900, through Hebecrevon, five kilometers to the D77 intersection)

The bomb line for Operation COBRA ran two kilometers east and five kilometers west of this point to a southern depth of 2.5 kilometers. The saturation ratio was ten bombs (500 pounds or less) per acre. Short bombing on the 30th Infantry Division disorganized their jump off time. As the infantry moved from their start line 500 meters north of the intersection they were strafed and bombed by US fighter-bombers. Colored identification panels were obscured by the dust and smoke.

The division's objectives were to clear the D77 road southward for the armor follow through, clear the Germans west of St. Lo and the Vire River, and secure the Vire River bridge three kilometers south of St. Lo against possible German counterattacks into the eastern flank of the COBRA southern thrust.

The 119th Regiment came from the north towards the intersection. Just a few meters north the Germans had established a three (Panther) tank roadblock across the road and on both sides of D77. A three company attack including armor was unsuccessful. Three Shermans remained smoking in the fields. Outflanking was unsuccessful. The bombing had failed to destroy resistance nests in the hedgerows. Advances by the 4th Infantry Division on the Americans right flank threatened the German positions. Renewed attacks gained ground and the intersection was seized. Of the six roads running south, the axis of the American operation D77 and D29 (4 kilometers west) were the widest and best developable for rapid armor mobility. From the road fork the D900 road to St. Lo yielded quick access to the Vire River and its western bank. Easily driven today but desperately fought over in 1944. The 119th Infantry Regiment led the way down the two mined roads, D77 and D900, maneuvering the tanks around the bombardment craters in daylight and in dark. By midnight Hebecrevon and its significant crossroads was in American hands. The day's gains of two kilometers had been small but here and to the west, the Marigny road, the initial defense had been overcome and the wider roads were available for armor exploitation. The defense of the ground between Hebecrevon and St. Lo was fanatical. The American advances had annihilated their forces in the bombardment, a regiment of the 275th Division moving up from Canisy was destroyed and the German flank south of St. Lo was exposed.

Leaving Hebecrevon along D900 towards St. Lo the 117th Regiment (30th Division) ran into stiff resistance at the ravine two kilometers to the east. Germans on the east side of the ravine supported by their artillery south of St. Lo arrested the regiment's advance. Five attempts to cross the ravine north of the D900 road were stopped. American 4.2 inch mortars broke the defense. The surviving Germans withdrew followed closely by the Americans. Rearguard skirmishes continued throughout the day. By midnight (July 26) the Vire River loop was in American hands.

From Hebecrevon two roads lead south to St. Giles. These and D77 from D900 were in use by the American's moving south. They were also under observation by the German artillery east of the Vire River and south of St. Lo. Southbound traffic was stopped until mid-afternoon (July 26) when US counter battery fire silenced the German guns.

The 2nd Armored Division's Combat Command A with the 22nd Regiment attached moved down the St. Giles road D77 in the afternoon (July 26). Sporadic fighting with pockets of resistance and craters slowed progress as they passed through the 2.5 kilometers of obliteration. Several hundred meters north of St. Giles German armor formed a roadblock across the road and into the neighboring fields. Dive bombers and tanks destroyed four Mark IV tanks and a self-propelled 88. St. Giles was taken by late afternoon.

The American armor and infantry continued south towards Canisy (three kilometers south). The defending Panzer Lehr Division no longer existed. Fire from the German 352nd Division artillery south of St. Lo continued to harass the advance. Bomb craters and minefields were the significant delays.

The railroad overpass 500 meters north of Canisy crossing the D77 road was a problem. A bomb had tumbled the overpass onto the road. The Germans reinforced the roadblock establishing a defense line. The Americans maintained fire into the rumble as a force passed east of the road, crossed the railroad tracks, and fired point blank into the pocket of resistance. By passing the obstruction the Americans moved towards Canisy. Dive bombers had set half the town ablaze. The end of the day saw the Americans through the town's crossroads fanned out and moving south down three roads. By running throughout the night, by the next afternoon (July 27) the three columns were seven kilometers south of Canisy on an 11 kilometer front. The American advance was gaining momentum. Masses of armor were moving through the gap and down the destroyed roads. Eastern flank protection against a 352nd Division counterattack was a consideration. Engineers had to repair the roads not designed to withstand bombs and heavy tank treads. The collapsed railroad pass had to be removed.

A few hundred meters north of Canisy is the Canisy Chateau, site of an American hanging August 14. At Vierville-sur-Mer, a kilometer inland from OMAHA's Beach Exit D-1, Private Clarence Whitfield, 240th Port Company of the 494th Port Battalion, at gun point raped Aniela Skrzyniarz, a Polish farm girl. This was the first rape case in Normandy. Whitfield was drunk on the local alcoholic apple cider, Calvados. A general court-martial was held in Vierville June 20. He was found guilty and sentenced to death by hanging. The Judge Advocate General in Britain confirmed the verdict on July 24. A gallows was constructed in the chateau's kitchen garden. Whitfield arrived on August 13 and helped dig the three-meter pit beneath the gallows. Guards were posted at the chateau garden wall's shell holes to keep out the curious. The only civilian witness was Monsieur Amiable Lehoux whose recollections of 1944 include Whitfield went to his death smoking a cigar.

Related battle sites are Marigny Road, St. Lo and Quibou.

15.5 St. Jean-des-Baisants

(9 kilometers southeast of St. Lo. Travel east on D972 1 kilometer to D11, the road south to St. Jean-des-Baisants (7 kilometers) and Caumont)

The American breakout, Operation COBRA, west of St. Lo commenced July 25. South (Hill 101) and east (St. Jean-des-Baisants Ridge) of St. Lo the German positions on these elevated prominences overviewed the COBRA advancing line just 7 kilometers west. German artillery from here threatened to slow the advances and cause high casualties. German troops could be shifted westward to counterattack the American eastern flank.

Seizing Hill 101 and the ridge would eliminate the artillery and pin down the German troops from moving westward.

The ridge, seven kilometers long, ran from St. Jean-des-Baisants southwest to Ste. Suzanne-sur-Vire. Its capture would encircle the Germans on Hill 101 (two kilometers south of St. Lo) forcing them to withdraw.

The nearest American force, the 2nd Infantry Division, was 4 kilometers north of St. Jean-des-Baisants along the D972 highway. Northeast the 5th Infantry Division was 5 kilometers away.

The terrain benefited the defenders. Hedgerowed, small, sloping fields where a two week lull had given the Germans ample time to apply their proven bocage defensive tactics.

The American 5th Infantry Division had just arrived in line and lacked the battlefield experience. Numerically the four attacking regiments (38th, 23rd, 9th and 2nd) outnumbered the Germans. Twenty artillery and two tank destroyer battalions were in support. Ammunition was plentiful.

July 25, dawn, 136 guns opened a 20 minute bombardment along the front. New tactics for armor support of the infantry were implemented. Tanks with two 2-meter spears welded to the chassis rammed into the hedgerows. Pulling back, bangalore torpedoes were inserted then exploded creating a passable gap into the enclosed field. The thin-skinned underside of the tank was not exposed as it had been when it mounted the hedgerow. Another technique was to attach a cutter on the tank and ram through the hedgerow with mass and speed while firing its machine guns across the field. The hedgerow mound still on the tank added protection against antitank weapons. The cutters were made from the steel beach obstacles cut and welded into sharp teeth that sliced through the dense roots in the hedgerow. Tanks alone would cut through several fields opening up avenues for infantry follow-through.

Starting from St. Germain and Montrabot (five kilometers northeast) the 9th and 2nd Regiments advanced in spite of artillery and mortar fire almost to the Caumont road (D11). From Hill 192, due north of St. Jean-des-Baisants (four kilometers) the 38th and 23rd Regiments made it to les Marecheaux at the D90-D59 crossroads. Strong resistance stopped the 38th Regiment.

Gains for the day were good. Enemy artillery fire had caused 1,000 casualties. As planned the American pressure had held German troops to this battlefield.

The following day saw further advances up to the ridge crest and the closing of the two kilometer gap between the regiments created the first day. American gains west of St. Lo outflanked the Germans on Hill 101 and along the St. Jean-des-Baisants ridge. They withdrew to a new defense line on the 27th. The next day the 38th and 9th Regiments occupied the ridge.

Related battle site is Hill 192.

Chapter 16 Breakout

On the eve of Operation COBRA General Eisenhower wrote General Bradley, "Pursue every advantage with ardor verging on recklessness and with all your troops without fear of major counter offensive from the forces the enemy now has on his front. The results will be incalculable."

In the last six warm sunny days of July the US 1st Army captured 20,000 Germans. Following the COBRA bombardment July 25 the enemies' communications were destroyed and in disarray. The rapid American deployment southwards continued to disrupt the remaining communications as advancing troops cut all lines. The integration of armor, infantry and engineers, all with radio linkage to overhead fighter-bombers brought the German term blitzkrieg back on themselves. Initially Collins' 7th Corps was to thrust south and then west to be behind the German northern line facing the 8th Corps. With speed and before the Germans escaped he hoped the 7th and 8th Corps would encircle 16,000 Germans. General Bradley by the 28th saw bigger opportunities to develop and exploit the breakthrough. By redirecting the 7th Corps south instead of west the Americans could maximize the use of the southbound roads to Avranches and Pontaubault and breakout into Brittany and central France. General Patton's 3rd Army was in place and set to move. Patton took over the supervision of the 8th Corps as it advanced down the Contentin's Atlantic coast to Avranches. The quicker they got to Brittany the sooner his 3rd Army would be activated.

Although the Germans were withdrawing numerous obstacles delayed the American follow-up. Rearguards caused frequent stops to clear out the resistance pockets. Withdrawing the Germans scattered mines. Those with new technology took longer to disarm. Many bridges were demolished. The numerous prisoners were just disarmed and told to head north with little or no escort. The roads had been bombed and strafed. Booby-trapped wreckage had to be cleared. Heavy trucks and treaded armor chewed up the asphalt. However, the biggest problem was the congestion created by the breakout's success. The 1st Army's enormous power of men and material was unleashed along a relatively narrow front. The armored funnel pointed to the bridges across the See and Selune River at Avranches and Pontabault

50 kilometers south. The exploitation and developments between July 25 and 31 moved from a breakout to a breakthrough.

16.1 Torgini-sur-Vire

(11 kilometers southeast of St. Lo on N174)

By July 29 the US 5th Corps was 5 kilometers south of D11 the St. Lo – Caumont road. The corps' west flank bordered the Vire River. Its front line facing south ran 11 kilometers east to the western flank of the British 2nd Army. The 35th Infantry Division was only 1.25 kilometers north of Torgini. The east-west secondary road, D53, was the front line. Torgini, an important road junction, was to be seized quickly. The well trained and equipped German 3rd Parachute Division was defending an extended line facing the 35th and 2nd US Infantry Divisions. US intelligence estimated the opposition as "a few tired old Austrians". The bocage hills favored the defense. German rear guard squads and platoons were numerous using machine guns, mortars, and artillery effectively. The July 30 attack from D53 to Torgini gained little ground but caused 1,000 casualties to the 35th Division north of Torgini and the 2nd Division attempting to bypass the town to its east.

A plan for a successful attack on July 31 was drawn up. The Germans made a tactical withdrawal during darkness. Although void of combat the July 31 advances were delayed by minefields and artillery fire.

16.2 Tessy-sur-Vire

(16 kilometers south of St. Lo via D28)

The COBRA breakout created a significant, threatening gap in the German front line. Field Marshal Guenther von Kluge rushed the 2nd and 116th Panzer Divisions and remnants of the 352nd Infantry Division (under the command of the 47th Panzer Corps) into the area north and west of Tessy. Tessy's Vire River bridge became a critical factor to the defenders and attackers. Major General Charles Corlett (19th Corps Commander) wanted the bridge and the high ground south of the town seized as soon as possible.

On July 27 the 2nd Panzer Division crossed the bridge from east to west and into the new German defense line from Moyon, 5 kilometers northeast of Tessy to Troisgots, 4 kilometers north of Tessy. The armored division's infantry support came from the remnants of the mauled 352nd Division that had been in battle since OMAHA Beach, June 6. A small river south of both villages paralleled the front line creating a natural barrier to the attackers. Troisgots was a strongly fortified defense bastion. Two attempts by the three regiments of the 30th Infantry Division were stopped. The artillery support and bombardment was three times more powerful than used in standard attacks. Six of nineteen American tanks were destroyed but any plans for the Germans to move north were stopped.

Simultaneous to the 30th Division attack the American 2nd Armored Division's Combat Command B attacked from the west along D13 from Villebandon (8 kilometers west of Tessy). The CCB was also stopped at Beaucoudray hamlet (6 kilometers west of Tessy). American tanks attempting to move south from Beaucoudray and Villebaudon came under intense shellfire from the German guns on the high ground south of Tessy. German heavy tanks impervious to the American Shermans lighter guns entered the Beaucoudray intersection blocking movement in all directions.

Elements of the German 116th Panzer Division entered the area July 30 threatening to overrun Villebaudon. American fighter-bombers attacked Tessy and its bridge leaving impassable rubbled streets.

Attacks from the north and west on July 31 made little progress. The ravine 1.5 kilometers east of Beaucoudray on D13 was impassable even though fighter-bombers strafed and bombed the defenders' emplacements on the slopes.

To the north at Troisgots the 119th Regiment and 34 tanks broke into the town with a three sided attack destroying several German tanks and self-propelled guns. The all-day battle ended successfully that evening. Lieutenant H. F. Hansen (743rd Tank Battalion) was awarded the Distinguished Service Cross.

August 1 witnessed the Germans west of the Vire River withdrawing behind a strong rearguard action. Von Kluge's plan to plug the gap had failed. The American advances elsewhere left Tessy untenable. However, the rearguard actions north and west were designed to buy time for the German withdrawal so they could form a new defense line.

The 30th Division pressed into Tessy from the north while the CCB came in from the west through the fields north and south of D13 with two armored battalions. By noon the 22nd Regiment and tanks were in Tessy and crossing the bridge to establish a bridgehead east of the Vire River.

German harassment artillery fire rained down on Tessy throughout August 2 until the bridgehead was expanded beyond the Germans effective visible range.

16.3 le Chene – Gueran

(23 kilometers south of St. Lo via D999 to Percy, 19 kilometers, east on D58 and D208, 8 kilometers)

Half a kilometer west of Le Cheme – Guerain on D208 are the wartime sites of American and German cemeteries across the road from each other. The American cemetery on the north side was closed first as the remains were returned to the United States or re-interned in the St. Laurent and St. James cemeteries.

The German cemetery was closed in 1957 when the last remains were re-interned in the Marigny Cemetery.

16.4 Vire

(40 kilometers south of St. Lo via N174)

Vire is built on a hill amphitheater fashion that overlooks and dominates the bocage countryside. The Vire River meanders around the southern and western edges of the town. Six roads converge on this artistic and religious center.

In anticipation of German reinforcements rushing north to the invasion beaches the town was almost obliterated by allied bombers on June 6 and 7. The clogged streets and destroyed bridges were a repeatable allied tactic throughout the Normandy campaign. The presence of a German radar site in Vire was an additional motivation and benefit of the bombing.

Although the allied air force dominated the daylight skies taking a heavy toll on German movements, expediency forced the Germans to take their chances. As the Panzer Lehr Division extracted itself from the rubble and moved north on D377, the fighter-bombers pounced on the traffic. The Germans called the road "Jabo Rennstreche", fighter-bomber race course.

By August 2, British tanks (11th Armored Division) were several kilometers to the north. The Vire area was being held by a German battle group of the 353rd, 363rd and 3rd Parachute Divisions. The defenders holding the high ground had excellent artillery fire control positions. Roadblocks with antitank weapons covered the entrance roads. The battle that unfolded destroyed the town's few remaining buildings.

On August 4 after a hard fight, down the 24-kilometer road, D52, from Tessy-sur-Vire, the US 29th Infantry Division and Combat Command A of the 2nd Armored Division reached the northwestern outskirts. The British armor vacated their positions to the US 2nd Infantry Division and proceeded southeast to Flers. The 29th Division and CCA were to take the town.

The following day a spearhead of the CCA drove into the northern suburb Martilly down the D52, Tessy Road. German resistance in the neighboring fields was pushed aside. Nineteen Shermans collected to cross the stone Vire River bridge. Concentrated fire knocked out ten. Four more were destroyed crossing the bridge. The soft river bottom prohibited fording the river.

The Americans moved south taking Hill 219 one kilometer southwest of Vire but still west of the river. German counterattacks throughout August 5 threatened the American's precarious hold on the hill. The 116th Regiment moved from Martilly south through the well defended fields making it to the top of Hill 219 by evening.

The next evening under German observation and shellfire the 116th Regiment descended the steep eastern slope, forded the river, climbed the ravine wall, raced across the road and up the gentle slope into the gutted houses. House to house fighting ensued throughout the night until dawn. With the town captured roadblocks were established on the roads leading east and south. No counterattack developed.

16.5 Camprond

(19 kilometers west of St. Lo via D972, 19 kilometers to la Chapelle, north on D52 2.5 kilometers)

The hill at Camprond and its two sister hills a few kilometers to the west were dominating features for whoever held them. In German hands they would impede the American westward advance on D972 to Coustances. In American hands they overshadowed the few escape routes the Germans had to withdraw south through Coustances.

On July 27 the 1st US Infantry Division with the Combat Command B of the 3rd Armored Division pivoted west from Marigny down D972. After overcoming and side slipping sporadic resistance the force cut across the terrain occupying the hill near the Camprond village by mid-afternoon.

The relief battalion of the 18th Infantry Regiment was not as fortunate. As it came up the hill from la Chapelle German tank and infantry groups fought delaying actions at roadblocks and in the adjacent fields. Close support by the fighter-bombers one by one overcame the resistance pockets. By midnight the battalion was on the hill releasing the holding force to continue its westward thrust to Cambernon (3 kilometers southwest)

Related battle sites are Marigny and Coustances.

16.6 Coustances

(27 kilometers southwest of St. Lo via D972)

The town is a religious and judicial center built on a hill dominated by a cathedral. As a significant northern route for German reinforcements to the Contentin Peninsula, it was severely bombed twice on June 6 causing the citizens to flee to the neighboring country side.

The following day a third bombing completed the town's destruction. An incendiary raid on June 13 burned the cathedral, town hall and hospital.

The breakout of Operation COBRA threatened to entrap the six German divisions north facing the American 8th Corps. The American rapid advance southward and then west towards Coustances along the D972, St. Lo highway, placed the German forces in a rapidly deteriorating position. German delaying tactics on D972 held open their escape route through the town. Combat Command B of the 4th Armored Division entered Coustances July 28 against minimum rearguard opposition.

The rubbled streets strewn with mines became a bottle neck as the 8th Corps passed southward in pursuit

In early August General Bradley established his 12th Army Group command post (code named "Eagle Rear") as a tent city in a magnificent estate a few kilometers north of Coustances.

Related battle site is Camprond.

16.7 Brehal

(45 kilometers southwest of St. Lo via D972 to Coustances and D971 south 18 kilometers)

The American 6th Armored Division advanced southward towards Brehal on D971 (from Coutances) and D20 (from Montmartin-sur-mer) on July 30.

Combat Command B on D971 had little more opposition than small arms fire. Using the proven technique of firing high explosives and canister into potential resistance areas the CCB had advanced rapidly.

At the outskirts of Brehal a roadblock of logs and a rolling steel gate blocked the route. Four P47 Thunderbolts unsuccessfully strafed and bombed the obstruction. In frustration the lead Sherman rammed the roadblock opening up the street for other Americans to enter the town. The quick show of force caused the small German rearguard to surrender in the village square.

An abandoned roadblock south of Brehal was passed through. The 6th Division split into three columns headed southbound for Granville and Avranches.

16.8 Granville – Jullonville

(26 kilometers northwest of Avranches via D973)

This small seaport was evacuated by the Germans on July 30 and occupied by elements of the US 6th Division the following day. Recognizing the seaport's value to the allies the German demolition engineers denied its use by blowing up the wharf facilities, sinking barges and boats throughout the harbor including a barge in the damaged lock. Although the town had been spared from allied bombers, the port was in shambles. By September adequate repairs were made to accommodate small vessels from southern Wales to bring in coal for the French population. German POWs were the unloading labor force.

In mid-August General Eisenhower established his advanced headquarters 3 kilometers east of Granville. Here on August 20, a rainy afternoon, under a tarpaulin, Ike, General deGaulle and General Bradley discussed the pros and cons of either going into Paris to relieve the Free French Resistance uprising, or bypassing the city to optimize the pursuit of the retreating Germans. Supplies were still limited. Large ports were not yet cleared or captured. Ships were still being unloaded at the invasion beaches. There was concern at the time, as the dynamic battlefield situation was demanding huge amounts of supplies for the allies' mobile army.

SHAEF (Supreme Headquarters Allied Expeditionary Force) and URRA (United Nations Relief and Rehabilitation Administration) occupied the previous Gestapo interrogation center in the Normandy Hotel on the beachfront. (Note: The three story addition is of recent years). The cells on the top floor still had the prisoners' blood on the floors and walls when the URRA personnel used them as bedrooms. The hotel became SHAEF signals center mid-August.

In March, 1945, the Germans stockaded on the British Guersey Islands, raided Granville with the objective of capturing supply ships, destroying the harbor facilities and capturing staff officers for interrogation. The surprise attack, so late in the war, caught the small American force by surprise. German POWs were released and taken back to Guersey. A few American and British personnel were captured and some damage was done to the facilities.

Casualties were three Germans and four Americans killed. The British freighter crews and the French civilians had higher casualties as the German commandos automatic weapon fire raked the buildings and ships indiscriminately to create chaos. Numerous tombstones in the cemetery mark March 9, 1945 as a day of fruitless wasted deaths 800 kilometers behind the front lines with peace two months away.

Jullonville (8 kilometers south on D911)

SHAEF Forward Headquarters was established here in the La Colonie Scolaire de St. Ouen school grounds September 1. (It moved to the Trianon Palace Hotel in Versailles, September 20.) The largest building housed the communications center, the War room, messes and female billets. Tents and prefab huts housed the 750 officers and 2500 men.

An Advanced Landing Strip, A-56, was established on the small hilltop overlooking the school.

General Eisenhower's accommodations were 5 kilometers south at St. Jean-le-Thomas in the Villa Montgommery overlooking Mont St. Michel 10 kilometers south. (The owner Monsieur E. H. Benois, at the time, owned and operated a pharmacy in Carentan). In early September, returning from a meeting with General Bradley in Chartres, General Eisenhower transferred at Pontorson from his C47 to his light liaison aircraft, L-5, piloted by Dick Underwood. Bad weather made it difficult to find the Jullonville landing strip causing the pilot to land on the hard sand beach. With a rising tide threatening to swamp the plane the pilot and general pushed the plane off the beach, but in the process General Eisenhower sprained his knee badly. Underwood carried the general to the highway where a passing jeep picked them up and took them to the Villa. The time lapse since leaving Pontorson had created much concern. The general's knee was put in a cast and he convalesced in the Villa for the next two weeks. Although the pain persisted long after the cast was removed, he suppressed his anguish throughout his demanding schedule. Only his closest aids were conscious of the continuing knee problem.

16.9 Gavray

(31 kilometers southwest of St. Lo via D38)

Gavray on the north side and la Planche on the south side straddle the east-west running Sienne River.

On July 30 Combat Command B, 3rd Armored Division, entered Gavray from St. Denis-le-Gast, D38. The reconnaissance troop in the early afternoon found the river bridge demolished and la Planche well defended in strength. The wooded hill to the south had numerous German observation posts and artillery batteries.

In the late afternoon, following a fifteen minute bombardment of the village and hill, the US infantry waded across the meter and a half deep river. German fire poured into the attackers. In one case when the infantry was faltering Lieutenant Colonel L. L. Doan dismounted from his tank and personally led the assault. (awarded the Distinguished Service Cross for this action).

Within a few hours the village and hill were in American hands. The engineers completed a new bridge during the night for the following mornings' advance to continue.

Related battle sites are St. Denis-le-Gast and Lengronne.

16.10 St. Pois

(23 kilometers northeast of Avranches via D911 to Brecey, 16 kilometers, and D39 to St. Pois, 9 kilometers)

Northeast of the village 1.5 kilometers stands the prominent Hill 232, and to the southeast 1.5 kilometers is Hill 211. The two hills and village were held by elements of the 116th Panzer Division.

From St. Pois westward to the coast the American forces had overrun the opposition and were rushing southward. American strategy was to widen the gap by pushing the Germans out of St. Pois eastwards. German strategy called for closing the gap and cut off the American 3rd Army.

The 4th Infantry Division's three regiments attacked the 116th Panzer's position on August 4. The 12th Regiment against Hill 232, the 22nd Regiment against the village, and the 8th Regiment against Hill 211. Hill 211 was taken and strong gains made on Hill 232. Although surrounded on three sides the forces in the village held out.

Other American forces to the south of St. Pois were successful driving eastward threatening the St. Pois defenders retreat routes. On August 5 under a rain of shells and fighter-bombers the 116th Panzer remnants pulled out on the Cherence-le-Roussel road running eastward past the church at the village square. Seventy-five percent of the village was destroyed.

Chapter 17 Roncey Pocket

Operation COBRA for its many opportunities had potential for disasters. The southwestern thrust of the 7th Corps planning to encircle the German 84th Corps facing north against the 8th Corps became vulnerable to German counterattacks all along its southeastern flank. The Combat Command B of the US 2nd Armored Division had rushed headlong through the COBRA breach bullying its way through the congestion to Canisy. At Canisy, with their 82nd Reconnaissance Battalion leading, the Combat Command B turned southwest onto D38 towards the western coast. Their objectives were to move quickly to cut off the German 84th Corps southern escape route and create flank protection against expected German counterattacks from the east in their attempt to open escape routes for the encircled 84th Corps. To close the southern escape route Combat Command B had to drive 22 kilometers southwest down D38 from Canisy to Lengronne then turn north to Cambry four kilometers. The majority of the retreating Germans had concentrated around Montpinchon and Roncey, west of D38. The surrounded area became known as the Roncey Pocket.

17.1 Canisy - Roncey Road

(Drive southwest from St. Lo on D999 three kilometers to the road fork. Take D38 to Canisy, four kilometers)

Canisy: Combat Command B (CCB) of the 2nd: Division, under the command of Brigadier Isaac D. White entered Canisy from the north (D77) mid-afternoon July 27, pivoted southwest onto D38 and proceeded towards Quibou.

Half a kilometer northeast of Canisy is the Chateau Canisy. In its kitchen garden, August 14, 1944, was hanged Private Clarence Whitfield for the rape of a polish woman at Vierville-sur-Mer (OMAHA Beach) June 14. He and three other soldiers of the 494th Port Battalion, who were unloading supply ships raped Aniela Skrzyniarz and her sister Zofia, the former at gunpoint. Zofia was able to escape the drunken soldiers to return with officers and Aniela's husband. The General Court Martial in Vierville, June 20, found Whitfield guilty and sentenced to death. The Judge Advocate General in England confirmed the sentence July 24. A gallows was erected in the chateau's kitchen garden. Whitfield arrived August 13 and helped dig the pit under the gallows. The following day guards were posted at the shell holes in the surrounding walls. Monsieur Aimable Lehoux was the only civilian witness. Whitfield went to his death smoking a cigar.

Quibou: (2 kilometers) The CCB's rapid movement down D38 was halted two kilometers later by an enemy roadblock on the outskirts of the Quibou village. The 78th Armored Field Battalion laid down a barrage from a distance of only one kilometer. Fighter bombers waiting to pounce were called in. The roadblock and positions on the ridge overlooking the village were blasted. Resistance crumbled. The American blitzkrieg moved through.

Dangy: (3 kilometers southwest of Quibou on D38)

The day previous, July 26, Lieutenant General Fritz Bayerlein Commander of the Panzer Lehr Division was expounding on the realities of their situation to Oberstleutnant (Lieutenant Colonel) von Kluge (son of Field Marshal von Kluge who had replaced Field Marshal Rommel after being strafed and wounded July 17). Bayerlein's command post was in a Dangy home close to the highway. An explosion rocked the house blowing in the windows and doors.

American fighter-bombers had hit an ammunition dump. Mines, shells, ammo and rockets went off in all directions. The following day Bayerlein was trying to determine if his panzer division still existed. Then he looked out through the broken windows and saw the American armored spearhead racing by. He and his headquarters staff narrowly escaped being captured. The American intent was to close the southern escape route without being delayed or handicapped by prisoners. American history states Bayerlein was in Dangy however, German history describes the staff moving south to Pont Brocard after the ammo dump explosion.

Pont Brocard: (3 kilometers southwest of Dangy on D38)

Late afternoon July 27 an antitank gun and small arms fire briefly delayed the Americans. Overcoming the opposition the armored column crossed the Soulle River and continued its rush down D38.

Bayerlein's headquarters staff of half a dozen officers and fourteen radio operators and runners had moved into a farmhouse bordering the river that morning. Late afternoon American tanks rumbled up the river bank firing at the farmhouse. The only exit door faced the American tanks. Last to leave the burning building, Bayerlein successfully dodged the tank's shells and machine gun fire. Running south he escaped the 84th Corps encirclement. He and a few others were the sole survivors of Germany's most powerful armored division decimated in the previous weeks battles northwest of St. Lo and its conclusive annihilation during Operation COBRA.

Just after midnight, July 28, Germans (remnants of a battalion of the 2nd SS Panzer Division, the 275th Division and miscellaneous other units) extracting themselves from encirclement entered Pont Brocard at the intersection from the Cerisy-la-Salle road (D52). The thin American line of the 183rd Field Artillery Battalion broke. A flood of escapees rushed across the bridge and down the Laubressiere Road (D52).

The division reserve moved in from Canisy closed the breach and reinforced the thin line to Notre Dame-de-Cenilly.

Notre Dame-de-Cenilly: (2 kilometers southwest of Pont Brocard on D38)

The 2nd Armored Division.'s Combat Command B moving rapidly along D38 from Canisy seized the village July 28 at 2 a.m. The CCB had covered 11 kilometers in 10 hours. The mobile army previously bogged down in the hedgerows where advances were measured in meters or yards was now a steel juggernaut. Brigadier White's orders were to move to Lengronne (11 kilometers southwest) thereby narrowing the German escape route, simultaneously strengthen the D38 frontline to prohibit escapees across the road from the north and defend against counterattacks from the south trying to open escape routes. The Americans manning the road were to keep it open for traffic and ward off attacks from the fields on either side. The division's reserve and the 8th Regiment (4th Infantry Division) bolstered the defenses. The major German escape efforts were expected between Notre Dame-de-Cenilly and Lengronne. Aerial reconnaissance had identified sizeable German forces around Montpinchon (four kilometers northeast) and Roncey (5 kilometers west).

Les Hogues: (4 kilometers southwest of Notre Dame-de-Cenilly on D38 at the junction of D58 to Roncey)

Elements of the 2nd Armored Division's Combat Command B passed through this hamlet intersection in the predawn hours of July 28 in their head long rush to stop the German retreat southward.

The stream of American mobile might kept rolling down D38 with follow-up troops securing the flanks and blocking German penetrations across the roadway.

Before dawn, 24 hours later (July 29) the Germans came down D58 from Roncey. A company of American infantry and tanks were holding the area. Leading the attack was a SP (self-propelled 88mm gun on tank treads) followed by 30 tanks and armored vehicles. German infantry flanked the SP along both ditches. The SP barged through the American defenses, crossed D38 and stopped. Rifle fire had killed the driver and gunner. The twelve tanks following could not bypass the SP now blocking their escape road to the southeast. American tanks were on D38 blasting into the iron cauldron. The infantry closed in and hand to hand fighting ensued until dawn. The Germans pulled back leaving 17 dead and 150 wounded plus tanks and armored cars. The SP still loaded and running had a driver change and moved off the roadway. D38 was reopened. The American losses were 50 dead and wounded, a tank and a half track destroyed.

St. Denis-le-Gast: (4 kilometers southwest of les Hogues on D38)

The village was captured on July 28 morning by units of the 2nd Armored Division's Combat Command B who then continued on to Lengronne (3.5 kilometers southwest) and Cambry (6 kilometers northwest). German counterattacks from the north and south were expected as the American encirclement pressured the Germans to break out, be captured, or be killed.

A coordinated German attack on the village from the south and north started shortly after midnight July 29. Up D38 from Gavray a diversionary attack was designed to pull the American firepower away from the two-column attack of 1,000 men and 100 armored vehicles entering the village from the north on D38 and the adjacent fields. Greatly outnumbered the Americans pulled back opening the D38 as a narrow short lived escape corridor. There was no intent by the Germans to hold the route open for following escapees. This group wanted out. The American pressure to recapture the village kept the intended escapees in close combat. The D13-D38 intersection was the focal point and witnessed much hand to hand combat. By dawn the Americans had closed the gap. Casualties were high. Germans, 130 killed, 124 wounded, 500 captured, 7 tanks and 18 vehicles destroyed. Americans, 100 men dead or wounded and 12 vehicles destroyed.

In the confusion of the night time battle a Luftwaffe radar unit of eleven vehicles turned west onto D13 to Lengronne (3 kilometers) unable to continue south on D38 through the blocked intersection. This was an American held road prepared to repel German attacks from the north and south. Half way to Lengronne the Luftwaffe vehicles passed into the 78th Armored Field Artillery Battalion bivouac area. The vehicle convoy coming along D13 into their area surprised the American guards on the alert for infantry infiltration. Vehicles and darkness on an American held road delayed the American reaction time. The vehicles passed through an antitank gun roadblock and were half way through the battalion area when the Americans and Germans realized what was happening. The American howitzers and tank destroyers opened up at point blank range. The action was so close that the shrapnel from the exploding vehicles was whizzing over the artillery men's heads. The flames and explosions silhouetted the fleeing Germans caught in the crossfire from the fields on both sides of the road. The Germans lost 90 killed, 200 prisoners, 11 vehicles destroyed. American losses, 5 killed and 6 wounded. A Distinguished Service Cross was posthumously awarded to Captain Naubert O. Simand, Jr. for his actions in manning an exposed machine without regard of his own safety.

Lengronne: (3 kilometers west of St. Denis-le-Gast on D13)

Captured by the 2nd Armored Division's Combat Command B on the afternoon of July 28. The armored spear moving so rapidly and decisively had taken the retreating Germans by surprise. From Canisy to Lengronne enemy crossroads had been left guarded by the Americans. All German retreating vehicular traffic had to pass through these manned intersections. Few attempts were successful. However, the open fields and night darkness allowed many of the Roncey pocket survivors to escape in small groups on foot.

Cambry: (4 kilometers north of Lengronne on D7 at the intersection of D49, named les Hauts Vents, "High Winds")

The intersection was occupied by a small American force from St. Denis-le-Gast (D49) July 28. A roadblock was established with a machine gun on the northwest corner that could cover the road north (D7) and east (D49).

West on D49, at Trelly, the 2nd SS Panzer Regiment (2nd SS Panzer Division) had established its headquarters the previous day. Its much decorated commander SS Oberstrumbannfuhrer (Lieutenant Colonel) Christian Tychsen, 34, nine times wounded, was returning from Coustances. Unaware the Americans had occupied the intersection in his absence his open kubelwagen (German jeep) came into the intersection from the north. The machine gun fired. The much admired German hero bled to death. He was the first of hundreds to die here.

Just before midnight, July 29, from the north 2500 Germans made a break for it through the crossroads and adjacent fields. The American roadblock was overwhelmed. Sergeant Hulan B. Whittington, an infantryman (41st Armored Infantry Regiment) jumped up on an American tank hosing the attackers with the turret machine gun. He directed the tank driver to maneuver so as to blunt the main thrust of the attack. The Germans faltered. US artillery zeroed in creating chaos. The battle lasted six hours. Sergeant Whittington was awarded the Medal of Honor. Casualties were Germans, 450 killed, 1,000 wounded, 100 vehicles destroyed. American: 50 killed and 60 wounded.

Roncey: (6 kilometers northeast by D7 and D438)

The squeeze by the US 7th and 8th Corps entrapped elements of the Germans 243rd, 353rd, 91st and 2nd SS Panzer Divisions into the Roncey-Montpinchon (4 kilometers northeast) area.

On July 29 the Americans 9th Tactical Air Force discovered the Roncey pocket of 500 armored vehicles. Many were abandoned for lack of fuel, their occupants having elected to battle their way through the American lines on foot. For six hours Roncey, the surrounding roads and fields were pounded by strafing dive-bombers, artillery and tank fire. The newness of the town bears witness to its destruction. The tank hulks that littered the intersection no longer surround the modern rebuilt church. One hundred tanks and 250 vehicles were destroyed within the one kilometer radius of the town's center.

By July 30 the German resistance had stopped. The battle of the Contentin was complete.

Chapter 18 End Run

The launching of Operation COBRA broke open the stalemated Battle of Normandy.

The sunshine and warm weather in the last week of July gave the opportunity for the 9th Tactical Air Command to develop ground-air radio communications previously unknown. Fighter bombers destroyed all forms of mechanized equipment, railroads, bridges, ammo dumps and troops. Relays of four fighter-bombers flew in half hour shifts over the lead tank columns. VHF radios between the tanks and fighter-bombers gave the ground forces "eyes of steel in the air".

German communications were either non-existent or intercepted by the allied receivers. Their commanders, lacking clear intelligence of their disintegrating left flank, were powerless to command effectively. Allied air supremacy negated German movements defensively or offensively. Allied delayed time bombs were dropped in the daylight hours on road intersections that would explode during the night hours as the Germans were predictably passing through safely under the cover of darkness. Field Marshal von Kluge described the situation by phone to Berlin "It's a mad house here."

The opportunity presented to the Americans exceeded their optimistic expectations. Their mobile air supported army by destroying the German left flank had created an end run that could swing east behind the Germans front line and drive west to seize the ports along the Bay of Biscay. The last objective to success was seizing the bridges at Avranches and Pontaubault and securing the connecting road, D104, from counterattacks and bombardment.

18.1 Avranches

Lieutenant General George Patton's 3rd Army exploited the gateway from Normandy into Brittany on July 31, 1944. The area known for its unique Avranchin sheep witnessed numerous major military successes the following month.

The town of less than 8,000 souls was spared devastating bombing on June 6 but in the three days following the business center was completely razed. Several major roads converge here including the route to and from Brittany – a source of German reinforcements.

Avranches on a bluff is situated between the See and Selune Rivers 7 kilometers apart. The capture of the bridges and the connecting road (D104) was paramount in the US development plan.

Major General John S. (Tiger Jack) Wood's 4th Armored Division's Combat Command B reconnaissance battalion advanced on Avranches from the northwest along D973 the afternoon of July 30. CCB's battalion's advance had been so surprisingly rapid that a major German headquarters in the les Portes chateau (5.5 kilometers northwest and 2 kilometers west of D973) was unknowingly bypassed. This was the 7th German Army headquarters. SS General Paul Hausser, Generalmajor Christoph Freiherr Gersdorff, and numerous general staff officers were west of the American advance highway. The Germans fled on foot across the highway between gaps in the CCB's armored traffic to regain their lines and vehicles for a more appropriate means of retreating east. Hausser's last communique to Berlin before evacuating the chateau described the Germans' position on their western flank as "Reisensauerei"-one hell of a mess.

Arriving at Avranches' outskirts, American recon units confirmed that the two See River bridges at le Pont Gilbert (D973) and Ponts (N175) in the northeast sector of Avranches were intact. The main body of CCB entered the unoccupied town that evening. Outposted roadblocks were established as far east as Tirepied (7 kilometers) and at the south and southeast of Avranches. CCB's speed had put it ahead of their support forces. It was isolated in enemy territory at least until daybreak.

Two German columns from the coastal region in retreat moved against the northwestern bridge position down D973 from D911. The first column was stopped after a brief battle. Prisoners taken included an ammo carrying red cross ambulance. The second column resumed the attack forcing the Americans to abandon their positions just after midnight. The Germans positioned artillery on the bluffs over the bridge to fire onto D973 when needed. A large body moved into town looking for eastern escape routes. A group moving south ran into the armored infantry at the roadblock. Private W. N. Whitson (awarded a Distinguished Service Cross posthumously) put up a strong defense. With a .30 caliber machine gun Whitson killed 50 Germans in 20 vehicles before dying. The Germans pulled back to regroup and re-attack at daylight. The attack collapsed. Several hundred surrendered.

Brigadier Holmes E. Dager ordered the company that had withdrawn from le Port Gilbert bridge to re-occupy the D9111-D973 crossroads at sunrise. A few hours later the German artillery on the bluffs fired upon the main body of the CCB coming south on D973 towards the bridge. The American infantry forded the river, scaled the bluff, and put the artillery pieces out of action. It was noon July 31.

That afternoon the CCB fanned out four task forces to secure their flanks and move south of Pontaubault and the road junction to its south. As the fluidity of the battlefield progressed, Advanced Landing Grounds were built in the area by the 9th Engineer Command i.e., Avranches, A-30C, Granville A-56, Pontorson A-28.

Today there is a memorial square to General Patton in which a monument stands on the site of the General's billet.

In Le Val St.-Pere, 3 kilometers southwest of Avranches via N175 there is a WWII museum.

Related battle sites are Pontaubault and Mortain and the American cemetery at St. James and the German cemetery at Huisines sur Mer.

18.2 Pontaubault

(6 kilometers south of Avranches via N175)

The new expressway from Avranches to Pontorson passes east and south of Pontaubault village. The road and railroad line of 1944 are still in use. A railline running east, north of the Selune River, has been removed. The road and railroad bridges north of the village were vital to General Patton's 3rd Army breakout plan.

American troops of the 4th Armored Division from Avranches entered Pontaubault July 31 afternoon. They were disbelieving of aerial reconnaissance reports that the two bridges still stood. Having failed to demolish the See River bridge in Avranches, was it possible the Germans made a second mistake at the Selune River? Expecting the bridges to explode under their feet the troops ran across fanning out defensively into the south side fields and orchards.

Fieldmarshall von Kluge, German Army Group B commander, had to stop the influx of American forces by closing the open door at Pontaubault. He ordered his Brittany Commander, Generalleutenant Wilhelm Fahrmbacher, to recapture Pontaubault and Avranches with troops from the St. Malo area. In reality the only troops available were coastal battery static troops without transport and remnant forces that had narrowly escaped the American blitzkrieg. Fahrmbacher chose Colonel Rudolf Bacherer's remnant 77th Division re-enforced with some 5th Parachute Division paratroopers and 14 assault guns "to re-capture Avranches and hold at all cost. On it stands or falls the outcome in the west." Bacherer with less than a thousand men in light transport vehicles set out from Pontorson to stop Patton's 100,000-man, mobile 3rd Army. Some progress was made against the American recon force around Pontaubault. House to house fighting ensued along the streets leading to the road bridge. Several two-man teams made it into the southern outskirts of Avranches. By late afternoon armored elements of the CCA entered the battle with their fighter-bomber escorts. Bacherer's force retreated as an American company moved close to his headquarters.

With Bacherer's attack defeated, nothing stood in General Patton's way. The road and railroad lines were immediately lined with a strong force of antiaircraft guns from Avranches to Pontaubault. Overhead an umbrella of fighters kept all marauders at bay. From August 3 to 7 the Luftwaffe tried to bomb the Pontaubault bridges unsuccessfully. Only one bomb did minor damage. As an exemplary feat of organization in a three-day period, seven divisions, 100,000 men with 15,000 vehicles passed through the village. The opportunity of encircling the German front lines that faced the British and Canadian armies to the east was possible and developing.

18.3 St. James – The American Brittany Cemetery

(17 kilometers south of Avranches via D798)

Site of the American Battle Monument Commission cemetery. One of fourteen overseas military cemeteries for the dead of World War II. Temporary wartime cemeteries were closed out following the war and the remains were either returned to the United States (61%) or re-interned in collective cemeteries. A white marble headstone marks every burial (Star of David for the Jewish, a Latin cross for all others regardless of religious belief). There are memorials bearing the names of the missing.

This cemetery contains 4,410 burials and the names of 498 missing.

18.4 Huisines-sur-mer – A German cemetery

(9 kilometers southwest of Avranches via N175, D43 and D75)

Site of the German War Graves Welfare Organization cemetery (Volksbund Deutsche Kriegsgraberfursorge). This is one of six large German cemeteries established from 1,400 temporary war time sites in Normandy. It contains 11,956 burials. Additionally, 2,238 German remains are in ten British cemeteries.

The total German burials in Normandy, excluding those in French community cemeteries, is 59,645.

Chapter 19 Counterattack LUTTICH

(The battlefield is in the Mortain area that is 30 kilometers east of Avranches via D5 to la Tournerie, then south on D977 3 kilometers).

On July 25, west of St. Lo, the American forces blasted through the German lines opening a gap now referred to as the "Breakout at St. Lo." With the characteristic order, "Drive, worry about your objective, not your flanks," General George S. Patton's 3rd Army raced southward seizing the towns and bridges of Avranches and Pontabault on July 30 and 31 respectively.

To the Germans a catastrophe was at hand. Patton had opened a gateway into France's interior through which the vast mobile American army could pass. The single road and its two bridges crossing the See and Selune Rivers had to be recaptured.

A limited counterattack by Colonel Bacherer's remnant 77th Infantry Division did reoccupy Pontabault and a few buildings on Avranches' south side on July 31 morning. The morning rain, the German ally, ceased, the clouds disappeared, the American fighter-bombers and tanks appeared. Bacherer's troops retreated to the south and west. Demolition of the Selune River bridge was thwarted by the rapid American advance.

Patton's rapid deployment organization took control of the opportunity. Both sides of the 6 kilometers of road between the two bridges were lined with antiaircraft guns. Overhead the air force formed an impenetrable defense against the Luftwaffe dive-bombers. Only one bomb slightly damaged the southern most bridge.

Within a three day period 100,000 men and 15,000 vehicles moved through this gateway into France's heartland.

As Patton's 3rd Army advanced, the US 1st Army widened the corridor to 25 kilometers by moving southeast from St. Lo. Even Hitler was impressed by "Patton, the crazy cowboy's" dramatics. On August 3 Hitler planned Operation "Luttich", a counterattack by 10 armored divisions and 1,000 airplanes to push west from Mortain to the ocean. His plan envisioned plugging the gap and isolating the 3rd Army from their supply lines. He reasoned the 3rd Army would capitulate soon after. His mind could not envision the probable American contingency plan to air supply their army and utilize the Bay of Biscay ports and beaches. Hitler viewed his plan as utopic.

The opportunity to throw the allied armies back into the sea. Field Marshal Guenther von Kluge, Rommel's replacement, was surprised at Hitler's lack of realistic expectations. General Paul Hausser, the 7th Army Commander, under von Kluge, could see the capture of Avranches but to push north and throw the allies out of France was completely incomprehensible.

The German westward attack, Operation "Luttich" with only four panzer divisions, totaling 120-190 tanks and 300 aircraft, commenced late August 6 from a line east of Mortain and northward 10 kilometers to Sourdeval.

19.1 Mortain

(30 kilometers east of Avranches via D5 to la Tournerie, then south on D977 3 kilometers)

The 1st US Division following through on opportunities since the breakthrough at St. Lo, July 25th, was ordered "to envelop the enemy's left flank and exploit the breakthrough of his defenses by seizing the high ground and road centers in the Mortain area." In combination with Combat Command A of the 3rd Armored Division the 1st Division fought towards Mortain from the northwest. The German 275th Division fought to hold every meter of ground as they withdrew from le Mesnil-Adelee, Juvigny, St. Barthelemy into Mortain on the afternoon of August 3. Holding the 1600 inhabitant town was a reconnaissance battalion of the 2nd Panzer Division. The Germans retreated east with the Americans taking up positions on the defensive high ground a kilometer east of the town. From Mortain 20 kilometers north to Vire the German front line held doggedly against the American pressure. The German's loss of Mortain threatened their left flank.

When the German 2nd SS Panzer Division and the 17th SS Panzer Grenadier Regiment attacked at 1 a.m. August 7 without a forewarning artillery barrage the town was held by elements of the 30th Infantry Division and the 3rd Armored Division. The two German columns passed to the north and south of the town to seize the heights west of the town. Although the US battalion command post was overrun and Mortain captured two US roadblocks hampered and delayed the German advances. One US roadblock was on the south side of town where D907, from Barenton, comes into D977 running southwest to St. Hilaire. The Americans faced down the Barenton road. The second roadblock was north of Mortain where the road to the neighboring village, St. Barthelemy, passes under the railroad very close to the Abbaye Blanche. Here the Americans with antitank guns faced north and successfully stayed in action destroying forty enemy vehicles August 7 and 8.

The panzers moved rapidly halfway to St. Hilaire (12 kilometers southwest) along D977, occupying Romagny and Fontenay by noon hour. The night darkness and morning fog had given the Germans their best progress.

East of Mortain, on the long thin rock ridge (Hill 317) the 2nd Battalion, 120th Regiment (30th Division) was surrounded but became, in the next five days, historically one of the outstanding unit achievements in the Western Europe Campaign. With the battalion command post overrun in Mortain, Captain Reynold C. Erichson (awarded the Distinguished Service Cross for leadership) assumed command of the battalion's force on Hill 317. The 17th SS Panzer Grenadiers surrounded and attacked Erichson's men continuously. The hilltop location afforded his 7th Corps artillery observers excellent targets within a 40 kilometers radius. German flak disrupted cargo air drops of essential medical, food and ammo supplies so smoke canisters filled with the essentials were fired onto the hill. The penicillin and morphine ampoules smashed on landing. This method was abandoned leaving the battalion without re-supply of basic water, ammunition, dressings and medicines. Food was smuggled through the German lines by local farmers.

The German-forecasted misty day dawned clear and cloudless. American and British fighter-bombers zeroed in on the German tank columns relentlessly and successfully blunting their westward thrust. Hitler's promised 300 Luftwaffe airplanes were destroyed on and around their Paris airfields. The German panic plan to shift three armored divisions from the Caen area was canceled when coincidentally the British and Canadian armored divisions attacked south of Caen threatening a breakthrough. Within 24 hours the Americans had 2 armored and 5 infantry divisions countering the German attack. By August 12 the US forces converged on Mortain from the northeast, the west, the southwest and the south. 100 German tanks smoldered in the Mortain area. Of the original 700 Americans on Hill 317 only 400 walked down to the relief force on August 12.

Although Mortain was severely damaged, the Abbaye Blanche and the fine church Saint-Evroult were saved once more from centuries of its warlike history created by its location on a prominent rocky spur.

Picture 18: Mortain - Looking North
July 3, 1948

Patton's Breakout and Breakthrough brought the American 30th Division and a few tank squadrons of the 3rd Armored Division into Mortain August 3 (D-day +58). The Germans launched a major counterattack westward five days later bypassing Mortain to the north and south. Roadblocks at the town's entrances slowed the attack. On the rocky prominence (top right) called Hill 317 the 2nd Battalion of the 120th Regiment held out for five days. Ammo, food and medical supplies were shot onto the hill unsuccessfully. French citizens using little known paths kept the Americans supplied. This is one of the most historically outstanding unit achievements in the Western European Campaign.

19.2 le Mesnil-Tove

(8 kilometers northeast of Mortain via D33 to St. Barthelemy through Belle Fontaine, north 0.5 kilometers and left onto le Mesnil-Tove road)

The German 2nd Panzer Division launched their westward attack late (early morning August 7) and only at half strength from the north-south road 2 kilometers east to le Mesnil-Tove. The armored column achieved surprise and watched as the withdrawing Americans set fire to their ammunition dump and field train, then rolled through the village along the secondary road to a point 2 kilometers west of le Mesnil-Adelee. The clear dawn brought forth the allied fighter-bombers and the American artillery. The Germans faced the 4th and 30th Infantry Division to the west, the 3rd US Armored Division's Combat Command B to the southwest (Reffuveille), and on their northern flank the 2nd Armored Division. Artillery and fighter-bombers pounded them incessantly. The Germans withdrew back to le Mesnil-Tove August 8 night. Gravel roads converged on this old stone village of 50 buildings that was soon demolished and pulverized by American artillery and fighter-bombers.

Hard fighting on August 10 and 11 by the 119th Infantry Regiment and the 3rd Armored Division's Combat B recaptured the smoking ruins. Dismembered dead littered the streets, fields and ditches a half a kilometer radius from the intersection. The field on the village's south side was cratered and contained a burning German tank and two crashed fighter planes. One of the pilots was trapped upside down eight days as the crash had sealed his canopy. The battle had raged back and forth across the field for several days. A depleted regiment (1,000 men) of the 2nd Panzer Division had been annihilated in the area.

Chapter 20 Falaise Pocket

The American Operation COBRA brought their armored spearheads to Avranches and Pontaubault July 31. Overcoming a futile German counterattack at Pontaubault the 3rd Army poured through the break into Brittany and the French heartland. The forces driving west to the Bay of Biscay were intent on making more transatlantic ports available. The forces that passed south and then east were driving for the Seine River. Steadily the Americans at Avranches widened the opening making more roads available to further increase the flow of traffic. By August 7 the "open door" was 30 kilometers wide. Hitler envisioned slamming the door shut with a major ten panzer division counterattack from Mortain to Avranches. He thought the US 3rd Army would be cut off from supplies and be defeated readily. Pressure on the British-Canadian front held the proposed panzer divisions in place. The "major" Operation "LUTTICH", August 7, had only three divisions without air cover. Little gains were made but resulted in further severe losses. Without hesitation the Americans continued to flood south, west and east. By August 8 elements of Patton's 3rd Army had driven 110 kilometers southeast to le Mans.

12th Army Group Commander Lieutenant General Omar Bradley outlined his German encirclement plan to General Eisenhower on August 8. The US 1st and 3rd Armies pushing east to the Seine turned north towards the back of the German lines that faced north against the British and Canadians. The Canadians and the 1st Polish Armored Division south of Caen were to drive south in a series of operations. The two allied armored armies would meet, complete the encirclement, and "bag" twenty German divisions. Closing the pocket was expected to be between Falaise and Argentan hence the historic description the "Falaise Pocket".

The "Pocket" was conclusively closed by August 22. Accurate figures on the numbers who escaped are not available. About 20,000 to 50,000 men and 50-70 tanks are the generally accepted numbers. 100,000 were left behind as casualties or prisoners and approximately 3,000 mobile pieces of equipment including 187 tanks and self-propelled guns. The roads and fields in the Argentan, Trun, Chambois triangle were packed with abandoned burning equipment intermingled with dead and crazed horses and thousands of corpses, the aftermath of a horse-drawn army being bombed, shelled and strafed continuously for ten days.

As the mouth of the pocket closed by the convergence of the allied armies the escape funnel focused on St. Lambert-sur-Dives and Chambois. The funnel's spout became the corridor of death. Unable to remove and bury the dead rotting in the hot August sun after the battle, the only sanitary recourse was to bulldoze the remains into funeral pyres, which flamed for days, and massive grave pits. Recovering the battlefield scrap from the agriculturally productive fields went on for twenty years.

The battle for Normandy cost the Allies 206,703 casualties. The Germans lost 460,900 men, 1300 tanks, 20,000 vehicles, 500 assault guns and 1500 field guns.

Picture 19: The Escape Corridor - Looking East Today

This August 4, 1944 photo (top right) shows this road, one of three used for German retreat from the Falaise Pocket, littered with destroyed tanks, vehicles, wagons, slaughtered horses and slain soldiers. Two Polish Sherman tanks are seen standing on the grassy slope to the left, their guns aimed toward the road. The Polish Armored Division moving from the north fought up to this hilltop overlooking the German eastbound retreat route between Chambois and Vimoutier. The Polish firepower combined with artillery support and fighter bombers decimated the trapped Germans. Attacks to dislodge the Poles from their positions were costly to both sides.

20.1 Argentan

(23 kilometers southeast of Falaise on N158)

A hillside town overlooking the junction of the Orne and Ure Rivers.

The town was severely bombed by allied planes on June 6 to encumber German reinforcements from moving north towards the invasion beaches. The town was burning June 7 as the Panzer Lehr Division moved west on D924 towards Ecouche and Flers. The Orne River bridge was badly damaged and the streets blocked with rubble. The panzers cut through the fields and crossed a temporary bridge to bypass the town.

With daylight low-level medium bombers attacked again. One crash landed north of the town. The three surviving US airmen were brought to the Sarrenjanes farm just north of town, on N158, and shot behind the barn.

The American 5th Armored Division moving north towards Argentan on August 11 was delayed at Montree (13 kilometers south via N158) due to a fuel shortage and the French 2nd Armored Division using the N158 road. The six hour delay gave the German 116th Panzer Division time to occupy defensive positions around Argentan. The Germans now recognizing the threat of encirclement were fighting to hold open a wide escape corridor. On the 12th a battalion of panzers moved down N158 attacking the 5th Armored Division near Montree. The next day a patrol of the French 2nd Armored Division in Ecouche (7 kilometers west on D924) entered Argentan briefly but was quickly driven out. Attempts by the Americans on the Montree road to move against Argentan made little progress. German artillery north of Argentan took a heavy toll of the Americans south and east of the town. As the tankers vented their frustrations the 1st SS and 2nd Panzer Divisions entered Argentan in their eastward retreat.

The following day General Bradley stopped any further attacks northward for understandable reasons. The allied air forces had scattered delayed action time bombs between Argentan and Falaise. The German divisions withdrawing far outnumbered the thin American line. The British, Canadian and Polish forces coming towards the Americans from the north could easily suffer from friendly fire. As the southern jaw held its positions for the next five days, the German army fled the pocket. From the north the upper jaw kept moving southeast from Falaise towards Chambois. Two Canadian and a Polish armored divisions fought through the scramble of the fleeing twenty German divisions.

On the morning of August 18 the American 318th Regiment (80th Infantry Division) side-slipped Argentan to the east starting from Point 1641.5 kilometers south of Bordeaux (3 kilometers east on D14). By nightfall the German exit, road D14, to le Bourg St. Leonard had been cut. German artillery from higher ground inflicted tragic losses on the regiment in the orchards around Sal and Bordeaux. The panzers fought tenaciously to hold open the narrowing corridor.

Continuing their struggle the following day against the fanatical defenders, the decimated American regiment pressed north to the Argentan-Trun road, D916, crossing it 2 kilometers north of Argentan. A costly gain to narrow the escape corridor by 2 kilometers.

August 20, the regiment entered Argentan from the north down the Trun road. The 116th Panzer Division remnants held the town firmly throughout the day. House to house, tanks and infantry battled in close combat until days end when the few embattled surviving defenders surrendered.

Although the town has been rebuilt over the years, to the sharp eye the shrapnel, sprang and pock marks in the masonry evidence the deeper scars of 1944.

There is a monument to the French Resistance fighters of the region on the south edge of town along N158 to Sees. Also, 4 kilometers west, on D924, to Ecouche stands a Sherman tank memorial to the 2nd French Armored Division. At the intersection of D2 and D219 one kilometer south of the Sherman tank is a monument commemorating the headquarters site of the 2nd French Armored Division Commander, Major General Jacques Phillipe Leclerc.

Four kilometers north of Argentan, on D916 to Trun, the road passes through the Foret (forest) de Gouffern. The forest stretches northwest and southeast six kilometers on either side of D916. The August foliage afforded the easterly retreating German armor some respite from the allied dive-bombers and strafing fighters. The roads and tracks throughout the forest were packed with men and equipment. Aerial reconnaissance, August 18, observed large enemy concentrations throughout the area of the forest and the roads to Trun.

The 2nd and 9th Tactical Air Forces concentrated Spitfires, Typhoons, Mustangs, Lightnings and Thunderbolts on the forest and roadways. Relaying squadrons spent the afternoon and evening destroying whatever could be seen. As the fuel fed fires burned off the foliage more armor was revealed. That day the 2nd Tactical had flown 1,471 sorties and claimed 1,100 vehicles and 90 tanks destroyed, 1,500 vehicles and 100 tanks damaged. By days end the pilots reported "little movement seen, most vehicles already destroyed." The following day the massacre continued under clear skies subdued by the black smoke from the burning tanks and trucks.

As the pocket shrank from the pressure of the British, Canadian and American armies the air force pilots could not differentiate friend from foe. Forty air strikes fell against British and Canadian front line troops. The 53rd British Division was hardest hit sustaining casualties that blunted their pursuit.

West of D916, August 20, the American 11th Armored Division moved through the forest to the village of Bailleul. A local resident, Maurice Dornois, described his village a few days later. "There was not an acre of ground without its wreckage from the German debacle. The roads were marked with skeletons, burned trees, metal hulks blackened by fire, war material and abandoned loot, corpses of men and horses teeming with worms."

The forest east of the road still harbored remnants of three panzer divisions. The German pocket was then six kilometers deep with only a two kilometer opening north of Chambois for the German retreat.

Related stories: le Bourg St. Leonard/Chambois, Coudehard

20.2 le Bourg St. Leonard and Chambois

(24 kilometers southeast of Falaise via N158 south from Falaise to Argentan, 22 kilometers, east on N26 to le Bourg St. Leonard, 10 kilometers)

The 90th US Infantry Division moving from the south to north were in positions on the southern edge of the town August 16. To the west lay the Gouffern Forest whose foliage hid masses of German armor and men moving in an easterly retreat. Three possible escape roads leading south from St. Leonard were roadblocked by the Americans. Units of the 2nd SS Panzer and 116th Panzer Divisions attacked the roadblocks in an attempt to counterblock the American threat to their retreat routes eastward. St. Leonard's elevation overlooking the open land to the north dominated the escape route. The German afternoon attack pushed the Americans off the ridge and out of the town. An evening counterattack with infantry and tanks repulsed the Germans. The battle for the town see-sawed back and forth over the next 24 hours. The strength and organization of the German forces indicated there were more well-equipped German forces still encircled than the allied intelligence estimates indicated. Shifting of American forces had placed only two US divisions and seven artillery battalions along the southern shoulder of the escape route that stretched from Ecouche (18 kilometers west) to Exmes (6 kilometers east). On the 17th the German infantry, armor and artillery overwhelmed the St. Leonard positions. Fighting continued throughout the day but the ridge stayed firmly in the enemy's hands. That evening the Americans successfully regained the ridge. Casualties had reduced the Germans to a remnant battalion of 80 men. The 2nd SS Panzer Division had moved east out of the pocket leaving the 116th Panzer Division to hold the southern line against the American advance.

On August 18 the 90th Division from their positions three kilometers east of St. Leonard moved north on D305 then northwest across the open fields to intersect the St. Leonard-Chambois road (D16) at its mid-point. Tenacious Germans stopped further advances until the next day (19th) when the Americans supported by units of the 2nd French Armored Division were able to push north into Chambois.

Chambois

By August 19 the remnants of the German 5th Panzer and 7th Armies had been compressed into 130 square kilometers west of D13, the Chambois-St. Lambert-sur-Dives road. From the west two British divisions were at Pierrefitte and Necy. The British 11th Armored Division had swept around the west end of the pocket to attack from Putanges in the southwest. The US 80th and 90th Infantry Divisions were moving north through the Gouffern Forest. East of St. Leonard the 2nd French Armored Division was advancing north to cut the D13 road running east out of Chambois.

Canadian armored units had moved south to St. Lambert-sur-Dives two and a half kilometers north of Chambois on D13. The 1st Polish Armored Division was a few kilometers due north of Chambois moving onto hilltops 262 and 252 that overlooked the eastern escape roads. The narrow escape corridor was 3 kilometers wide and 8 kilometers long from D13 east to Champosoult. Here the 2nd SS Panzer Corps was preparing to attack into the "corridor of death" to hold open the escape paths. Above the medley of compressed armies rained down artillery shells, mortar rounds, dive-bombers and strafing fighters.

Chambois with its D16 road running east was crucial to the Germans escaping. This and the roads at Moissy (1 kilometer northwest) and St. Lambert (2 kilometers northwest) were the only serviceable easterly routes for mobile equipment. The German soldiers could cut across the fields but not the armor and vehicles. The Canadian, Polish and Americans had to join up, cut the escape routes and seal the pocket. As the 90th Division fought their way from St. Leonard, dive-bombers tore Chambois apart destroying enemy equipment and blocking the streets with building rubble. The intersection of D13 and D16, the town's center, was no longer identifiable.

The Polish 10th Armored Rifle Regiment units entered across the fields from the north. A German antitank gun in the cemetery knocked out a Cromwell tank. Major Zgorzelski sped past the cemetery onto D16 with 3 tank squadrons, light armor and a six pound artillery piece. From the southwest entered the US 359th Regiment (90th Division). Both forces claimed the capture of Chambois. The troops met August 19, Saturday, 7:20 p.m. Captain Laughlin E. Waters and Major Zgorzelski shook hands briefly.

The Polish had aggressively swept through the town but the Americans added numerical equipment and strength. After a short sharp fight on the eastern outskirts, on D16, with two Germans antitank guns the Polish 24th Lancer Regiment entered the town and re-enforced the position. Unable to close the escape route the Poles set up resistance points within the corridor surrounded by a sea of Germans.

The Americans in the meantime sent L Company up the hardtop road D13 to meet the Canadians near Moissy at 8:30 p.m. The link was tenuous. The overwhelming German motivation to escape eastward made it impossible to establish a solid connection with the allied forces available at that time.

August 20 witnessed the heaviest fighting in the pocket. Around its perimeter rear guards attempted to slow the allied squeeze while along D13 from Trun to Chambois attacks and re-attacks punctured the thin Canadian line blocking the eastbound intersections. The Poles on elevated ground in the escape corridor were surrounded and under attack from all directions.

August 21 afternoon brought the Canadian 4th Division down D13 to Chambois in sufficient strength to seal the German's fate.

The destruction of buildings, equipment, civilians and German soldiers was indescribable. Chambois was in flames and everywhere there was the unbearable stench of death from burned flesh and the corpses of humans, horses and cattle. Bulldozers were brought in to clear paths and push the corpses aside.

In Chambois a "Closing the Gap" monument commemorates the actions without detail.

The town cemetery north, on D13, on the east side of the road has numerous civilian headstones reminding us of the non-combatants who lost their lives those grim days of August.

In the Trun, Argentan, Chambois triangle lay 10,000 human bodies, 2,000 dismembered horses, and over 3,000 destroyed vehicles. Along the three escape roads running east of D13 to Vimoutiers the shambles was just as gruesome. In the hot August sun decomposition and putrification was rapid. The ground and water were poisoned. For months water had to be trucked in from Caen. The bulldozers opened grave pits 25 meters deep and pushed in thousands of bodies.

German prisoners dragged their dead comrades from the fields and stacked the rotting bodies along the road edge 2 meters high. Within a few days decomposition had so deteriorated the bodies they had to be carried on planks, doors and stretchers as the arms and legs would fall off when lifted.

After the war a Franco-German Commission was established to find and identify every skeleton still in the fields and woods. Every square meter was scrutinized for body remains including the mass burial pits. All the German Falaise Pocket remains are buried 85 kilometers east in Ste Andre-de-l'Eure.

Related stories: Argentan, Coudehard

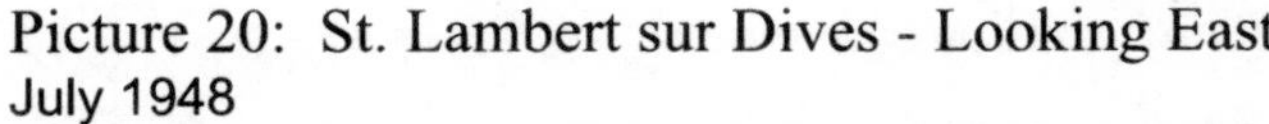

Picture 20: St. Lambert sur Dives - Looking East

July 1948

On August 19, a German Tiger tank occupied the town intersection facing north holding open one of the three escape routes for the defeated and surrounded German army in Normandy. As the Germans fled eastward along the road and neighboring fields and orchards the Allied airforce incessantly bombed and strafed. Canadian artillery added to the inferno. With the road from the north as its axis of advance, B Company of the Argyll and Sutherland Highlanders (Canadian Infantry) and C Squadron of the South Albert regiment knocked out the Tiger tank. Canadian Commander Major David Currie (awarded the Victoria Cross) renewed the artillery fire to further help close the escape route successfully. The town was pulverized, the roadways littered with hundreds of abandoned and destroyed vehicles and equipment. Hundreds of horses and thousands of German soldiers lay dead within the limits of the photograph.

Picture 21: Chambois - Looking Northwest
July 6, 1948

The road running from bottom left to top right was one of three German escape roads from the "Cauldron" in mid-August. American units of the 90th Infantry Division moved towards the town intersection from the bottom of the photo. Elements of the Polish 10th Armored Rifle Regiment moved towards the intersection from the top of the photo. American Captain L.E. Waters and Polish Major Zjorzelski met and shook hands at the intersection at 7:20 PM August 19. Although closing this route, the retreating Germans continued to flee eastwards across fields and orchards. The Allied linkup was tenuous.

20.3 Coudehard

(20 kilometers southeast of Falaise via D13, 18 kilometers to Trun then take D242, 7 kilometers to Coudehard.)

The three hundred-meter ridge half a kilometer east of the village dominates the region. By August 18 the surrounded German armies were fleeing the pocket along all routes leading northeast to Vimoutiers. D16 passing between Hills 262 and 252 was of great significance. Seizing and holding the two points was tactically significant. In the rapidly shrinking pocket (12 kilometers wide and 14 kilometers long) were the remnants of six infantry divisions, a parachute division, five panzer divisions, and splinter divisions that no longer existed consisting of stragglers, service personnel and supply units.

German General Eugen Meindl planned for August 19 a 2nd Parachute Corps (3rd Parachute and 353rd Divisions) attack between Trun and Chambois to secure the Mont Ormel ridge (Hill 262 and 252). From the elevated positions they would hold open the corridor for an organized fighting retreat of the remaining units from the "kettle" as the Germans called their surrounded position. On the 19th, before the breakout plan could materialize a Canadian force of 175 men, 15 tanks, and 4 self-propelled antitank guns took St. Lambert-sur-Dives (5 kilometers southwest), closing the easterly road D710. The Canadian commander Major D. V. Currie was awarded the British Commonwealth's highest award, the Victoria Cross, for this action.

Also, the 1st Polish Armored Division left their positions 4 kilometers north of Coudehard to seize Mont Ormel and Chambois. By mid-afternoon (August 19), after a short battle, they occupied the Mont Ormel's northern high point 262. Moving along D242, the ridge road, they intersected D16 (Chambois-Vimoutiers road). The Polish tanks surprised a long column of German vehicles and armor moving to the east. The Poles opened fire destroying the column. Dense smoke and dusk reduced visibility making further movement impossible. By midnight, two Polish armored regiments and three battalions of motorized infantry (1,500 men and 80 tanks) were concentrated on Mont Ormel's northern ridge, Hill 262. The Poles had occupied the German objective before their planned attack had started.

As the Poles consolidated their positions on Mont Ormel's north point two Polish regiments a kilometer west of Coudehard moved towards Chambois where they linked up with G Company of the 90th US Infantry Division.

Dawn, August 20, a cloudy rainy day. General Meindl's attack plan had fallen apart. He with 15 paratroopers having crawled through the Canadian lines was a kilometer west of Coudehard observing his objective the Mont Ormel northern ridge now in Polish hands. From Hill 262 the German columns west and north were clearly visible. Tank fire bombarded the retreating Germans winding through the burning hulks and putrefying bodies. At 9 a.m. the Polish perimeter was attacked from the northeast. Steadfastly the Poles held their ground until the Germans withdrew at 10:30. However, at 10 a.m. panzers from the east re-entering the escape corridor were seen climbing Hill 239 two kilometers due north of Hill 262. An attempt to stop the ascent was unsuccessful and by 11 o'clock German shells were falling on the Polish positions quickly knocking out five tanks. The pressure on Hill 262 prohibited the Poles from following their previous day's plan to occupy the other Hill 262 on the southern portion of the Mont Ormel ridge. On Hill 262 they were completely surrounded and running low on essential supplies. In combination with the tank fire from Hill 239 German infantry attacked the Polish position throughout the day from the north and south. Lack of radios prohibited coordination of the attacking units. The bad weather benefited the attackers as the allied air force was grounded. At 5 p.m. the Germans breached the northern defenses. The Poles were tenacious in closing the gap. Their fighting quality was enhanced by the reality that their battles would take them home through Germany. A second penetration along the Chambois-Vimoutiers road was blocked and the perimeter re-secured by 7 p.m. The Germans' limited successes had, however, compressed the Polish position enabling the Germans to reopen the two roads immediately north of Hill 262, to Champosont. General Meindl organized an identifiable Red Cross convoy to carry the seriously wounded through the burning maze to Champosont. For an hour the shelling ceased but resumed as the last marked vehicle disappeared in the distance. The road stayed open as a heavy rain fell on the withdrawing units. Meindl's headquarters was at the crossroads of D242 and the Champosont road, under the shadow of Hill 262. Before dawn, August 21, the rear guard of a panzer division reported they were the last. Meindl's group left the junction at 5 a.m unaware there were Germans, who had spent the night crossing the Dives River near St. Lambert, had moved into Coudehard shortly after dawn. In a suicidal attack up Hill 262 from the church they failed to overrun or even penetrate the Polish lines. The Polish machine guns cut them down in their final and futile effort.

The 22nd Canadian Armored Regiment reached Hill 262 that afternoon bringing in water, food, medical supplies, and ammunition. A thousand prisoners including General Otto Elfedt, Commander of the 84th Corps, were marched to POW cages. Three hundred and fifty Polish wounded were transported to field hospitals. Eleven tanks had been damaged or destroyed.

By 4 p.m. all German movement had ceased in the corridor.

From the air the ridge had the shape of a gigantic mace. Today it's known by its Polish translation "Maczuga".

As the Germans pulled out of Normandy they looted shops and homes stuffing all that could be moved into tanks, trucks, cars and horse drawn carts. As their exit routes narrowed to a few roads the loot was abandoned. When the guns fell silent the French civilians looted the battlefield across its entirety. Clothing, sheets, linens, lingerie, woollens, layettes, office materials, toilet articles, hardware, pharmaceuticals, tires and vehicles. The victorious allied soldiers, less disdainful of corpses and the thousands of prisoners, looted cameras, watches, pens, wallets and gold rings. "Soldaten Buchs", the soldiers' identification and record books, were taken as souvenirs leaving little for graves registration to confirm the "missing" as "dead". All this happened within hours before the weather could damage the goods or the death stench created its own barriers.

There is monument on Maczuga, a Sherman tank and an armored scout car beside an arched wall symbolizing the blocking of the exit route. Also, the adjacent museum offers a panorama view of the Falaise Pocket.

Related stories: Chambois ,Argentan.

20.4 Vimoutiers

(East of Falaise via D63, 18 kilometers to Trun and D916, 19 kilometers to Vimoutiers.)

The strafing and wounding of Field Marshal Erwin Rommel occurred on road D579, 500 meters north of Vimoutiers, July 17, around 6 p.m.

The British and Canadians had not taken Caen. Operation GOODWOOD, the encirclement of Caen from the east and west was to be launched July 18. British and Canadian armor had crossed the Orne Canal and River north of Caen into the British airborne bridgehead. The massive build-up was visible to German observers south of Caen from the elevated Bourgebus ridge. Vibrating ground stakes sensed and measured the British armor activity. The wide expanse of the wheat fields favored armored warfare. The generals conferred in preparation for the predictable allied armored attack.

Rommel left SS Oberstgruppenfuhrer (Lieutenant General) Sepp Dietrich's 1st SS Panzer Corps headquarters in St. Pierre-sur-Dives (16 kilometers northwest) at 4 p.m. to return to his Army Group B headquarters in Roche Guyon on the east bank of the Seine River. From St. Pierre-sur-Dives, Rommel's Horch took D4 towards Livarot. Observing fighter-bombers over Livarot, Daniels, Rommel's driver turned south on D155 a kilometer before the town. At la Breviere the car turned east, joined D579, then turned south. To avoid "death by strafing" commanders cars remained inconspicuous by travelling without escorts and minimal dust clouds. The open convertible allowed the aircraft spotter Feldweber (Technical Sergeant) Holke to stand in the front passenger foot well and scan the skies in all directions. In the spacious back seat from left to right were the Field Marshal, Major Neuhaus and Hauptman (Captain) Helmuth Lang (Rommel's personal aid since March).

After passing through Ste Foy de Montgommery, Holke looking behind spotted two Spitfires flying south at tree top level. The Horch sped towards the Usine (factory) Laniel entrance ahead a kilometer on the right. Too far and too late! The eight machine guns of the Spitfire IX flown by Bill Switzer, RAF 602nd Squadron, ate up the road lacing the left side of the Horch. Daniel's left arm and shoulder disappeared in a cloud of dirt and gore. Neuhaus' pistol took a round punching the gun into his pelvis breaking his hip. The Field Marshall was unconscious his face streaming blood from glass cuts, his left cheek bone destroyed, a wound in his left eye, severe skull fractures in the temple and at the base near the spine. Out of control the automobile careened past the gatekeeper's lodge at the factory's entrance, swerved left across the road and slammed into a tree (since removed) 3 meters before the short bridge crossing the tributary of the Vie River. Rommel lay on the road 20 meters back. The second Spitfire, the wingman, dropped two bombs into the scene without further damage. Lang and Holke dragged Rommel and Neuhaus to the shelter of the gatekeeper's cottage. Daniels although mobile was in shock and bleeding profusely. He died a short time later. A passing army truck took the group to the "Pharmacy" in Livarot for first aid. Rommel was then transported to the Luftwaffe hospital in Bernay, Room 9. On July 23 he was transferred to the hospital in le Visnet outside Paris. To dispel belief that he had been killed he attended a Paris press conference August 1. He hid his pain allowing only his intact right face to be seen and photographed. On August 8 he returned home for convalescence and treatment by specialists from the nearby Tubingen University Clinic. During his weeks of recovery his death warrant was being prepared. Militarily he knew the war was lost. He believed Germany should make peace with the western powers so the German resources could be focused on the Russians. The conspirators of the July 20 plot to kill Hitler in Ratsenburg had been unsuccessful in soliciting Rommel's support. Although disagreeing with Hitler on military matters he recognized der Fuhrer as Germany's chosen leader. Hitler however was convinced that Rommel was in the plot. On October 14 Generals Burgdorf and Maisel and Major Ehrensperger arrived at the Field Marshal's Herrlingen home. He was "accused of complicity in the plot on Hitler's life". He would be tried for treason, found guilty, be shot and his wife Lucie and son Manfred be imprisoned, or he could commit suicide, that would be explained as post battle injuries, have a heroes funeral and the family be forever honored. Rommel bid farewell to his wife and son. A few minutes later, having taken a poison pill, he died in the back seat of Burgdorf's Mercedes stopped on the road to Wippingen, a kilometer from his home.

The official state funeral took place Wednesday, October 18 in Ulm from the town hall. Fire bombed on December 17 it has been rebuilt with the same façade and now houses the Movenpick Restaurant. After cremation the urn was interned in the Herrlingen churchyard. Lucie Rommel, who died September 26, 1971, is buried next to her husband.

One kilometer south of Vimoutiers on D979 is a Tiger tank monument signifying the relationship of this, the German escape route from the Falaise Pocket.

Picture 22: Rommel Strafed - Looking North Today

Field Marshall Erwin Rommel, returning from the Bourgebus Ridge battlefield on July 17 at 6:30 PM, was strafed by a British Spitfire here. Racing quickly, Rommel's driver came over the hill attempting to turn into the factory driveway by the gatehouse. Under machine gun fire the car careened into the ditch in the right-hand foreground. Rommel lay in the middle of the road at the 6th white line with head injuries. He was rushed to the Bernay hospital.

Picture 23: The Vimoutiers Tiger Today

The Tiger tank monument facing west is on the eastern exit road at Vimoultier. Panzers were used to keep open the German escape corridor from the Falaise Pocket (the "Cauldron") in late August. The tank facing west is symbolic of this action. There are many Tigers in museums but only one or two are outdoor monuments in France.

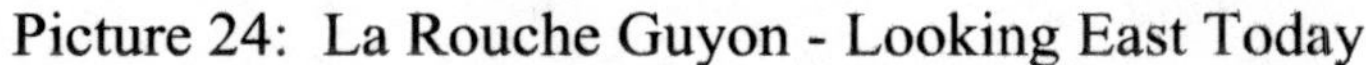
Picture 24: La Rouche Guyon - Looking East Today

Forty miles north of Paris on the Seine River's eastern bank, La Roche's 67 citizens were occupied by 937 Germans as this was Field Marshal Erwin Rommel's Army Group B Headquarters. His office was behind the three windows above the lamp post to the right. The chateau entrance is to the right in the photo. The lower buildings to the left are the horse stalls and carriage house. Rommel rushed back on June 6 from his wife's birthday party arriving late that evening. He was returning from the battlefield south of Caen July 17 when his Horsch car was strafed and he was wounded.

Chapter 21 Military Cemeteries

21.1 The United States Cemeteries

American Cemeteries on foreign soils i.e. other than in the United States, or its territories and possessions, are constructed and permanently maintained by the American Battle Monuments Commission.

At the end of World War II there were a dozen temporary cemeteries in Normandy and Brittany. Two permanent cemeteries were selected and the smaller temporary cemeteries were vacated and closed. About 40% of the total recovered remains of the battle of Normandy, including "unknowns", are buried in the two United States Cemeteries. The remains of the other 60% of the "fallen" were returned home at the request of their families.

There can be no further burials in these cemeteries except those remains found in the battlefields.

The cemeteries are open weekdays Sundays and holidays. An American superintendent is stationed at each cemetery to provide information and assist visitors. Each cemetery has a Visitor's Building with a comfortably furnished reception room.

The Normandy Cemetery is located midway along Omaha beach on the bluffs overlooking the historic battlefield and the English Channel. From Bayeux the Cemetery is reached by taking highway N13 westward 16 kilometers to Formigny. At the intersection turn north on D517 to St. Laurent-sur-Mer (3 kilometers). Turn east on D514 to Colleville-sur-Mer 2 kilometers to a well marked fork indicating the road north to the cemetery.

The site encompasses 172 acres and contains 9,386 graves. The cemetery was consecrated in 1956.

Brigadier General Theodore Roosevelt, Jr., eldest son of President Theodore Roosevelt, is buried here. He died of a heart attack near St. Jores and was initially interned in the Ste. Mere-Eglise #2 temporary cemetery.

The majestic semi-circular memorial colonnade looms significantly atop the bluffs. Four ceramic wall maps on the concave walls depict the allied military operation in northwest Europe. East of the colonnade inscribed on the formally constructed, crescent, red brick wall bordering the sunken gardens, can be found the names of the 1, 557 "missing", whose final resting place remains unknown. The beauty and tranquility of these grounds, immaculately groomed lawns, shrubs and walkways is a fitting tribute to the men who sacrificed their lives for freedom's cause.

The Brittany Cemetery **Error! Bookmark not defined.** is located in the southwest corner of Normandy. From Avranches, take highway N175 south 6 kilometers, through Pontaubault, to the junction of N998. Proceed south on D998, 11 kilometers to St. James. From the town's center intersection go east on D30 one kilometer to D230. Turn right. The cemetery is one kilometer on the right.

The site encompasses 28 acres and contains 4,410 graves. The cemetery, also consecrated in 1956, contains the casualties of the Normandy and Brittany campaigns. On the curved retaining wall of the memorial terrace are inscribed the names of 498 missing whose final resting place remains unknown.

The Breton Chapel simply constructed of native granite contains two maps depicting the allied military operations in northwest Europe.

21.2 British Cemeteries

Military cemeteries of the British Commonwealth countries are constructed and permanently maintained by the Commonwealth War Graves Commission. The Commission's expenses are met by contributions from the participating Commonwealth governments.

Throughout the world the Commission maintains 15,551 cemeteries containing the graves of World War II servicemen. In Normandy there are seventeen British and two Canadian cemeteries. Many graves are still located and maintained in French civilian cemeteries.

The British cemeteries are more numerous and generally smaller than the Canadian cemeteries, as the latter concentrated the burials from small temporary cemeteries. The British improved and constructed their permanent cemeteries on the sites of the war time temporary cemeteries. It is not uncommon to find Canadian and German graves within the British cemeteries. Canadian and German authorities are not planning to re-intern the remains in their national cemeteries.

There have been very few transferals of the remains to the respective homeland, and therefore, the total number of graves listed are the total mortal casualties on the battlefield, with the exclusion of those who may have died of wounds in British hospitals.

The cemeteries are open every day of the year.

Banneville la Campagne Cemetery

Situated 9 kilometers east of Caen on N175. The cemetery is situated on the south side of the highway.

It contains the graves of 2,150 British, 11 Canadian, 5 Australian, 2 New Zealand, 5 Polish and 2 unidentified.

Bayeux Cemetery

Located in the southwest section of the city on the south side of the N13 bypass road.

The cemetery contains the graves of 4,018 British, 181 Canadian, 25 Polish, 40 from seven allied countries, 1 unidentified and 466 German.

Brouay Cemetery

The village of Brouay is 14 kilometers west of Caen and 1.5 kilometers south of the Caen-Bayeux highway (N13). The cemetery is located on the northern edge of Brouay.

The cemetery contains the graves of 375 British and 2 Canadian servicemen.

Cambes en Pleine Cemetery

The village of Cambes-en-Pleine is 6 kilometers north of Caen and one kilometer west of the Caen-Lion-sur-Mer highway (D60). The cemetery is 0.5 kilometers north of the village on the east side of the road to Ainsy.

The cemetery contains the graves of 224 British servicemen.

Fontenay le Pesnel Cemetery

The village of Fontenay le Pesnel is 16 kilometers west of Caen on the Carpiquet road (D9). The cemetery is one kilometer south of the village on the east side of the road to Vendes.

The cemetery contains the graves of 457 British, 4 Canadian and 59 German servicemen.

Hermanville Cemetery

The town of Hermanville is 12 kilometers north of Caen on the Caen-Lion sur Mer road (D60). The cemetery is on the eastern edge of the town several streets from its center.

The cemetery contains the graves of 986 British, 13 Canadian, 3 Australian and 3 French servicemen.

Hottot les Bagues Cemetery

The village of Juvigny sur Seulles is 19 kilometers west of Caen on the Carpiquet road (D9). The cemetery is one kilometer west of the village on the north side of the road.

The cemetery contains the graves of 965 British, 34 Canadian, 3 Australian, 2 New Zealand, 2 South African, and 132 German servicemen.

Jerusalem Cemetery

The cemetery is located 8.5 kilometers south of Bayeux on the Bayeux-Tilly sur Seulles (D6) road, on the east side.

The cemetery contains 47 British and 1 Czech servicemen.

La Delivrande Cemetery

The cemetery is 13 kilometers north of Caen on the Caen-Langrune sur Mer road (D7), on the east side.

The cemetery contains 927 British, 11 Canadian, 3 Australian, 1 Polish and 180 German servicemen.

Ranville Cemetery

The village of Ranville is 9.5 kilometers northeast of Caen and 1.5 kilometers north of Herouvillette via the Caen-Cabourg highway (D513). The cemetery is 0.5 kilometers south of the Ranville intersection on the west side of the secondary road to Longueval.

The cemetery contains the graves of 2,153 British, 76 Canadian, 1 Australian, 3 New Zealand, 5 French, 1 Polish, 1 Belgian, 1 unidentified and 322 German servicemen. In the adjoining churchyard are 47 British paratroopers buried along the perimeter wall.

Ryes-Bazenville Cemetery

The road intersection of Les Noyaux is 7.5 kilometers northeast of Bayeux on the road of Ver-sur-Mer (D12). The cemetery is 0.5 kilometers east of the intersection on the north side of the secondary road (D87) to Villers le Sec.

The cemetery contains the graves of 630 British, 21 Canadian, 1 Australian, 1 Polish, and 326 German servicemen.

One of the Canadian graves is a re-internment from the Abbey of Ardennes, where 20 Canadian prisoners were shot by their German captors, buried in shallow graves, and discovered in the spring of 1945.

St. Charles de Percy Cemetery

From Caen take N175/E401, southwest past Villers-Bocage 26 kilometers to the Vire Highway, D577. Proceed south on D577 1.5 kilometers to the la Ferroniere intersection. Turn left onto D56 and right after a few hundred meters. The cemetery is on the left.

The cemetery contains the graves of 795 British and 4 Canadian servicemen.

St. Desir Cemetery

The cemetery is located 3 kilometers west of Lisieux in the St. Desir de Lisieux quarter through which the highway to Caen (N13) passes. The cemetery is on the well-marked road to La Pommeraye (D159) going north as one leaves the western outskirts of St. Desir de Lisieux. The British cemetery is 500 meters along the road and backs on to a German military cemetery.

The British cemetery contains the graves of 569 British, 16 Canadian, 6 Australian, 1 New Zealand, and 5 South African and 1 American servicemen. In addition, 4 British soldiers from WWI have been re-interned here.

St. Manvieu Cemetery

The village of St. Manvieu is 10.5 kilometers west of Caen on the Carpiquet road (D9). The cemetery is on the north side of the north side of the road 500 meters west of the village, past the St. Manvieu-Cheux road.

The cemetery contains the graves of 1,623 British, 3 Canadian, 1 Australian, and 556 German servicemen.

Secqueville en Bessin Cemetery

The village of Bretteville l'Orgueilleuse is 12.5 kilometers northwest of Caen on the Caen-Bayeux highway (N13). Secqueville en Bessin village is 2 kilometers north of Bretteville l'Orgueilleuse. The cemetery is on Farringdon Way on the west side of the village.

The cemetery contains the graves of 98 British, 1 unidentified and 18 German.

Tilly sur Seulles Cemetery

The town of Tilly sur Seulles is 12.5 kilometers southeast of Bayeux on highway D6. The cemetery is 1 kilometer west of the town on the south side of the road (D13) to Lingevres.

The cemetery contains the graves of 986 British, 1 Canadian, 1 Australian, 2 New Zealand and 232 German servicemen.

Tourgeville Cemetery

Midway between the town of Honfleur, at the mouth of the Seine River, and Cabourg, at the mouth of the Dives River, is the seashore town of Deauville. Tourgeville is 4 kilometers south of Deauville at the intersection of highway D278 and D27. The cemetery is 1 kilometer west of the town on the south side of highway D27.

The cemetery was developed for World War I casualties and in this connection contains the graves of 193 British, 7 Canadian, 8 Australian, 1 New Zealander, and 57 German servicemen. The Germans died as prisoners of war.

In August 1944, as the British and Canadian forces rushed eastward towards the Seine River, the cemetery became the last resting place of 12 British, 2 Canadian, and 32 German servicemen.

21.3 Canadian Cemeteries

4,926 Canadian casualties lie buried in the two cemeteries Beny sur Mer and Cintheaux. 349 additional Canadian graves are located in the British Cemeteries, Banneville la Campagne, Bayeux, La Delivrande, Ranville Ryes-Bazenville, St. Charles de Percy, St. Desir, St. Manvieu, Tilly sur Seulles and Tourgeville.

Beny-sur-Mer Cemetery

The town of Beny-sur-Mer is 14 kilometers northwest of Caen on the highway D7 and D404 to Courseulles-sur-Mer. 1.5 kilometers north of Beny-sur-Mer at the D35 intersection turn west to Reviers. The cemetery lies 1 kilometer west of the intersection on the north side of the Reviers road, at the top of a gentle rolling hill overlooking the Canadian invasion beaches.

The cemetery contains the graves of 2,044 Canadian, 4 British and 1 French servicemen. Seven of twenty Canadian prisoners shot by their German captors in the Abbey of Ardennes are buried here.

Bretteville-sur-Laize

The cemetery is on the west side of the Caen-Falaise road (N13) 14 kilometers south of Caen, 500 meters north of Cintheaux.

The cemetery contains the graves of 2,872 Canadian, 80 British, 4 Australian, 1 New Zealander, and 1 French servicemen. Eleven of twenty Canadian prisoners shot by their German captors in the Abbey Ardennes are buried here.

21.4 Polish Cemetery

The Granville-Langannerie Cemetery is situated 18.5 kilometers south of Caen on the road to Falaise (N158). The cemetery is on the west side of the road immediately north of the village of Vieille Langannerie.

The cemetery containing 650 graves was designed and constructed by the Commonwealth War Graves Commission. However, maintenance and general upkeep are not the Commission's responsibility, nor does the Polish government assume or contribute monies to meet these expenses. It is maintained by the French Ministry of Anciens Combattants. Polish workers in the area donate maintenance time and financial contributions are received from Polish veterans associations throughout the world. There are also 25 Polish burials in Bayeux, 1 in Ryes, 1 in La Delivrande, 1 in Ranville and 5 in Banneville-la-Campagne.

The 1st Polish Armored Division landed in early August. At noon August 8, as the division was marshalling southeast of Cormelles, it was erroneously bombed by the allied air force in support of Phase II of Operation TOTALIZE. The Poles' first casualties were 65 killed and 250 wounded.

The division fought relentlessly and ardently just east of the Caen-Falaise highway south to Chambois. At Chambois the Polish and US forces linked up to close the German escape corridor from the Falaise Pocket. Remnants of the defeated German army continued to withdraw eastwards escaping through the encircling allied lines. The Polish division seized commanding heights at Coudehard over the escape routes, thereby thwarting and arresting the enemies withdrawal.

21.5 German Cemeteries

At the conclusion of World War II there were 250,000 German casualties interned in 8,000 cemeteries in France. Between 1956 and 1961 the West German Government developed twenty-one concentration cemeteries by the re-internment of approximately 220,000 remains from the many scattered and isolated temporary wartime burial locations.

The German dead from the Normandy campaign are located in the six German cemeteries; Marigny, Mont-de-Huisnes, La Cambe, Orglandes, St. Andre de L'Eure and St. Desir de Lisieux.

A unique feature of each German cemetery is the Kamerdergraven, a centralized common grave for the unknown fallen.

Ten British cemeteries contain 2,238 German graves; Bayeux, Fontenay le Pesnel, Hottot les Baques, La Delivrande, Ranville, Ryes-Bazenville, St. Manvieu, Secqueville en Bessin, Tilly sur Seulles, Tourgeville. The British Government does not wish exhumations thereby disturbing the cemeteries that were completed soon after the war's end.

Marigny Cemetery

The town of Marigny is 11 kilometers west of St. Lo. It is easily reached via the St. Lo-Constance highway (D972). Two kilometers to the north of Marigny on the Montreuil road (D29) is the hamlet and intersection of L'Aubrie. From the intersection proceed east 500 meters to the cemetery, on the north side of the road, readily identified by the Norman church at its entrance.

On July 25, 1944 the United States forces punctured the German defense line with a massive aerial and artillery bombardment in this area.

American infantry and armor poured through the breach and fanned out to encircle the defenders to the west. Powerful armored thrusts southward produced chaos amongst the German forces preparing to counterattack. Before the German defense lines could be re-established the breakout from the Normandy bridgehead had been achieved. A month later, as a consequence of this operation in combination with the British, Canadian and Polish successes to the east, the German army in Normandy was surrounded and defeated.

The cemetery was developed in late July 1944 as a consequence of the American and German losses in the battles of the "Breakout". In 1945 and 1946 the Americans removed their dead for re-internment in the United States and their Normandy Cemetery.

At that time 4,246 German graves remained. Ten years later, when suitable agreements were reached between the French and West German governments; the Germans commenced re-internments from the thousands of temporary wartime graves. Today there are 11,169 burials.

Mont-de-Huisnes Cemetery:

In the southwest corner of Normandy, at the juncture of the Brittany Peninsula stands the solitary island of Mont St. Michel, one of the great French monuments known throughout the world. On the mainland and 4 kilometers east of the island is Mont de Huisnes, bordering the Baie du Mont St. Michel, and the site of the cemetery. The cemetery is 1 kilometer north of the village of Huisne and is accessible via the coastal road, D75.

The cemetery is unique. The absence of the never ending rows of crosses is striking. In their place is a two-floor rotund consisting of 64 rooms. In each room wall crypts harbor the remains of the fallen.

There are 11,956 burials of the Normandy and Brittany campaign casualties.

La Cambe Cemetery

The village of La Cambe is 24 kilometers west of Bayeux on the highway to Carentan N13). The cemetery is 1 kilometer west of the village on the south side.

The cemetery was established in June 1944 for American and German burials. In 1945 and 1946 the Americans re-interned their fallen either in the United States or in the Normandy Cemetery overlooking Omaha Beach. This latter cemetery had been a temporary burial site for German casualties of the Omaha Beach battle.

In 1944 the La Cambe Cemetery contained 8,000 German graves. As a result of closing out temporary war time cemeteries and re-internments, the cemetery has 20,864 grave sites. Additionally,

296 unknown lie together in a mass grave under the grassed mound, the cemetery's focal point.

Orglandes Cemetery

The village of Orglandes is 10 kilometers south of Valognes on D24. The cemetery is 500 meters north of the village on the west side.

In June 1944 the cemetery was developed with the internment of American and German casualties. In 1945 the Americans removed their dead for re-internment in the United States or the Normandy Cemetery overlooking Omaha Beach. As a result of German re-internments from the many temporary wartime cemeteries the cemetery has grown from 7,358 in 1944 to 10,152 burials today.

St. Andre-de-L'Eure Cemetery

Evreux is 100 kilometers northwest of Paris on the highway to Caen (N13). Ste. Andre-de-L'Eure is 16 kilometers south of Evreux on the highway (D52) to Dreux. The cemetery is 3 kilometers south of the town (D53) south of the hamlet of Ferriere.

St. Andre and its cemetery, although in Normandy, are east of the geographical limits of the Normandy campaign. However, many of the 19,795 German burials are from the last great battle in Normandy, the German encirclement and breakout from the Falaise Pocket.

The allied encirclement of the German army in Normandy was of such a disastrous magnitude to the Germans that for four days and nights the trapped, decimated remnants of their army battled its way out through the closing allied vice. The final battle left 10,000 German soldiers lying in the fields and 40,000 prisoners of war.

In addition, the casualties sustained during the allied army's rush to the Seine River and Paris are also buried in this cemetery that was initially developed by the United States Army Graves Registration.

St. Desir de Lisieux Cemetery

Three kilometers west of Lisieux on highway N13 to Caen, a well marked road to La Pommeraye (D159) leads off to the north, as one leaves the western outskirts of St. Desir de Lisieux. Five hundred meters along the road, on the east side, is a British cemetery. Five hundred meters further a road leads into the German cemetery. The two cemeteries share a common boundary.

The cemetery contains the graves of 3,735 German servicemen killed in the battle for Normandy and as a consequence of the allied push to the Seine River.

Chapter 22 Normandy Campaign Museums

Arromaches-les-Bains

Musee du Debarquement. (Emphasis - Mulberry harbor floated over from England). 8 kilometers (5 miles) northeast of Bayeux on the coast.

Avranches

Musee (Emphasis - The 3rd Army breakout into Brittany). 3 kilometers (2 miles) south of Avranches in le Val St. Pere.

Bayeux

Musee Memorial de la Bataille de Normandie (Emphasis - Broad view of the campaign). Southwest side of city on the by-pass road.

Benouville

Musee des Troupes Aero-portees, Pegasus Bridge (Emphasis – British glider troops capturing the bridge). 6 kilometers (3.6 miles) northeast of Caen.

Carentan

Musee de la Liberte (Emphasis – American paratroop actions in the area). On N13 400 meters past the town hall.

Caen

Memorial, Un Musee Pour la Paix (Emphasis – Reunification of wartime differences). Northwest side of Caen via the by-pass expressway.

Cherbourg (Fort du Roule)

Musee de la Guerre et de la Liberation (Emphasis – The battles around Cherbourg.) South side of Cherbourg via N13.

Colleville – Montgomery

SWORD Museum (Emphasis – The British landings in this area). 11 kilometers (7 miles) north of Caen on the coast.

Coudehard

Musee (Emphasis – Closing the Falaise Pocket). 30 kilometers (20 miles) southeast of Caen via Falaise and Trun.

Crisbecq

Musee Batterie (Emphasis – The Battery battle). 8 kilometers (5 miles) northeast of Ste. Mere-Eglise.

Grandcamp – Maisy

Musee des Rangers (Emphasis – The rangers at Pointe du Hoc). 10 kilometers (6 miles) west of OMAHA Beach on the coast.

Merville

Merville Battery Museum (Emphasis – The British glider troops capturing the battery). 14 kilometers (9 miles) northeast of Caen east of the Orne River.

Ouistreham

Musee No. 4 Commando (Emphasis – The Commando landings). 10 kilometers (6 miles) northeast of Caen on the coast.

Musee Le Mur de l'Atlantique (A representative structure of the Atlantic Wall). 10 kilometers (6 miles) northeast of Caen on the coast.

Port-en-Bessin

Recovery Museum (Emphasis – Sunken equipment recovered). 9 kilometers (5.5 miles) northwest of Bayeux.

Quineville

Musee (Emphasis – General). 16 kilometers (10 miles) northeast of Ste. Mere-Eglise on the coast.

Ste. Mere-Eglise

Airborne Museum (Emphasis – The US Airborne landings). 10 kilometers (6 miles) west of UTAH Beach.

C-47 Museum (Emphasis – Paratroop aircraft "Argonia"). 10 kilometers (6 miles) west of UTAH Beach, next to the Airborne Museum.

Surrain

Musee de la Liberation de Normandie (Emphasis – General). 11 kilometers (7 miles) west of Bayeux on N13.

UTAH Beach

Musee du Debarquement (Emphasis – The D-Day assault).

Vers-sur-Mer

Musee America/GOLD Beach (Emphasis – British Intelligence Service and the beach assault). 14 kilometers (9 miles) northeast of Bayeux on the coast.

Vierville-sur-Mer

Exposition OMAHA (Emphasis – Omaha landings). West end of OMAHA Beach inland .0.5 kilometers (0.3 miles).

Picture 25: Asnelles sure Mer - Looking North
June 14, 1948

This is the British 30th Corp Gold-Jig Beach D-day assault area. Asnelles is the village in the center of the photo. Close support by the airforce and navy subdued the beach defenses quickly, causing relatively light casualties to the attacking British 50th Division. The 231 Brigade moving west; however, met stiffened resistance as they moved along the coast road towards le Hamel and Arromanches. The 56th and 151st Brigades supported by the 7th Armored Division moved rapidly south reaching the Bayeux outskirts D-day evening.

Picture 26: Abbey Ardennes - Today

The old Abby of the 13th century was a farming commune in 1944. The German 12th SS Panzer Division occupied it D-day afternoon. Its tall turreted chapel afforded excellent observation of the southerly advancing Canadians. The following afternoon the SS men attacked the exposed Canadian flank at Authie. Canadian POWs were shot on site. Eighteen were brought singly into this garden, shot in the back of the head and buried in shallow graves. Colonel Kurt Meyer, the officer in charge, was held accountable, tried and condemned to be shot. The authorities dismissed his sentence. He was released and after a beer salesman career selling to the allied army clubs, died of a heart attack at age 63.

Picture 27: Bayeux - Looking North
July 2, 1946

The city was not bombed, shelled or fought in. The magnificent cathedral and the site of the Bayeux Tapestry Museum were spared war's destructive force. It was liberated by the British on D-day +1. Bayeux's narrow, ancient streets prohibited the rapid flow of military traffic so the British engineers built bypass roads to the north and south. In the photo (lower left) is the British wartime cemetery containing 4018 British, 181 Canadian, 25 Polish and 466 German gravesites, all casualties of the battles to the south. The British do not permit exhumations and transfers of remains to other national cemeteries.

Picture 28: Chateau Adrieu - Today

The chateau was occupied by a regiment of the 12th SS Panzer division D-day +1. The area saw much fighting with British and Canadian troops. POWs were brought here and twenty were shot by their guards along this wall. The officer responsible was later killed along with the perpetrators of the murders. The chateau has been rebuilt and is now a five star hotel with shrapnel in the ceiling of the higher rooms as evidence of the battle.

Picture 29: Courseulles sur Mer - Looking West

The western end of the Canadian 3rd Infantry Division D-day assault beach east of the breakwater was codenamed "Nan-Green Beach" and was attacked by the Regina Rifles Regiment. Note the concrete blockhouse on the shoulder of the coast road is still present as are several more in the dunes west of the breakwater. West of the river mouth Mike Green and Mike Red beaches were assaulted by the Royal Winnipeg Rifles. Coordination of tank and infantry landing together overcame the German resistance quickly without heavy losses to the two Canadian regiments.

Picture 30: Creully - Looking South Today

Field Marshal Bernard Law Montgomery's headquarters for two weeks in June 1944. His sleeping caravan was kept under the trees to the right. The front lines were two miles to the left. Winston Churchill spent a day here. A week later King George visited but upon his return to London the British press described the chateau's location so completely that the Germans started shelling the area forcing Montgomery to abandon the site and move to Blay near Bayeux.

Picture 31: Le Hamel - Looking East
June 14, 1948

The British Hampshire Battalion of the 50th Infantry Division assaulted Gold-Jig-Red-West Beach at 7:30 AM D-day at the sandy beach top left. Beach obstacles, minefields and enemy resistance took 200 casualties in the first hours. Only five of their sixteen tanks made it beyond the minefields. Moving west accompanied by one tank the Hamshires attacked a 75mm strongpoint on the town's west side. German resistance was completely overcome by 4:30 that afternoon. The battalion continued to Arromanches where the following day British engineers commenced building Port Churchill assembled with components floated across the English Channel.

Picture 32: Longues Battery - Looking South Today

Four 155mm guns in thick concrete casements were positioned along the bluffs between Arromanches and Onaha Beach. A hard fought duel was fought between te guns and the battleship HMS Warspite. One of the 16-inch naval shells entered the gun embrasure exploding among the ammunition. The explosion vaporized the German crew blowing the casement apart like giant toy blocks. British troops captured the position late D-day. The site has changed little and is readily accessible by automobile including the observation and fire control bunker built into the cliff face.

Picture 33: Mont St. Michel

The thousand year old church and village are located on an island half a mile off the coast connected by an elevated causeway. On the mainland a short distance away is the German Mont de Huisenes Cemetery, an ossuary of 11,956 remains from the battle casualties on Brittany.

Picture 34: Port en Bessin - Looking North
June 14, 1948

Captured by the 47th Royal Marine Commandos the morning of D-day +1 entering from the south along the main road. By D-day +6 the port was reopened with off loading of about 8,000 tons per day. In early July floating pipelines connected fuel and oil tankers to the large petrol dump immediately west of the town. The German pill boxes on the west and east headlands overlooking the harbor and its approaches are still present. The commandos cleared the town quickly and continued westward to link up with the American forces moving eastward from Omaha Beach. The four storied building on the east side of the port entrance was demolished in the making of the movie "The Longest Day" in 1963.

Picture 35: Pegasus Bridge - Looking East
June 12, 1944

The lift bridge spanning the Orne Canal was captured by British 6th Airborne Division glider troops in the first few hours of D-day. The three Horsa gliders, visible in the top right brought Major John Howard and his troopers in on time, accurately placing them in position to seize the bridge by rapid surprise. Lt. Den Brotheridge, the first allied death on D-day was killed where the Jeep is standing as he and his men rushed across the bridge from the eastern side. A Bedford 4x4 engineer's truck is returning from the airborne headquarters area to secure supplies from Sword Beach. The drivers, although in Europe, are still driving on the left side as in England.

Chapter 23 Bibliography

Ambrose, Stephen. Citizen Soldiers. New York: Simon &Schuster, 1997.

Ambrose, Stephen. D-Day June 6, 1944. New York: Simon & Schuster, 1994.

Ambrose, Stephen. Pegasus Bridge. New York: Touchstone, 1985.

Bando, Mark. The 101st Airborne at Normandy. Osceola, WI: Motorbooks International, 1994.

Bauer, Eddy. The History of World War II. New York: Galahad, 1979.

Bell, Ken. Not in Vain. Toronto: University of Toronto Press, 1985.

Bell, Ken. The Way We Were. Toronto: University of Toronto Press, 1988.

Blumenson, Martin. The Duel For France 1944. Boston, MA: Houghton Miffin, 1963.

Blumenson, Martin. U.S. Army in World War II. Breakout and Pursuit. Washington: U.S. Government Printing Office, 1961

Bookman, John and Powers, Stephen. The March of Victory, Niwot, CO: University Press of Colorado, 1986

Breuer, William B. Death of A Nazi Army. New York: Stein and Day, 1985.

Brokaw, Tom. The Greatest Generation. New York: Random House, 1998.

Campbell, Ian J. Abbaye D'Ardenne June 1944. Paris: Canadian Embassy, 1984.

Cooper, Benton. Death Traps. Novato, CA: Presidio Press, 1998.

Copp, Terry. A Canadian's Guide to the Battlefields of Normandy. Waterloo, Ontario: Wilfred Laurier Unversity Press, 1994.

D'Este, Carlo. Decision in Normandy. New York: Dunton, 1983.

Dear, I.C.B. and Foot, M.R.D. World War II. New

York: Oxford University Press, 1995.

Dubosq, Genevieve. My Longest Night. New York: Seaver, 1981.

Eisenhower, Dwight D. Crusade in Europe. New York: Doubleday, 1948.

Florentin, Eddy. The Battle of the Falaise Gap. London: Elek Books, 1965.

Forty, George. World War II Tanks. London: Osprey, 1995.

Goldstein, Donald M., Dillon, Katherine V., Wenger, J. Michael. D-Day Normandy. New York: Brassey, 1994.

Goodenough, Simon. War Maps. New York: Simons, 1982.

Harrison, Gordon. U.S. Army in World War II. Cross Channel Attack. Washington: U.S. Government Printing Office, 1951

Hastings, Max. Victory in Europe. Toronto: Little & Brown, 1985.

Historical Division, Department of the Army. Omaha Beachhead. Washington: US Government Printing Office, 1946.

Historical Division, Department of the Army. Utah Beach to Cherbourg. Washington: US Government Printing Office, 1947.

Holt, Tonie and Valmai. The Visitor's Guide to Normandy Landing Beaches. Ashbourne, UK: Moorland, 1989.

Keegan, John. Six Armies in Normandy. London: Pimlico, 1993.

Keegan, John. The Rand McNally Encyclopedia of World War II. Greenwich, CT: Bison, 1977.

Keeney, L. Douglas, and Butler, William S. Day of Destiny. New York: William Marrow, 1998.

Lefevre, Eric. Panzers in Normandy, Then and Now. London: Battle of Britain Prints International, 1983.

Lucas, Laddie. Wings of War. London: Hutchison, 1983.

Martin, Charles Cromwell. Battle Diary. Toronto: Dundurn Press, 1994.

Masters, Charles J. Glidermen of Neptune. Carbondale, IL: Southern Illinois Unversity Press, 1995.

Meyer, Hubert. The History of the 12th SS Panzer Division "Hitlerjugend." Winnipeg, Manitoba: J.J.Fedorowicz, 1994.

Morgan, Kay Summersby. Past Forgetting. New York: Simon & Schuster, 1976.

Natly, Bernard C. and Pritchard, Russ A. D-Day, Operation Overlord. New York: Smithmark, 1993.

Neillands, Robin and DeNorman, Roberick. D-Day, 1944 Voices From Normandy. Osceola, WI: Motorbooks, 1993.

Nowarra, Heinz J., Feist, Uwe and Maloney, Edward The Tiger Tanks. Fallbrook, CA: Aero, 1966.

Olof, Brian. D-Day and The Liberation of Normandy 1944. Petersfield, UK. Easiguides, 1993.

Pimlott, John. Rommel, In His Own Words. London: Greenhill, 1994.

Preston, Antony. Jane's Fighting Ships of World War II. New York: Military Press, 1989.

Ramsey, Winston G. D-Day, Then and Now. London: Battle of Britain Prints International, 1995.

Rasmussen, Henry. D-Day Plus Fifty Years. Novato, CA: Top Ten, 1994.

Reynolds, Michael. Steel Inferno. New York: Dell Publishing, 1997.

Ryan, Cornelius. The Longest Day. New York: Touchstone, 1959.

Sommerville, Donald. World War II, Day By Day. Greenwich, CT: Brompton, 1989.

Sorley, Lewis. Thunderbolt. New York: Simon & Schuster, 1992.

von Luck, Hans. Panzer Commander. New York: Dell, 1989.

Williamson, Gordon. Infantry Aces of The Reich. London: Arms and Armour Press, 1991.

Wood, Herbert Fairlie and Swettenham, John. Silent Witnesses. Toronto: Hunter Rose, 1974.

Wright, Michael. Illustrated History of World War II. London: The Readers Digest Association, 1989.

Zaloga, Steven and Balin, George. D-Day Tank Warfare. Hong Kong: Concord, 1997.

INDEX

Referenced by Chapters

Picture 36: Campaign Time Line

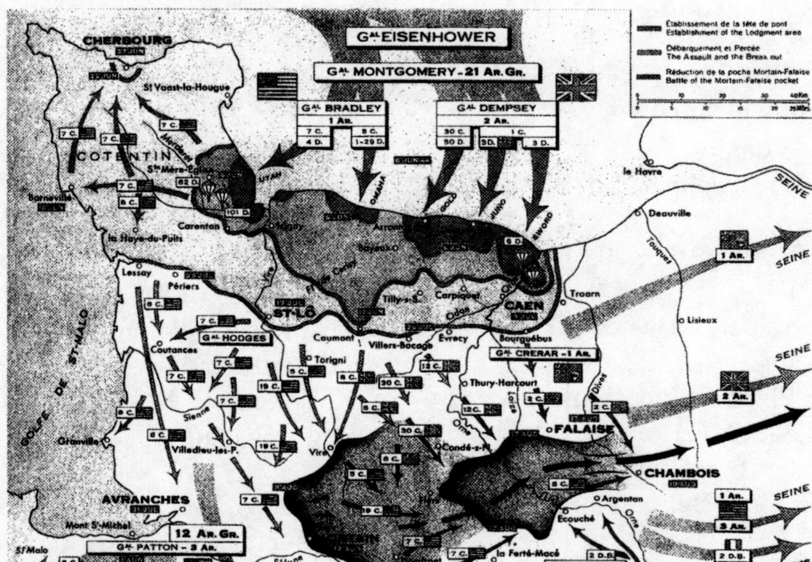

The invasion was started by American and British Airborne divisions creating flank protection to the east and west of the five invasion beaches and ended seventy-seven days later after the American 12th Army Group out flanked the German west end defense line and raced eastward to link up with the Canadian and Polish forces at Chambois.

Picture 37: US Forces First Ten Days

CPSIA information can be obtained at www.ICGtesting.com
Printed in the USA
LVOW11s2214051213

364134LV00001B/342/A